Ferrari
On The Road

All rights reserved. Apart from any fair dealing for the purpose of private study, research, criticism or review, as permitted under the terms of the Copyright, Design and Patents Act of 1988, no part of this book may be reproduced or transmitted in any form or by any means, electronic, electrical, chemical, mechanical, optical including photo-copying, recording or by any other means placed in any information storage or retrieval system, without written permission from the author or the publisher. All photographs are, wherever possible, credited to their source. Every effort has been made to ensure the accuracy of picture credits but if, for any reason, an illustration is not properly credited, or is not credited at all, the publisher apologises for any inconvenience caused and undertakes to correct such errors in future editions of this work.

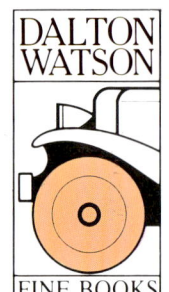

Ferrari
On The Road

Stanley Nowak
with Rob de la Rive Box
and Julian McNamara

CONTENTS

      6 Foreword
        by Richard F. Merritt

      7 Introduction

      9 Acknowledgements

Chapter 1   10 **The Beginnnings**
           166 Sport & Inter (1947-1949)
           195 Inter (1949-1951)

Chapter 2   24 **The Big Bangers**
           340 America (1951-1952)
           342 America (1952-1953)
           375 America (1953-1954)
           375 Mille Miglia (1953-1955)

Chapter 3   40 **A Step Forward**
           212 Inter (1951-1952)

Chapter 4   53 **Towards Production**
           250 Mille Miglia (1953-1954)
           250 Europa (1953-1954)

Chapter 5   58 **For The Elite**
           410 Superamerica (1956-1959)

Chapter 6   66 **Production Begins**
           250 Europa GT (1954-1955)
           250GT Boano/Ellena (1956-1958)
           250GT Tour de France (1955-1959)
           250GT Pininfarina Coupé (1958-1960)

Chapter 7   86 **Alfresco Elegance**
           250GT Series 1 Convertible (1957-1959)
           250GT Spyder California (1957-1962)
           250GT Series 2 Convertible (1959-1962)

Chapter 8   112 **The Elegance Expands**
           250GTE 2+2 (1960-1963)
           250GT Lusso Berlinetta (1962-1964)

Chapter 9   121 **Limited Edition Luxury**
           400 Superamerica (1959-1964)
           500 Superfast (1964-1966)
           365 California (1966-1967)

Chapter 10   138 **The Family Ferraris**
           330 America (1963)
           330GT 2+2 (1963-1967)

Chapter 11   146 **Burgeoning Berlinettas**
           250GT SWB (1959-1963)
           275GTB (1964-1966)
           275GTB/4 (1966-1968)

Chapter 12   162 **Sumptuous Spyders**
           275GTS (1964-1966)
           330GTS (1966-1968)
           275GTB/4-S NART Spyder (1967-1968)
           365GTS (1969)

FERRARI ON THE ROAD
First published in 1988
Second edition 1993

© 1988, 1993 The Estate of Stanley Nowak
and Dalton Watson Fine Books

ISBN 1-85443-105-6

British Library Cataloguing in Publication Data:-
Nowak, Stanley
Ferrari cars
I-Ferrari-On The Road
History
I–Title
629.2222

Published by Dalton Watson Fine Books,
P.O. Box 2, Belton, Loughborough, Leicestershire LE12 9UW.
Printed and bound by Stamford Press Pte Limited,
48 Lorong 21, Singapore 1438.

Chapter 13 172 **'The Best All Around V12'**
  330GTC (1966-1968)
  365GTC (1968-1970)

Chapter 14 177 **Family Luxury**
  365GT 2+2 (1967-1971)
  365GT4 2+2 (1972-1976))

Chapter 15 182 **The Final V12 Sports Cars**
  365 GTC/4 (1971-1972)
  365 GTB/4 'Daytona' Berlinetta (1968-1973)
  365 GTS/4 'Daytona' Spyder (1971-1973)

Chapter 16 196 **2+2 Redefined**
  400GT (1976-1979)
  400iGT (1979-1985)
  412 (1985-)

Chapter 17 202 **Compromised Performance**
  206GT (1968-1969)
  246GT (1969-1973)
  246GTS (1972-1974)

Chapter 18 218 **The V8 Emerges**
  308GT4 2+2 (1974-1980)
  308GTB, GTBi & GTB QV (1976-1985)
  308GTS, GTSi & GTS QV (1977-1985)
  208s Models (1980-)
  328GTB (1985-)
  328GTS (1985-)
  Mondial 8 & QV (1983-1985)
  3.2 Mondial (1986-)

Chapter 19 242 **The Flat 12 Sports Cars**
  365 GT4/BB Boxer (1973-1976)
  BB 512 (1976-1981)
  BB 512i (1981-1984)
  Testarossa (1985-)

Chapter 20 258 **Prototypes and Special Models For The Road**
  Prototypes
  28GTO (1984-1986)
  F40 (1987-)

Chapter 21 273 **The Next Five Years 1988-93**

Appendix
The Numbers

FOREWORD TO THE FIRST EDITION

Stan Nowak and I have known each other for over twenty-five years and in the early years we competed with each other over the purchase of what were then considered 'those funny old Ferraris'. At about the same time we both decided to try to keep track of these old Ferraris by chassis and engine numbers, partly to locate the cars but also to try to understand the Ferrari factory numbering system.

After a few years of corresponding Stan and I finally met and as often as possible would get together to compare notes and those precious numbers! Our information came from our own observations of specific cars, from owners, Ferrari Club of America records, and from the factory in the form of the invaluable 'assembly sheets'. Overall information from the factory was sparse indeed and personal visits to Modena and Maranello produced some lists but none of it was definitive. More of the gaps were filled in by the publication of coachbuilder records such as those of Pininfarina and Touring. When all is said and done it is amazing that a book of this nature can be done at all without any official help from the manufacturer!

This is a monumental job and I am delighted that one of the true early enthusiasts of the Ferrari marque has been able to get it all into print. Make no mistake it is a book that never will be 100% complete or correct as each and every day we continue to learn more about the wonderful machines that Enzo Ferrari has created for us.

This book on the road cars will be the bible for all true Ferraristi. Thank you, Stan, for making this possible.

Richard F. Merritt
Bethesda, Maryland

AUTHOR'S NOTE TO THE SECOND EDITION

Taking up where any author has laid off is always difficult. Filling Stanley's pages is almost impossible. My acquaintance with him was cordial, if brief. I would see him in the Dalton Watson offices, usually hunched over the tables contained in the back of this volume.

Our conversations tended to be humorous asides on the business of writing. Later, I had occasion to call on his help in various Ferrari matters and always found him both charming and helpful. It was always clear that he dealt with questions from a deep and abiding love of his subject.

Further information has also come to this book with the kind help of Peter Frater and his team at Maranello Concessionaires, now based in Dover, as well as from other sources in Great Britain. Hopefully, for those coming to this book for the first time, the joins will not be too evident.

Julian McNamara
London 1993

INTRODUCTION

My life long love affair with unusual automobiles began in 1939 when my family lived near a gentleman who owned a 1937 Lagonda Rapide Tourer. My unending interest in Ferraris began in 1948 when I attended the first Bridgehampton Road Race and saw Briggs Cunningham's Type 166 Inter Spyder Corsa in action. Twelve years later I bought my first Ferrari, 004C, another Spyder Corsa and the oldest Ferrari known to exist at that time.

I began to research the history of 004C and discovered that only one book on Ferrari existed, 'Ferrari' by Hans Tanner. To my surprise this book contained no information about these early Ferraris. With the help of Franco Gozzi at the Ferrari factory and Corrado Millanta, the famous Italian photographer, I was able to put together a definitive history of 004C. To corroborate the information obtained I read all the 1947 and 1948 issues of Auto Italiana, Motor Italia, Inter Auto, Motor, Autocar, and Motor Sport. My article on 004C appeared in the September 1966 issue of Road & Track, and later I gave Hans Tanner permission to use this material to create a new chapter for the next edition for his book (ably carried into further editions by Doug Nye).

In 1960 I began trying to keep track of Ferrari chassis and engine numbers. Dick Merritt and I and a few other mid-western early birds began buying and selling old Ferraris and as these cars were offered I wrote down the numbers. In Europe I began to work with A. F. 'Bart' Loyens (first from Amsterdam and later from Luxemburg), Rob Box in Switzerland, and Corrado Cupellini, Tom Meade and Pete Coltrin in Italy. Further down the road I got to know Ed Niles in California. Dick Merritt was still in Detroit and through him I met Ernie Beutler, Fred Leydorf and John Delameter. In Europe I heard from Viviano Corradini and Gus Vignole, both of whom had moved back to Italy after years in the U.S.

As cars were offered, bought and sold, I kept track of the numbers. Slowly but surely patterns began to emerge and I saw that in the early years Ferrari liked to give competition cars even numbers and road cars the odd numbers - except when they didn't! I also saw that the road cars ran almost in a straight line from 001S whereas the race cars started with a three digit series and shortly after to a new four digit series (forgetting the possible one or two digit series of the first three 1947 cars). I also began to see that the early specifications published in Ferrari brochures and handed out to the press didn't necessarily describe any car that had actually been produced. Conversely it became obvious that cars that actually ran in early events were of a specification that was never published. 001S is a perfect example. As the first 'road' car one might expect it to have a conservative specification. On the contrary, engine compartment photos clearly show three carburettors and two magnetos. This would indicate a race engine with a compression ratio of as high as 9.0 to 1. We know from Briggs Cunningham that these early cars ran on an AVGAS/alcohol fuel mixture to obtain as high an octane rating as possible. All this would indicate a horsepower of 140 to 150 at 7,000 RMP for 001S! This is in contrast to the published specification of 90HP at 5,600 RPM with one carburettor and two distributors and a compression ratio of only about 7.0 to 1.

It can be fairly said that official specifications were only an indication of what was really happening. Production was so small that each car was really unique and <u>no two cars were alike.</u> This was true of every Ferrari made through at least 1954. The factory made changes and improvements car by car. In addition each customer could order special features to suit his whims. This early period is particularly fascinating as six different coachbuilders were used and even cosmetically no two cars were alike. In most cases positive identification of a specific car can be made from contemporary photographs thus enabling the historian to establish the history of a particular car.

Slowly but surely Enzo Ferrari did aim toward standardising his cars but in Ferrari's lexicon that is a loose term and exceptions abounded. The exception was the rule. Beware to the Ferrari historian and to the Ferrari Concours d'Elegance judge.

Our fascination with the Ferrari automobile became a mania with some of us, and the lack of help from the factory and the U.S. importer of that era, Luigi Chinetti, made us all the more eager to find the 'truth'. Some of us made the pilgimage to the factory and cooled our heels in the cell-like rooms in Modena waiting for an invitation to come inside. If we passed that test we might have been allowed to enter the gates at Maranello - but only by specific appointment. John Bond, the long time publisher of *Road & Track*, was made to wait two days to take delivery of his new 330 America. Ron Tonkin, who has been a Ferrari dealer longer than anyone in the U.S.A., did not meet Mr. Ferrari until 1985.

Through extensive correspondence I got to know Dr. Franco Gozzi, Mr. Ferrari's personal assistant and Public Relations chief for the racing team, and in 1969 when he was the factory's racing team manager, I met him in New York. He had come over with Mauro Forghieri and the entire team for the U.S. Grand Prix at Watkins Glen. I went with the team to the Glen and got to know Franco Gozzi very well. When I pressed him for more information about the older cars he told me he could not help as no one had the time to go through the archives, and anyway 'people like you, Stan Nowak, and Dick Merritt, know more about the old cars than anyone at the factory.'

The mysteries only deepened and the mystique continued to grow. Those of us who were persistent were rewarded, and for five years I received the latest edition of the factory year book with Ferrari's compliments. When I requested the fabled 'assembly sheets' for a specific car I usually got them. When I owned 002C and 004C I was blessed with letters from Franco Gozzi and reports of Luigi Bazzi, that practical engineer who took the designs of Colombo and Lampredi and others and made them work. Although retired and of advanced age he came to the factory one or two days a week 'to straighten out the archives' - a job he never finished.

In any case, over the years hundreds of assembly sheets were sent out along with dribs and drabs of information like small pieces of a very large, very intricate jigsaw puzzle. Some of it didn't fit and we now know that some of the factory information was incorrect. We also know that engines were changed and/or renumbered and the same was true of chassis numbers. Human error crept in and we know of a 400 Superamerica we have carefully examined that is correctly numbered on the engine and the frame tube but the wrong number is on the original factory maker's plate (it is stamped the same number as a Lusso Berlinetta that is elsewhere in the U.S.).

Looking back on all this I cannot help but ask why we have all become so fascinated with Ferraris and everything that concerns Ferraris. And remember, we did not just read about them, we owned them, we drove them, we raced them - and by stretching our finances a bit we managed to afford them! And we sold them and bought others. We discovered, early on, that we never lost money doing this. We never really made any money, but wasn't it wonderful to have a hobby that didn't cost anything? But this was just the icing on the cake. What was the overall magnetic attraction? Surely it was the genuine creative genius of Enzo Ferrari and the aesthetic appeal of the mechanical marvels he caused to be produced. The look! The sound! The smell! The shape! The power! The feel!

Thank you, Enzo Ferrari, the last of the great original automotive geniuses, on your fortieth anniversary.

Stanley Nowak
Scottsdale, Arizona.

ACKNOWLEDGEMENTS

No serious book on the subject of Ferrari automobiles can be written without the use of information obtained by others. This is only fully appreciated when one realizes that the Ferrari factory provides no information officially. I am indebted to Rob Box for providing a master list of all Ferraris up to chassis number 11,183. My own Ferrari register, which I started in 1960, was added to this. I am also indebted to pioneer Ferrari enthusiast Dick Merritt who added his register to mine; Dick started his as long ago. Over the years an immense amount of information has been gathered from public sources all over the world. This includes magazines, worldwide Ferrari club publications, books, countless Ferrari owners, former owners, enthusiasts, and Ferrari dealers. It is simply not possible to thank everyone, but I must single out a special few who in the past have always been willing to share their knowledge. In addition to Robby Box and Dick Merritt I must include Ed Niles, Fred Leydorf, George Carrick, Jess Pourret, Antoine Prunet, Gerald Roush, John Barnes, Dyke Ridgely, Alan Boe, Peter Sachs, Joel Finn, Lorenzo Boscarelli and Angelo Tito Anselmi. I also must thank John Geils, Brian Brunkhorst, Marcel Massini, and Kurt Miska. Special thanks must also go to Tony Singer for his wonderful colour photography.

Stanley Nowak

I wish to thank the following enthusiasts who were helpful in giving their knowledge and opinions and in some cases photographs: A. van Bever, G. Dardenne, A. Flach, R. Hunziker, Manfred Lampe, Fred Leydorf, Hil Raab, B. Rosman, P. Sachs, R. Scheuchzer, G. Sutterfield, Richard Veen, Geoff Willoughby, A. Prunet, and Paul Schouwenburg. Also for their cooperation: Carrozzeria Bertone and Carrozzeria Pininfarina.

Rob de la Rive Box

Above The first Ferrari closed car 003S, had a unique coupé body built by Carrozzeria Allemano. This car won the 1948 Mille Miglia but was really Ferrari's first attempt at a dual-purpose sports/racing car.

Right Built for a private customer, this is believed to be chassis number 001S, the first odd-numbered car to be built for the road but also used for competition. The coachbuilder is believed to be Allemano, but this is not confirmed.

CHAPTER ONE

THE BEGINNINGS

166 Sport & Inter (1947-1949)
195 Inter (1949-1951)

Enzo Ferrari began planning his own new automobile in 1946, with Italy still involved in World War II. Guiding his engineer, G. Colombo, the design of the new car took shape. At the heart of the concept was a small V12 engine, mounted in a rugged tubular frame, driving a live rear axle through a 5-speed gearbox. By early 1947 the first two cars had become a reality.

The Type 166 road car of 1948 evolved from the first three Ferraris built in 1947. They began as Type 125 sports/racing cars with 1.5-litre V12 engines and by May 1947 they began their racing history at Piacenza in the hands of Franco Cortese. Each cylinder of these cars had a swept volume of approximately 125cc (x 12 = 1500cc) and this method was used by Ferrari to name each of his early models. By mid-1947 the engines were enlarged to 1900cc - the Type 159 - and by September 1947 the first Type 166 (2000cc) emerged to win the Grand Prix of Turin.

As the founder of the illustrious Scuderia Ferrari in 1929 it was instinctive for Enzo Ferrari to establish the new company's reputation through racing, and all of the cars built or sold in 1947 and 1948 were intended to be raced by the factory or by their wealthy customers. In some cases the new company's cash flow requirements no doubt led to a reduction in the standard of driving acceptable to qualify for the purchase of a new car.

During 1948 about eleven new cars were built or sold, including the original two Type 166 Spyder Corsas that had been developed from the earlier 1947 cars. All of these were intended for competition and were designated 'Sport' chassis although some were referred to as having 'Inter' chassis.

By early 1949, production began on the first cars truly intended for road use, beginning with C/N 005S. As these were really dual purpose cars an argument

CHAPTER ONE

can be made to include C/N 001S and 003S. The two earlier cars are believed to have been built on a wheelbase of 2620mm with subsequent cars using a shorter wheelbase of 2420mm.

The year 1949 proved to be extraordinary for the Type 166 and outright victories were won in the most prestigious road races in the world: the Mille Miglia (003S), the Targa Florio (001S) and the Le Mans 24 Hour Race (000 8M). Of the three, 003S looked most like a true road car with its unexceptional coupé body by Allemano. All of this did nothing but assist Ferrari in establishing his new car factory in Maranello, Italy as a viable enterprise.

By Autumn 1950 a total of 40 Type 166 road cars had been produced, utilizing the talents of the following coachbuilders: Allemeno, Touring, Stabilimenti Farina, Ghia, Vignale and Bertone. The Type 195 was really a variation and a development of the Type 166 with the engine enlarged to 2340cc and horsepower increased accordingly. The first 195s were 166s modified by the factory - usually for racing purposes. The first car built as a Type 195 was probably 081S. We believe 27 of the Type 195 Inter were made by early 1952.

Above This is an example of the first version of Carrozzeria Touring's realization of the 166 Inter, probably on chassis 007S. The Cabo steel wheels and Ferrari hubcaps appeared only on 3 or 4 cars.

Top right This variation on the first version of the 166 Inter includes Borrani wire wheels and side vents to allow fresh air directly into the car. This is probably 005S after it had been updated. A second version had a notch-back with continuous sides.

Right This third version introduces a major change to the shell of the 166 Inter: continuous sides and a fastback top. A further development was the sculptured effect around the rear tail lights. This is probably 075S built for Giannino Marzotto.

Centre right Another example of the third version of the 166 Inter by Touring. This is 077S built for Sig.I. Bernabei of Rome.

THE BEGINNINGS

CHAPTER ONE

Above A more typical example of Vignale's work on the 166 Inter chassis. At least seven were made to look very much like this one but each with details that differ!

Top right A superb example of the mastery of Carrozzeria Vignale, inspired by a design of Giovanni Michelotti. The chassis number is 065S.

Centre A mystery car, this 166 Inter with a unique body by Bertone vanished after 1951 and may have been rebodied. Its chassis number can only be guessed (possibly 061S).

Bottom right A rare interior view of the mysterious Bertone convertible, showing typical Ferrari instrumentation of the period.

THE BEGINNINGS

15

CHAPTER ONE

Above An average example of the efforts of Carrozzeria Ghia, this 195 is chassis number 0121S. While generally more conservative than Vignale's work, the Ghias usually were endowed with more opulent interiors.

Above right This rear view of 0121S is more graceful and appealing than many of the Ghia creations.

Below right This early engine photo of 0121S clearly shows the water-heated manifold for the single Weber carburretor installation, common to most of the 195 Inters.

THE BEGINNINGS

CHAPTER ONE

Stabilimenti Farina had been established in 1896 and began supplying bodies to Ferrari two years before Pinin Farina, who had left the old family business in 1930 to establish his own coachbuilding business. This example of Stabilimenti Farina's work looks much like the Pinin Farina design for the Fiat 1100S, and the Simca 8 Sport and may have been a combined effort. This is chassis number 011S.

More striking and original than 011S is this creation by Stabilimenti Farina on chassis number 063S.

CHAPTER ONE

SPECIFICATIONS

	166 Sport
Type	166
Model	Sport
Years made	1948
Chassis range	001/S-005S
Number produced	3
Coachbuiders	Allemano & Touring
Body styles	Coupé
Body material	Aluminium
Seating capacity	2 and 2+2
Engine type	V12 60° Colombo
Displacement	1995cc
Bore and stroke	60mm x 58.8mm
Cyl. head	SOHC, single inside plug, finger followers
Ignition	2 magnetos or 2 distributors
Compression	8.5 to 1
Carburation	3 x 30 DCF
Lubrication	Wet sump
Horsepower	140 @ 7,000
Chassis/Drivetrain	Engine/gearbox in front
Frame	Tubular steel with elliptical maintubes
Transmission	5 speed
Axle ratio	5.0 to 1 (& others)
Brakes	Hydraulic drum
Wheels	Borrani wire 5.50 x 15
Front suspension	Independent, A-arms, transverse leaf lever shocks
Rear suspension	Live axle, semi elliptic springs and lever shocks
Curb weight	1900/2000 lbs (est)
Wheelbase	2620mm
Track front	1270mm
Track rear	1250mm

	166 Inter
Type	166
Model	Inter
Years made	1948-1950
Chassis range	007S-079S
Number produced	36
Coachbuiders	Touring, Vignale, Ghia, Stabilimenti Farina, Bertone
Body styles	Coupé, Berlinetta, Convertible
Body material	Aluminium
Seating capacity	2 and 2+2
Engine type	V12 60° Colombo
Displacement	1995cc
Bore and stroke	60mm x 58.8mm
Cyl. head	SOHC, single inside plug, finger followers
Ignition	2 distributors
Compression	8.0 to 1
Carburation	1 x 32 DCF
Lubrication	Wet sump
Horsepower	110/115bhp @ 6,000rpm
Chassis/Drivetrain	Engine/gearbox in front
Frame	Tubular steel with elliptical maintubes
Transmission	5 speed
Axle ratio	5.0 to 1 (& others)
Brakes	Hydraulic drum
Wheels	Borrani wire 5.50 x 15
Front suspension	Independent, A-arms, transverse leaf lever shocks
Rear suspension	Live axle, semi elliptic springs and lever shocks
Curb weight	2000 lbs (est.)
Wheelbase	2500 and 2420mm
Track front	1250mm
Track rear	1250mm

THE BEGINNINGS

195 Inter

Type	195
Model	Inter
Years made	1950-1952
Chassis range	081S - 0195 EL
Number produced	27
Coachbuiders	Ghia , Touring , Vignale and Ghia-Aigle
Body styles	Coupé and Berlinetta
Body material	Aluminium
Seating capacity	2 and 2+2
Engine type	V12 60°
Displacement	2341cc
Bore and stroke	65mm x 58.8mm
Cyl. head	SOHC, single inside plug, finger follower
Ignition	2 distributors
Compression	7.5 to 1
Carburation	1 x 32DCF
Lubrication	Wet sump
Horsepower	130bhp @ 6,000rpm
Chassis/Drivetrain	Engine/gearbox in front
Frame	Tubular steel with oval maintubes
Transmission	5 speed
Axle ratio	5 to 1
Brakes	Hydraulic drum
Wheels	Borrani wire 5.90 x 15
Front suspension	Ind., A-arms, transverse leaf springs, lever shocks
Rear suspension	Live axle,semi elliptic springs and lever shocks
Curb weight	2100/2200 lbs
Wheelbase	2500mm
Track front	1270mm
Track rear	1250mm

Note. All colour photographs were taken by Everett Anton Singer, except # R. Hunziker *Stan Nowak, and † Alessandro Stefannini.

A superb example of the 'third version' coachwork on the 1950 166 Inter chassis by Carrozzeria Touring. This is chassis number 077S.#

The first Ferrari bodied by Pinin Farina was this perfectly proportioned 1952 212 Inter Cabriolet, Chassis Number 0177E. It was originally delivered to Scuderia Filipinetti in Switzerland. The car was restored by Pininfarina and 'redelivered' to its present owner on February 18, 1988, the 90th birthday of Enzo Ferrari. The photographs were taken at the Pininfarina Research and Development Centre, Cambiano, Italy.

Above Carrozzeria Ghia provided this elegant solution to clothe the chassis of the 340 America, a competition chassis that was adopted for road use. Note the door handle on the fender outline of the door. Similar 340 Americas went to dictator Peron in Argentina and Tony Parravano in California. The latter car finished 5th overall in the 1952 Carrera Panamericana!

Right The second 342 America built was this unusual convertible created by Pinin Farina in 1952 for King Leopold of Belgium. It bears chassis number 0234AL.

CHAPTER TWO

THE BIG BANGERS

340 America (1951-1952)
342 America (1952-1953)
375 America (1953-1955)
375 Mille Miglia (1953-1955)

This series of large bore and stroke big-bangers was the direct result of Aurelio Lampredi's answer to the problem of finding a way to beat the Alfa Romeo Formula I cars of 1949. Ferrari's 1.5-litre supercharged monoposto was not able to do the job and this small Colombo-designed V12 could not be enlarged to 4.5-litres. Lampredi set about designing a new V12, engine with the goal of developing it to 4.5-litres for use in a new unsupercharged Formula I car.

Within two years, by the end of 1951, it had accomplished its purpose, and Alfa Romeo withdrew from racing. Lampredi's new engine also spawned a whole new series of Ferrari sports cars.

Early in 1950 the first version of the new engine was installed in a Touring-bodied Barchetta Spyder for Ascari and Villoresi to drive in the Mille Miglia. This was a 275 engine of 3.3-litres. In July a 4.1-litre version was installed in a new Formula I chassis that ran at the Swiss Grand Prix and by September the full 4.5-litre engine was in action at the Italian Grand Prix.

A 4.1-litre sports car, the 340 America, was debuted at the October 1950 Paris Salon. In March 1951, Ferrari displayed a Touring-bodied Berlinetta at the Turin Motor Show. Subsequently 340 Americas were pro-

duced with coachwork by Vignale, Ghia and Touring with the last one completed by the factory on 23 July 1952 (a Vignale coupé). Of the 22 built, about eight were for the road.

The 342 America was designed as a pure road car with a 4-speed all synchromesh gearbox and was generally beefed up to be more reliable than the sports/racing-oriented 340. Only six were built, starting in the fall of 1952 and ending in early 1953.

At the Paris Salon in October 1953 Ferrari introduced the new 375 America and the 250 Europa. The two were very much alike and a number of 250 Europas were converted by the factory to 375 specifications simply by installing the larger engine. Some confusion was also engendered by the fact that a few 375 Mille Miglia chassis were fitted with pure touring car coachwork. In one case a 375 Plus engine was used but in such cases it is impossible to know exactly what was done without a thorough study of the assembly sheets prepared by the factory as the car was built. The last pure 375 America was completed at the end of May 1954.

Left This front view of 0234AL accentuates its overly decorated shapes in the hood area. However, its basic shape is a Pinin Farina classic.

Above This 342 America is another Pinin Farina variation on their then current theme. This one is cleaner, less fussy than 0234AL.

Top right A typical Pinin Farina's instrument panel for a 342 America. The symmetrical display of gauges is not the most pragmatic approach for a Ferrari.

Right The last 342 America was this Pinin Farina convertible which was shown at the 1953 New York Auto Show. It is a somewhat refined version of the earlier King Leopold car. This one is chassis number 0248AL.

THE BIG BANGERS

CHAPTER TWO

Top left This 375 America shows Pinin Farina's ability to develop simpler and more pleasing forms. This is chassis number 0329AL, which was completed by the coachbuilder in April 1954.

Top Pinin Farina made no two 375 Americas exactly alike. This is another variation on the theme, probably with some room for luggage or children behind the front seats.

Left 0193AL was first shown at the 1953 Paris Salon. The prominent chrome trim on the 375 America's grill surround seems restrained compared to some of Vignale's more aggresive designs of the same period.

Above This 375 America seems to reflect a backward step for Pinin Farina as its approach seems far too conservative for a Ferrari.

CHAPTER TWO

Above The last 375 America was this styling exercise by Pinin Farina, first shown at the 1955 Turin Motor Show. It then became the property of FIAT head, Giovanni Agnelli. Though striking from some angles, it seems to introduce too many styling ideas in one package. The overall result lacks cohesion. It is chassis number 0355AL.

Top right One of Pinin Farina's most successful styling experiments was this special 375 Mille Miglia for movie director Roberto Rossellini. It was first shown at the 1954 Paris Salon. It featured concave panels behind the front wheels that were found a few years later on the production Corvette! It is chassis number 0456AM.

Right From the rear, 0456AM is equally disarming and eloquent. These forms influenced Pinin Farina styling for another 30 years.

THE BIG BANGERS

CHAPTER TWO

Top left For the 1955 Turin Motor Show the usually conservative Ghia chose to show a prototype that featured a Z paint-break and a rather American-looking grille. This is chassis number 0476AM, a 375 Mille Miglia.

Above This particular 375 Mille Miglia was probably never raced. It was built for Dr. Wax in Genoa and was intended for high-speed touring, although it looks identical to those built solely to win races. It is chassis number 0378AM.

Left The interior of 0476AM seems to have been directly influenced by American styling clichés. The traditional Ferrari wood steering wheel offers a bold contrast.

CHAPTER TWO

Above Pinin Farina's supreme moment came with the creation of this one-off design for King Leopold of Belgium. It is the quintessential Ferrari convertible shape. Built at the end of 1954, it used a 375 Plus engine. It is a design that looks as new today as it did when created.

Right Another outstanding prototype was designed on chassis number 0490AM by Pinin Farina. This 375 Mille Miglia for the road was shown at the 1955 Turin Motor Show, and forecast the shape of the 250GT Long Wheelbase Tour de France of the future.

Top right Even more bizarre was this 375 Mille Miglia built for Emperor Bo-Dai of Thailand. The Emperor lived in Paris and this vehicle was strictly for touring. It is chassis number 0450AM.

THE BIG BANGERS

35

CHAPTER TWO

SPECIFICATIONS

340 America

Type	340
Model	America
Years made	1951-1952
Chassis range	0122A - 0150A
Number produced	8
Coachbuiders	Touring, Vignale & Ghia
Body styles	Coupé & Berlinetta
Body material	Aluminium
Seating capacity	2
Engine type	V12
Displacement	4101cc
Bore and stroke	80mm x 68mm
Cyl. head	SOHC, single inside plug, finger follower
Ignition	2 distributors
Compression	8.0 to 1
Carburation	3 x 40DCF
Lubrication	Wet sump
Horsepower	220bhp @ 6,000rpm
Chassis/Drivetrain	Engine/gearbox in front
Frame	Tubular steel with oval maintubes
Transmission	5 speed
Axle ratio	Various
Brakes	Hydraulic drum
Wheels	Borrani wire 5.90 x 16
Front suspension	A-arms, transverse leaf spring, lever shocks
Rear suspension	Live axle, semi-elliptical springs, lever shocks
Curb weight	2400 lbs
Wheelbase	2420mm
Track front	1278mm
Track rear	1250mm

342 America

Type	342
Model	America
Years made	1952-1953
Chassis range	0232AL - 0248AL
Number produced	6
Coachbuiders	Pinin Farina & Vignale
Body styles	Coupé, Berlinetta & convertible
Body material	Aluminium
Seating capacity	2 & 2+2
Engine type	V12 60° Lampredi
Displacement	4101cc
Bore and stroke	80mm x 68mm
Cyl. head	SOHC, inside plug, finger follower
Ignition	2 distributors
Compression	8 to 1
Carburation	3 x 40DCF
Lubrication	Wet sump
Horsepower	200bhp @ 5,000rpm
Chassis/Drivetrain	Engine/gearbox in front
Frame	Tubular steel with oval maintubes
Transmission	4 speed
Axle ratio	Various
Brakes	Hydraulic drum
Wheels	Borrani wire 6.40 x 15
Front suspension	A-arms, transverse leaf springs, lever shocks
Rear suspension	Live axle, semi-elliptical springs, lever shocks
Curb weight	2400lbs
Wheelbase	2650mm
Track front	1325mm
Track rear	1320mm

THE BIG BANGERS

375 America

Type	375
Model	America
Years made	1953-1954
Chassis range	0293AL - 0355AL
Number produced	12
Coachbuiders	Pinin Farina, Vignale & Ghia
Body styles	Coupé
Body material	Aluminium & steel
Seating capacity	2
Engine type	V12 60°
Displacement	4523cc
Bore and stroke	84mm x 68mm
Cyl. head	SOHC, single inside plug, finger follower
Ignition	2 distributors
Compression	8.0 to 1
Carburation	3 x 40DCF
Lubrication	Wet sump
Horsepower	300bhp @ 6300rpm
Chassis/Drivetrain	Engine/gearbox in front
Frame	Tubular steel with oval maintubes
Transmission	4 speed
Axle ratio	Various
Brakes	Hydraulic drum
Wheels	Borrani wire 7.10 x 15
Front suspension	A-arms, transverse leaf springs, lever shocks
Rear suspension	Live axle, semi-elliptical springs, lever shocks
Curb weight	2500lbs
Wheelbase	2800mm
Track front	1325mm
Track rear	1320mm

375 Mille Miglia

Type	375
Model	Mille Miglia
Years made	1953-1955
Chassis range	0368AM - 0488AM
Number produced	5
Coachbuiders	Pinin Farina, Vignale & Ghia
Body styles	Coupé & convertible
Body material	Aluminium & steel
Seating capacity	2
Engine type	V12 60°
Displacement	4522cc
Bore and stroke	84mm x 68.5mm
Cyl. head	SOHC, single inside plug, roller rockers
Ignition	2 magnetos
Compression	9.0 to 1
Carburation	3 x 40IF4C or 3 x 42DCZ
Lubrication	Wet sump
Horsepower	340bhp @ 7,000rpm
Chassis/Drivetrain	Engine/gearbox in front
Frame	Tubular steel with oval maintubes
Transmission	4 speed
Axle ratio	Various
Brakes	Hydraulic drum
Wheels	Borrani wire
Front suspension	Independent, A-arms, coil spring, lever shocks
Rear suspension	Live axle, semi-elliptical springs, lever shocks
Curb weight	2300 lbs
Wheelbase	2600mm
Track front	1325mm
Track rear	1320mm

NOTE. Probably only 5 were built specifically for high speed touring; 0368AM, 0402AM, 0456AM, 0476AM, 0488AM.

This is certainly one of the finest examples of the successful blending of the talents of Ferrari and Pinin Farina. In this case it produced what many consider to be the ultimate Ferrari road car. For this reason we have featured it on the dust jacket of this book, and here we explore its styling and mechanical features more thoroughly. This is a 1954 375 Mille Miglia, chassis number 0488AM, built specially for King Leopold of Belgium for his use on the road. These outstanding photographs were taken by Everett Anton Singer at the 1984 Monterey Ferrari celebration.

Above The limousine 'look' of the Ghia-bodied 212EL (Export Lungo for long chassis) 2+2 has not endeared it to Ferraristi, though it did forecast the 250GTE 2+2 of years later.

Right A rare photo of the original interior of the Ghia 2+2 shown above. Indeed, it qualifies as the 'family' Ferrari.

CHAPTER THREE

A Step Forward

212 Inter (1951-1952)

Again the original Colombo-designed V12 engine was enlarged - and again it was based on racing experience and a need for increased performance. One great advantage of a V12 engine is that only small increases in bore and/or stroke are needed to increase the overall cubic capacity. Compared to the type 195, the engine was increased in bore from 65mm to 68mm and the stroke remained at 58.8mm - the same stroke as the final version of the 166. This precluded any need to change the crankshaft.

The usual confusion over nomenclature was heightened by the fact that the 212 Inter series of cars used three different suffixes after their chassis numbers: E, EL and EU. Despite this, it seems that most likely all the odd numbered 212s did have a wheelbase of 2600mm. Even 0237EU, which was raced by Franco Cornacchia, had the longer wheelbase of the 212 Inter.

Mechanically the 212 Inters could be quite different, and some, such as 0237 EU, were fitted with engines fully up to 212 Export road-racing specifications. As no more than two cars were produced each week there was no need for standardization. The customer could have exactly what he wanted: a luxury body and interior to satisfy his wife and/or mistress and a racing engine and chassis to satisfy himself.

The Vignale designs were by far the most exciting and some of these on the long 2600mm chassis were as daring and compelling as those built strictly for competition. Ghia and Touring began to lose favour and while Vignale produced one triumph after another, Pinin Farina emerged as Ferraris own favorite coachbuilder.

CHAPTER THREE

A sporty version of the 212 Inter, this 2-window coupé on chassis number 0213EL is probably the most attractive of all the Ghia-bodied Ferraris.

Left Another view of 0213EL - restrained, elegant and purposeful - altogether a very successful design.

A STEP FORWARD

Three views of Ghia's second solution for a viable 2+2. This one as a fastback coupé with two seats in the back for the children or extra luggage space. This is chassis number 0201EL.

CHAPTER THREE

One of the most unusual bodies ever to clothe a Ferrari chassis was this effort by British coachbuilder Abbott. This drophead body on the 212 Export Lungo chassis was not a success and was separated from the chassis some years later. This is chassis number 0165EL.

Right A most attractive 212 Inter Coupe is this Pininfarina-built design, the lines of which would do credit to a much later car.

A STEP FORWARD

CHAPTER THREE

A STEP FORWARD

Left Pinin Farina's first convertible on a Ferrari chassis seems a very well thought out exercise. Its lines are classic even today. Built on chassis number 0177E, it made an impressive debut in mid-1952.

Below left Another view of 0177E showing it's elegant interior. The first owner was Mr. Filipinetti of Switzerland who later became famous as the sponsor of the renowned Swiss Ferrari racing team Scuderia Filipinetti.

Below Pinin Farina's second Ferrari convertible, on chassis number 0235EU, was more restrained and more elegant. It was sold to movie director Roberto Rossellini.

CHAPTER THREE

This elegant Vignale coupé started life in 1952 as a 212 Inter, chassis number 0239EU, and was raced in the 1952 Carrera Panamericana. It then returned to the factory and was converted with a 212 Mille Miglia engine and renumbered 0292M. These six photos show the details of this Vignale creation: an excellent example of their unique work that was based on designs by Giovanni Michelotti.

A STEP FORWARD

CHAPTER THREE

Although this is a 212 Export, C/N 0080E, on the short chassis, it was obviously never intended for serious competition. It is, in any case, a superb example of the perfection that was brought about by the collaboration of Vignale and designer Michelotti.

CHAPTER THREE

SPECIFICATIONS

212 Inter

Type	212
Model	Inter
Years made	1951-1952
Chassis range	0107ES-0297EU*
Number produced	80
Coachbuiders	Touring, Vignale, Ghia and Pinin Farina
Body styles	Coupé, Berlinetta & convertible.
Body material	Aluminium
Seating capacity	2 & 2+2
Engine type	V12 60° Colombo
Displacement	2562cc
Bore and stroke	68mm x 58.8mm
Cyl. head	SOHC, single inside plug, finger followers.
Ignition	2 distributors.
Compression	7.5/8.0 to 1
Carburation	1 x 36 DCF & 3 x 32 DCF
Lubrication	Wet sump
Horsepower	150/170bhp @ 6500rpm
Chassis/Drivetrain	Engine/gearbox in front
Frame	Tubular steel with oval maintubes
Transmission	5 speed
Axle ratio	5 to 1
Brakes	Hydraulic drum
Wheels	Borrani wire 5.90 x 15 & 6.40 x 15
Front suspension	A-arms, transverse leaf springs, lever shocks
Rear suspension	Live axle, semi-elliptical rear springs, lever shocks.
Curb weight	2200lbs
Wheelbase	2600mm
Track front	1270mm
Track rear	1250mm

Note. 0292M, (originally 0239EU), was fitted with an experimental 212MM engine by the factory.

Above Pinin Farina continued to refine and simplify their shapes, and this unique convertible attests to the success of their efforts. This is chassis number 031EU, the only convertible built on the 250 Europa foundation.

Right Another variation of the Pinin Farina approach to the 250 Europa/375 America chassis. This 5-window coupé is not as attractive from a rear three-quarter view.

CHAPTER FOUR

TOWARDS PRODUCTION

250 Mille Miglia (1952-1954)
250 Europa (1953-1954)

Early in 1952 at least one Colombo 225 engine was enlarged to a bore and stroke of 73mm x 58.8mm. Once again, only the bore was increased. This change brought the engine size up to 2,953cc. So the 250 series was born, with this Colombo 3-litre engine installed in chassis number 0156ET, which had started life as a 225 Sport. (About 20 of these had been made in 1952 with a bore and stroke of 70mm x 58.8mm.)

In May of 1952 the experimental 250 Sport (C/N 0156ET) was catapulted into fame when it became the overall winner of the Mille Miglia, beating the factory-entered Mercedes Benz 300SL. The driver was an impetuous and gifted amateur named Giovanni Bracco who had talked his way into a factory drive based on his surprising success with marginally competitive cars.

The 250S engine that powered Bracco's winning Ferrari has in some books been described as being based on the Lampredi engine, but the evidence, photographic and otherwise, does not support this. The same car, C/N 0156ET, was entered by the factory in the 1952 Le Mans 24 Hour Race in 1952, a few months after its incredible victory in the Mille Miglia. The official entry shows the engine to be a 250S with a bore and stroke of 70mm x 58.8mm. Also a photo of the engine compartment taken at Le Mans shows it to be a Colombo-based engine.

While the racing department at Maranello was developing the Colombo 3-litre engine the commercial department was preparing a 3-litre version of the larger Lampredi-designed engine, the 342 America. While the 342 America had a bore and stroke of 80mm x 68mm (4101cc), the new Europa 250 engine, as it was to be called, was 68mm x 68mm. At the same time the 375 America was being developed with an 84mm x 68mm bore and stroke.

In 1952 the Ferrari factory was actually building more competition cars than road cars and the customer racing department was a beehive of activity and influence. The lighter Colombo-based engine was preferred by the Ferrari owner drivers and it's continued development was ensured. Those "in the know" always insisted on the latest factory modifications and it is most likely that a small number of Colombo-based 3-litre engines were installed in 212 Inter chassis. One of these was 0237EU, raced by one of their most active Italian dealers, Franco Cornacchia. Another special 250 engine was installed in C/N 0265EU for Roberto Rossellini, the famous Italian movie director who was also one of Ferrari's best customers. Another special car, 0295EU, a Vignale coupé, may have been built with a 3-litre Colombo engine. No such model existed officially but it might have been called the 250 Inter.

The 212 Inter chassis had a 2600mm (102.4 inch) wheelbase. The new 250 Mille Miglia wheelbase was about 8 inches shorter, at 2400mm, but it was longer

CHAPTER FOUR

Above A more satisfactory solution was this 2-window coupé with wraparound rear window. This led directly to the 250 Europa design.

Left Another view of the classic front invented by Pinin Farina for their favorite customer-Ferrari.

than the 212 Export and the 225 Sport which both had a wheelbase of 2250mm. Experimentation with the 212 Inter and 225 Sport chassis led to the median proportions of the new 250 Mille Miglia, which also carried on the direct line of Colombo-based engines, while the 250 Europa veered off with a physically larger engine, based on the big Lampredi engine. (To identify these engines count the number of capped nuts at the bottom edge of the valve cover. The Colombo engine has six; the Lampredi has seven.) In addition to the unknown number of possible 250 Inters, there may also have been a few 250 Colombo engines installed in 250 Europa chassis. Without access to all of the factory assembly sheets - or the cars themselves - it is impossible to be certain. In addition, a few 250MMs were built for road use only (this could include rally use) and these include 0334M and 0356M.

This unique Vignale-bodied 250 Mille Miglia was obviously not built for pure racing. It was a compromise intended for high speed touring or rally use. It is chassis number 0334M.

Another view of C/N 0334M shows its capacious rear indicating more than adequate room for luggage. Certainly, this is not a feature of a standard competition 250MM.

Undoubtedly the 250 Europa was the commercial department's answer to standardizing engine production and, when taken together with the 375 America, chassis production as well. The larger, heavier 3-litre Lampredi engine was to last less than a year, and only about 18 were produced. By mid-1954 it was out of production. The Lampredi engine survived, but as an even larger displacement engine, at 4.9 litres, in a large luxury touring car, the 410 Superamerica. The Colombo continued its unbroken development from 1947 through all of the 250GTs and directly to the 275GTB of 1964.

CHAPTER FOUR

Two views of one of the rare 250 Europas bodied by Vignale. This is C/N 0313EU, which is believed to be the car first shown by Luigi Chinetti at the 1954 New York Auto Show. This is a dechromed version of the car after it arrived in California some years ago.

TOWARDS PRODUCTION

SPECIFICATIONS

250 Mille Miglia

Type	250
Model	Mille Miglia
Years made	1953-1954
Chassis range	0230M - 0390M *
Number produced	31
Coachbuiders	Pinin Farina and Vignale.
Body styles	Spyders, coupés & Berlinettas
Body material	Aluminium
Seating capacity	2
Engine type	V12 60°
Displacement	2953cc
Bore and stroke	73mm x 58.8mm
Cyl. head	SOHC, 6 Ports, single inside plug, roller rockers
Ignition	2 distributors
Compression	9.0 to 1
Carburation	3 x36IF4C
Lubrication	Wet sump
Horsepower	240bhp @ 7,200rpm
Chassis/Drivetrain	Engine/gearbox in front
Frame	Tubular steel with oval maintubes
Transmission	4 speed
Axle ratio	5 to 1
Brakes	Hydraulic drum
Wheels	Borrani wire 5.50 x 16 front 6.00 x 16 rear
Front suspension	Ind., A-arms, transverse leaf springs, lever shocks
Rear suspension	Live axle, semi-elliptical leaf springs, lever shocks
Curb weight	2300lbs
Wheelbase	2400mm
Track front	1300mm
Track rear	1320mm

* Possibly only 2 built for road use: 0334M & 0356M

250 Europa

Type	250
Model	Europa
Years made	1953-1954
Chassis range	0301EU-0351EU
Number produced	18/20
Coachbuiders	Pinin Farina & Vignale
Body styles	Coupé
Body material	Aluminium & steel
Seating capacity	2
Engine type	V12 60° Lampredi
Displacement	2963cc
Bore and stroke	68mm x 68mm
Cyl. head	SOHC, single inside plug, roller rockers
Ignition	2 Distributors
Compression	8.0 to 1
Carburation	3 x 36DCF
Lubrication	Wet sump
Horsepower	200/220bhp @ 6,000rpm
Chassis/Drivetrain	Same as 250MM
Frame	Same as 250MM
Transmission	4 speed
Axle ratio	Various
Brakes	Hydraulic drum
Wheels	Borrani wire
Front suspension	Ind., A-arms, transverse leaf springs, Houdaille shocks
Rear suspension	Live axle, semi-elliptical springs, Houdaille shocks
Curb weight	Est. 2500/2600lbs
Wheelbase	2800mm
Track front	1325mm
Track rear	1320mm

The Series 1 410 Superamerica chassis proved to provide ideal proportions for Pinin Farina to be able to achieve a long, low purposeful stance.

CHAPTER FIVE

FOR THE ELITE

410 Superamerica (1956-1959)

The large Lampredi engine was in it's glory when utilized in the 375 America on the road, and in the 375 Mille Miglia and 375 Plus on the track. Wayne Golomb, who has owned some of the most important ones in the world, states the case quite eloquently: "It is unfortunate that Lampredi engines are so rare and that more people have not had the chance to experience them. Anyone who has driven a car with a large displacement Lampredi engine will tell you that, depending on the gearing, it has Cobra-like acceleration and phenomenal top speed, especially considering the tyre capabilities and aerodynamics of the era."

The 410 Superamerica was but more of the same - a continuation of the lofty Lampredi heritage. The engine was enlarged from the 84mm x 68mm of the 375 America to 88mm x 66mm, giving an engine of 4962cc. The 340 horsepower was up from 300. The chassis was strengthened and the suspension modernized. The comfortable, stable, long wheelbase of 280mm was retained as being totally appropriate to its

Another version of Pinin Farinas classic coupé design for the 410 Superamerica.

CHAPTER FIVE

its luxurious demeanour. The first one was unveiled at the 1956 Brussels Motor Show and was a classic Pinin Farina design, derived from the theme supplied by their 250 Europa, but longer, sleeker and more purposeful. No two were alike in detail and production was limited to about one a month. The customer list was impressive and included royalty and captains of industry from the U.S., France, Great Britain and Switzerland, not to mention Emperor Bao-Dai of Thailand who lived in exiled splendour in Paris. Of the 23 Series 1 and 2 made, at least 14 were of the basic Pinin Farina coupé design shown at Brussels. The Series 1 cars had a wheelbase of 2800mm and the Series 2 car had the shorter wheelbase of 2600mm. The difference was hardly noticeable.

A number of unique body styles were produced on the 410 Superamerica chassis. The most bizarre was by the coachbuilding house of Ghia, using a design by Ing. Savonuzzi that had been developed for Chrysler, called the Gilda. It was pure auto-show fantasy, and it is surprising that it was sold to an American, Bob Wilke, who sponsored many Indy cars. The engine of this Ghia prototype was a 510 (supposedly of 6120cc!) specially made by Ferrari for Mr Wilke.

Most notable of all the 410 Superamericas was the Pinin Farina Superfast I mounted on the Series I long wheelbase chassis. This very special styling exercise

FOR THE ELITE

Herewith, three views of the anomalous Ghia body mounted on the 510 Superamerica, chassis number 0473SA. To be kind, it is simply not appropriate to a Ferrari.

first appeared at the Paris Salon in October 1956. It's single most unique feature was its cantilevered top with no windshield posts. However, before the car was sold to its first owner, oil man William Doheney of Los Angeles, windshield posts were added. The car was rarely ever used and years later a subsequent owner discovered that the engine featured twin ignition - 24 spark plugs - and was probably a development engine for the 410 Sport, which revived and updated the old 375 Formula I engine of 1950/51.

Carrozzeria Boano, who were concurrently building a series of 250GT coupés decided to construct three very special prototype Ferraris and two of these were 410 Superamericas. One was the only convertible built on the 410SA chassis and was first shown at the 1956 Turin Motor Show. These Boanos seemed derivative in their use of American-inspired fins but three decades later they seem, on closer inspection, to achieve a validity of their own which is based on the

61

lightness and refinement of their details. This is further reinforced by the smaller scale of the Ferraris.

Totally unexpected was the one contribution by Scaglietti on chassis number 0671SA. It was over-decorated, over-styled and rarely photographed or seen. Far more important was the special coupé built for NART supporter Jan de Vroom. This was an extraordinary exercise that redefined Pinin Farina's approach to the high-powered luxury coupé concept. It was, and is, a landmark design and led directly to the Series 3 410 Superamericas. All 12 were variations on the deVroom theme (C/N 0719SA). These final 410 Superamericas were the last Lampredi engined Ferraris and also were the largest Ferrari engines ever to power a road model until the introduction of the BB512 in 1976.

Superfast I - while somewhat overblown with cliché fins, the basics are solid and original and lead naturally to a new concept direction for Pinin Farina. The interior photo clearly shows the original cantilevered roof with a total lack of windshield support, except for the glass itself.

Top This very special design, (C/N 0719SA) for a very special customer, Jan de Vroom, is a distillation of the best in Superfast I and presented with conviction a new road for Pinin Farina to follow.

Above An open headlight version of one of the Series 3 cars - this could be 1423SA - was more staid and less successful than the covered headlight versions.

SPECIFICATIONS

410 Superamerica Series 1

Type	410
Model	SA Series 1
Years made	1956
Chassis range	0423SA -0501SA
Number produced	17
Coachbuiders	Pinin Farina, Ghia, Boano
Body styles	Coupé & convertible
Body material	Aluminium & steel
Seating capacity	2
Engine type	V12 60° Lampredi
Displacement	4962cc
Bore and stroke	88mm x 68mm
Cyl. head	SOHC, single inside plug
Ignition	2 distributors
Compression	8.5 to 1
Carburation	3 x 40DCF
Lubrication	Wet sump
Horsepower	340bhp @ 6000rpm
Chassis/Drivetrain	Engine/gearbox in front
Frame	Tubular steel with oval maintubes
Transmission	4 speed all synchromesh
Axle ratio	3.44 to 1
Brakes	Hydraulic drum
Wheels	Borrani wire 6.50 x16
Front suspension	Independent, coil springs, A-arms, lever shocks
Rear suspension	Live axle, semi-elliptical springs, lever shocks
Curb weight	Est. 3600lbs
Wheelbase	2800mm
Track front	1455mm
Track rear	1450mm

410 Superamerica Series 2

Type	410
Model	SA Series 2
Years made	1957
Chassis range	0671SA - 0721SA
Number produced	6
Coachbuiders	Pinin Farina & Scaglietti
Body styles	Coupé & Berlinetta
Body material	Aluminium & steel
Seating capacity	2
Engine type	V12 60° Lampredi
Displacement	4962cc
Bore and stroke	88mm x 68mm
Cyl. head	SOHC, single inside plug
Ignition	2 distributors
Compression	8.5 to 1
Carburation	3 x 40DCF
Lubrication	Wet sump
Horsepower	340bhp @ 6000rpm
Chassis/Drivetrain	Engine/gearbox in front
Frame	Tubular steel with oval maintubes
Transmission	4 speed all synchromesh
Axle ratio	3.99 to 1
Brakes	Hydraulic drum
Wheels	Borrani wire 5.50 x16 front 6.50x16 rear
Front suspension	Independent, coil springs, Houdaille shocks
Rear suspension	Half elliptical springs, Houdaille shocks
Curb weight	Est. 3600lbs
Wheelbase	2600mm
Track front	1455mm
Track rear	1450mm

410 Superamerica Series 3

Type	410
Model	SA Series 3
Years made	1958-1959
Chassis range	1015SA - 1495SA
Number produced	12
Coachbuiders	Pinin Farina
Body styles	Coupé
Body material	Steel
Seating capacity	2
Engine type	V12 60° Lampredi
Displacement	4962cc
Bore and stroke	88mm x 68mm
Cyl. head	SOHC, single outside plug
Ignition	2 distributors
Compression	9.0 to 1
Carburation	3 x 42 DCF
Lubrication	Wet sump
Horsepower	400bhp @ 6500rpm
Chassis/Drivetrain	Engine/gearbox in front
Frame	Tubular steel with oval maintubes
Transmission	4 speed
Axle ratio	3.44 to 1 (and others)
Brakes	Hydraulic drum
Wheels	Borrani wire, 6.60 x16
Front suspension	Independent, coil springs, Houdaille shocks
Rear suspension	Semi-elliptical springs, lever shocks, Houdaille shocks
Curb weight	Est. 3600lbs
Wheelbase	2600mm
Track front	1455mm
Track rear	1450mm

Note. First Ferrari model with outside plug engine.

Two examples of the 'standard' 250GT Europa as created by Pinin Farina. The one posed on the marble floor is one of the original production cars with a 2-tone paint scheme.

CHAPTER SIX

Production Begins

250 Europa GT (1954 - 1955)
250 Boano/Ellena (1956-1958)
250GT Tour De France (1955-1959)
250GT Pininfarina Coupé (1958-1960)

At the annual Paris Salon in October 1954, the Colombo engine rejoined the main stream of Ferrari engine development for their road cars. The larger and heavier 3-litre Lampredi engine was abandoned in favour of the compact, lighter and more efficient Colombo design. (Development of the larger Lampredi engines continued in the three series of 410 Superamericas.) The new car together with the new engine was soon to be called the 250GT. It was a refined road version of the very popular competition-oriented 250 Mille Miglia.

At a quick glance it looked like a 250 Europa but it was built on a new, shorter chassis with a wheelbase of 2600mm. On closer inspection it was a tighter, sleeker package. About 35 250GT Europas were built and about 10 of these were special bodies that can be considered as prototypes or 'show cars' and many were built for special customers. But keep in mind that even the 25 'standard' cars did differ in detail. Total standardisation was on the way but it had not yet arrived.

Pinin Farina was now Ferrari's prime supplier of coachwork, and the last Vignale-bodied Ferrari was built on 250GT chassis number 0359GT for Princess de Rethy of Belgium. With few exceptions Pinin Farina, renamed Pininfarina late in 1958, was now responsible for all of Ferrari's coachwork requirements. Of the very special cars built by Pinin Farina during this period, four of them looked like the 250MM Competition Berlinetta and two forecast the design of the 14-louvre Tour de France Berlinetta.

Ferrari was now determined to put a road car into production and the Pinin Farina experiments were crystalised in a new design that was first shown to the public at the Geneva Motor Show in March 1956. Although the prototype cars were designed and built by Pinin Farina, the final version was given to Carrozzeria Boano to put into genuine series production. However the Boano coachbuilders shield did not appear on these cars it appeared only on a few prototypes that Boano built for Ferrari, the last of which is chassis number 0531GT, an elaborate show version of the standard 250GT Boano coupé.

By mid-1957 Mario Boano had gone to FIAT to head a new central styling department. The Boano works were taken over by his partner, Luciano Pollo, and his son-in-law Ezio Ellena. A few cars appeared with the new Ellena badge but in general no coachbuilders identification was used on these cars. About 50 of the Boano/Ellena coupés were made by mid-1958, when production ceased.

At Pinin Farina, 250GT convertibles were being experimented with, and along with these a few special 250GT coupés were produced, such as the one (C/N 0751GT) built for the irrepressible Princess Liliana de Rethy of the Belgium Royal Family. At the same time Pinin Farina had begun building prototypes for the new model that was to replace the ageing Boano/Ellena Coupé. By September 1958 the new 250GT Pininfarina 'notchback' coupé was in production at their own expanded factory where they could control the quality themselves. The earliest of the new run featured an engine with a single distributor, which proved troublesome and was retrofitted in most cases with two distributors at factory expense. Very soon the 128F engine was adopted with outside spark plugs and a new 4-speed gearbox using an electrically actuated 5th-speed overdrive. By early 1959 most of the cars in this group were fitted with disc brakes as standard equipment. Despite the new pressure of production responsibilities Pininfarina continued to issue prototypes and 'specials' of great quality and ingenuity.

The 250GT Tour de France is included in this

CHAPTER SIX

chapter as it evolved out of the lessons learned with the 250 Mille Miglia and the 250 Europa. The very first official 250GT was C/N 0357GT, a 250GT Europa built for competition with an all-aluminium body built by Pinin Farina in 1955, but not released until March 1956. Between April and July 1955 Pinin Farina built three more 250GTs that were 250MM lookalikes: 0369GT, 0383GT and 0385GT. A bit later, in October 1955, 0393GT appeared at the 1955 Paris Salon and presented a new design that included many louvres on the sail panel. Pininfarina made two more prototypes (0403GT and 0415GT) before Scaglietti themselves appeared at the 1956 Geneva Motor Show with their own prototype for the limited production Tour de France 250GT competition coupé - this was 0425GT with the 14-louvre sail panels. The first production 14-louvre was 0585GT built in November 1956. The production of the competition-orientated 250GTs was now in the hands of Scaglietti in Modena.

Left The interior of the 250GT Europa is well laid out for the convenience of the driver but lacks the luxury look that many expected of such an expensive car. Not surprisingly it sold primarily to enthusiasts who valued its performance over its limited amenities.

Above & right A good example of a production 250GT Boano coupé with the low roof. This is chassis number 0510GT. The chain that shows in the interior photo controlled the radiator blind that was standard equipment on this model.

CHAPTER SIX

PRODUCTION BEGINS

Above left An interesting Pinin Farina variation on chassis number 0407GT. This is one of the studies that led to the final version of the Boano-built coupé. Note the windshield wipers on the rear window.

Below left First shown at the Paris Salon in 1955 this unusual prototype presented an almost finished design for the Tour de France competition berlinetta of two years later. This is C/N 0393GT.

Above These views show a very special one-off, C/N 0403GT, with a rear end treatment echoing the 375MM coupé built for Roberto Rossellini (C/N 0456AM) a year earlier. The chassis numbers, odd vs. even, are not synchronized, as Ferrari was building many more competition cars than road cars during that period.

CHAPTER SIX

Top This photograph clearly shows the Boano/Ellena high roof design initiated when Ellena took over production. This feature does seem to disturb the smoothness of the pure Pininfarina/Boano version that came before. No doubt it did allow more head room. This is C/N 0835GT, one of the last built.

Above This is believed to be one of the pre-production prototypes built in 1958. The final result was the Pininfarina 250GT 'notchback' coupé.

PRODUCTION BEGINS

Top Another pre-production prototype, this shows the final version for production.

Above This is one of two identical early Pininfarina prototypes that were sold to the same French family. These are C/N's 0841GT and 0843GT.

CHAPTER SIX

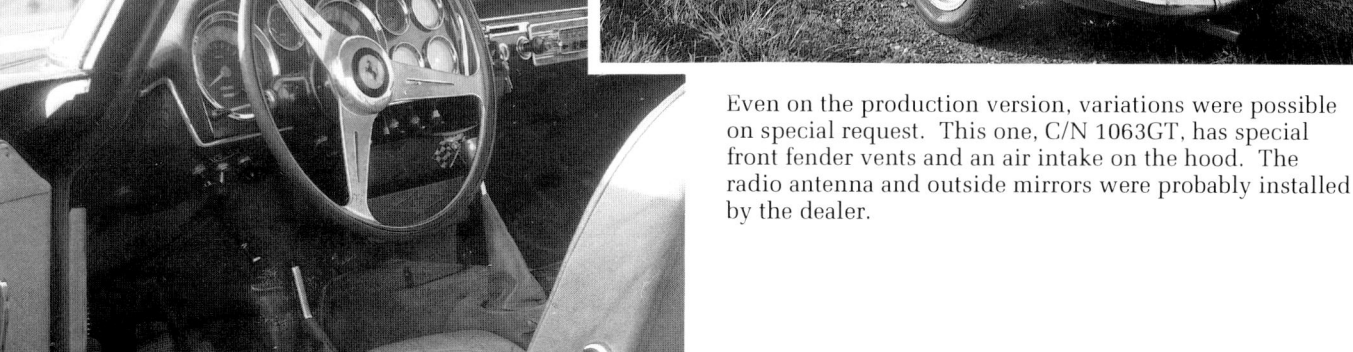

Even on the production version, variations were possible on special request. This one, C/N 1063GT, has special front fender vents and an air intake on the hood. The radio antenna and outside mirrors were probably installed by the dealer.

While this appears to be a 410 Superamerica it is in fact a 250GT specially built for Prince Bernhard of Holland. This body was built on C/N 0725GT.

CHAPTER SIX

Two revealing photos of C/N 1273GT probably taken when the car was being delivered to a Swiss dealer.

A particularly elegant variation, C/N 0853GT, was built for Prince Bertil of Sweden, also a notable Bugatti fancier.

CHAPTER SIX

Above left This variation included bumperettes, a polished rocker panel strip and very special form-fitting bucket seats. It is believed to be a later car than 0853GT and was built for Dr Wax of Genoa, Italy.

Below left, above & right In this case, a stock 250GT, C/N 1777GT, was shortened in wheelbase and rebodied by Neri and Bonnacini along lines suggested by American Tom Meade. Tiny chrome bumpers had been removed by the time these photos were taken. The lines are similar to those used on the Nembo convertible created by the same team about 1965.

CHAPTER SIX

PRODUCTION BEGINS

SPECIFICATIONS

Above Another 250GT Speciale, this time for Ferrari's loyal client Princess Lilian de Rethy of Belgium. It was created on C/N 0751GT.

Left Probably the most unusual body built on the 250GT notchback coupé chassis is this superb interpretation by Pininfarina on chassis number 1187GT. It was first shown at the 1959 Geneva Motor Show.

250GT Europa

Type	250GT
Model	Europa
Years made	1954-1955
Chassis range	0357GT-0427GT
Number produced	35
Coachbuiders	Pinin Farina & Vignale
Body styles	Coupé & Berlinetta
Body material	Aluminium & steel
Seating capacity	2
Engine type	V12 60° Colombo
Displacement	2953cc
Bore and stroke	73mm x 58.8mm
Cyl. head	SOHC with roller rockers, single inside plug
Ignition	2 distributors
Compression	8.5 to 1
Carburation	3 x 36DCF
Lubrication	Wet sump
Horsepower	220bhp @ 7000rpm
Chassis/Drivetrain	Engine/gearbox in front
Frame	Tubular steel with oval maintubes
Transmission	4-speed all synchromesh with engine
Axle ratio	4.57 to 1 (and others)
Brakes	Hydraulic drum
Wheels	Borrani wire , 6.00 x16
Front suspension	Independent, A-arms, coil springs, Houdaille shocks
Rear suspension	Live axle, semi-elliptical springs, Houdaille shocks
Curb weight	Est. 2800lbs
Wheelbase	2600mm
Track front	1354mm
Track rear	1349mm

SPECIFICATIONS

250GT Boano

Type	250GT
Model	Boano
Years made	1956-1957
Chassis range	0429GT-0675GT
Number produced	70-80
Coachbuiders	Boano
Body styles	Coupé - lowroof
Body material	Aluminium & steel
Seating capacity	2
Engine type	V12 60° Colombo
Displacement	2953cc
Bore and stroke	73mm x 58.8mm
Cyl. head	SOHC with roller rockers, single inside plug
Ignition	2 distributors
Compression	8.5/8.8 to 1
Carburation	3 x 36DCF
Lubrication	Wet sump
Horsepower	220/240bhp @ 7000rpm
Chassis/Drivetrain	Engine/gearbox in front
Frame	Tubular steel with oval maintubes
Transmission	4 speed all synchromesh with engine
Axle ratio	4.57 to 1 (and others)
Brakes	Hydraulic drum
Wheels	Borrani wire , 6.00 x16
Front suspension	Independent, A-arms, coil springs, Houdaille shocks
Rear suspension	Live axle, semi-elliptical springs, Houdaille shocks
Curb weight	Est.2800lbs
Wheelbase	2600mm
Track front	1354mm
Track rear	1349mm

250GT Boano/Ellena

Type	250GT
Model	Boano/Ellena
Years made	1957-1958
Chassis range	0679GT-0887GT
Number produced	50
Coachbuiders	Ellena
Body styles	Coupé -high roof
Body material	Aluminium & steel
Seating capacity	2
Engine type	V12 60° Colombo
Displacement	2953cc
Bore and stroke	73mm x 58.8mm
Cyl. head	SOHC with roller rockers, single inside plug
Ignition	2 distributors
Compression	8.5/8.8 to 1
Carburation	3 x 36DCF
Lubrication	Wet sump
Horsepower	220/240bhp @ 7000rpm
Chassis/Drivetrain	Engine/gearbox in front
Frame	Tubular steel with oval maintubes
Transmission	4 speed all synchromesh with engine
Axle ratio	4.57 to 1 (and others)
Brakes	Hydraulic drum
Wheels	Borrani wire , 6.00 x16
Front suspension	Independent, A-arms,coil springs & Houdaille shocks
Rear suspension	Live axle, semi-elliptical springs & Houdaille shocks
Curb weight	Est.2800lbs
Wheelbase	2600mm
Track front	1354mm
Track rear	1349mm

PRODUCTION BEGINS

250GT Pininfarina Coupé

Type	250GT
Model	Pinin Farina Notchback
Years made	1958-1960
Chassis range	0851GT-2081GT
Number produced	350
Coachbuiders	Pinin Farina and Pininfarina
Body styles	Coupé
Body material	Steel
Seating capacity	2
Engine type	V12 60° Colombo
Displacement	2953cc
Bore and stroke	73mm x 58.8mm
Cyl. head	SOHC with roller rockers Single inside plug*
Ignition	1 or 2 distributors*
Compression	8.57/9.0 to 1
Carburation	3 x 36DCF
Lubrication	Wet sump
Horsepower	240bhp @ 7000rpm
Chassis/Drivetrain	Engine/gearbox in front
Frame	Tubular steel with oval maintubes
Transmission	4 speed and (1960) 4 speed plus overdrive
Axle ratio	4.25 (and others)
Brakes	Hydraulic drum or (1960) discs on all wheels
Wheels	Borrani wire 6.00 x16 &185 x 400
Front suspension	Independent, A-arms, coil springs, lever shocks †
Rear suspension	Live axle, semi-elliptical springs, lever shocks †
Curb weight	2800lbs
Wheelbase	2600mm
Track front	1354mm
Track rear	1349mm

* 1960 cars had single outside plugs with 2 distributors.
† Telescopic shocks were added from about 1960

250GT Tour de France

Type	250GT
Model	Tour de France
Years made	1955-1959
Chassis range	0383GT-1401GT
Number produced	84
Coachbuiders	Pinin Farina , Scaglietti & Zagato
Body styles	Berlinetta
Body material	Aluminium
Seating capacity	2
Engine type	V12 60° Colombo
Displacement	2 953cc
Bore and stroke	73mm x 58.8mm
Cyl. head	SOHC with roller rockers, single inside plug
Ignition	2 distributors
Compression	8.8-9.5 to 1
Carburation	3 x 36DCL/DCZ
Lubrication	Wet sump
Horsepower	230/280bhp @ 7000rpm
Chassis/Drivetrain	Engine/gearbox in front
Frame	Tubular steel with oval maintubes
Transmission	4 speed
Axle ratio	4.0 to 1 and others
Brakes	Hydraulic drum
Wheels	Borrani wire 6.00 x16
Front suspension	Independent, A-arms, coil springs lever shocks
Rear suspension	Live axle semi-elliptical springs, lever shocks
Curb weight	2600lbs
Wheelbase	2600mm
Track front	1354mm
Track rear	1349mm

A beautifully restored example of the 1956 410 Superamerica Series 1 seen entering the field at the 1984 Pebble Beach Concours. This is chassis number 0475SA.

While this looks like the '4.9 Superfast'(a very special Series 2 410 Superamerica prototype) it is in fact a 250GT built by Pinin Farina expressly for Prince Bernhard of Holland. It is chassis number 0725GT built in 1957.

Pinin Farina's first 250GT convertible was this unusual creation with an English-inspired cut-down door for the driver. It first appeared at the 1957 Geneva Motor Show. The overall shape was clean and well-resolved but some of the details detracted from the final result. The chassis was number 0655GT.

CHAPTER SEVEN

ALFRESCO ELEGANCE

250GT Series 1 Convertible (1957-1959)
250GT Spyder California (1957-1962)
250GT Series 2 Convertible (1959-1962)

As Ferrari expanded their production, Pinin Farina's ability to service their burgeoning client grew by leaps and bounds. In addition to building special coupés on both 410 Superamerica and 250GT chassis, they began to build a series of open Spyder prototypes. Strictly speaking, the first 250GT convertible was the work of Carrozzeria Boano on chassis number 0461GT. The series 1 Pinin Farina convertibles started with chassis number 0655GT, a special design for an Italian customer, which was taken over very quickly by Ferrari factory driver Peter Collins. The public first saw it at the 1957 Geneva Motor Show.

About 40 of these 'first series' 250GT Pinin Farina convertibles were built from late 1957 to very early in 1959. The best did resemble the long wheelbase (LWB) Spyder Californias and certainly the design of the California must be credited to Pinin Farina although the prototype was built by Scaglietti. A study of the prototype in bare metal indicates that some experiments were carried out with the width and shape of the top of the front fenders. This prototype, C/N 0769GT, was completed in December, 1957, and was an open version of the Tour De France Berlinetta which Scaglietti had been making since April 1956. The car before 0769GT and the two cars after were all Scaglietti bodied Tour De France Berlinettas with all-aluminium bodies. Despite this, 0769GT was built with a steel body with aluminium hood, trunk, lid, doors and firewall. Steel was probably chosen to impart some extra stiffness to the open structure. The Californias were built to a more sporting specification and at least 8 of the LWB Californias had all-aluminum

CHAPTER SEVEN

Here is 0655GT some time later, repainted for its first owner, Cav. Fassio of Italy. It gained more notoriety as the personal car of Peter Collins, a Ferrari factory Grand Prix driver at that time.

bodies and were intended for competition. The second of these, C/N 1451GT, finished 5th overall in the 1959 Le Mans 24-Hour Race.

Like the Series 1 Pinin Farina convertibles, most of the Californias had covered headlights but there was no pattern to how and when they occurred. For example, 1451GT had open headlights. A more consistent feature was the outside fuel filler cap in the all-aluminium LWB California.

At the introduction of the short wheelbase (SWB) California in 1960 disc brakes and the outside plug (128F) engine became standard equipment. (A few outside plug engines had been fitted in special LWB Californias in 1959). The SWB California was the open version of the SWB Berlinetta and both shared the same chassis with a wheel-based of 2400mm. Both were available with either steel or aluminum bodies and in various states of tune. The LWB Californias with all-aluminium bodies had been known to be somewhat flexible in the chassis department and this did adversely effect handling in competition. Perhaps for this reason only 3 LWB Californias were made with all-aluminium bodies. The 250GT of choice for racing was the much more predictable SWB Berlinetta. Despite the negatives the Spyder Californias had an aura of their own as the most sporting of all Ferraris of the late 1950s and early 1960s. Combined with their very limited availability (about 49 LWBs and 55 SWBs) they have become known as the 'in' car to own among Ferraristi.

ALFRESCO ELEGANCE

Pinin Farina's next experiment in open coachwork for the 250GT chassis took the form of a Spyder Competitzione for a Belgian customer. It is chassis number 0663GT, and has since been equipped with a more usual top and windshield.

The 250GT Series 2 Pininfarina convertible was first shown at the 1959 Paris Salon, always held in October so that most manufacturers could preview their new models for the following year. This convertible was strictly for road use and was, quite simply, an open version of the new Pininfarina 250GT 'notchback' coupé. They shared the same chassis and mechanical features and were built side by side by Pininfarina (their new name) until 1962. About 200 were built and as far as is known only one was equipped with covered headlights as new from Pininfarina. Quite a few exist now and must be considered as altered after the fact without proof to the contrary. It was the end of an era, for no more Ferrari convertibles were available before 1965.

CHAPTER SEVEN

Above & left, below left, left Pinin Farina's third and fourth attempts looked like this and were realized on chassis numbers 0705GT and 0709GT (these photos are of the former). Certainly this example defines more clearly Pinin Farina's ultimate intentions. Mechanically it is the same as the 250GT Boano coupé with the inside plug engine. The luxury look did not extend to the instrument panel, which is finished in black crackle paint.

CHAPTER SEVEN

Top A rare right-hand drive example of the Series 1 is on chassis number 0811GT.

Above A good example of an early covered headlight LWB California, C/N 0937GT, first sold to Brigitte Bardot.

ALFRESCO ELEGANCE

Above The interior of 1217GT. Note the instrument panel in crackle black paint. The non-standard device behind the gearshift is probably to support a small child.

Left An uncluttered rear view of 1217GT which is representative of the early run of LWB Californias.

Below An early LWB California with open headlights and the optional hardtop. This is C/N 1217GT.

CHAPTER SEVEN

In this photo of the SWB California it looks only slightly stubbier than the LWB. This is C/N 2505GT, a good example of the open-headlight version.

Right This is a good sample of the middle range SWB California, showing clearly the standard feature of the air intake scoop being indented in the hood. The interior shows the use of leatherette on the instrument panel and a somewhat longer than standard gear-shift lever. This is C/N 3301GT.

ALFRESCO ELEGANCE

CHAPTER SEVEN

This SWB California was the next to the last made and shows this model in its final form. With the top up or down it is equally attractive. This particular car, C/N 4131GT, uses air horns only on the carburettors.

CHAPTER SEVEN

Pininfarina gave the new production model Series 2 convertible a three-way look: top down, top up and hardtop mounted.

By 1960 Pininfarina was building very few special cars. This exception is on a SWB (2400mm) chassis number 1737GT and was first displayed in public at the 1960 Geneva Motor Show.

CHAPTER SEVEN

Three different views of C/N 2029GT. Unlike the Californias these Series 2 convertibles were all made by Pininfarina and bore their badge on both sides.

ALFRESCO ELEGANCE

CHAPTER SEVEN

This Series 2 Convertible has been in France since new. It is C/N 1727GT. Note the covered headlights and special side intakes. This work could have been done by Pininfarina themselves but authenticity would have to be confirmed.

Another unique modification - this time incorporating a flush sunroof in a Pininfarina hardtop. This is C/N 2489GT.

CHAPTER SEVEN

SPECIFICATIONS

250GT Series 1

Type	250GT
Model	Series I
Years made	1957-59
Chassis range	0461GT-1475GT
Number produced	41
Coachbuiders	Pinin Farina
Body styles	Convertible
Body material	Steel
Seating capacity	2
Engine type	V12 60°
Displacement	2953cc
Bore and stroke	73mm x 58.8mm
Cyl. head	SOHC single inside plug, roller rockers
Ignition	1 or 2 distributors
Compression	8.5 to 1
Carburation	3 x 38 DCN
Lubrication	Wet sump
Horsepower	220/248bhp @ 7000rpm
Chassis/Drivetrain	Engine/gearbox in front
Frame	Tubular– maintubes oval
Transmission	4 speed
Axle ratio	Various
Brakes	Hydraulic drums
Wheels	16" Borrani wire
Front suspension	Independent, A-arms, coil springs & shocks*
Rear suspension	Live axle ,semi-elliptical springs & shocks
Curb weight	2400lbs
Wheelbase	2600mm
Track front	1354mm
Track rear	1349mm

*Telescopic shocks were introduced in 1958 and 1959

250GT LWB California

Type	250GT
Model	LWB California
Years made	1957-60
Chassis range	0769GT-1715GT
Number produced	49
Coachbuiders	Scaglietti
Body styles	Spyder
Body material	Steel & aluminium
Seating capacity	2
Engine type	V12 60°
Displacement	2953cc
Bore and stroke	73mm x 58.8mm
Cyl. head	SOHC single inside plug, roller rockers. †
Ignition	2 distributors
Compression	9.1/9.6 to 1
Carburation	3 x 36/40DCL 6
Lubrication	Wet sump
Horsepower	240/250bhp @ 7000rpm
Chassis/Drivetrain	Engine/gearbox in front
Frame	Tubular– maintubes oval
Transmission	4 speed
Axle ratio	Various
Brakes	Hydraulic drums or discs
Wheels	16" Borrani wire
Front suspension	Independent, A-arms, coil springs & shocks*
Rear suspension	Live axle ,semi-elliptical springs & shocks
Curb weight	2300lbs
Wheelbase	2600mm
Track front	1354mm
Track rear	1349mm

*Telescopic shocks were introduced in 1958 and 1959
† Some outside plug engines fitted

ALFRESCO ELEGANCE

250GT SWB California	
Type	250GT
Model	SWB California
Years made	1960-63
Chassis range	1795GT-4167GT
Number produced	55
Coachbuiders	Scaglietti
Body styles	Spyder
Body material	Steel and aluminium
Seating capacity	2
Engine type	V12 60°
Displacement	2953cc
Bore and stroke	73mm x 58.8mm
Cyl. head	SOHC, single outside plug, roller rockers
Ignition	2 distributors
Compression	9.2/9.5 to 1
Carburation	3 x 40DCL6
Lubrication	Wet sump
Horsepower	280bhp @ 7000rpm
Chassis/Drivetrain	Engine/gearbox in front
Frame	Tubular– maintubes oval
Transmission	4 speed
Axle ratio	Various
Brakes	Hydraulic discs
Wheels	15" Borrani wire
Front suspension	Independent, A-arms, coil springs & shocks*
Rear suspension	Live axle, semi-elliptical springs & shocks
Curb weight	2400lbs
Wheelbase	2400mm
Track front	1378mm
Track rear	1374mm

*Telescopic shocks were introduced in 1958 and 1959

250GT Series 2	
Type	250GT
Model	Series II
Years made	1959-62
Chassis range	1537GT-3803GT
Number produced	200
Coachbuiders	Pinin Farina
Body styles	Convertible
Body material	Steel
Seating capacity	2
Engine type	V12 60°
Displacement	2953cc
Bore and stroke	73mm x 58.8mm
Cyl. head	SOHC, single inside plug, roller rockers †
Ignition	2 distributors
Compression	8.8 to 1
Carburation	3 x 38 DCN
Lubrication	Wet sump
Horsepower	240bhp @ 7000rpm
Chassis/Drivetrain	Engine/gearbox in front
Frame	Tubular– maintubes oval
Transmission	4 speed + overdrive
Axle ratio	Various
Brakes	Hydraulic discs
Wheels	16" Borrani wire
Front suspension	Independent, A-arms, coil springs & shocks*
Rear suspension	Live axle, semi-elliptical springs & shocks
Curb weight	2644lbs
Wheelbase	2600mm
Track front	1354mm
Track rear	1349mm

*Telescopic shocks were introduced in 1958 and 1959
† Outside plug phased in 1959 and 1960

The next to the last Series 1 Pinin Farina Convertible, chassis number 1439GT, begins to look more like the Series 2 production car, but still could be mistaken for a California Spyder.

An early example of an open headlight LWB California Spyder, this is chassis number 1505GT built around the middle of the run of only about 49 LWBs.

Right This is an early example of the LWB California Spyder. The outside filler cap indicates that it is an all aluminium car with some possible competition history. As the owner could not be found we must guess that it is chassis number 1085GT.

The steel gray car was built in May 1960, and is chassis number 1795GT, the first SWB California Spyder built. The red car with the silver hardtop is a rare example of a SWB with open headlights.

One of the pre-production prototypes, which appears to be identical to the early production cars.

Right This is believed to be the car which was first shown at the 1960 Paris Salon.

CHAPTER EIGHT

THE ELEGANCE EXPANDS

250GTE 2 + 2 (1960-1963)
250GT Lusso Berlinetta (1962-1964)

By the end of 1958, Ferrari had built a total of about 685 road cars, of which 183 had been produced in 1958. It was Ferrari's aim to increase their sale of road cars to be able to better support their racing effort. This had to mean new road models that would appeal to a larger audience. The close cooperation of Ferrari with Pininfarina produced two new models that would double the sale of road Ferraris within three years.

The first challenge was the proposal of a 2+2 in an overall package that would look and handle like a thoroughbred *gran turismo*. The wheelbase of 2600mm was chosen despite the fact that the wheelbase of the 2-seater notchback Pininfarina coupé was the same.

With a subtle repositioning of the engine slightly forward, Pininfarina was able to create a marginal 2+2, and this was just enough to make it a logical choice for Ferrari admirers who needed only the promise of two extra seats in the back to turn them into buyers. It stayed in production through 1963 and continues in concept through 1987 with the 412.

The new 250GTE 2+2 was announced at the Paris

CHAPTER EIGHT

THE ELEGANCE EXPANDS

Left Chassis number 2255GTE shows some minor changes but still represents the early first version.

Below left, *Below* Two views of C/N 2657GTE showing the second series one-piece tail lights. By the end of 1962 fog lights were added on either side of the grille and the parking lights moved further out.

Right The interior of C/N 2657GTE showing the oil-pressure gauge between the two large gauges (speedometer and tachometer) in front of the driver.

CHAPTER EIGHT

Motor in October 1960. The mechanical features were as advanced as might be expected for a road Ferrari. The horsepower was 240 at 7,000 rpm! At the end of 1962 further improvements and changes were made before it was replaced at the end of 1963 by the 330 America.

The 250GT Pininfarina 'notchback' coupé ceased production at the end of 1960, and was not replaced as Pininfarina was fully occupied in developing and putting into production the all-new 250GTE 2+2 . A *lusso* (de luxe) version of the SWB Berlinetta continued to be produced by Scaglietti, which along with the Competition version, grew into the GTO. The SWB *lusso* model was replaced by the new model which came to be known as the 250GT/L Berlinetta Lusso and was afterward commonly referred to as the Lusso.

A prototype of this new Lusso appeared at the Paris Motor in October 1962. The new Pininfarina design was a stylistic triumph. It was mounted to a new chassis with a 2400mm wheelbase that bore a great resemblence to the immortal 250GTO.

The remarkable shape of the new Lusso was striking indeed, and its pure sculptural form was for many the most attractive ever to grace a production-line Ferrari. Its performance and road-holding was up to Ferrari's high standard, but it suffered from a first gear ratio and a final drive ratio that were simply too high. Changing the rear axle ratio to 4.56 (as used on the 250GTE 2+2) proved to be a great improvement for normal legal driving speeds.

Ferrari began to tackle more seriously the problems of comfort and reliability and the Lusso boasted as standard equipement a thermostatically-operated radiator fan to preclude the overheating that had been reported in some markets such as the U.S.A. A driver-operated radiator blind was also included to induce a high enough water temperature to allow the heater and defroster to work properly in the winter. The

Above & left Pininfarina had the inspired habit of inventing new classics every year and the Lusso was no exception. Every line was perfection but the nose was vulnerable as the bumper was not as far forward as the nose!

Right Although the interior door trim was still spartan, Pininfarina was trying to create a more luxurious interior. The pleated seats and the padded instrument panel certainly helped. The grab handle on the passenger side was soon replaced with a foot bar (the white switch is not original).

switchable electric fuel pump (always included in all Ferraris) continued to be part of the standard specification, to avoid the indignity of vapour lock on a hot summer's day or in high altitudes. The Lusso proved to be a beautiful and reliable machine for everyday transport.

CHAPTER EIGHT

Two versions of C/N 4335GT, a 1963 special version built for the personal use of Mr. Pininfarina. The second version included covered headlights.

THE ELEGANCE EXPANDS

The vulnerability of the nose was overcome by many different 'after market' solutions. One of these was a custom built front bumper!

CHAPTER EIGHT

SPECIFICATIONS

250GTE 2+2

Type	250
Model	GTE 2 +2
Years made	1960-1963
Chassis range	1895-4961
Number produced	950
Coachbuiders	Pininfarina
Body styles	Coupé
Body material	Steel
Seating capacity	2+2
Engine type	V12 60° Colombo
Displacement	2953cc
Bore and stroke	73mm x 58.8mm
Cyl. head	SOHC, single outside plug, roller rockers
Ignition	2 distributors
Compression	9.2 to 1
Carburation	3 x 40 DCL/6
Lubrication	Wet sump
Horsepower	235bhp @ 7 000rpm
Chassis/Drivetrain	Engine/gearbox in front
Frame	Tubular– maintubes oval
Transmission	4 speed + overdrive
Axle ratio	4.56 to 1 and others
Brakes	Hydraulic discs
Wheels	15" Borrani wire
Front suspension	Independent A-arm, coil springs, telescopic shocks
Rear suspension	Live axl ,semi-elliptical springs, telescopic shocks
Curb weight	3150lbs
Wheelbase	2600mm
Track front	1395mm
Track rear	1387mm

250GT Berlinetta Lusso

Type	250
Model	GT/L Lusso
Years made	1962-1964
Chassis range	3849-5955
Number produced	350
Coachbuiders	Pininfarina & Scaglietti
Body styles	Berlinetta
Body material	Steel
Seating capacity	2
Engine type	V12 60° Colombo
Displacement	2953cc
Bore and stroke	73mm x 58.8mm
Cyl. head	SOHC, single outside plug, roller rockers
Ignition	2 distributors
Compression	9.2 to 1
Carburation	3 x 36DCS
Lubrication	Wet sump
Horsepower	240bhp @ 7,500rpm
Chassis/Drivetrain	Engine/gearbox in front
Frame	Tubular– maintubes oval
Transmission	4 speed
Axle ratio	4.0 to 1 and others
Brakes	Hydraulic discs
Wheels	15" Borrani wire
Front suspension	Independent, A-arms, coil springs, telescopic shocks
Rear suspension	Live axle,semi-elliptical spgs, telescopic shks,Watts linkage
Curb weight	2700lbs
Wheelbase	2400mm
Track front	1395mm
Track rear	1387mm

CHAPTER NINE

*L*IMITED *E*DITION *L*UXURY

400 Superamerica (1959-1964)
500 Superfast (1964-1966)
365 California (1966-1967)

This unique styling exercise is chassis number 1517SA and is believed to be the first 400 Superamerica. Once again the intended customer was Giovanni Agnelli. Cluttered with American styling clichés, it is not considered a great success.

The 400 Superamerica (it could also be written SuperAmerica as is sometimes found on the cars themselves) body style that truly represents this model best evolved from a prototype show car, the Superfast II (or SuperFast II), that was introduced to the public at the Turin Motor Show early in 1960. It represented the pinnacle of Pininfarina's creative art and an elegant new way to look at high-speed luxury transport. As the design was developed in the wind tunnel, it was even used for several 250GTO racing prototypes.

This totally new 'Coupé Aerodinamico' took some time to get into even limited production, so the first six or seven 400 Superamerica were of alternate designs. The first is believed to be C/N 1517SA, a unique special for the head of FIAT, Giovanni Agnelli.

CHAPTER NINE

In addition to Superfat II, six convertibles, one California-like Spyder, and a conventional 2+2 were built before the first production Coupé Aerodinamico arrived in early 1961. One more convertible and a very special Scaglietti Berlinetta had been built by August, 1962 when the last Series 1 (short wheelbase) C/N 3747SA was completed.

The first Series 2 (long wheelbase) was introduced at the London Motor Show in 1962 with C/N 3931SA. By the end of January 1964 21 more had been built, about one a month, of which three were convertible.

Throughout both series the coupés were a random mixture of closed-and open-headlight versions. In addition, each car was different in small details. Special interiors were often requested to fill special orders and within reasonable limits Pininfarina would accommodate these individual demands.

In March 1964 the new 500 Superfast was premiered at the Geneva Motor Show. It was a larger, more powerful and more luxurious replacement for the 400 Superamerica. The Series 1 ran to about 25 cars and the last, C/N 6679, was completed in September 1965 for the English actor, Peter Sellers. Of course it had right-hand drive, as did all of the last four built.

The Series 2 500 Superfast appeared late in 1965 and was featured at the 1966 Brussels Motor Show. Its appearance was little altered but did include new side louvres in the fenders and a new synchromesh 5-speed gearbox (the overdrive was discontinued). The last one was completed on August 1, 1966 for Col. Ronnie Hoare, the founder and head of Maranello Concessionaires Ltd., the Ferrari importer for Great Britain. It was a sad day, as it was the last of the

This is C/N 2207SA showing the first of many versions of Superfast II. It made a sensational first showing at the Turin Motor Show in 1960.

LIMITED EDITION LUXURY

limited-production closed Ferraris. While the newest 412 is technically superior it is not possible to personalize one to the extent that was permitted and encouraged when the 500 Superfast was built at the rate of only one a month!

Before the last 500 Superfast was completed the prototype of the new 365 California convertible was finished and made its debut at the 1966 Geneva Motor Show. A continuation of the 500 Superfast line, the 365 California used a new 4.4-litre engine based on the SOHC V12, proven in the racing 365P. The styling was based on Pininfarina's latest experiments and it was really a prototype show car put into limited production. Unaccountably, the handling was not up to Ferrari's usual standard and one new owner (who had owned and loved many earlier Ferraris) remarked that its handling was as bad as his wife's Ford Mustang! (Perhaps this chassis could not operate properly without the rigidity supplied by a closed body.) Only fourteen of these special open cars were made and production ceased in August 1967.

Three views of an early 400 Superamerica (probably C/N 1611SA or 2407SA) it illustrates clearly how Pininfarina's experiments with the Series 2 Convertible continued with the early 400 Superamericas. Note the quarter windows are attached to the removable hardtop.

CHAPTER NINE

This is a rare photo of Superfast II at the Brussels Motor Show in 1961. Here the hood intake has been added but the covers are still on the rear wheels. On a later version of Superfast II the rear wheel covers were removed.

Right This 1961 production version shows how features of the Superfast II were adopted. This is probably C/N 2373SA.

LIMITED EDITION LUXURY

CHAPTER NINE

This Superfast III - rebuilt from Superfast II and showing the revised styling for the 'greenhouse' and the controllable horizontal air intake for the radiator.

Top One of the later 400SA convertibles was C/N 3309SA which was shown at the 1962 New York Auto Show.

Above & right Superfast IV is a revision of Superfast III and is still C/N 2207SA. This time the ungainly 4-headlight set up represents a backward step - one of the few ever made by Pininfarina but destined to effect the styling of the 330GT 2+2 . Also shown here is a rare view of the interior.

CHAPTER NINE

This page & below right A good example of a Series 2 (LWB) 400 Superamerica. This is C/N 4111SA.

LIMITED EDITION LUXURY

Above & right The 500 Superfast was a less dramatic visual development of the 400 Superamerica. It was Ferrari's last limited production luxury car in closed form.

CHAPTER NINE

LIMITED EDITION LUXURY

The 365 California incorporated styling features from various Pininfarina prototypes - and not all of them for Ferrari. The door treatment forecast the 206GT Dino of two years later. This was the last limited production road Ferrari until the arrival of the 288GTO in 1985.

Chapter Nine

Specifications

400 Superamerica Series 1 & 2

Type	400
Model	SA Superamerica
Years made	1959-1964
Chassis range	1517-5139
Number produced	47
Coachbuiders	Pininfarina and Scaglietti
Body styles	Berlinetta and Scaglietti
Body material	Steel and aluminium
Seating capacity	2
Engine type	V12 60° Colombo
Displacement	3967cc
Bore and stroke	77mm x 71mm
Cyl. head	SOHC, single outside plug
Ignition	2 distributors
Compression	8.8 to 1
Carburation	3 x 42DCN and others
Lubrication	Wet sump
Horsepower	340bhp @ 7,000rpm
Chassis/Drivetrain	Engine/gearbox in front
Frame	Tubular–maintubes oval
Transmission	4 speed + overdrive
Axle ratio	Various
Brakes	Hydraulic discs
Wheels	15" Borrani wire
Front suspension	Independents, A-arms, coil springs, telescopic shocks
Rear suspension	Live axle, semi-elliptical springs, telescopic shocks
Curb weight	3500lbs (Est.)
Wheelbase	S1(SWB)2420mm S2(LBW)2600mm
Track front	S1(SWB)1359mm S2(LWB)1395mm
Track rear	S1(SWB)1350mm S2(LWB)1387mm

500 Superfast Series 1&2

Type	500
Model	SF Superfast
Years made	1964-1966
Chassis range	5951-8897
Number produced	37
Coachbuiders	Pininfarina
Body styles	Coupé
Body material	Steel
Seating capacity	2
Engine type	V12 60°
Displacement	4961cc
Bore and stroke	88mm x 68mm
Cyl. head	SOHC, single outside plug
Ignition	2 distributors
Compression	8.8 and 9.0 to 1
Carburation	3 x 40DCZ/6
Lubrication	Wet sump
Horsepower	400bhp @ 6500rpm
Chassis/Drivetrain	Engine/gearbox in front
Frame	Tubular–maintubes elliptical
Transmission	S1 4-speed + overdrive /S2 5-speed
Axle ratio	Various
Brakes	Hydraulic discs
Wheels	15" Borrani wire
Front suspension	Independent, A-arms, coil springs, telescopic shocks
Rear suspension	Live axle, semi-elliptical springs, telescopic shocks
Curb weight	3400lbs
Wheelbase	2650mm
Track front	1397mm
Track rear	1389mm

LIMITED EDITION LUXURY

365 California

Type	365
Model	California
Years made	1966-1967
Chassis range	8347-10369
Number produced	14
Coachbuiders	Pininfarina
Body styles	Convertible
Body material	Steel
Seating capacity	2
Engine type	V12 60°
Displacement	4390cc
Bore and stroke	81mm x 71mm
Cyl. head	SOHC, single outside plug
Ignition	2 distributors
Compression	8.8 to 1
Carburation	3 Weber carburettors
Lubrication	Wet sump
Horsepower	320bhp @ 6600rpm
Chassis/Drivetrain	Engine/gearbox in front
Frame	Tubular– maintubes oval
Transmission	5-speed
Axle ratio	Various
Brakes	Hydraulic discs
Wheels	15" Borrani wire
Front suspension	Independent, coil springs, telescopic shocks
Rear suspension	Live axle, coil springs, telescopic shocks
Curb weight	3300lbs
Wheelbase	2650mm
Track front	1405mm
Track rear	1397mm

133

The SWB Berlinetta shown is an example of the 'street' version built in 1961. Notable features include indentations at the rear for the license plate and the vent above the rear window. This particular yellow car, chassis number 2111GT, is unusual in having a round lockable cover over the gas filler cap.

This Zagato-bodied Ferrari started life as a SWB Berlinetta, chassis number 2491GT. *

Is the 4-headlight 330GT 2+2 really ugly ?

Right Judge for yourself in this comparison with the later 2-headlight version. Other differences : the earlier model had small louvres on the sides of the fenders, the later car had three large openings.

CHAPTER TEN

THE FAMILY FERRARIS

330 America (1963)
330GT 2+2 (1963-1967)

For some time, Ferrari had been quietly developing a replacement engine for the 250GTE 2+2. The new design was based on the 4-litre 400 Superamerica engine. Improvements included lengthening the distance between the cylinder-bore centres to allow better water circulation and, at the top end, to allow for a more efficient combustion chamber design. The official horsepower rating of 300 at 6600rpm was certainly conservative, as the less efficient 400SA engine was rated at 340 horsepower at 7000 rpm.

At the end of 1963, Ferrari began delivering 250GTE 2+2s equipped with the new 330 engine, and the 50 or so cars produced were called the 330 America. The new model looked exactly like any late production 1963 250GTE 2+2 except that some of them had the script 'America' on the trunk lid. It seems likely that production of this engine came along faster than expected and the new Lusso had sold more quickly than predicted thus using up the supply of 250GT engines. In fact 493 road Ferraris were produced in 1962 and 598 in 1963!

The all-new 330 GT 2+2 was formally announced and shown at Ferrari's traditional January press conference in 1964. Compared to the 250GTE 2+2 it was a new car. The wheelbase was 50mm greater, allowing for increased interior space. The disc-braking system was improved by installing totally separate systems front and rear. Later in the run, after mid-1965, cast alloy wheels replaced the traditional Borrani wire wheels though they were still available as an option. Toward the end of the run even power steering and air conditioning were fitted on demand by the factory.

The styling of the new 330GT 2+2 has been a subject of controversy among Ferrari enthusiasts since the day it was introduced. The overall effect was softer and less positive than the 250GTE 2+2 and the copycat 4-headlight installation, inspired by American car usage and the same treatment on the Superfast IV, did nothing to enhance the otherwise traditional pure lines laid down so successfully by Pininfarina. The general negative clamour did not effect Ferrari immediately, but a year and a half later two of the four headlights were deleted by popular request.

As far as is known, Pininfarina built no special coachwork on the 330GT 2+2. An unknown chassis number may have received the Lilian de Rethy Special type of coupé bodywork that we know graced at least four 330GTC chassis. Aside from unconfirmed possibilities, it seems that it was left to Luigi Chinetti, the American importer at that time, to commission three specials. Two of these, C/N 6109GT and another (C/N unknown), were designed and built by Giovanni Michelotti, who started his own coachbuilding house after severing his long cooperation with Alfredo Vignale. The third car was a 'station wagon' built by Vignale, based on a finished design by artist Bob Peak. The body was steel and was overly heavy. This caused the rear suspension to bottom out at the slightest bump in the road. It, C/N 7963, is memorable as the last Ferrari bodied by Vignale. With the 250GTE 2+2 and

the 330GT 2+2 Ferrari achieved their goal of creating a mass production Ferrari. About 950 of the former were sold followed by 50 of the interim 330 America and 1120 or so of the later car. To sum it up, from 1960 to 1967 about 2120 2+2 Ferrari were sold.

In the U.S.A. Luigi Chinetti began experimenting with the use of an automatic transmission in the 330GT 2+2. This model seemed to cry out for this option and Chinetti's General Manager Dick Fritz began studying the possibilities very seriously. The General Motors Hydromatic transmission of the type used in the Chevrolet Corvette was finally chosen as it had the ability to handle well over 300 horsepower. A new 1966 330GT 2+2 was chosen for this experiement (possibly C/N 6191) and unofficial assistance was obtained from General Motors. Detail modifications were made and the result was an extremely smooth, well matched engine/transmission unit which received compliments from every one who drove it. The results of this successful experiment were transmitted to the Ferrari Factory but no action was taken.

Chassis number 5755GT is a good example of the early, 4-headlight, 4-speed-plus-overdrive version of the 330GT 2+2.

THE FAMILY FERRARIS

CHAPTER TEN

Luigi Chinetti's in Greenwich, Connecticut, now an office complex, provided the venue for this photo of the Michelotti-designed and bodied 330GT 2+2, chassis number 6109GT.

The final version, with 2-headlights and 5-speed gearbox, represented by C/N 8753GT.

SPECIFICATIONS

330 America

Type	330
Model	America
Years made	1963
Chassis range	4953 -5125
Number produced	50
Coachbuiders	Pininfarina
Body styles	Coupé
Body material	Steel
Seating capacity	2+2
Engine type	V12 60° Colombo
Displacement	3967cc
Bore and stroke	77mm x 71mm
Cyl. head	SOHC, single outside plug
Ignition	2 distributors
Compression	Est. 8.8 to 1
Carburation	3 Weber
Lubrication	Wet sump
Horsepower	300bhp + @6,600rpm
Chassis/Drivetrain	Engine/gearbox in front
Frame	Tubular - maintubes oval
Transmission	4-speed + overdrive
Axle ratio	Various
Brakes	Hydraulic discs
Wheels	15" Borrani wire
Front suspension	Independent, A-arms, coil springs, telescopic shocks
Rear suspension	Live axle, semi-elliptical springs, telescopic shocks
Curb weight	3200lbs
Wheelbase	2600mm
Track front	1395mm
Track rear	1387mm

330GT 2+2

Type	330
Model	GT 2+2
Years made	1963-1967
Chassis range	4963 -10193*
Number produced	1080
Coachbuiders	Pininfarina
Body styles	Coupé
Body material	Steel
Seating capacity	2+2
Engine type	V12 60° Colombo
Displacement	3967cc
Bore and stroke	77mm x 71mm
Cyl. head	SOHC, single outside plug
Ignition	2 distributors
Compression	Est. 8.8 to 1
Carburation	3 x 40DCZ6
Lubrication	Wet sump
Horsepower	300bhp+@6600rpm
Chassis/Drivetrain	Engine/gearbox in front
Frame	Tubular -maintubes oval
Transmission	see below.*
Axle ratio	4.25 to 1 and others
Brakes	Hydraulic discs
Wheels	15" Borrani wire / 15" cast alloy
Front suspension	Independent, A-arms, coil springs, telescopic shocks
Rear suspension	Live axle, semi-elliptical springs, telescopic shocks
Curb weight	3300lbs
Wheelbase	2650mm
Track front	1397mm
Track rear	1389mm

*1963-1965 4 headlight, 4 speed +overdrive 4963-6937(500)
1965 4 headlight, 5 speed 6939-7547(125)
1965-1967 2 headlight, 5 speed 7553-10,193 (455)

This is the next to the last Series 2 400 Superamerica Coupé Aerodinamico, chassis number 5131SA, built in 1963.

This is a good example of the 1961/1962 style-SWB Berlinetta. The earlier version had the filler cap in the top left corner of the trunk lid.

CHAPTER ELEVEN

Burgeoning Berlinettas

250GT SWB Berlinetta (1960-1963)
275GTB Berlinetta (1964-1966)
275GTB/4 (1966-1968)

For most Ferrari enthusiasts the ideal Ferrari is the one that is most like their racing cars and yet practical enough to drive on public roads. What these enthusiasts actually buy depends on their driving ability, their egos, how extrovert they are, and the possible effect such a car might have on their neighbours, their families, their wives or girlfriends. Ferrari and Pininfarina tried to ring all the changes, and 2-seater cars were made available at many different levels at the same time. In 1962, for example, one could choose from the following : 250GT Lusso Berlinetta, 250GT SWB Berlinetta (in *lusso* trim for road use), 250GT SWB Competition Berlinetta, 250GTO Berlinetta, 250GT SWB Spyder California, and a 400 Superamerica - a remarkable array of variations on the V12 Ferrari theme.

The 250GT Pininfarina 'notchback' coupé had really started a new line of restrained and elegant 2-seater Ferraris. The 250GT LWB Tour de France had come directly from the 250 Europa GT and directly led into the Interim LWB Berlinetta and ultimately the SWB Berlinetta. The all-aluminium Competition SWB Berlinetta led directly to the 250GTO, a very special car that was entrusted only to experienced race drivers.

The *lusso* or de luxe version of the SWB Berlinetta was somewhere between the 250GT Lusso Berlinetta and the 250GT Competition Berlinetta and eventually led to the 275 GTB Berlinetta. Ferrari buyers want the Ferrari mystique and performance, but it is Ferrari's job to find out just how far they will go. Putting 2-seater Ferraris of various configurations into the market place is the ultimate test.

The first 21 SWB Berlinettas were Competition models. The street or *lusso* version was not available in any quantity until the end of November, 1960. By that time the Competition version was achieving notable racing successes : 4th and 5th overall at the 1960 Sebring 12-Hours race and 4th and 5th overall at the 1960 Le Mans 24-Hours Race. The *lusso* version offered the opportunity to acquire an outwardly identical car more suitable for the public roads. Of the approximately 167 Berlinetta made about 93 of them were the *lusso* street version. The last was C/N 4065GT, completed in February 1963. Some specials were built on this chassis and these included C/N 2613GT and 2821GT, both of which look like a cross between a 400SA (the rear) and a 250GTE (the front) but are slightly different. Another special was C/N 3469GT which is identical to C/N 1737GT. The outstanding special on the SWB street Berlinetta chassis was not by Pininfarina. It was a remarkable creation, a unique prototype coupé by Bertone which should have been put at least into limited production. This most attractive effort was mounted on C/N 3269GT.

With the end of the SWB Berlinetta models and all their variations, Scaglietti was able to concentrate on increasing production of the 250GT Lusso Berlinetta, which seemed to appeal to a far wider audience. Once again, Ferrari and Pininfarina began to think of the future and decided what mix of models would be made next. The factory began by designing a revolutionary new chassis that was to include independent rear suspension together with a 5-speed gearbox unified with the rear axle to allow better weight distribution.

The new engine was still basically a Colombo-derived design, with the traditional stroke of 58.8mm.

CHAPTER ELEVEN

The bore was 77mm, giving a total engine size of 3280cc (about 275cc per cylinder). The factory had already proven this design in the 275P and 250LM (with 275 engine) racing cars. At the same time the new 275GTS convertible was introduced. This model shared the same basic chassis but with a body made by Pininfarina themselves. This model is fully covered in chapter twelve.

In the new 275 GTB, the engine would produce about 280 horsepower with 3 Weber carburettors and approached 300 when fitted with the optionally available 6 Weber carburettors. Other options included outside quick-filler cap, an all-aluminium body, and Borrani wire wheels, as handsome new cast alloy wheels were now standard equipment.

Toward the end of 1965, a revised 275 GTB was introduced with a longer nose, a slightly larger rear window and exposed trunk hinges. In addition, the sometimes troublesome open driveshaft was replaced with a solid torque tube. (With proper maintenance the open driveshaft with constant velocity joints was a reliable solution and was used exclusively on the competition 275 GTBs and on all the 275 GTSs after the initial use of the single-bearing open shaft at the beginning of the run of both the GTB and the GTS).

Some special competition cars were made and the experience gained with these eventually led to the

This particular street SWB Berlinetta was given a special body by Pininfarina for Ferrari's very good customer Prince Bernhard of Holland. Except for the nose, it uses the design of the 400 Superamerica. This is C/N 2613GT. A similar car was built on C/N 2821GT.

A design rendering by Bertone proved not to be as attractive as the finished product. The very talented Giorgio Giugiaro, a Bertone stylist at that time, was responsible for this design. It is on a SWB street Berlinetta, chassis number 3269GT. Certainly more than one deserved to be made.

construction of a special series called the 275 GTB/C of which about 12 were made. A few of these were never raced but only because racing customers could not be found. These special competition cars are fully described in Volume II, of this work to be called *Ferrari - Forty Years on the Track*.

Ferrari was never first to introduce dramatic technical innovations. After all, Jaguar had been producing double, overhead camshaft engines in their production cars since 1949. Ferrari were content with

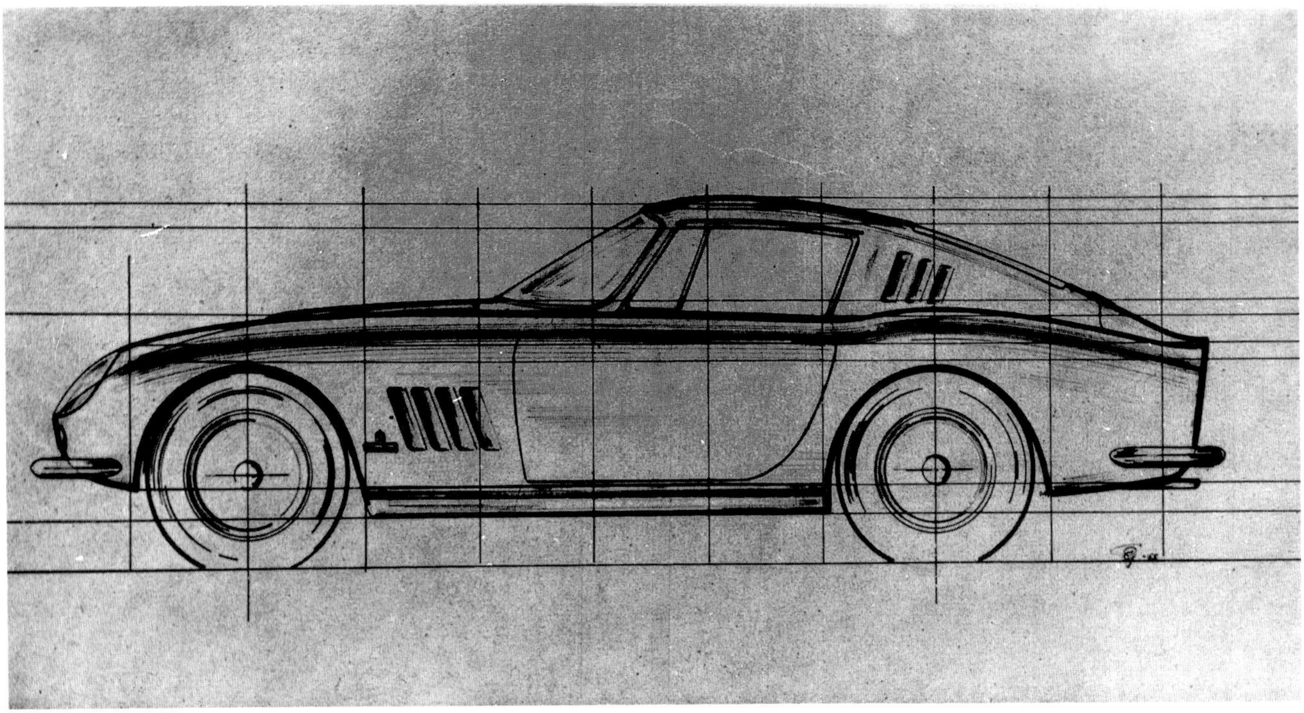

CHAPTER ELEVEN

A study by Pininfarina showing an almost final version of the design for the 275GTB. The photograph shows one of the Pininfarina prototypes used to display the new model at the 1965 Frankfurt Motor Show.

Right A short nose 275GTB (C/N 6841) in front of the first Ford factory. Compare this with the long nose (C/N 7923) in the darker colour. The difference is subtle and we wonder how many enthusiasts have purchased a short nose, convinced it was a long nose.

BURGEONING BERLINETTAS

CHAPTER ELEVEN

A rear view of a long nose showing the slightly larger rear window.

The instrument panel of an early short nose 275 GTB. The red line on the tachometer is 7500rpm! The other most important small instruments, oil pressure and water temperature gauges, are directly in front of the driver.

their single-overhead cam engines and had never felt it necessary to put a DOHC engine into production. For their racing cars Ferrari would try anything and were always on the cutting edge of race car engine development. However, more and more road cars were being produced with DOHC engines, and by 1965 these included not only Jaguar, but Aston Martin, Alfa Romeo, Maserati, and newcomer Lamborghini as well. It was time for Ferrari to step forward with the additional prestige of a DOHC engine - not to mention the additional power and efficiency it made possible.

The new 275TB/4 was born in 1966 and introduced to the public at the Paris Salon in October, 1966. The specification was dramatic and impressive. Never before had Ferrari offered such a competition-oriented specification to the public in a road car: DOHC-dry sump lubrication - six twin-throat Weber carburettors –300 horsepower at 8000 rpm ! Developed from Ferrari's racing experience, it was the 228GTO of its time : an incomparable dual-purpose machine that could challenge the driving ability of anyone. Like all of the best Ferraris, driving it automatically focused

The 6-carburettor option on the 275GTB. Those originally delivered this way are usually referred to as a 275GTB/6C.

one's concentration on getting the most out of it. It responded in kind. The more one puts into it, the more one gets out of it. Like most Ferraris it is intended for serious drivers.

By mid-1968 production of the 275GTB/4 ceased. The U.S.A. had imposed strict regulations, beginning in 1968, which limited the amount of hydrocarbons (HC) and carbon monoxide (CO) that a car's engine could emit. Safety standards were also imposed and eventually these required that new models be crashed to prove the safety of their bumper designs.. Each year the requirements became more difficult and as there was no precedent for this type of restriction and few technical alternatives available to enable a small manufacturer to meet the laws, Ferrari were forced to withdraw from the U.S.A. temporarily. In 1969 only 619 road Ferraris were produced, less than were made five years earlier. Early in 1968 production of the 275GTB/4 was terminated. It was replaced by the completely new 365GTB/4 Daytona, but deliveries did not commence until the middle of 1969, and a U.S. legal version was not available until 1970.

CHAPTER ELEVEN

Three views of the 275GTB/4 showing the great similarity to the 275GTB long nose. The easiest way to spot the difference is to look for the bulge on the hood that is found only on the 4-cam. This is C/N10259.

BURGEONING BERLINETTAS

The impressive architecture of the 275 GTB/4 engine.

CHAPTER ELEVEN

SPECIFICATIONS

250GT SWB Berlinetta
(Road Version Only).

Type	250GT
Model	SWB Berlinetta
Years made	1960-1963
Chassis range	1993GT-4065GT *
Number produced	93 *
Coachbuiders	Scaglietti, Pininfarina and Bertone
Body styles	Berlinetta
Body material	Steel or aluminium
Seating capacity	2
Engine type	V12 60° Columbo
Displacement	2953cc
Bore and stroke	73mm x 58.8mm
Cyl. head	SOHC, single outside plug, roller rockers
Ignition	2 distributors
Compression	8.8 to1
Carburation	3 x 40DCL6 or 36DCL6
Lubrication	Wet sump
Horsepower	240bhp @ 7,000rpm
Chassis/Drivetrain	Engine/gearbox in front
Frame	Tubular steel– maintubes oval
Transmission	4-speed
Axle ratio	Various
Brakes	Hydraulic discs
Wheels	15" Borrani wire
Front suspension	Independent, A-arms, coil springs, telescopic shocks
Rear suspension	Live axle, semi-elliptical springs, telescopic shocks
Curb weight	2400lbs
Wheelbase	2400mm
Track front	1354mm
Track rear	1349mm

* Chassis range and number produced:
 1960 body style: 1993GT-2389GT (18)
 1961 body style: 2399GT-4065Gt (75)

275GTB

Type	275
Model	GTB
Years made	1964-1966
Chassis range	6003-8979
Number produced	460
Coachbuiders	Scaglietti
Body styles	Berlinetta
Body material	Steel or Aluminium
Seating capacity	2
Engine type	V12 60° Columbo
Displacement	3285cc
Bore and stroke	77mm x 58.8mm
Cyl. head	SOHC, single outside plug, roller rockers
Ignition	2 distributors
Compression	9.2 to1
Carburation	3 x 40DCZ6 or 6 x 40DCN/3
Lubrication	Wet sump
Horsepower	Approx. 280bhp @ 7600rpm
Chassis/Drivetrain	Engine front/gearbox rear
Frame	Tubular steel– maintubes oval
Transmission	5-speed transaxle
Axle ratio	3.55 to1
Brakes	Hydraulic discs
Wheels	14" cast alloy
Front suspension	Independent, A-arms, coil springs, telescopic shocks
Rear suspension	Independent, A-arms, coil springs, telescopic shocks
Curb weight	2700lbs
Wheelbase	2400mm
Track front	137mm
Track rear	1393mm

275GTB/4

Type	275
Model	GTB/4
Years made	1966-1968
Chassis range	8769-11069
Number produced	350
Coachbuiders	Scaglietti
Body styles	Berlinetta
Body material	Steel or aluminium
Seating capacity	2
Engine type	V12 60°
Displacement	3285cc
Bore and stroke	77mm x 58.8mm
Cyl. head	DOHC single outside plug
Ignition	2 distributors
Compression	9.2 to1
Carburation	6 x 40 DCN17
Lubrication	Dry sump
Horsepower	300bhp @ 8,000rpm
Chassis/Drivetrain	Engine front / gearbox rear
Frame	Tubular steel– maintubes oval
Transmission	5-speed transaxle
Axle ratio	3.55 to 1
Brakes	Hydraulic discs
Wheels	14 " cast alloy
Front suspension	Independent, A-arms, coil springs, telescopic shocks
Rear suspension	Independent, A-arms, coil springs, telescopic shocks
Curb weight	2750lbs
Wheelbase	2400mm
Track front	1401mm
Track rear	1417mm

* 275GTB Driveshaft Configuration

Short nose
C/N 6003-7801 (approx)
open with single centre bearing.
Long nose
C/N 7803-8309 (approx)
open with constant velocity joints.
Long nose
C/N 8311-8979 (approx)
torque tube

This beautifully restored Ferrari is a fine example of a 1967 330GTS. This one is chassis number 9749.

Parked at the Monterey Historic Races in 1984 this is one of the 330GTC Specials inspired by the Lillian de Rethy car.

An impressive engine compartment : the 275GTB/4 in all of its mechanical glory !

Two immaculate examples of the classic 275GTB/6C

The first version of the 275GTS used side vents in the front fenders similar to those found in the first version of the 330GT 2+2. The Borrani wire wheels were standard on the 275GTS unlike the 275GTB, which featured cast alloy wheels as standard.

Right Early in 1965 new side vents were adopted on the 275GTS and were later used on the 330GTC. The hardtop was an option designed by Pininfarina.

CHAPTER TWELVE

Sumptuous Spyders (And Convertibles)

275GTS (1964-1966)
330GTS (1966-1968)
275GTB/4-S NART Spyder (1967-1968)
365GTS (1969)

The difference between a Spyder and a Convertible became less defined as time went on. In the 1950s, a Spyder was an open competition car with no top and no windows ; a convertible had a water-resistant, foldable top and wind-up windows. By the mid-1960s only the feel of the car made the difference. With the four open cars described in this chapter only the NART Spyder had the proper heritage to earn the title Spyder. The others were unquestionably road cars and could thus only be Convertibles. All of this became part of the ever-growing Ferrari mystique.

The 275GTS replaced the 250GT SWB California Spyder in time, but was really a much more conservative styling conception and mechanically was better suited to everyday driving. In terms of spirit and intent the California Spyder was not replaced until the arrival of the NART Spyder in 1967. It is noteworthy that both models were inspired by Luigi Chinetti for the American market.

163

CHAPTER TWELVE

Early experience of the 275GTS in Great Britain was not altogether pleasant and this applied to those parts of the U.S.A. that are subject to frequent spells of rain and snow. The car was something of a Jekyll and Hyde, performing like a true champion in dry weather but turning evil in even the slightest amount of moisture. The problem was solved with chassis tuning and a better choice of tyres, but before the cure could be found at least one loyal Ferrari customer in England returned his new 275GTS to the importer and demanded (and obtained) a full refund ! Subsequently about half a dozen right-hand drive 275GTSs remained unsold at the factory. Luigi Chinetti finally took them to the states after they were all fitted with 6 carburettors ! Most of them seem to have been sold in Texas and Southern California.

The 330GTS seemed a great mechanical improvement, with its more powerful engine and better road holding under all weather conditions. It was also better looking with its new long nose (shared with the 330GTC Coupé). The rigid torque tube (never used on the 275GTS) was standard on the 330GTS, as were the cast alloy wheels.

Luigi Chinetti's most inspired concept for a road car proved to be the 275GTB/4-S NART Spyder ! This unofficial model was possible only because of Chinetti's long association with Ferrari and was accomplished with the tacit agreement of the factory. These ten or so cars were of course 275GTB/4 Berlinettas that were converted into NART Spyders on the assembly line. It is certain that Scaglietti built most of them but it seems that a few were farmed out to Drogo and/or Fantuzzi who were housed in either end of the same building in Modena at the time. Aside from the top itself, there were substantive differences between the Berlinetta and the Spyder. For full details you should obtain the appropriate back issue of the Ferrari Market Letter published by Gerald Roush, Roush Publications inc., P.O. Box 1498, Stone Mountain, GA 30086-1498. As a number of unauthorized conversions were made in later years, in California and also by Scaglietti themselves, it is very important to carefully check the chassis and engine numbers before buying one !

In the context of the NART Spyder we must mention the special that was built by Neri and Bonacini in Modena, to suggestions by American Tom Meade. This very special Spyder was built in early 1966 on a

250GT chassis (C/N 1777GT). Of all the specials not authorized by the factory this one, called the Nembo, must be considered the most successful or at least the most visually attractive. Luigi Chinetti did see it and it did inspire the creation of the NART Spyder which it resembles.

The 365GTS was little heard of in the U.S.A. as even by 1969 Ferrari was only beginning to make an effort to meet the U.S. requirements. During 1968 and 1969 most of the research on how to meet the new requirements was done by Dick Fritz, at that time the general manager of Luigi Chinetti's. The hardware was obtained in the U.S.A. and sent to the factory. As a result, a few 365GTSs were brought into the American market. In later years even more were brought in and proved to be a revelation to their new owners as the performance of the 365GTS proved to be comparable to the 365GTB/4 Daytona!

Left & above The 275GTS had a taut look that was in character with its short, crisps nose line. At the rear the '275' in chrome numerals usually appeared just below the Ferrari script on the trunk lid.

Right The 330GTS was substantially identical to the 330GTC. The new long nose gave the car a softer look.

CHAPTER TWELVE

SUMPTUOUS SPYDERS

Left The 365GTS looked much like the 330GTS, but with the side vents moved to the top of the hood.

Above The 275GTB/4-S NART Spyder was originally offerred with cast alloy wheels but the Borrani wire wheels on this example were optional equipment.

Right The Nembo, created by Neri and Bonacini, was built on C/N 1777GT, E/N 2271GT about a year before the NART Spyder.

CHAPTER TWELVE

SPECIFICATIONS

275GTS

Type	275
Model	GTS
Years made	1964-1966
Chassis range	6001-8653 *
Number produced	200
Coachbuiders	Pininfarina
Body styles	Convertible
Body material	Steel
Seating capacity	2
Engine type	V12 60°
Displacement	3285cc
Bore and stroke	77mm x 58.8mm
Cyl. head	SOHC, single outside plug, roller rockers
Ignition	2 distributors
Compression	8.8 to1
Carburation	3
Lubrication	Wet sump
Horsepower	260bhp @ 7000rpm
Chassis/Drivetrain	Engine ft/5spd transaxle rear
Frame	Tubular steel– maintubes oval
Transmission	5-speed transaxle
Axle ratio	3.3 to 1
Brakes	Hydraulic discs
Wheels	14" Borrani wire
Front suspension	Independent, A-arms, coil springs, telescopic shocks
Rear suspension	Independent, A-arms, coil springs, telescopic shocks
Curb weight	2800lbs
Wheelbase	2400mm
Track front	1377mm
Track rear	1393mm

330GTS

Type	330
Model	GTS
Years made	1966-1968
Chassis range	889-11713
Number produced	100
Coachbuiders	Pininfarina
Body styles	Convertible
Body material	Steel
Seating capacity	2
Engine type	V12 60°
Displacement	3967cc
Bore and stroke	77mm x 71mm
Cyl. head	SOHC, single outside plug, roller rocker
Ignition	2 distributors
Compression	8.8 to1
Carburation	3 x 40DCZ6
Lubrication	Wet sump
Horsepower	300bhp @ 7,000rpm
Chassis/Drivetrain	Engine ft/5spd transaxle rear
Frame	Tubular steel– maintubes oval
Transmission	5-speed transaxle
Axle ratio	3.3 to1
Brakes	Hydraulic discs
Wheels	14" cast alloy
Front suspension	Independent, A-arms, coil springs, telescopic shocks
Rear suspension	Independent, A-arms, coil springs, telescopic shocks
Curb weight	3250lbs
Wheelbase	2400mm
Track front	1401mm
Track rear	1417mm

SUMPTUOUS SPYDERS

275GTB4/S NART Spyder

Type	275
Model	GTB4/S
Years made	1967-1968
Chassis range	8437-11057
Number produced	10
Coachbuiders	Scaglietti
Body styles	Convertible
Body material	Steel or aluminium
Seating capacity	2
Engine type	V12 60°
Displacement	3285cc
Bore and stroke	77mm x 58.8mm
Cyl. head	DOHC single outside plug
Ignition	2 distributors
Compression	9.2 to1
Carburation	6 x 40 DCN17
Lubrication	Dry sump
Horsepower	300bhp @ 8,000rpm
Chassis/Drivetrain	Engine front/gearbox rear
Frame	Tubular steel– maintubes oval
Transmission	5-speed transaxle
Axle ratio	
Brakes	Hydraulic discs
Wheels	14" cast alloy
Front suspension	Independent, A-arms, coil springs, telescopic shocks
Rear suspension	Independent, A-arms, coil springs, telescopic shocks
Curb weight	2800lbs
Wheelbase	2400mm
Track front	1401mm
Track rear	1417mm

365GTS

Type	365
Model	GTS
Years made	1969
Chassis range	12163-12493
Number produced	20
Coachbuiders	Pininfarina
Body styles	Convertible
Body material	Steel
Seating capacity	2
Engine type	V12 60°
Displacement	4390cc
Bore and stroke	81mm x 71mm
Cyl. head	SOHC, single outside plug, roller rockers
Ignition	2 distributors
Compression	8.8 to1
Carburation	3 x 40DRI
Lubrication	Wet sump
Horsepower	320bhp @ 6600rpm
Chassis/Drivetrain	Engine ft/5spd transaxle rear
Frame	Tubular steel– maintubes oval
Transmission	5-speed transaxle
Axle ratio	3.3 to1
Brakes	Hydraulic discs
Wheels	14" cast alloy
Front suspension	Independent, A-arms, coil springs, telescopic shocks
Rear suspension	Independent, A-arms, coil springs, telescopic shocks
Curb weight	3350lbs
Wheelbase	2400mm
Track front	1401mm
Track rear	1417mm

Two outstanding examples of the very rare 275GTB/4-S NART Spyder. The cream coloured one is the first to be made. It is unusual in having an all aluminium body. It was raced at Sebring and appeared in the movie 'The Thomas Crown Affair'. It is chassis number 9437.

Every view of a 330GTC is a flattering one. Its understated elegance stands the test of time very well. Note that the full side view shows a car with earless knock-offs as required by U.S. safety regulations. The other car has the optional Borrani wire wheels with the 3-eared knock-offs traditional since about 1955. The interior photo fails to show the exposed gate for the gearshift, a race-proven feature that became standard on all transaxle-equipped Ferraris.

CHAPTER THIRTEEN

'THE BEST ALL AROUND V12'

330GTC (1960-1968)
365GTC (1968-1970)

When production of the 250GT Lusso Berlinetta ceased at the end of 1964 it was not replaced. The Lusso had been positioned between the 250GTE 2+2 and the 250GT SWB Berlinetta street version. By 1965 there was no closed model between the 330GT 2+2 and the 275GTB. Obviously Ferrari and Pininfarina believed there was a market for an intermediate 2-seater closed car. While the 275GTS convertible might fill the bill in the U.S.A., it would not be the answer for the rest of the world where convertibles are simply not in great demand. The answer was a closed version of the 275GTS with a larger engine and other refinements to create a smoother and quieter car.

The new 330GTC was first shown to the public at the Geneva Motor Show in March, 1966. Particularly in Europe, it seemed the ideal high speed express for

CHAPTER THIRTEEN

2 people and their luggage. It has since been referred to as "the best all around V12 Ferrari"! While its styling is understated in the best Pininfarina grand touring mode - it is no head turner - it is, from the occupants point of view, a superb means of getting from point A to point B. Like a professional Minolta 9000, it has a surplus of everything else in the field. It gives the driver the feeling of being totally in control and superior to everything on the road.

Fewer and fewer special cars were being made, but Pininfarina made an exception with the 330GTC. At least four 330GTC Specials were built (three more are yet to be confirmed). The first was for Princess Lilian de Rethy of Belgium. At least three more were made, one of which was for Dr. de Bakey, the eminent American heart surgeon and long time Ferraristi. This limited edition utilized the front styling of the 365 California together with a rear treatment suggested by 206S Pininfarina prototype of 1965 (see Chapter Seventeen).

The 365GTC replaced the 330GTC at the end of 1968. Some exterior changes were made but these had already been incorporated in the last of the 330GTCs and included moving the vents to the top of the hood near the windshield. Horsepower was increased to 320 but more important was an even greater increase in torque. Within one year production ceased and 150 to 200 were produced. Like the 365GTS the performance of this rare Ferrari is almost equal to the Daytona coupé. A few were brought to the U.S.A. but they were almost unknown outside of Europe. It is a great Ferrari that was forced out of production due to the new and very tough American regulations.

The 330GTC Special had an exceptional amount of overhang at the rear, thus providing a truly cavernous trunk area. The overall proportions made the wheelbase of only 2400mm almost unbelievable.

Right The 365GTC was distinguished by its lack of front fender vents.

Below The vents had been moved to the rear of the hood. The interior is almost identical to its predecessor.

'THE BEST ALL ROUND V12'

CHAPTER THIRTEEN

SPECIFICATIONS

330GTC

Type	330
Model	GTC
Years made	1966-1968
Chassis range	8329-11613
Number produced	600
Coachbuiders	Pininfarina
Body styles	Coupé
Body material	Steel
Seating capacity	2
Engine type	V12 60°
Displacement	3967cc
Bore and stroke	77mm x 71mm
Cyl. head	SOHC, single outside plug, roller rockers
Ignition	2 distributors
Compression	8.8 to1
Carburation	3 x 40DCZ6
Lubrication	Wet sump
Horsepower	300bhp @ 7,000rpm
Chassis/Drivetrain	Engine ft/5spd transaxle rear
Frame	Tubular steel–maintubes oval
Transmission	5-speed transaxle
Axle ratio	3.3 to1
Brakes	Hydraulic discs
Wheels	14" cast alloy
Front suspension	Independent, A-arms, coil springs, telescopic shocks
Rear suspension	Independent, A-arms, coil springs, telescopic shocks
Curb weight	3050lbs
Wheelbase	2400mm
Track front	1401mm
Track rear	1417mm

365GTC

Type	365
Model	GTC
Years made	1968-1969
Chassis range	11823-12795
Number produced	150
Coachbuiders	Pininfarina
Body styles	Coupé
Body material	Steel
Seating capacity	2
Engine type	V12 60°
Displacement	4390cc
Bore and stroke	81mm x 71mm
Cyl. head	SOHC, single outside plug, roller rockers
Ignition	2 distributors
Compression	8.8 to1
Carburation	3 x 40 DRI
Lubrication	Wet sump
Horsepower	320bhp @ 6600rpm
Chassis/Drivetrain	Engine ft/5spd transaxle rear
Frame	Tubular steel–maintubes oval
Transmission	5-speed transaxle
Axle ratio	3.3 to1
Brakes	Hydraulic discs
Wheels	14" cast alloy
Front suspension	Independent, A-arms, coil springs, telescopic shocks
Rear suspension	Independent, A-arms, coil springs, telescopic shocks
Curb weight	3350lbs
Wheelbase	2400mm
Track front	1401mm
Track rear	1417mm

CHAPTER FOURTEEN

Family Luxury

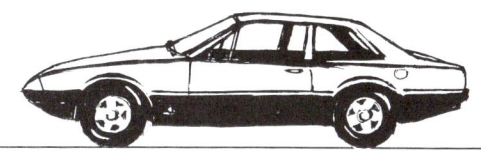

365GT 2 + 2 (1967-1971)
365GT4 2 + 2 (1972-1976)

Intent on seriously competing in the worldwide luxury car market, Ferrari introduced a totally new state-of-the-art 2 + 2 at the Paris Salon in October 1967. Called the 365GT 2 + 2, it resembled the 330GTC Special that had been built for Belgium's Princess de Rethy and was shown at the Brussels Motor Show in January 1967 (see Chapter thirteen). It also strongly resembled the 500 Superfast.

Ferrari's ability to design and produce competitive racing cars might seem at odds with its desire to provide competition for Rolls-Royce, but, in fact, the challenges are both in terms of controlling the chassis and in providing an appropriate environment for the driver (and passengers in the case of the new 365GT 2+2). The new car was a technical triumph! It was the first Ferrari 2 + 2 with four-wheel independent suspension. Extreme measures were taken to insulate the occupants from noise and vibration by stabilising the engine, gearbox and rear axle case in one unit and mounting it all at four points on special rubber bushes. The rear axle also contained a differential with a limited slip feature. The independent rear suspension was similar to that found on the GTB and GTS but with the addition of hydro-pneumatic devices that automatically controlled the ride height of the rear of the car to keep it constant regardless of the load. This self-levelling system was developed jointly by KONI, the famous Dutch maker of high performance and racing car shock absorbers, and Ferrari themselves. A further innovation was the installation of power steering as standard equipment. In addition, the standard specification included air conditioning.

During 1968, 1969 and 1970 Ferrari produced 2,276 cars for the road, of which about 800 were 365GT 2 + 2's. The success of this elegant and powerful automobile was quite amazing, considering that only a hundred or so had been brought to the U.S.A. Luigi Chinetti also arranged for six specially-prepared GM automatic transmissions to be sent to the factory and these were installed in six U.S.-specification 365GT 2 + 2s during 1969 and 1970. The technical work to make this possible was handled by Dick Fritz, who was the general manager at Chinetti's at that time. At the beginning of 1971, production ceased.

No real replacement was available until the end of 1972 when the 4-cam 365GT4 2 + 2 was introduced. (The interim 365GTC/4 will be covered in Chapter 15). This newest and grandest of all of Ferrari's 2 + 2s thus far was first seen by the public on the occasion of the Paris Salon in October 1972. Longer and wider but lower than the previous 2 + 2, it again included as standard every possible luxury, but much refined and improved. Most important was the double overhead cam engine. Like Rolls-Royce, no horsepower figure was quoted, but surely it was at least 320. More important was its massive amount of torque. Taken together with the turbine-like characteristics of the V12 engine, it mattered little which gear one was in or at what speed.

CHAPTER FOURTEEN

The 365GT 2+2 carried on the legacy of Ferrari's Pininfarina designed and executed luxury cars. This time '2+2' was taken more literally and, four adults could actually use all the seats for more than a few minutes at a time. One further detail remained to be cleared up : neither the designer nor the factory had provided compatible outside rearview mirrors.

FAMILY LUXURY

179

CHAPTER FOURTEEN

Totally redesigned, the new 365GT4 2+2 was longer and lower with an exterior design that was taut and cohesive from one end to the other. The impressive engine with its side-draft Weber carburettors was inherited from the 365GTC/4 and allowed for a particularly low hood profile.

FAMILY LUXURY

SPECIFICATIONS

365GT 2+2

Type	365GT
Model	2+2
Years made	1967-1971
Chassis range	10791-14099
Number produced	800
Coachbuiders	Pininfarina
Body styles	Coupé
Body material	Steel
Seating capacity	2+2
Engine type	V12 60°
Displacement	4390cc
Bore and stroke	81mm x 71mm
Cyl. head	SOHC single outside plug
Ignition	2 distributors
Compression	8.8 to 1
Carburation	3 x 40 DFI/5
Lubrication	Wet sump
Horsepower	320bhp @ 6600rpm
Chassis/Drivetrain	Engine/gearbox in front
Frame	Tubular steel— maintubes oval
Transmission	5-speed *
Axle ratio	3.3 to 1
Brakes	Hydraulic discs
Wheels	15 " cast alloy
Front suspension	Independent, A-arms, coil springs, telescopic shocks
Rear suspension	Independent, A-arms, coil springs, telescopic shocks †
Curb weight	3550lbs
Wheelbase	2650mm
Track front	1483mm
Track rear	1468mm

* 6 with automatic transmission were made for the U.S.A.
† with self-levelling hydro-pneumatice ride control

365GT4 2+2

Type	365GT4
Model	2+2
Years made	1972-1976
Chassis range	15897-19709
Number produced	524
Coachbuiders	Pininfarina
Body styles	Coupé
Body material	Steel
Seating capacity	2+2
Engine type	V12 60°
Displacement	4390cc
Bore and stroke	81mm x 71mm
Cyl. head	DOHC single outside plug
Ignition	2 distributors
Compression	8.8 to 1
Carburation	6 x 38DCOE
Lubrication	Wet sump
Horsepower	340bhp @ 7,000rpm
Chassis/Drivetrain	Engine/gearbox in front
Frame	Tubular steel— maintubes oval
Transmission	5-speed
Axle ratio	3.3 to 1
Brakes	Hydraulic discs
Wheels	15" cast alloy
Front suspension	Independent, A-arms, coil springs, telescopic shocks
Rear suspension	Independent, A-arms, coil springs, telescopic shocks †
Curb weight	4250lbs
Wheelbase	2700mm
Track front	1470mm
Track rear	1500mm

† with self-levelling hydro-pneumatic ride control

The 365GTC/4 looks more attractive today than when it was new in 1972. The sharp edges of the design did not convey the traditional Ferrari look. Note the exceedingly busy engine compartment, mostly due to the use of six dual-throat sidedraught Weber carburettors which allowed Pininfarina to achieve an especially low hood line. Compared to previous Ferraris the interior is particularly elegant and was carried on to the 365GT4 2+2.

CHAPTER FIFTEEN

THE FINAL V12 SPORTS CARS

365GTC/4 (1971-1972)
365GTB/4 'Daytona' Berlinetta (1968-1973)
365GTS/4 'Daytona' Spyder (1971-1973)

While the 365GTB/4, unofficially but immediately dubbed the 'Daytona' by the press, was first introduced at the Paris Salon in October, 1968, deliveries did not commence in any numbers until the last half of 1969. Although it was the first Ferrari to be built in quantity to meet the U.S. regulations, the European version was marketed first, and U.S. legal cars from the factory were not available on a regular basis until mid-1970; real quantities did not arrive until early 1972, when the new U.S. Ferrari importers took over. In the eastern United States a partnership was formed by Luigi Chinetti with Al Garthwaite, called Chinetti-Garthwaite Imports, headquartered in Paoli, Pennsylvania. In the West, the importer was Modern Classic Motors in Reno, Nevada-owned by Bill Harrah, the famous owner of gambling establishments in Reno and Las Vegas, Nevada. The western arrangement had been made about a year earlier. These changes provided the financial resources needed to give Ferrari serious distribution throughout the U.S.A. for the first time.

The timing was good, for in mid-1971 Ferrari had presented another new model at the Geneva Motor Show. This was the 365GTC/4, offered as a more civilised version of the Daytona, but really much closer in design to the 365GT 2 + 2 which it had replaced on Pinnfarina's assembly line. Perhaps Ferrari felt it had saturated the market with the large and somewhat un-Ferrari-like 2 + 2, for the C/4, as it came to be called, had 2 seats in the back that were good only

for small children, luggage, or emergency use only by no more than one adult, probably sitting sideways. Although it was physically attractive, as a piece of industrial design, it did not look like a Ferrari - or so said the Ferrari traditionalists. On the other hand, it was a far more pleasant car to drive than the Daytona. The power steering (standard equipment) made all the difference. Taken together with the plush Pininfarina interior that included separate reclining seats for driver and passenger it was an attractive package that could be sold to those who found the Daytona too much for everyday driving and to those who knew nothing about Ferraris but wanted a powerful luxury sports car that could hold more than two persons in a pinch.

I suspect that Ferrari and Pininfarina saw the C/4 as a more logical and more Ferrari-like 2 + 2. After all, there was no more room in the rear seats of a Porsche. If it had caught on it would have been offered with an automatic transmission; allowance had been made in the width of the console to accomodate the GM Hydramatic transmission! Most of the C/4s produced were sold in the U.S. and almost all of these were made in 1972. It was not a great sales success, and the last new ones were not sold until late in 1974. Production was stopped completely around October, 1972, when the new 365GT4 2+2 was introduced at the Paris Auto Show. The new 2 + 2 was really just a long wheelbase version of the C/4.

In 1972 and 1973 I had my first experience with new Ferraris as a partner in a new Ferrari dealership near New York City. I had the opportunity to drive C/4s, Daytonas and 246GTS Dinos every day. Of the three, my own favourite for every day driving was the C/4. It felt almost as powerful as the Daytona whilst requiring a good deal less effort. It was also more comfortable. But, the C/4 was an acquired taste and one had to live with it on a day to day basis to accept and love it for what it was. Ferrari had educated us to lust after a brute like the Daytona - that was its heritage. Ferrari did the right thing in cancelling the C/4, as it was neither a brute nor a real four-passenger car. The new 365GT4 2+2 had a wheelbase of 2700mm (106.3") and really would hold four in high speed comfort.

The Daytona was another world. It looked the part of the most powerful 2-seater sports car of its time. It was what an enthusiast felt a real Ferrari should be. Purposeful, agressive, demanding and somewhat intimidating. The Daytona was all of these things and it was a machine that could not be taken for granted. To get the best out of it took great concentration and demanded 100 per cent of the driver. The fact that the air conditioning was inadequate was really not a sales deterrant; it was adequate up to about 85 degrees Fahrenheit and 70% humidity. Beyond that you turned it off and opened the windows - and enjoyed the sound of the glorious V12 engine. Who needs air conditioning?

Almost all the Daytonas sold in the U.S. were equipped with every option available from the factory. These included an outside rearview mirror, air conditioning, full leather seats, and an electrically- operated radio antenna. The installation of a radio was left to the selling dealer. Normally all U.S.-specification Daytonas arrived with the 'star' cast alloy wheels as standard.

The Daytona was first shown with the headlights in fixed position, covered by clear plastic. This did not meet the U.S. height requirement, so Pininfarina designed pop-up units operated by electric motors. This was put into production for all Daytonas during the last half of 1970 and was on all U.S.-specification cars except for a few brought in by Luigi Chinetti that were legalised in the U.S.A.

The Daytona 'Spyder', also known as the 365GTS/4 (except on those officially imported to the U.S.A., which were stamped '365GTB/4' on the makers plate!), was first shown at the Frankfurt Motor Show in September 1969. About 150 were made through early 1973. About 100 of them were imported into the U.S.A. Surprisingly, they were not that easy to sell and were regularly discounted in the U.S. market off the list price of the about $26,000. In 1973 a used one with a very low mileage remained unsold for 6 months at a price of less than $20,000.

Due to the tremendous interest in this model in recent years and the fact that many replicas have been created by converting Daytona Berlinettas it is important to identify those that are original. In detail, these cars are quite different in substantive ways and full specifications of the differences are available from the invaluable Ferrari Market Letter (contact Roush Publications Inc., PO Box 1498, Stone Mountain, GA 30086-1498, U.S.A.).

The day of the special was just about over, but the Pininfarina could not resist the opportunity to produce one based on the new Daytona Spyder. This was really a non-removable hard-top, with a rear window that was removable. It was exhibited at the Paris Salon in October 1969.

Further special coachwork on the 365GTB/4 chassis was limited. The best were the work of Luigi

This clearly shows the fixed headlight treatment on the early Daytonas. The extra lights on the bumpers were added to meet local European requirements.

Chinetti in collaboration with Italian and American designers. The first and perhaps the most attractive was a Spyder NART in 1974 for actor Steve McQueen (picture reference P1/327). It featured clean lines with cut down doors integrated with great character and with a fixed-leather-covered roll bar.

Another was a NART coupé with removable top, built for Luigi Chinetti by Michelotti (C/N 15965). This seemed less successful as it resembled too closely the Chevrolet Corvette. A third collaboration with Michelotti was shown at the 1980 Turin Motor Show. This was a pure wedge design with a convertible top and less adventurous than the others, (C/N 15,003).

Last, but not least, was a 2-door station wagon designed by American Gene Garefinke, financed by Bob Gittleman and realised by the Panther works in England. (C/N 15275). (Picture reference FM/260).

Alas, at the end of 1973, production of the 365GTB/4 stopped and it was replaced by the all-new rear-engined 365GT4/BB. Ferrari had entered a new era they did not totally understand or agree with. They were obliged to compromise the U.S. market due to the technical difficulties of the U.S. safety and emission standards. Ferrari had little choice. On September 1, 1974 the U.S. exemption that allowed the minimal standard bumpers on the C/4, the Daytonas and the 246GTs expired.

CHAPTER FIFTEEN

With the 365GTB/4 Ferrari, Pininfarina and Scaglietti combined to produce a product that was fully mature and totally professional in execution. Not just a one-off special but a production car that could be sold competitively in the world market. In the engine photo the standard large air cleaner had been replaced with the very attractive velocity stacks.

CHAPTER FIFTEEN

The very first Daytona Spyder had the fixed headlight treatment. It is believed that all the others had pop-up lights. The U.S. version had additional built in rectangular side lights front and rear to meet U.S. legal requirements.

THE FINAL V 12 SPORTS CARS

The one and only special on the Daytona Spyder chassis produced by Pininfarina was first shown at the Paris Salon in October 1969. The top was fixed but the rear window was removable.

CHAPTER FIFTEEN

The 1975 Geneva Auto Show was the venue for the first public showing of this NART Coupé with removable roof panels. The Corvette-like aura did nothing to endear it to lovers of Ferrari. The design was a collaboration of Luigi Chinetti Jr. with Michelotti.

THE FINAL V 12 SPORTS CARS

Possibly the last Special Daytona commissioned by Luigi Chinetti and realised by Michelotti was this Spyder NART shown at the Turin Motor Show in 1980. It resembles the Steve McQueen Spyder NART but its pure wedge design is less innovative, (C/N 15,003).

CHAPTER FIFTEEN

SPECIFICATIONS

365GTC/4

Type	365
Model	GTC/4
Years made	1971-1972
Chassis range	14179-16289
Number produced	500
Coachbuiders	Pininfarina
Body styles	Coupé
Body material	Steel
Seating capacity	2 (+2)
Engine type	V12 60°
Displacement	4390cc
Bore and stroke	81mm x 71mm
Cyl. head	DOHC, single outside plug
Ignition	2 distributors
Compression	8.8 to1
Carburation	6 x 38DCOE
Lubrication	Wet sump
Horsepower	320bhp @ 6200rpm
Chassis/Drivetrain	Engine/gearbox in front
Frame	Tubular steel– maintubes oval
Transmission	5-speed
Axle ratio	3.3 to 1
Brakes	Hydraulic discs
Wheels	15" cast alloy
Front suspension	Independent, A-arms, coil springs, telescopic shocks
Rear suspension	Independent, A-arms, coil springs, telescopic shocks
Curb weight	3500 lbs
Wheelbase	2500 mm
Track front	1470 mm
Track rear	1470 mm

Note. Power steering was standard equipment. Air conditioning was optional in Europe and standard on all U.S. spec. cars.

365GTB/4 'Daytona'

Type	365
Model	GTB/4 'Daytona'
Years made	1968-1973
Chassis range	12037 - 17087
Number produced	1300
Coachbuiders	Scaglietti
Body styles	Berlinetta
Body material	Steel
Seating capacity	2
Engine type	V12 60°
Displacement	4390cc
Bore and stroke	81mm x 71mm
Cyl. head	DOHC, single outside plug
Ignition	2 distributors
Compression	9.3 to 1
Carburation	6 x 40DCN 20
Lubrication	Dry sump
Horsepower	352bhp @ 7500rpm
Chassis/Drivetrain	Engine front /transaxle rear
Frame	Tubular steel– maintubes oval
Transmission	5-speed transaxle
Axle ratio	3.3 to1
Brakes	Hydraulic discs
Wheels	15" cast alloy
Front suspension	Independent, A-arms, coil springs, telescopic shocks
Rear suspension	Independent, A-arms, coil springs, telescopic shocks
Curb weight	3150 lbs
Wheelbase	2400 mm
Track front	1440 mm
Track rear	1425 mm

Note. Air contitioning was optional in Europe, and standard on all U.S. spec. cars.

365GTB/4 – GTS/4 'Daytona Spyder'

Type	365
Model	GTB/4 GTS/4 'Daytona Spyder'
Years made	1969-1973
Chassis range	12851 - 17073
Number produced	123
Coachbuiders	Scaglietti
Body styles	Convertible
Body material	Steel
Seating capacity	2
Engine type	V12 60°
Displacement	4390cc
Bore and stroke	81mm x 71mm
Cyl. head	DOHC
Ignition	single outside plug 2 distributors
Compression	9.3 to 1
Carburation	6 x 40DCN 20
Lubrication	Dry sump
Horsepower	352bhp @ 7,500rpm
Chassis/Drivetrain	Engine front/transaxle rear
Frame	Tubular steel– maintubes oval
Transmission	5-speed transaxle
Axle ratio	3.3 to 1
Brakes	Hydraulic discs
Wheels	15" cast alloy
Front suspension	Independent, A-arms, coil springs, telescopic shocks
Rear suspension	Independent, A-arms, coil springs, telescopic shocks
Curb weight	3150 lbs
Wheelbase	2400 mm
Track front	1440 mm
Track rear	1425 mm

This particular 246GTS was built in 1974 and is one of the rare ones equipped with flared fenders and wide Campagnolo wheels. It may or may not be equipped with Daytona-style seats.

Above & right The 400 Automatic was the flagship of the line. Its refinement and mature development paved the way for future 4-seater Ferraris that would compete with the finest luxury sedans in the world.

CHAPTER SIXTEEN

2+2 Redefined

400GT (1976-1979)
400i GT (1979-1985)
412 (1985-)

At the 1976 Paris Salon, Ferrari's favourite occasion to announce any new model, a new 2 + 2 was announced, equipped with an automatic transmission as standard equipment. The transmission chosen was the General Motors Hydramatic unit as basically used in the Cadillac. It was the same one that had been chosen by Rolls-Royce and Jaguar years before. It was the same basic unit that had been pioneered by the work of Dick Fritz at Chinetti Motors. Ironically, this new model was not to be officially imported into the U.S.A. where it certainly would had had its largest potential market. So devastating was the cost of meeting all the US requirements, including crashing two cars, that it was not economically feasible: the price of the car would have been too high.

In 1977, the first full year of production, only 161 400GTs were produced. In 1978 production increased to 213. Most of these were sold in Europe. In 1979 fuel injection was finally introduced. The fuel injection system had been engineered by Bosch with Ferrari and used the latest K-Jetronic unit specially modified for the V12 Ferrari engine. The use of fuel injection seemed to encourage the rumour that the new car would be imported into the U.S.A. It did make the car easier to legalise and more found their way to the U.S.A. via the grey market, despite the fact that the makers warranty was inoperative and parts were not stocked.

About 1982, Ferrari North America, who had replaced Chinetti-Garthwaite Imports and Modern Classic Motors as the sole U.S. importer in 1980, made the decision to allow U.S. Ferrari dealers to take orders for the European specification 400i for delivery at the factory in Maranello. This was partly as the result of

pressure brought by the dealers who wanted to be able to compete with the grey market on Ferrari models not officially imported. As Ferrari North America is a direct branch of the factory, it became easier to steer the factory in the direction of marketing decisions that would benefit the North American Market.

The Ferrari 2 + 2 concept was further refined with the introduction of the revised 400i at the Paris Salon in October 1982. Horsepower and torque were improved, the self-levelling rear suspension was revised and improved with gas shock absorbers and the interior was completely redesigned. The option of dual (front and rear) air conditioning with climate control was continued and some leeway was allowed in the ability to order special interior colour schemes. There were limits however, and an American Ferrari dealer's request for a sun roof on a 400i ordered for himself was turned down.

In 1985, at the Geneva Motor Show, the 2 + 2 was again redefined with the introduction of the new 412. The styling was developed from the 400i and included a larger trunk and again a totally new interior, with the latest in touch sensitive switches and electrically controlled seats. While the GM automatic transmission was standard equipment, the traditional 5-speed Ferrari gearbox was still available as an option. Production continued at Pininfarina at the rate of about 250 each year and so the Ferrari V12 engine remained in production. At the end of 1987 rumour had it that the V12 would be revised, but would be used in whatever replacement for the 412 was finally announced and would be fully compatible with future U.S. standards.

Above A major improvement took place in late 1979 when the 400 engine was equipped with the latest Bosch K-Jetronic fuel injection.

Below & right With the 412, Ferrari produced an outstanding luxury automobile that met the highest possible standards in safety, performance and comfort - but it still did not meet all of the U.S. legal requirements.

2+2 REDEFINED

CHAPTER SIXTEEN

SPECIFICATIONS

400(2+2)

Type	400
Model	(2+2)
Years made	1976-1979
Chassis range	20093 -
Number produced	502
Coachbuiders	Pininfarina
Body styles	Coupé
Body material	Steel
Seating capacity	2 + 2
Engine type	V12 60°
Displacement	4823cc
Bore and stroke	81mm x 78mm
Cyl. head	DOHC single outside plug
Ignition	2 distributors
Compression	8.8 to 1
Carburation	6 x 38DCOE
Lubrication	Wet sump
Horsepower	340bhp @ 6500rpm
Chassis/Drivetrain	Engine/gearbox in front
Frame	Tubular steel– maintubes oval
Transmission	5-speed or automatic
Axle ratio	3.3 to1
Brakes	Hydraulic discs
Wheels	15" cast alloy bolt-on
Front suspension	Independent, A-arms, coil springs, telescopic shocks
Rear suspension	Independent, A-arms, coil springs, telescopic shocks †
Curb weight	4500 lbs
Wheelbase	2700 mm
Track front	1470 mm
Track rear	1500 mm

†with hydro-pneumatic self-levellers

400i(2+2)

Type	400i
Model	(2+2)
Years made	1979 - 1985
Chassis range	?? – 55523
Number produced	1308
Coachbuiders	Pininfarina
Body styles	Coupé
Body material	Steel
Seating capacity	2 + 2
Engine type	V12 60°
Displacement	4823cc
Bore and stroke	81mm x 78mm
Cyl. head	DOHC single outside plug
Ignition	2 distributors
Compression	8.8 to1
Carburation	Bosch K-Jetronic F.I.
Lubrication	Wet sump
Horsepower	310bhp @ 6400rpm *
Chassis/Drivetrain	Engine/gearbox in front
Frame	Tubular steel– maintubes oval
Transmission	5-speed or automatic
Axle ratio	3.3 to1
Brakes	Hydraulic discs
Wheels	15" cast alloy bolt-on
Front suspension	Independent, A-arms, coil springs, telescopic shocks
Rear suspension	Independent, A-arms, coil springs, telescopic shocks †
Curb weight	4500 lbs
Wheelbase	2700 mm
Track front	1470 mm
Track rear	1500 mm

* 315bhp @ 6400rpm after September 1982
† With hydro-pneumatic self-levellers

412(2+2)

Type	412
Model	(2+2)
Years made	1985 -
Chassis range	56275-
Number produced	Est. 250 per year
Coachbuiders	Pininfarina
Body styles	Coupé
Body material	Steel
Seating capacity	2 + 2
Engine type	V12 60°
Displacement	4943cc
Bore and stroke	82mm x 78mm
Cyl. head	DOHC single outside plug
Ignition	Marelli Microplex
Compression	9.6 to1
Carburation	Bosche K-Jetronic F.I.
Lubrication	Wet sump
Horsepower	340bhp @ 6000rpm
Chassis/Drivetrain	Engine/gearbox in front
Frame	Tubular steel– maintubes oval
Transmission	5-speed or automatic
Axle ratio	3.3 to 1
Brakes	Hydraulic discs with ABS
Wheels	15" cast alloy bolt-on
Front suspension	Independent, A-arms, coil springs, telescopic shocks
Rear suspension	Independent, A-arms, coil springs, telescopic shocks †
Curb weight	4300 lbs
Wheelbase	2700 mm
Track front	1470 mm
Track rear	1500 mm

† With hydro-pneumatic self-levellers

The first hint of the new Dino production car was this Pininfarina Special officially called the Dino 206GT Speciale. It was first shown at the 1965 Paris Salon and was mounted on C/N 0834, a 206S sports racing chassis.

CHAPTER SEVENTEEN

*C*OMPROMISED *P*ERFORMANCE

206GT (1968-1969)
246GT (1969-1973)
246GTS (1972-1974)

Enzo Ferrari had never been intimidated by unusual engine configurations and even before he had his own car company, before World War II, he had been responsible for developing engines of all kinds: straight 4-, 6- and 8-cylinders, and V12 and even 16s. But he had never been attracted to the V6. This changed when his only legitimate offspring, Dino, who died a youth in 1956, put forth some convincing arguments in its favour. In his memoirs, Ferrari has written that he and Vittorio Jano, one of Italy's greatest automobile engineers, had spent "long hours at his (Dino's) bedside discussing with him the design of a 1.5-litre engine." Although ill most of his life, Dino had acquired an engineering degree and had earlier presented his arguments for a V6 high-performance engine in a two part article in the Italian magazine *Velocita*. Enzo Ferrari continued, "For reasons of mechanical efficiency he finally came to the conclusion that the engine should be a V6 and we accepted his decision. There was thus born the famous 156 which burst into song for the first time five months after Dino had passed away."

The death of his only legitimate child was a severe blow, (Dino had suffered from nephritis or muscular dystrophy since he was born) and he was determined to honour his memory to the best of his ability. Over a period of 10 years a series of 3 different types of V6 Dino engines were designed, built and utilised for Formula 1, Formula 2, sports racing and GT road cars. The first was the Jano/Dino Ferrari design of 1956 for the forthcoming Formula 2: the Dino 156F2, a twin-ignition DOHC V6 that developed 175 horsepower at 8300 rpm. Jano designed another Dino V6-engined, this time a SOHC that seemed more appropriate for private owners. A third series was the work of the brilliant Mauro Forghieri and an engineer who had emerged from Ferrari's design departments, Franco Rocchi. This DOHC V6 led to the production engine made in collaboration with FIAT to ensure production of at least 500 engines, thus meeting the new regulations for Formula 2 racing engines.

The advent of a production V6 Dino engine was pushed forward with the stillborn V6 engine Ferrari designed for Innocenti to be used in an Innocenti production car in 1964. This never happened but the Ferrari factory gave the V6 program a real shot in the arm by introducing a small series of sports racing cars that were put into production for use in the 1966 racing season. This was the Dino 206S with the engine at the rear, but ahead of the rear axle. The engine, the Forghieri/Rocchi design, was a 65 degree V6 with double overhead cams and a bore and stroke of 86mm x 57mm which achieved 218 horsepower @ 9000rpm! About eighteen of these were built.

The first hint of serious production activity with a small V6 rear-engined Ferrari came with the showing of a Pininfarina special at the Paris Motor Show in October 1965. This was called the Dino 206GT Speciale and was actually built on C/N 0834, a prototype for the 206S sports racing car. The Speciale and the 206S had the engined mounted longitudinally in the rear, ahead of the rear axle. The final version of the 206S was first shown at Ferrari's January press conference in 1966.

The next step was the showing of the Pininfarina

CHAPTER SEVENTEEN

special called the Dino Berlinetta GT which appeared on display at the 1966 Turin Motor Show. This too had the engine in the longitudinal position. The third prototype was more definitive, as it had the engine mounted sideways, but still ahead of the rear axle. This proved to be the final production version and was in unit with a special Ferrari-designed 5-speed gearbox - actually a transaxle. This pre-production prototype was first displayed at the Turin Motor Show in November 1967. An additional prototype appeared at the 1968 Brussels Motor Show. The 206GT finally went into production at Scaglietti's in the early months of 1969. By the end of 1969 about 150 had been built, all of them with left-hand drive with all aluminium bodies and front vents in the side windows, which all of the prototypes lacked. The 206GT was also unusual in being the first production Ferrari to be given only even chassis numbers, (previous road Ferraris had - with a few exceptions - always been given odd numbers).

The new Dino 206GT production car was somewhat schizophrenic. The name Ferrari appeared nowhere on the outside but in fact the car was legally a Ferrari and Dino 206GT was the model name. The production of the new V6 was so low that almost all were sold in Italy or on the continent. Only a handful were brought in to the U.S.A. by Luigi Chinetti.

The 246GT was a more serious effort, and an official U.S. version was included in the production plans. This new car was slightly longer in wheelbase and its body was of steel except for the horizontal moving panels. The increase in engine size and horsepower (2.4 litres and 195 horsepower) was substantive. The U.S. version was rated at 180 horsepower and needed only an airpump and minor changes in timing to meet the tough U.S. emission requirements. Production began slowly in late 1969 and hit its stride in

Above, right & right above The second Pininfarina Dino prototype was shown at the 1966 Turin Motor Show. This is closer to the final production version but the engine is still mounted longitudinally.

COMPROMISED PERFORMANCE

Above Another 206GT prototype - this one may have been made by Scaglietti as no Pininfarina identification is visible.

CHAPTER SEVENTEEN

Above & right This is yet another Pininfarina Dino prototype which was displayed at the 1967 Brussels Motor Show.

1971 and 1972, with over 800 built each of those years. Sales in the U.S.A. began in earnest in 1972 with the formation of the new U.S. importers, Chinetti-Garthwaite Imports in the east and Modern Classic Motors in the west. The 246GT joined the 365GTB/4 Daytonas and the 365GTC/4 as the only legal Ferraris available on the American market. Sadly, the Canadian government imposed restrictions that were effectively the same as those in the U.S.A.. As a result, the Ferraris sold in Canada were the same as those in the U.S.

Late in 1972 Ferrari introduced a new 246 Dino model, the 246GTS. The 'S' is for Spyder which in this case meant a removable roof copying Porsche's popular Targa. It was an obvious idea but apparently one that had not been foreseen by Pininfarina or Ferrari. In any case it was a successful modification (the well-designed fibreglass top could be stored neatly in an upright position behind the seats.) In the U.S.A. the new model was treated as a replacement for the 246GT Coupé, but the factory kept both models in production until 1974 when both models were discontinued. Before production had ended some American dealers pleaded for a special version of the 246GTS. The factory offered in late 1973 and 1974 flared fenders with wide (Campagnolo) wheels as an option. Another option were Daytona seats but the two options did not always go together. The so called 'chairs and flairs' is a misnomer. Otherwise all 246GTSs were sold with every option available, and these included power windows, air conditioning, leather seats and an electrically-operated antenna. Radios were left to the dealers to install. The U.S. safety laws mandated marker lights in all four fenders and upright parking lights (not flush) in the nose.

While the Dino 246 was not the strongest Ferrari ever built, it was a sales success partly due to its voluptuous design which was instantly appealing. Its demise came as a complete surprise to the U.S. dealers. As the 365GTC/4 had been discontinued at the end of 1972 and the 365GTB/4 Daytona bit the dust in 1973 it left the U.S. market with only one Ferrari to sell: the controversial new Bertone-bodied 308GT4 2+2.

From Ferarri's point of view there was one substantive problem that was not generally known at the time. The U.S. government had granted an exemption that allowed 2-seater cars to be approved without 10-mph crash-worthy bumpers. All three Ferraris being imported into the U.S. were illegal after September 1st, 1974! With too little advance planning Ferrari found themselves required to design a whole new range of models that would meet all of the U.S. requirements. A further exemption was possible for small manufacturers who pleaded poverty, but Ferrari would not do this.

CHAPTER SEVENTEEN

COMPROMISED PERFORMANCE

This Scaglietti-built production version of the 206GT is correct except for a few dealer installed extras such as the plastic headlight covers and the prancing horse in the grill (C/N 00112). The two backup lights are believed to be original, although later in production only one was used.

CHAPTER SEVENTEEN

With the arrival of the 246GT, bolt-on cast alloy wheels replaced the traditional knock-offs. This is a European specification car with non-original headlight covers and prancing horse on the rear.

COMPROMISED PERFORMANCE

CHAPTER SEVENTEEN

The engine and transaxle of the 246GT(S) which shows that the driveshaft output is in front of the rear axle.

Above left & above The 246GTS had revised styling on the sail panels and a reinforced frame to increase structural rigidity. The outside rearview mirror shown is the type fitted by the factory on all the 246GTS built for the American market.

CHAPTER SEVENTEEN

These photos show clearly, front and rear, the flared fenders and wide wheels option available on a limited number of 246GTSs built for the U.S.A. The rectangular side lights front and rear were required by U.S. safety regulations. The special alloy wide wheels were built for Ferrari by Campagnolo and were sand cast magnesium alloy.

COMPROMISED PERFORMANCE

CHAPTER SEVENTEEN

SPECIFICATIONS

206GT

Type	206
Model	GT
Years made	1966 - 1969
Chassis range	00102 - 00404
Number produced	150
Coachbuiders	Scaglietti
Body styles	Coupé
Body material	Aluminium
Seating capacity	2
Engine type	V12 65° *
Displacement	1987cc
Bore and stroke	86mm x 57mm
Cyl. head	DOHC single outside plug
Ignition	1 distributor
Compression	9.0 to1
Carburation	3 x 40DCF
Lubrication	Wet sump
Horsepower	180bhp @ 8,000rpm
Chassis/Drivetrain	Engine/transaxle in rear
Frame	Tubular steel– maintubes oval
Transmission	5-speed transaxle
Axle ratio	
Brakes	Hydraulic discs
Wheels	14" cast alloy knock-ons
Front suspension	Independent, A-arms, coil springs, telescopic shocks
Rear suspension	Independent, A-arms, coil springs, telescopic shocks
Curb weight	2300 lbs
Wheelbase	2280 mm
Track front	1425 mm
Track rear	1400 mm

* Aluminium block

246GT

Type	246
Model	GT
Years made	1969-1974
Chassis range	00400
Number produced	2609
Coachbuiders	Scaglietti
Body styles	Coupé
Body material	Steel
Seating capacity	2
Engine type	V6 65° *
Displacement	2418cc
Bore and stroke	92.5mm x 60mm
Cyl. head	DOHC single outside plug
Ignition	1 distributor/dinoplex
Compression	9.0 to1
Carburation	3 x 40DCN F/7
Lubrication	Wet sump
Horsepower	195bhp @ 7600rpm *
Chassis/Drivetrain	Engine/transaxle in rear
Frame	Tubular steel– maintubes oval
Transmission	5-speed transaxle
Axle ratio	
Brakes	Hydraulic discs
Wheels	14" cast alloy bolt-on
Front suspension	Independent, A-arms, coil springs, telescopic shocks
Rear suspension	Independent, A-arms, coil springs, telescopic shocks
Curb weight	2700 lbs
Wheelbase	2340 mm
Track front	1425 mm
Track rear	1400 mm †

* cast iron block - U.S.A. 180bhp
† changed to 1430mm in 1970

COMPROMISED PERFORMANCE

246GTS

Type	246
Model	GTS
Years made	1972 - 1974
Chassis range	03408 - 08518
Number produced	1274
Coachbuiders	Scaglietti
Body styles	Coupé *
Body material	Steel
Seating capacity	2
Engine type	V6 65° †
Displacement	2418mm
Bore and stroke	92.5mm x 60mm
Cyl. head	DOHC single outside plug
Ignition	1 distributor/dinoplex
Compression	9.0 to1
Carburation	3 x 40 DCN F/7
Lubrication	Wet sump
Horsepower	195bhp @ 7600rpm †
Chassis/Drivetrain	Engine/transaxle in rear
Frame	Tubular steel– maintubes oval
Transmission	5-speed transaxle
Axle ratio	
Brakes	Hydraulic discs
Wheels	14" cast alloy bolt-on
Front suspension	Independent, A-arms, coil springs, telescopic shocks
Rear suspension	Independent, A-arms, coil springs, telescopic shocks
Curb weight	2700 lbs
Wheelbase	2340 mm
Track front	1425 mm
Track rear	1430 mm

* removable 'Targa' style roof
† cast iron block -U.S.A. 180bhp.
Note. First U.S.A. car was 03764

CHAPTER EIGHTEEN

THE V8 EMERGES

308GT4 2 + 2 (1974-1980)
308GTB, GTBi & GTB Qv (1976-1985)
308GTS, GTSi & GTS Qv (1977 - 1985)
208s Models (1980 -   )
328GTB (1985 -   )
328GTS (1985 -   )
Mondial 8 & Qv (1983-1985)
3.2 Mondial (1986 -   )

With the 308, Ferrari recognised the need to start with a clean sheet of paper to design a new power and chassis package that would satisfy the needs of markets throughout the world. The new 308GT4 2 + 2 was introduced at the Paris Salon in October 1973. The 90-degree V8 engine was related to the 1964 Formula 1 Ferrari 158. As is typical at Ferrari, no one person is given credit for the 308 engine design. It is probable that Franco Rocchi was responsible for this design, with possible assistance from engineer Angelo Bellei. Bellei had probably worked under Mauro Forghieri on the 158 racing engine in 1962 and 1963.

After a year's production in Europe the 308GT4 2 + 2 was legally ready for the fickle U.S. market. Shipments began at the very end of 1974 and the dealers received their first cars in January and February 1975. The response was negative, the new car was not a replacement for anything and it was not a 2-seater. Moreover, it was not a Pininfarina design and was lacking the sensuous curves for which Ferraris designed by Pinnfarina had become famous. It was a compromise, a 2+2 designed by Bertone. The design was a sharp contrast with previous Ferraris, a wedge devoid of curves. It did not look like anyone's idea of a Ferrari and - on the nose - it wore a badge that simply said 'Dino'. The name Ferrari was nowhere in sight!

Left & above These pictures illustrate a typical early 308GT4 built to European specifications. The neat European bumpers contrasted glaringly with the massive ones required for North America. The cloth interior shown was available in the U.S.A. but was a rare option, as most U.S. cars were fitted with full leather seats.

CHAPTER EIGHTEEN

Above & right Only one special was built on the 308GT4 2 + 2 chassis: it was a unique prototype built by Bertone on a chassis that had been shortened. It first appeared at the Turin Motor Show in 1976. The top could be retracted into the car without removing it and was the subject of a special patent. Called The Rainbow it is displayed from time to time and is still owned by Bertone.

THE V8 EMERGES

For the Ferrari dealers in the U.S.A. it was a rough period. From January 1975 to the fall of 1976 (when the new 308GTB finally arrived) the American dealers had only one model to sell - the 308GT4 2 + 2. Like most Ferrari dealers at the time this writer put a great many hours behind the wheel of this new model as no opportunity to demonstrate it was lost. We always had one full time demonstrator and kept two or three in stock at all times.

From the owner/driver point of view the 308GT4 was a winner! We really had no unhappy customers - just not enough of them. This new car was basically a 246GT with a slightly longer wheelbase and a more powerful engine. The U.S. version of the new V8 developed 230 horsepower, 20 less than the European version. To meet the U.S. standards Ferrari had fitted an air pump and some timing gimmicks. By simply disconnecting the air pump (removing the belt) about 10 of the missing 20 horsepower was recaptured. For those who were not put off by the styling it was - and still is - a hell of a car! The rear seats looked like a joke but again and again I would move the front passenger seat forward and jacknife my 6' frame into the back seat! I would not want to go to Philadelphia back there (about a 3.5 hour trip) but they are useable for around town.

No, it wasn't perfect. The first U.S. bumpers looked like battering rams and were eventually replaced at no cost to the customers with a more pleasing design. In addition, modifications were made to the air conditioning that included a new vent outlet to blow directly on the driver or passenger. Almost all of those sold in America were equipped with every option available from the factory. These included full leather seats, power windows, air conditioning and an electrically operated antenna. The radio was always dealer installed. On the 308GT4s built from 1974 through 1976 the Dino badge on the nose was standard but at the customer's request, dealers did fit Ferrari script and emblems and, in some cases, even the Ferrari badge to replace or add to the Dino badge. Finally, in 1978, the cars began to arrive from the factory with the Ferrari badge only, but still with the script Dino 308GT4 on the trunk lid.

The 308GT4 stayed in production into 1980 in Europe, but 1979 was its last year in the U.S.. From late 1978 through 1979 the U.S. model included a manually-operated steel sunroof as standard equipment but on these later U.S. cars the horsepower was reduced as the U.S. emission standards grew more stringent (starting in 1978 catalytic converters were required). The sale of 308GT4s was so poor in the U.S.

Right The inspired 308GTB styling solution will be difficult to improve upon. The top two photos show a standard 308GTB of 1982. The U.S. bumpers were very much the same, but protruded about 4 inches. The bottom photo shows a 208 Turbo, identified by the NACA duct just in front of the rear wheel. The large front spoiler on this car was offered as an option on all GTBs and GTSs.

Below The 308GT4 2 + 2 was built in 1977 through 1980. Note the Ferrari badge on the nose, the prancing horse on the hubs and the star wheels which became standard equipment. This particular car was built for the U.K. market and is right-hand drive. 'Dino 308GT4' still appeared on the trunk lid.

THE V8 EMERGES

CHAPTER EIGHTEEN

Above & right Pininfarina had given up the production of special cars but this one is an exception, although it was not built for a special customer and was subsequently scrapped! It was shown at the Turin Motor Show in 1977 and did forecast the use of the basket handle over the rear deck. The interior appears to be standard 1977 308GTB except for the special instrument panel, which is based on that used in the 365GT4 BB Boxer.

that dealers were still selling new 1975s in 1978.

The only real special on the 308GT4 chassis was a prototype built by Bertone on a slightly shorter wheelbase that was called The Rainbow. The only other out-of-the-ordinary cars were a small group equipped with a luggage area in place of the rear seats. This modification was designed and produced by Scaglietti, who built the cars to Bertone's design. For the Italian market Ferrari built a 2-litre version to take advantage of a loophole in the Italian tax laws. The 208GT4 2 + 2 was built in small quantities through 1980.

At the Paris Salon in October 1975, Ferrari debuted the totally new 308GTB 2-seat Berlinetta. The all-new design represented Pininfarinas very best efforts. It blended soft curves and crisp edges in a masterly way. Surprisingly the body was built entirely of fibreglass but the quality was so good that it could not be detected by even the most knowledgeable observer. It was a natural development of Ferrari's work with fibreglass in the past, which included the use of this material in the wheel wells and floorboards of the 246GT(S)s and the 365GTB/4 Daytonas.

THE V8 EMERGES

The 308GTB in fibreglass arrived in the U.S.A. in the fall of 1976. It was joyful day for the American dealers. The revolutionary new body styling was Pininfarina's answer to a stagnant American market. However, the first long drive in the new car was a bit disappointing as it did not handle quite as well as the 308GT4. The problem lay with the chassis and in due course the factory provided retrofit kits that included new coil springs and shocks. Over the next few years the handling was improved but the fibreglass body was scrapped and the steel replacement weighed at least 300 pounds more! Despite these teething problems, the 308GTB was a winner. Pininfarina's inspired new design became a sales success. This success was matched by the strength and reliability of the new 308 engine and gearbox.

In September 1977, the new 308GTS, inspired by the 246GTS, was announced as an addition to the line. Its Targa-style removable roof was an instant hit and very soon it led sales for all the 308 models. The 308GTB became almost a special order model. The 308GTS had been scheduled to be introduced before the 308GTB but was held up due to the open roof which had weakened the structural integrity of the entire car. The delay was due to the time needed to solve the frame flexing problems. On one early prototype, the roof had flown off at 90 mph on the testing circuit.

From 1977 to 1985 the GTB and the GTS went through a series of changes aimed at improving the quality of the product and at maintaining the horsepower available for the cars they built for North America. The change from carburettors to fuel injection in 1980 was a key step in the horsepower/emissions race and added a small 'i' to the model names. An even more radical move for 1982 was the complete redesign of the cylinder heads to include four valves per cylinder! Accordingly the models were renamed to add 'Qv' instead of 'i' although the fuel injection continued. The 'Qv' stood for *quottrovalvole* - Italian for four valve. The U.S. version showed an increase in horsepower, but even more important was the greater percentage increase in torque that was combined with a slight change in gear ratios to provide faster acceleration at speeds below 100 mph and a slightly lower top speed. Overall these models had become much

225

CHAPTER EIGHTEEN

Above The darker 308GTs with its top removed is a 1978 U.S. model. This is evident from the rectangular side lights and the very protruding front and rear bumpers. The other 308GTS is a slightly later example built to European standards. The later low-profile TRX tyres are a good clue.

Right The 1987 328GTS is a world car that looks the same in U.S. or European trim. The only substantive difference is horsepower: 260 for North America and 270 for the rest of the world.

smoother, faster and more luxurious.

For the Italian market, Ferrari had built a 2-litre carburetted version of the GTB and GTS from 1980 through 1982. Despite the modest 170 horsepower the GTB version had great success. In 1982 a fuel-injected turbocharged version was introduced and horsepower rose to 220. This version continued through 1985. Further engine improvements were made in 1986 that increased the horsepower to 254 at 6500 rpm.

Ferrari was still intent on offering a 2 + 2 model that could be approved for the U.S. market without having to approve a new engine. The answer was to use the existing 308 engine in a longer wheelbase chassis. The new Mondial 8 chassis was designed to allow the engine/transaxle unit to be easily removed with its surrounding framework! Pininfarina was back in business as Ferrari's exclusive source for new designs. While the look was new and different, the real breakthrough was in interior technology. New touch switches were utilised and a special trouble-shooting panel told the driver what was right or wrong with a variety of systems. Unusual were warnings of low oil level and a special signal to indicate that the car needed to be serviced. Another feature totally new to any Ferrari was the tiltable steering wheel. An electrically-operated sunroof was available, and this was standard equipment on those intended for North America. This new model was called the Mondial 8 to commemorate the race-winning Mondial of the 1950s.

The longer wheelbase, together with the redesigned steering and suspension, gave the new Mondial 8 a special feel that was at great contrast with the sportier GTB/GTS models. This was a Ferrari that could not be fairly judged in a short trip. It came into its own on journeys or at least 2 or 3 hours. Unfortunately it was not a great success in any market. Its marginal 2 + 2 configuration was at odds with its ideal long distance ride. Like the 365GTC/4 it was a compromise. The 4-valve engine and its increased power helped a bit, but sales did not really revive until the cabriolet version arrived in 1983. This 4-seater convertible did attract attention due to the rarity of 4-seater convertibles from any luxury car manufacturer. Besides, open Ferraris have always had a special appeal. In the U.S. market, the new cabriolet practically replaced the coupé, which became very scarce. For 1985 the new 3.2 Mondial brought the larger and more powerful 328 engine to the Mondial models. It mattered little, and this underrated model remained more popular in Europe than North America, though in Europe they prefer the closed version. In 1986 the factory built 303 coupés and 251 cabriolets. The Mondial is a model

CHAPTER EIGHTEEN

that cries out to be replaced by a slightly larger and more powerful model that will really hold four adults comfortably on a long trip.

No doubt the future will see a proud successor to the 328GTB/GTS. During 1986, 1467 GTSs were built and 373 GTBs. The disparity between the two models in terms of market appeal is clear; can we foresee some kind of rationalization and merging of the Mondial and 412 which might result in a totally new range built from scratch to meet all of the legal requirements worldwide? Something along these lines is clearly needed.

Right The interior of the Mondial coupé had Pininfarinas newest high-tech look - an unusual departure for Ferrari but note that analog instruments are retained.

Below The first Mondial 8 was this 2 + 2 coupé. It was a totally new look for Ferrari and Pininfarina.

Bottom The first version of the 1983 Mondial Cabriolet was the first true Ferrari convertible since 1967 when production of the 365 California ceased.

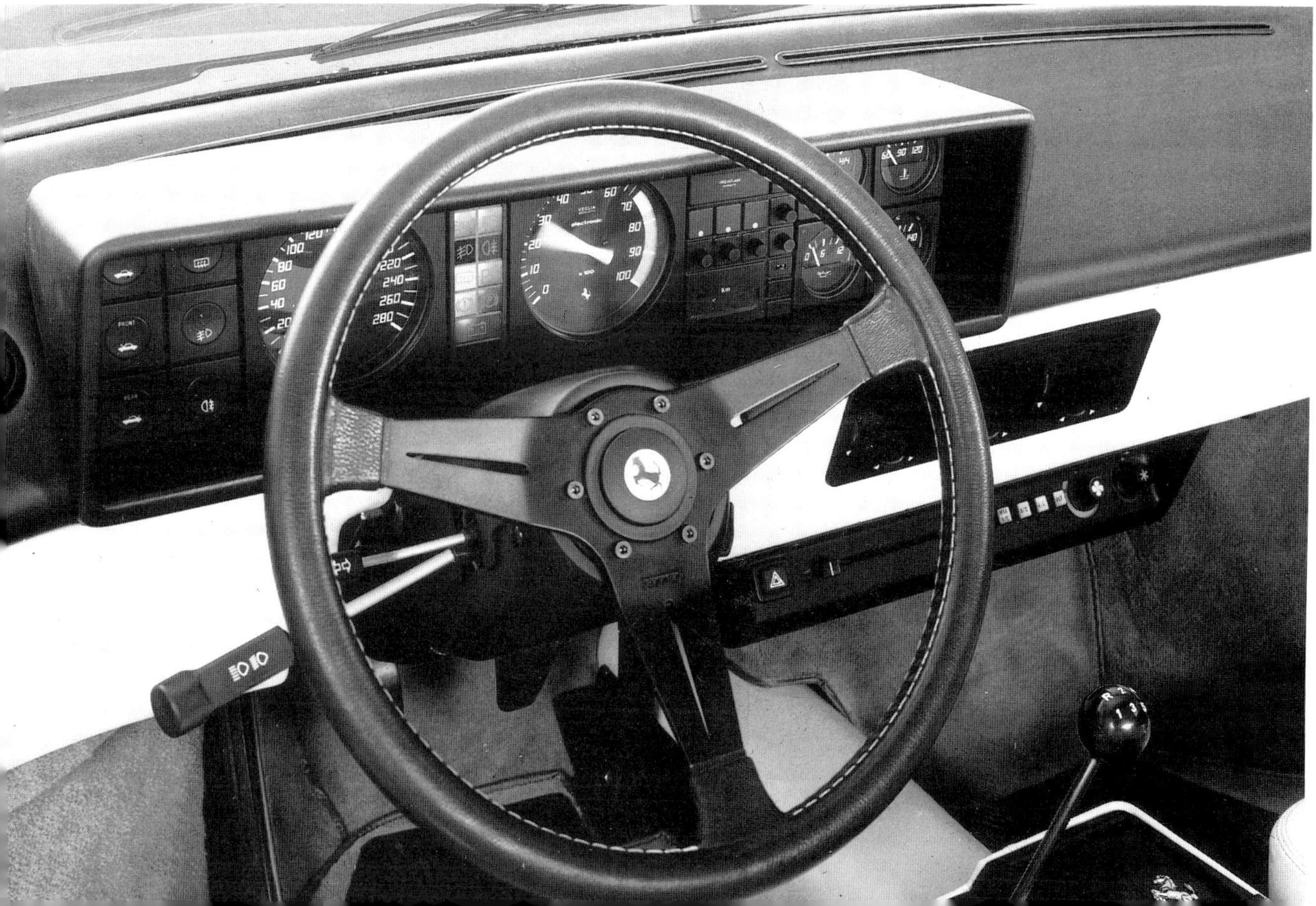
100
80
60
40
220
240
260
280
VEGLIA
electronic

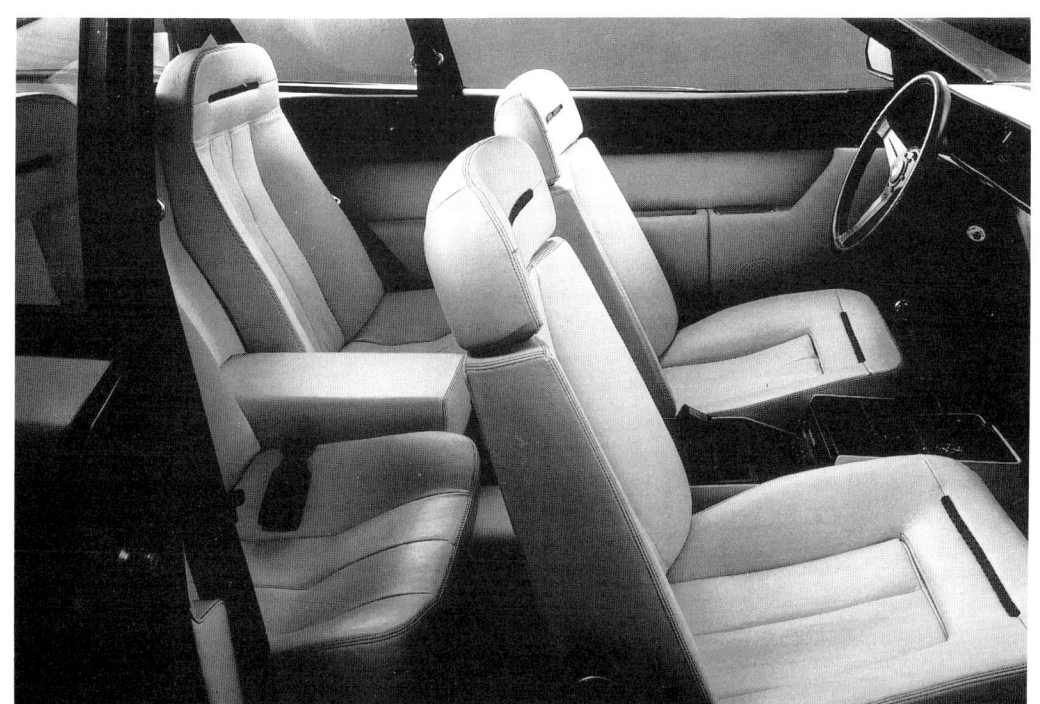

CHAPTER EIGHTEEN

The newest 3.2 Mondials are refined and improved versions of the previous Mondials. The U.S. version of the cabriolet is shown.

THE V8 EMERGES

SPECIFICATIONS

308GT4 2+2

Type	308
Model	GT4 2+2
Years made	1974 - 1980
Chassis range	07202 - 15604 *
Number produced	2826
Coachbuiders	Scaglietti
Body styles	Coupé
Body material	Steel
Seating capacity	2 + 2
Engine type	V8 90°
Displacement	2926cc
Bore and stroke	81mm x 71mm
Cyl. head	DOHC single outside plug
Ignition	1 or 2 distributors (U.S.A: 2)
Compression	8.8 to 1
Carburation	4 x 40DCNF
Lubrication	Wet sump
Horsepower	250bhp @ 7700rpm
Chassis/Drivetrain	Engine/transaxle in rear
Frame	Tubular steel– maintubes oval
Transmission	5-speed transaxle
Brakes	Hydraulic disc
Wheels	14" cast alloy bolt-on
Front suspension	Independent, A-arms, coil springs, telescopic shocks
Rear suspension	Independent, A-arms, coil springs, telescopic shocks
Curb weight	3200lbs
Wheelbase	2550 mm
Track front	1460 mm
Track rear	1460 mm

Note. U.S.A. 230bhp until 1978 and 215bhp later. The 208GT4 2 + 2 was made for Italy with a 2 litre engine of 170bhp @ 7700rpm (about 840 were made).

CHAPTER EIGHTEEN

SPECIFICATIONS

308GTB

Type	308
Model	GTB
Years made	1975 - 1980
Chassis range	18677 - 31001
Number produced	2897
Coachbuiders	Scaglietti
Body styles	Coupé
Body material	Fibreglass and steel
Seating capacity	2
Engine type	V8 90°
Displacement	2926cc
Bore and stroke	81mm x 71mm
Cyl. head	DOHC single outside plug
Ignition	1 or 2 distributors/Digiplex
Compression	8.8 to 1
Carburation	4 x 40DCNF
Lubrication	Dry or wet sump*
Horsepower	255bhp @ 7700rpm*
Chassis/Drivetrain	Engine/transaxle in rear
Frame	Tubular steel – maintubes oval
Transmission	5-speed transaxle
Brakes	Hydraulic discs
Wheels	14" cast alloy bolt-on
Front suspension	Independent, A-arms, coil springs, telescopic shocks
Rear suspension	Independent, A-arms, coil springs, telescopic shocks
Curb weight	3100 lbs
Wheelbase	2340 mm
Track front	1460 mm
Track rear	1460 mm

*U.S.A. Wet sump - 2 distributors -240bhp @ 6600 rpm (fibreglass cars ended with C/N 21289 and steel cars began with C/N 20805)

308GTBi

Type	308
Model	GTBi
Years made	1980-1982
Chassis range	31327 -
Number produced	494
Coachbuiders	Scaglietti
Body styles	Coupé
Body material	Steel
Seating capacity	2
Engine type	V8 90°
Displacement	2926cc
Bore and stroke	81mm x 71mm
Cyl. head	DOHC single outside plug
Ignition	Digiplex
Compression	8.8 to 1
Carburation	Bosch K-Jetronic F.I.
Lubrication	Wet sump
Horsepower	255bhp @ 6600rpm*
Chassis/Drivetrain	Engine/transaxle in rear
Frame	Tubular - maintubes oval
Transmission	5-speed transaxle
Brakes	Hydraulic discs
Wheels	14" cast alloy bolt-on
Front suspension	Independent, A-arms, coil springs, telescopic shocks
Rear suspension	Independent, A-arms, coil springs, telescopic shocks
Curb weight	3100 lbs
Wheelbase	2340 mm
Track front	1460 mm
Track rear	1460 mm

*U.S.A. 240bhp @ 6600 rpm

308GTB Qv

Type	308
Model	GTB Qv
Years made	1982 - 1985
Chassis range	N/A
Number produced	748
Coachbuiders	Scaglietti
Body styles	Coupé
Body material	Steel
Seating capacity	2
Engine type	V8 90°
Displacement	2926cc
Bore and stroke	81mm x 71mm
Cyl. head	DOHC, 4-valve, single outside plug
Ignition	Digiplex
Compression	8.8 to 1
Carburation	Bosch K-Jetronic F.I.
Lubrication	Wet sump
Horsepower	240bhp @ 7000rpm*
Chassis/Drivetrain	Engine/transaxle in rear
Frame	Tubular- maintubes oval
Transmission	5-speed transaxle
Brakes	Hydraulic discs
Wheels	14" cast alloy bolt-on
Front suspension	Independent, A-arms, coil springs, telescopic shocks
Rear suspension	Independent, A-arm, coil springs, telescopic shocks
Curb weight	3100 lbs
Wheelbase	2340 mm
Track front	1460 mm
Track rear	1460 mm

*U.S.A. 230bhp @ 6800 rpm

328GTB

Type	328
Model	GTB
Years made	1986 -
Chassis range	N/A
Number produced	373 (1986)
Coachbuiders	Scaglietti
Body styles	Coupé
Body material	Steel
Seating capacity	2
Engine type	V8 90°
Displacement	3185cc
Bore and stroke	83mm x 63.6mm
Cyl. head	DOHC, 4-valve, single outside plug
Ignition	Microplex
Compression	9.8 to 1
Carburation	Bosch K-Jetronic F.I.
Lubrication	Wet sump
Horsepower	270bhp @ 7000 rpm*
Chassis/Drivetrain	Engine/transaxle in rear
Frame	Tubular steel- maintubes oval
Transmission	5-speed transaxle
Brakes	Hydraulic discs
Wheels	16" cast alloy
Front suspension	Independent, A-arms, coil springs, telescopic shocks
Rear suspension	Independent, A-arms, coil springs, telescopic shocks
Curb weight	3140 lbs
Wheelbase	2350 mm
Track front	1473 mm
Track rear	1468 mm

*U.S.A. version 260bhp

CHAPTER EIGHTEEN

SPECIFICATIONS

	308GTS
Type	308
Model	GTS
Years made	1977-1980
Chassis range	22619-31001
Number produced	3219
Coachbuiders	Scaglietti
Body styles	Coupé
Body material	Steel
Seating capacity	2
Engine type	V8 90°
Displacement	2926cc
Bore and stroke	81mm x 71mm
Cyl. head	DOHC single outside plug
Ignition	Digiplex
Compression	8.8 to1
Carburation	4 x 40DCNF
Lubrication	Dry or wet sump
Horsepower	255bhp @ 7700rpm*
Chassis/Drivetrain	Engine/transaxle in rear
Frame	Tubular steel- maintubes oval
Transmission	5-speed transaxle
Brakes	Hydraulic discs
Wheels	14" cast alloy bolt-on
Front suspension	Independent, A-arms, coil springs, telescopic shocks
Rear suspension	Independent, A-arms, coil springs, telescopic shocks
Curb weight	3100 lbs
Wheelbase	2340 mm
Track front	1460 mm
Track rear	1460 mm

*U.S.A. version 240bhp @ 6600rpm

	308GTSi
Type	308
Model	GTSi
Years made	1980-1982
Chassis range	31327 -
Number produced	1743
Coachbuiders	Scaglietti
Body styles	Coupé †
Body material	Steel
Seating capacity	2
Engine type	V8 90°
Displacement	2926cc
Bore and stroke	81mm x 71mm
Cyl. head	DOHC single outside plug
Ignition	Digiplex
Compression	8.8 to1
Carburation	Bosch K-Jetronic F.I.
Lubrication	Wet sump
Horsepower	255bhp @ 6600rpm*
Chassis/Drivetrain	Engine/transaxle in rear
Frame	Tubular steel - maintubes oval
Transmission	5-speed transaxle
Brakes	Hydraulic discs
Wheels	14" cast alloy bolt-on
Front suspension	Independent, A-arms, coil springs, telescopic shocks
Rear suspension	Independent, A-arms, coil springs, telescopic shocks
Curb weight	3100 lbs
Wheelbase	2340 mm
Track front	1460 mm
Track rear	1460 mm

†with removable top
*U.S.A. version 240bhp @ 6600rpm

THE V8 EMERGES

308GTS Qv

Type	308
Model	GTS Qv
Years made	1982-1985
Chassis range	N/A
Number produced	3042
Coachbuiders	Scaglietti
Body styles	Coupé †
Body material	Steel
Seating capacity	2
Engine type	V8 90°
Displacement	2926cc
Bore and stroke	81mm x 71mm
Cyl. head	DOHC single outside plug
Ignition	Digiplex
Compression	8.8 to1
Carburation	Bosch K-Jetronic F.I.
Lubrication	Wet sump
Horsepower	255bhp @ 6600rpm*
Chassis/Drivetrain	Engine/transaxle in rear
Frame	Tubular steel - maintubes oval
Transmission	5-speed transaxle
Brakes	Hydraulic discs
Wheels	14" cast alloy bolt-on
Front suspension	Independent, A-arms, coil springs, telescopic shocks
Rear suspension	Independent, A-arms, coil springs, telescopic shocks
Curb weight	3100 lbs
Wheelbase	2340 mm
Track front	1460 mm
Track rear	1460 mm

†with removable top
*U.S.A. version 230bhp @ 6800rpm

328GTS

Type	328
Model	GTS
Years made	1986 -
Chassis range	N/A
Number produced	1467 (1986)
Coachbuiders	Scaglietti
Body styles	Coupé †
Body material	Steel
Seating capacity	2
Engine type	V8 90°
Displacement	3185cc
Bore and stroke	83mm x 73.6mm
Cyl. head	DOHC, 4-valve, single outside plug
Ignition	Microplex
Compression	9.8 to1
Carburation	Bosch K-Jetronic F.I.
Lubrication	Wet sump
Horsepower	270bhp @ 7000rpm*
Chassis/Drivetrain	Engine/transaxle in rear
Frame	Tubular - maintubes oval
Transmission	5-speed transaxle
Brakes	Hydraulic discs
Wheels	16" cast alloy
Front suspension	Independent, A-arms, coil springs, telescopic shocks
Rear suspension	Independent, A-arms, coil springs, telescopic shocks
Curb weight	3170 lbs
Wheelbase	2350 mm
Track front	1473 mm
Track rear	1468 mm

*U.S.A. version 260bhp
† with removable top

CHAPTER EIGHTEEN

SPECIFICATIONS

	Mondial 8
Type	Mondial
Model	8
Years made	1980-1982
Chassis range	33001+ - 41000 +
Number produced	494
Coachbuiders	Scaglietti
Body styles	Coupé
Body material	Steel
Seating capacity	2 + 2
Engine type	V8 90°
Displacement	2926cc
Bore and stroke	81mm x 71mm
Cyl. head	DOHC single outside plug
Ignition	Digiplex
Compression	8.8 to1
Carburation	Bosch K-Jetronic F.I.
Lubrication	Wet sump
Horsepower	255bhp @ 6600rpm
Chassis/Drivetrain	Engine/transaxle in rear
Frame	Tubular - maintubes oval
Transmission	5-speed transaxle
Brakes	Hydraulic discs
Wheels	14" cast alloy bolt-on
Front suspension	Independent, A-arms, coil springs, telescopic shocks
Rear suspension	Independent, A-arms, coil springs, telescopic shocks
Curb weight	3550 lbs
Wheelbase	2650 mm
Track front	1495 mm
Track rear	1517 mm

	Mondial Qv
Type	Mondial
Model	Qv
Years made	1982 -1985
Chassis range	41001+ - 58000+
Number produced	1145
Coachbuiders	Scaglietti
Body styles	Coupé
Body material	Steel
Seating capacity	2 + 2
Engine type	V8 90°
Displacement	2926cc
Bore and stroke	81mm x 71mm
Cyl. head	DOHC, 4-valve, single outside plug
Ignition	Digiplex
Compression	8.8 to1
Carburation	Bosch K-Jetronic F.I.
Lubrication	Wet sump
Horsepower	240bhp @ 7000rpm
Chassis/Drivetrain	Engine/transaxle in rear
Frame	Tubular steel- maintubes oval
Transmission	5-speed transaxle
Brakes	Hydraulic discs
Wheels	14" cast alloy bolt-on
Front suspension	Independent, A-arms, coil springs, telescopic shocks
Rear suspension	Independent, A-arms, coil springs, telescopic shocks
Curb weight	3550 lbs
Wheelbase	2650 mm
Track front	1495 mm
Track rear	1517 mm

Mondial Qv Cabriolet

Type	Mondial
Model	Qv Cabriolet
Years made	1983 - 1985
Chassis range	50001+ - 59001
Number produced	629
Coachbuiders	Scaglietti
Body styles	Convertible
Body material	Steel
Seating capacity	2 + 2
Engine type	V8 90°
Displacement	2926cc
Bore and stroke	81mm x 71mm
Cyl. head	DOHC, 4-valve, single outside plug
Ignition	Digiplex
Compression	8.8 to1
Carburation	Bosch K-Jetronic F.I.
Lubrication	Wet sump
Horsepower	240bhp @ 7000rpm
Chassis/Drivetrain	Engine/transaxle in rear
Frame	Tubular steel- maintubes oval
Transmission	5-speed transaxle
Brakes	Hydraulic discs
Wheels	14" cast alloy bolt-on
Front suspension	Independent, A-arms, coil springs, telescopic shocks
Rear suspension	Independent, A-arms, coil springs, telescopic shocks
Curb weight	3550 lbs
Wheelbase	2650 mm
Track front	1495 mm
Track rear	1517 mm

Mondial 3.2

Type	Mondial
Model	3.2
Years made	1986 -
Chassis range	61000 -
Number produced	303 (1986)
Coachbuiders	Scaglietti
Body styles	Coupé
Body material	Steel
Seating capacity	2 + 2
Engine type	V8 90°
Displacement	3185cc
Bore and stroke	83mm x 73.6mm
Cyl. head	DOHC, 4-valve, single outside plug
Ignition	Microplex
Compression	9.8 to1
Carburation	Bosch K-Jetronic F.I.
Lubrication	Wet sump
Horsepower	270bhp @ 7000rpm
Chassis/Drivetrain	Engine/transaxle in rear
Frame	Tubular steel- maintubes oval
Transmission	5-speed transaxle
Brakes	Hydraulic discs
Wheels	16" cast alloy
Front suspension	Independent, A-arms, coil springs, telescopic shocks
Rear suspension	Independent, A-arms, coil springs, telescopic shocks
Curb weight	3500 lbs
Wheelbase	2350 mm
Track front	1473 mm
Track rear	1473 mm

CHAPTER EIGHTEEN

SPECIFICATIONS

	Mondial 3.2 Cabriolet
Type	Mondial
Model	3.2 Cabriolet
Years made	1986 -
Chassis range	61000 -
Number produced	251
Coachbuiders	Scaglietti
Body styles	Convertible
Body material	Steel
Seating capacity	2 + 2
Engine type	V8 90°
Displacement	3185cc
Bore and stroke	83mm x 73. 6mm
Cyl. head	DOHC, 4-valve, single outside plug
Ignition	Microplex
Compression	9.8 to1
Carburation	Bosch K-Jetronic F.I.
Lubrication	Wet sump
Horsepower	270bhp @ 7000rpm
Chassis/Drivetrain	Engine/transaxle in rear
Frame	Tubular steel - maintubes oval
Transmission	5-speed transaxle
Brakes	Hydraulic discs
Wheels	16" cast alloy
Front suspension	Independent, A-arms, coil springs, telescopic shocks
Rear suspension	Independent, A-arms, coil springs, telescopic shocks
Curb weight	3500 lbs
Wheelbase	2350 mm
Track front	1473 mm
Track rear	1473 mm

	208GT4
Type	208
Model	GT4 2+2
Years made	1975 - 1980
Chassis range	08830 - *
Number produced	840
Coachbuiders	Scaglietti
Body styles	Coupé
Body material	Steel
Seating capacity	2 + 2
Engine type	V8 90°
Displacement	1991cc
Bore and stroke	66.8mm x 71mm
Cyl. head	DOHC, single outside plug
Ignition	1 distributor
Compression	9.0 to1
Carburation	4 x 34DCNF
Lubrication	Wet sump
Horsepower	170bhp @ 7700rpm
Chassis/Drivetrain	Engine/transaxle in rear
Frame	Tubular steel - maintubes oval
Transmission	5-speed transaxle
Brakes	Hydraulic discs
Wheels	14" cast alloy bolt-on
Front suspension	Independent, A-arms, coil springs, telescopic shocks
Rear suspension	Independent, A-arms, coil springs, telescopic shocks
Curb weight	2950 lbs
Wheelbase	2550 mm
Track front	1460 mm
Track rear	1460 mm

* even numbers
Note. No U.S. version available

THE V8 EMERGES

208GTB

Type	208
Model	GTB
Years made	1980 -1982
Chassis range	31219 -
Number produced	1743
Coachbuiders	Scaglietti
Body styles	Coupé
Body material	Steel
Seating capacity	2
Engine type	V8 90°
Displacement	1991cc
Bore and stroke	66.8mm x 71mm
Cyl. head	DOHC, single outside plug
Ignition	1 distributor
Compression	9.0 to1
Carburation	4 x 34DCNF
Lubrication	Wet sump
Horsepower	155bhp @ 6800rpm
Chassis/Drivetrain	Engine/transaxle in rear
Frame	Tubular steel - maintubes oval
Transmission	5-speed transaxle
Brakes	Hydraulic discs
Wheels	14" cast alloy bolt-on
Front suspension	Independent, A-arms, coil springs, telescopic shocks
Rear suspension	Independent, A-arms, coil springs, telescopic shocks
Curb weight	3100 lbs
Wheelbase	2340 mm
Track front	1460 mm
Track rear	1460 mm

Note. No U.S. version available

208GTS

Type	208
Model	GTS
Years made	1980 - 1982
Chassis range	31249
Number produced	703
Coachbuiders	Scaglietti
Body styles	Coupé *
Body material	Steel
Seating capacity	2
Engine type	V8 90°
Displacement	1991cc
Bore and stroke	66.8mm x 71mm
Cyl. head	DOHC, single outside plug
Ignition	1 distributor
Compression	9.0 to1
Carburation	4 x34DCNF
Lubrication	Wet sump
Horsepower	155bhp @ 6800rpm
Chassis/Drivetrain	Engine/transaxle in rear
Frame	Tubular steel - maintubes oval
Transmission	5-speed transaxle
Brakes	Hydraulic discs
Wheels	14" cast alloy bolt-on
Front suspension	Independent, A-arms, coil springs, telescopic shocks
Rear suspension	Independent, A-arms, coil springs, telescopic shocks
Curb weight	3100 lbs
Wheelbase	2340 mm
Track front	1460 mm
Track rear	1460 mm

* with removable top

Note. No U.S. version available

CHAPTER EIGHTEEN

SPECIFICATIONS

208 Turbo (GTB)

Type	208
Model	Turbo (GTB)
Years made	1981 - 1985
Chassis range	
Number produced	437
Coachbuiders	Scaglietti
Body styles	Coupé
Body material	Steel
Seating capacity	2
Engine type	V8 90°
Displacement	1991 CC
Bore and stroke	66.8 mm x 71 mm
Cyl. head	DOHC, single outside plug
Ignition	Digiplex
Compression	7.0 to 1
Carburation	T/C* Bosch K-Jetronic F.I.
Lubrication	Wet sump
Horsepower	220bhp @ 7800rpm
Chassis/Drivetrain	Engine and transaxle in rear
Frame	Tubular steel - maintubes oval
Transmission	5-speed transaxle
Brakes	Hydraulic discs
Wheels	14" cast alloy bolt-on
Front suspension	Independent, A-arms, coil springs, telescopic shocks
Rear suspension	Independent, A-arms, coil springs, telescopic shocks
Curb weight	3100lbs
Wheelbase	2340mm
Track front	1460mm
Track rear	1460mm

* Turbocharged
Note. No U.S. version available

208 Turbo (GTS)

Type	208
Model	Turbo (GTS)
Years made	1982 - 1984
Chassis range	
Number produced	250
Coachbuiders	Scaglietti
Body styles	Coupé †
Body material	Steel
Seating capacity	2
Engine type	V8 90°
Displacement	1991cc
Bore and stroke	66.8mm x 71mm
Cyl. head	DOHC, single outside plug
Ignition	Digiplex
Compression	7.0 to1
Carburation	T/C * Bosch K-Jetronic F.I.
Lubrication	Wet sump
Horsepower	220bhp @ 7800rpm
Chassis/Drivetrain	Engine/transaxle in rear
Frame	Tubular steel - maintubes oval
Transmission	5-speed transaxle
Brakes	Hydraulic discs
Wheels	14" cast alloy bolt-on
Front suspension	Independent, A-arms, coil springs, telescopic shocks
Rear suspension	Independent, A-arms, coil springs, telescopic shocks
Curb weight	3100 lbs
Wheelbase	2340 mm
Track front	1460 mm
Track rear	1460 mm

† with removable top
* Turbocharged
Note. No U.S. version available

THE V8 EMERGES

	GTB Turbo			**GTS Turbo**
Type	GTB		**Type**	GTS
Model	Turbo		**Model**	Turbo
Years made	1986 -		**Years made**	1986 -
Chassis range	N/A		**Chassis range**	N/A
Number produced	65 (1986)		**Number produced**	118 (1986)
Coachbuiders	Scaglietti		**Coachbuiders**	Scaglietti
Body styles	Coupé		**Body styles**	Coupé *
Body material	Steel		**Body material**	Steel
Seating capacity	2		**Seating capacity**	2
Engine type	V8 90°		**Engine type**	V8 90°
Displacement	1991cc		**Displacement**	1991cc
Bore and stroke	66.8mm x 71mm		**Bore and stroke**	66.8mm x 71mm
Cyl. head	DOHC, single outside plug		**Cyl. head**	DOHC, single outside plug
Ignition	Digiplex		**Ignition**	Digiplex
Compression	7.0 to1		**Compression**	7.0 to1
Carburation	T/C * Bosch K-Jetronic F.I.		**Carburation**	T/C * Bosch K-Jetronic F.I.
Lubrication	Wet sump		**Lubrication**	Wet sump
Horsepower	254bhp @ 6500rpm		**Horsepower**	254bhp @ 6500rpm
Chassis/Drivetrain	Engine/transaxle in rear		**Chassis/Drivetrain**	Engine/transaxle in rear
Frame	Tubular steel - maintubes oval		**Frame**	Tubular steel - maintubes oval
Transmission	5-speed transaxle		**Transmission**	5-speed transaxle
Brakes	Hydraulic discs		**Brakes**	Hydraulic discs
Wheels	14" cast alloy bolt-on		**Wheels**	14" cast alloy bolt-on
Front suspension	Independent, A-arms, coil springs, telescopic shocks		**Front suspension**	Independent, A-arms, coil springs, telescopic shocks
Rear suspension	Independent, A-arms, coil springs, telescopic shocks		**Rear suspension**	Independent, A-arms, coil springs, telescopic shocks
Curb weight	3100 lbs		**Curb weight**	3100 lbs
Wheelbase	2340 mm		**Wheelbase**	2340 mm
Track front	1460 mm		**Track front**	1460 mm
Track rear	1460 mm		**Track rear**	1460 mm

* Turbocharged
Note. No U.S. version available

* with removable top
Note. No U.S. version available

At the Turin Motor Show in 1968, Pininfarina presented a non-working prototype - a distillation of their best ideas for a rear-engined 12-cylinder (?) road car. This study pointed the way to the final design for the forthcoming 365GT4 BB. This design study was called the P6.

CHAPTER NINETEEN

THE FLAT-12 SPORTS CARS

365GT4 BB Boxer (1973-1976)
BB 512 (1976-1981)
BB 512i (1981-1984)
Testarossa (1985-   )

Ferrari are sensitive to criticism and to intimations of lack of prestige. The Maserati and Lamborghini factories in and near Modena had already put into production sophisticated rear-engined cars while Ferrari was still selling the Daytona as their premier sports car. Unquestionably the Maserati Bora and the Lamborghini Miuri were stealing sales from Ferrari. To achieve parity in the state of the art, Ferrari developed a new car from scratch. The engine was a 4.4 litre - of 12 cylinders in a flat configuration, 6 cylinders opposing 6 cylinders, as they had used in their Formula 1 cars. This is also known as a Boxer layout. For traditionally conservative Ferrari, it was an innovative step into the future and a dramatic replacement for the Daytona.

Driving the new car, the Boxer, was a special treat. Compared to the Daytona, it was light and responsive and a bit more forgiving. However, like the Daytona, surplus power was part of its performance envelope and could be intimidating if pushed to its outer limits.

The usual Ferrari development and improvement program took place and culminated in a new improved Boxer in 1976. The new model, called the 512 BB, used an enlarged version of the original Boxer engine, brought out to 4.9 litres, which enabled Ferrari to keep the horsepower about as before, but achieved a substantially higher torque rating. The oil capacity of the engine was increased by utilising a dry sump system with a separate oil storage tank.

The 365GT4 BB and the 512 BB had been brought into the U.S.A. as grey market cars only and independent specialist shops had been able to modify them to meet all of the U.S. requirements. However in 1980 the U.S. standard for emissions became much more difficult and the 1980 512 BB engine, still fitted with carburettors, was almost impossible to coax into meeting the standards.

By mid-1981 the 512 BB had been fitted with Bosch engineered K-Jetronic fuel injection units and renamed the 512 BBi. Again, horsepower was practically unchanged, but the power was available at lower engined speeds and again torque was increased. The cars were now much easier to convert for the U.S. and sales to that area increased, much to the annoyance of the U.S. Ferrari dealers who were not supposed to deal in these cars. Starting in 1983 Ferrari North America set up an official program which allowed and encouraged the American Ferrari dealers to sell the 512 BBi to their customers for delivery at the factory in Maranello. These cars were usually driven in Europe and then imported to the U.S. and legalised by companies specialising in the technology required. One of the best is Amerispec in Danbury, Connecticut, owned and managed by Dick Fritz, the former general manager of Luigi Chinetti Motors.

Obviously, Ferrari's long term goal is to create a family of cars than can all be sold throughout the world. To achieve this goal a new strategy was put into play in 1982. It was decided that all new models in future would be designed from scratch to meet all of the requirements throughout the world. In other words, all new cars would be designed first to meet the North American regulations (Canada and the U.S.A. have virtually identical laws relating to safety and emission standards) and then modified to meet the less difficult standards in the rest of the world. The first car to be approached this way was the unprece-

dented new Testarossa.

Late in September 1984 the Testarossa was unveiled in Modena on the site of the original Scuderia Ferrari facility in the heart of town. Every Ferrari dealer in North America was there to witness this unique event and they were not disappointed. While rumours had been legion, no one really knew all of the exciting details, such as the fact that water-cooling was moved from the front to either side of the car behind the doors. This allowed for better weight distribution and increased luggage capacity in the front. The following day the dealers (your author was on this historic trip, representing the Ferrari dealer in Connecticut) were treated to a ride in the new Testarossa at the Imola race track with a factory test driver behind the wheel. This only confirmed that the car performed as well as it looked.

By mid-1985 the first new Testarossas began to arrive in the U.S.A. and it was with heightened anticipation that I drove the first one to arrive at our dealership. Even a short test drive was enough to confirm that this was a far more sophisticated car than the previous Boxers. It was also a much more forgiving car, despite its abundance of surplus horsepower. It also felt smaller and more nimble, more like a the best 308 - with 100 horsepower added!

The Testarossa was destined to uphold Ferrari prestige throughout the 1980s. It's mixture of exceptional performance coupled with styling which owed much to the up-market customising of Willi Koenig, proving the ultimate status symbol. Still, as the 1990s drew on, a mood of refinement

Above Two views of the 365GT4 BB. This Swiss example used a dealer-installed outside rearview mirror.

was in the air and with increasing anti-pollution and crash legislation, the time had arrived for a major rejuvenation. In 1991 Ferrari unveiled the 512 TR, modestly proclaiming it "The Ultimate Ferrari".

The 5 litre boxer engine had been refined throughout, with additional rigidity and overall strength from revised block castings, allowing a power uplift to 428bhp gained from a completely redesigned cylinder head configuration allied to the Bosch Motronic M2.7 engine management system. The object of this reworking was to cut emission levels to meet any standards, existing or expected. In this it succeeded magnificently, although peak power arrived higher up the rev band at 6750rpm, while the redesign raised the red line to 7700rpm

and allowed sustained cruising at 7250rpm – quite a package!

A 12.5 per cent increase in torsional rigidity plus a revised suspension lay-out, incorporating double gas filled shocks at the rear, allowed even more precise handling, while attention to such details as the transfer gears improved the feel of the transaxle.

The styling underwent detail improvements. The flamboyant side strakes were moderated, a new engine cover, new front bumper with integral spoiler, new rear underbumper panel, black-light type rear lights and a third brake lamp faired into the roof on US spec models. Matching this was an improved interior with a redesigned instrument panel and centre console. New inner door panels matched the theme of the redesigned seats, which sat 13cm lower, and an improved air conditioning unit was incorporated.

Two similar views of the first 512BB point out a few differences including the NACA ducts on the sides and four rear lights instead of six. This car also features a two-tone paint scheme with flat black at the bottom. This became famous as the Boxer paint scheme, even when used on other models, such as the 308GT4 2+2, 308GTB and 308GTS.

Interestingly while rivals struggled to meet the same legislation without increasing weight, Ferrari managed to shed over 100 pounds in their repackage, quite an achievement.

CHAPTER NINETEEN

The interior of the 512BB offered leather seats upholstered in a pattern reminiscent of those used in the Daytona. Contrasting colours were possible for the inserts and the piping. The engine room view was awesome - in this case featuring four 3-throat Weber carburettors.

THE FLAT 12 SPORTS CARS

The 512BBi boasted special outside rearview mirrors on both sides of the car, designed by Pininfarina to blend with the car. The interior was not really changed from earlier versions. The fuel-injected engine featured belt-driven camshafts like the earlier Boxers and all the 308 engines.

CHAPTER NINETEEN

The rather exuberant design of the Testarossa satisfied those who thought that Ferrari should compete with the ostentatious Lamborghini Countach.

CHAPTER NINETEEN

The completely new Testarossa flat-12 engine looked very much like the 512BBi, but in fact has virtually no parts in common. This view of the Testarossa shows its rear design to the best advantage.

The newest 1987 Testarossa speaks for itself. The U.S.-mandated side lights are as unobtrusive as possible. Pininfarina-designed outside rearview mirrors, developed in their wind tunnel, are now standard on both sides of this unusual automobile.

CHAPTER NINETEEN

SPECIFICATIONS

365GT4BB Boxer

Type	365
Model	GT4 BB
Years made	1973 - 1976
Chassis range	17185 - 19323
Number produced	387
Coachbuiders	Scaglietti
Body styles	Coupé
Body material	Aluminium
Seating capacity	2
Engine type	Flat12
Displacement	4391cc
Bore and stroke	81mm x 71mm
Cyl. head	DOHC, single outside plug
Ignition	2 distributors
Compression	8.8 to 1
Carburation	4 x 40IF3C
Lubrication	Wet sump
Horsepower	344bhp @ 7,000rpm
Chassis/Drivetrain	Engine/transaxle in rear
Frame	Tubular steel– maintubes oval
Transmission	5-speed transaxle
Axle ratio	
Brakes	Hydraulic discs
Wheels	15" alloy knock-ons
Front suspension	Independent, A-arms, coil springs, telescopic shocks
Rear suspension	Independent, A-arms, coil springs, telescopic shocks
Curb weight	3200 lbs
Wheelbase	2500 mm
Track front	1500 mm
Track rear	1510 mm

Note. No U.S. version available

512BB

Type	512
Model	BB
Years made	1976 - 1981
Chassis range	19711 - 38001 (?)
Number produced	929
Coachbuiders	Scaglietti
Body styles	Coupé
Body material	Aluminium
Seating capacity	2
Engine type	Flat12
Displacement	4942cc
Bore and stroke	82mm x 78mm
Cyl. head	DOHC, single outside plug
Ignition	2 distributors
Compression	9.2 to1
Carburation	4 x 40IF3C
Lubrication	Dry sump
Horsepower	340bhp @ 6800rpm
Chassis/Drivetrain	Engine/transaxle in rear
Frame	Tubular steel– maintubes oval
Transmission	5-speed transaxle
Axle ratio	
Brakes	Hydraulic discs
Wheels	15" alloy knock-ons
Front suspension	Independent, A-arms, coil springs, telescopic shocks
Rear suspension	Independent, A-arms, coil springs, telescopic shocks
Curb weight	3800 lbs
Wheelbase	2500 mm
Track front	1500 mm
Track rear	1563 mm

Note. No U.S. version available

THE FLAT-12 SPORTS CARS

512BBi

Type	512
Model	BBi
Years made	1981 - 1984
Chassis range	38001(?) - 52935
Number produced	1007
Coachbuiders	Scaglietti
Body styles	Coupé
Body material	Aluminium with steel
Seating capacity	2
Engine type	Flat12
Displacement	4942cc
Bore and stroke	82mm x 78mm
Cyl. head	DOHC, single outside plug
Ignition	Digiplex
Compression	9.2 to 1
Carburation	Bosch K-Jetronic F.I.
Lubrication	Dry sump
Horsepower	340bhp @ 6,000rpm
Chassis/Drivetrain	Engine/transaxle in rear
Frame	Tubular maintubes oval
Transmission	5-speed transaxle
Axle ratio	
Brakes	Hydraulic discs
Wheels	15" alloy knock-ons
Front suspension	Independent, A-arms
Rear suspension	Independent, A-arms
Curb weight	3800 lbs
Wheelbase	2500 mm
Track front	1500 mm
Track rear	1563 mm

Note. No U.S. version available

Testarossa

Type / **Model**	Testarossa
Years made	1985 -
Chassis range	56,000 (?) -
Number produced	1985, 568 &1986, 819
Coachbuiders	Pininfarina
Body styles	Coupé
Body material	Aluminium with steel
Seating capacity	2
Engine type	Flat12
Displacement	4942cc
Bore and stroke	82mm x 78mm
Cyl. head	DOHC, 4 valves, single outside plug
Ignition	Digiplex
Compression	9.2 to 1
Carburation	Bosche K-Jetronic F.I.
Lubrication	Wet sump
Horsepower	390bhp* @ 6300rpm
Chassis/Drivetrain	Engine/transaxle in rear
Frame	Tubular maintubes oval
Transmission	5-speed transaxle
Axle ratio	
Brakes	Hydraulic discs
Wheels	16" alloy knock-ons
Front suspension	Independent, A-arms
Rear suspension	Independent, A-arms
Curb weight	3660 lbs
Wheelbase	2550 mm
Track front	1518 mm
Track rear	1660 mm

*The U. S. version develops 380bhp

The limited production 1985 288GTO road car became an overnight collectors' item.

The newest limited production 'road' car from Ferrari is the F40 to celebrate Ferrari's 40 years in production (1947-1987). This one will outperform the 288GTO and full racing versions will be available to establish racing teams. †

CHAPTER TWENTY

Prototypes And Special Road Models

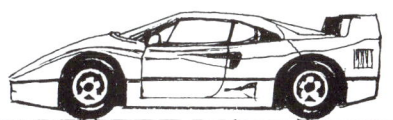

Prototypes
288GTO (1984-1986)
F40 (1987 -   )

During the 1950s and even into the early 1960s Pinin Farina (and later Pininfarina) had produced dozens of special cars, which ranged from simple modifications of existing basic designs to complete, unique one-of-a-kind prototypes. All of these were running, fully-functional cars and were sold to customers for their use on the public roads.

The prices charged for these cars were not out of line with those paid for the standard models and in some cases they were no more. The very special one-off cars were somtimes as much as 100% more than standard, but that was unusual. It was also possible to build models of which only 12 were made in one year, and where each one was slightly different inside and out. These cars were from 60% to 70% more expensive than the most popular model built at the same time.

All of this special work was made possible by the economics of the times. A very strong U.S. dollar, together with a low standard of pay for workers in Italy, made it feasible. Slowly but surely, the economy of Italy grew stronger, the standard of living in Italy became higher and higher, (at least in the industrial

Left & Below This special version of the rear-engined 250LM was designed and built by Pininfarina in 1965, possibly to indicate to Ferrari what could be done with a road version produced in larger quantities but based on the racing 250LM. Indeed, this particular car (C/N 6025) was never raced in earnest.

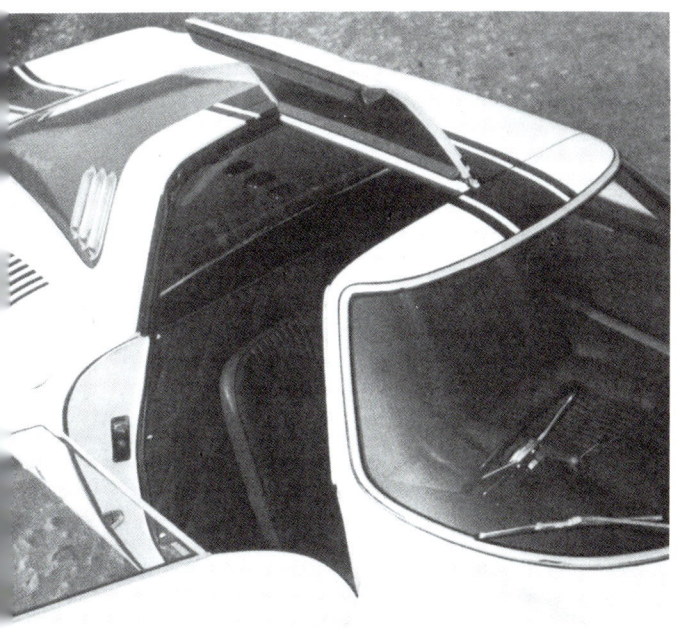

CHAPTER TWENTY

north, which included Modena and Maranello) and the hand-built custom, or even customized, automobile disappeared.

In their place we began to see special design studies, idea cars, non-working prototypes, and in small numbers. It is important for Ferrari and their designers, in most cases Pininfarina, to see their best ideas in full scale with painted surfaces. Even a full scale model in clay does not give the same impression as the identical design in polished paint.

Shown at the Paris Salon in October 1966, this is another Pininfarina effort to show Ferrari what could be done with a rear-engined production car. This one was based on the 365P race car and dared to put the driver in the middle of a 3-seat automobile.

PROTOTYPES AND SPECIAL ROAD MODELS

While some of these prototypes did not seem to relate to any later productions cars, they did point a way and provided directed inspiration to those actually designing the cars. Others are obviously connected directly to a specific model that went into production a year or two later.

The Ferrari factory also builds engineering prototypes to try out new ideas, new engines, and other mechanical components, and new configurations. In some cases the concept is pursued to the point where the prototype running chassis is given to the designer to impart a definitive shape. The result will be a working, running prototype in a form that is final enough to put into production.

In the case of the limited-production 288GTO the limited-production sports car. The technology included the use of turbochargers and of new materials, such as Kevlar.

With little specific information available, over 200 were sold in advance of the first production model being available! While no U.S. legal version was offered, the North American dealers were allowed to take orders for delivery at the factory. Although the suggested list price at the factory was about $76,000 the cars were actually sold sight unseen for an average price of around $95,000. It was quite a price to pay for a pig in a poke. Many of the original buyers were Ferrari enthusiasts, but they were also prepared to sell their unknown car if they did not care for it and it seemed likely that they would at least be able to get

This is another central-seating special similar to the previous one shown. This example was built later for the head of FIAT, Giovanni Agnelli (C/N 8815).

impetus seemed to come from the prestige gained by Porsche in dominating the sports car racing scene in cars that looked a great deal like those that can be bought at your nearest friendly Porsche dealer. The time seemed right for Ferrari to build a 2-seater that would be faster than any other road car in the world. The answer was to use the latest technology gleaned from Ferrari's Formula 1 experience and apply it to a

their money back.

I first drove the new 288GTO in Italy, in company with the new owner, who was fortunate enough to get one of the first ones. The first drive for both of us was a revelation and it was immediately obvious that the new Ferrari was something very special indeed. It was totally tractable and could be driven as slowly as a learner driver might try the second time out - and without distress to the car. Or - one can play Grand Prix driver touching 7,000 rpm in each gear and allowing the car to drift through the corners (provided you have the requisite talent). If you take your driving

CHAPTER TWENTY

Above This time, Pininfarina used the 206S racing chassis to indicate what might become a production 2-seater rear-engined car for the road (C/N 0032).

Right Called the P5, it was yet another design exercise by Pininfarina to point the way toward future Ferrari rear-engined production cars.

seriously, the 288GTO captures you. As a result, few are offered for re-sale and the market value at the end of 1987 was more than triple what was paid for it new.

While there were plans to build 20 for serious competitive racing, this never happened, as it was decided to pursue the design and production of an even more advanced car of the same general configuration. Production of the 288GTO ceased in early 1986. A total of 278 is believed to have been built, 41 in 1984, 230 in 1985 and 7 in 1986.

In July of 1987, Ferrari introduced the F40, the successor to the 288GTO, and was named to commemorate Ferrari's 40 years as a car manufacturer. It was first shown to the public at the Frankfurt Auto Show in September 1987. It was an immediate sensation. With second-hand GTO prices still climbing, the F40 was bound to create a stir, and it did. For the first time in a road car, Ferrari used high tech materials from the F1 programme. The bodyshell was a single moulding with trunk lid, hood, doors and side panels of composite materials, bonded to a

CHAPTER TWENTY

The dramatic Modulo of 1970 was Pininfarina's major effort to explore new ground for the future of rear-engined sports cars. Based on 512S racing chassis, it made the rounds of the auto-show circuit worldwide, and always attracted a tremendous amount of attention.

PROTOTYPES AND SPECIAL ROAD MODELS

265

CHAPTER TWENTY

At the 1974 Turin Motor Show Pininfarina presented this dream car, designed in their own wind tunnel. As the resistance coefficient was only 0.256 it was called the cr25. It utilised the 365GT4 BB engine, mounted in the front! Pininfarina was telling Ferrari that a car which was expected to hold four people, should have the engine in the front.

tubular frame by structural adhesives. The result was a light but immensely rigid structure, devoid of ornamentation and styled with an almost brutal elegance by Pininfarina.

Suspension was of transverse quadrilateral layout, comprising tubular carriers with coils over Koni hydraulic shock absorbers. This gave the capability of height variation at speed, while maintaining an essentially straightforward and well proven system. The 4-cam V8 was mid-mounted longitudinally, with two IHI turbochargers allowing a healthy 478bhp at 7000rpm, the red-line coming at 7700rpm.

Inside the theme of "a racer for the road" was carried over with a fervour approaching the masochistic. The seats were body-contoured, non-adjustable, and a fire-retardant, felt-like material was used as a lightweight dashboard covering. Little was done to deaden sound, the result being an experience few drivers unacquainted with endurance racing cars will ever experience.

The cars were introduced to the press by factory test drivers Claudio Ori and Giuseppi Carnia at Ferrari's test track at Fiorano. Those lucky enough to be chauffeured around the track emerged awe stricken. Even the most cynical motoring hacks were smitten by this new offering. While Porsche had dipped into the realms of electronic wizardry for their 959, the F40 was the logical progression from the GTO, itself a superb machine. Traditional engineering values were refined to the point of artform.

"Everything which can be improved has been." Proclaimed engineering chief Nicola Metarazzi, leaving the temporarily deafened international press contingent to search their thesauruses for new superlatives to describe it. The only extra was air-conditioning (almost vital given the glass area), though the factory proposed a choice of road-going synchromesh gearbox or non-synchro racing box. The latter was planned for a limited production run of pure track racers which never materialised.

PROTOTYPES AND SPECIAL ROAD MODELS

CHAPTER TWENTY

The reason for the profound impact of the F40 was not just bound up with its mechanical perfection. Quite apart from mind numbing acceleration plus exceptional handling and road-holding, the car emerged at the height of Ferrari madness as the greed driven boom years of the late 1980s drew to a close. With most Ferrari customers facing over a year from order to delivery, any 328 driver could expect to be approached at any time by dealers looking for a fast profit in the hyper-inflated used market.

Soon after the first cars began trickling to those Ferrari deemed worthy of them, advertisements started appearing offering massive profits to those owners, or even potential owners, who would relinquish their cars or even the sales contracts. Possibly the most publicised example arrived in August 1989 with the news that businessman David McKee was taking legal action against Ferrari F1 driver Nigel Mansell who, it was reported, had refused to honour an agreement to sell his personal F40 for £680,000 ($1 million). Quite a step-up from the UK list price of £170,000 ($250,000).

Faced with this type of demand, and unwilling to continue lining the pockets of the grey-market dealers, Ferrari responded pragmatically by quietly threatening to prolong the production of the F40 well beyond the 400 originally planned. The last few trickled to their owners in 1992.

This time Pininfarina built a 4-door Ferrari prototype called the Pinin. Again, Pininfarina presented a proposed new car that would hold four in comfort and again the engine is in the front.

Ferrari F40

CHAPTER TWENTY

Factory photos of the F40 clearly indicate the dynamic nature of the Pininfarina design.

PROTOTYPES AND SPECIAL ROAD MODELS

SPECIFICATIONS

288GTO

Type	288
Model	GTO
Years made	1984 - 1986
Chassis range	50253 - 58001 (?)
Number produced	278
Coachbuiders	Scaglietti
Body styles	Coupé
Body material	Kevlar, fibreglass, aluminium
Seating capacity	2
Engine type	V8 90°
Displacement	2855cc
Bore and stroke	80mm x 71mm
Cyl. head	DOHC, 4-valves, single outside plug·
Ignition	Weber Marelli
Compression	7.6 to 1
Carburation	Twin turbos + intercoolers
Lubrication	Dry sump
Horsepower	400bhp @ 7,000rpm
Chassis/Drivetrain	Engine and transaxle in rear*
Frame	Tubular steel– maintubes oval
Transmission	5-speed transaxle
Axle ratio	
Brakes	Hydraulic discs
Wheels	16"alloy
Front suspension	Independent, A-arms, coil springs, telescopic shocks
Rear suspension	Independent, A-arms, coil springs, telescopic shocks
Curb weight	2850 lbs
Wheelbase	2450 mm
Track front	1589 mm
Track rear	1563 mm

* Engine in longitudinal position

F40

Type Model	} F40
Years made	1988 -
Chassis range	70167
Number produced	950 est.
Coachbuiders	Scaglietti
Body styles	Coupé
Body material	Kevlar and fibreglass
Seating capacity	2
Engine type	V8 90°
Displacement	2936cc
Bore and stroke	82mm x 69.5mm
Cyl. head	DOHC, 4-valves, single outside plug
Ignition	Weber Marelli
Compression	7.8 to 1
Carburation	Twin turbos + intercoolers
Lubrication	Dry sump
Horsepower	478bhp @ 7,000rpm
Chassis/Drivetrain	Engine and gearbox in rear *
Frame	Tubular steel, Kevlar, carbon fibre and adhesive
Transmission	5-speed transaxle
Axle ratio	
Brakes	Hydraulic discs
Wheels	17" alloy forged
Front suspension	Independent, A-arms, coil springs, telescopic shocks
Rear suspension	Independent, A-arms, coil springs, telescopic shocks
Curb weight	2425 lbs
Wheelbase	2450 mm
Track front	1594 mm
Track rear	1610 mm

*Engine in longitudinal position

CHAPTER TWENTY-ONE

THE NEXT FIVE YEARS: 1988 - 1993

The 1986 pattern of success in sales of the Mondial continued, with orders growing over the next three years. But by 1989, there was a need for a more sophisticated package. It was met with the launch of the Mondial t.

Outwardly, little had changed, but under the skin, Ferrari had added a technological package capable of taking the Mondial into the next century. The gearbox came from 1970s Grand Prix practice, being transversely mounted to allow better weight distribution (hence the "t" suffix), though it was also aimed at smoothing out some of the "notchiness" of the original box. Also new was electronic damping control, while other touches which took the car out of the traditional mould were: power steering and, for 1993, a Valeo clutchless gearbox option. This transmission option was a highly sophisticated device, essentially similar to the much-maligned Porsche Sportomatic insofar as it allows full driver control through a gate-change shift, electronic sensors monitoring the movement of the gearstick and harmonizing the change.

As Europe jumped on the catalyst bandwagon, the 348 engine replaced the 328 unit. The result was an exceptional motor car by any standard. However, although the Mondial carried the same level of tune as the 348t and ts models, its extra weight made it a little slower. Even so, its performance was still impressive, with a 0-60mph time of 6.3 seconds and a top speed of 160 miles per hour.

On the road, the Mondial was a revelation, but the gearshift still called for skilful movement into and out of second. The handling remained superb, complemented by an extra 30bhp, and it now took some effort to provoke the traditional oversteer, though once provoked, it was easily caught.

The technological refinement was not just confined to the car, though. Speaking to the British "Car" magazine, the then-President of Ferrari, Ing Giovanbattista Razelli (he later went to work his miracles at the Alfa Romeo plant in Arese), was at pains to stress the higher build quality which had resulted from an ongoing modernisation program at Modena. The idiosyncrasies of hand-build production were to be a thing of the past. Only those eccentricities the owners wanted, such as the raw edge of sound, the precision of the gearshift and a positive bias towards skilled performance driving were to be retained.

Razelli went on at that time to discount rumours that a new, downmarket Ferrari might emerge to challenge the Porsche 944, making the comment: "We have to stay exclusive". He went on to say that future Ferraris would be hand finished and implicitly sporting, but the age of Connolly leather, air conditioning and power options was definitely here to stay. His comments were a good curtain-raiser to the launch of the 348. As Autumn 1989 arrived, so the motoring press gradually shifted up a gear to give the new car a deservedly warm welcome. "The 348 will be lighter, faster and more economical than its predecessors" predicted one of their number. The market was not disappointed.

There is a close family resemblance between the 348 and the superseded 328. That, according to Ferrari,, was deliberate. Underneath Pininfarina's smooth skin, which carried over the side strakes from the twelve-cylinder cars, Maranello had worked its magic and produced a whole new car. The 348 engine was the same as that seen in the Mondial t. Giving a useful 295bhp via its Bosch

CHAPTER TWENTY-ONE

The Mondial Coupé inside and out.

M2.7 Motronic engine management system, it was built to beat even the most stringent anti-pollution laws. To allow for finer weight distribution and make room for two water radiators plus an oil cleaner, the engine was mounted longitudinally with the transverse gearbox behind it.

This arrangement allowed the engine to be lowered five inches in the chassis, so lowering the centre of gravity. The chassis itself marked a departure from previous Ferrari practice. Described by the factory as a "complex self-supporting frame", it was basically a semi-monocoque with the engine and transmission carried in separate demountable rear tubular frame. Introduced in two initial variants, the tb (trasversale berlinetta) and ts, which featured a targa top, the cabriolet was delayed until 1993. As the lynch-pin of the range, the car had to offer a very special driving environment, immediately at ease in busy traffic, but relaxing on long journeys. Increased leg and headroom were a major feature, while Connolly hide, air conditioning, electric windows, power door mirrors and central locking added to the sense of refinement.

The ride of the new 348 was refined, lacking the abruptness of earlier cars. While the unequal-length

The year 1989 saw the revised Mondial model, in both Coupé and Cabriolet versions. These two views of the Cabriolet show the clean and well-balanced line of the car.

wishbones at front and rear maintained a link with previous models, gas-filled dampers and revised spring rates allowed the same taut feeling, but with more compliance. Coupled with the improvement in weight distribution, the result was a fine, neutral handling car, which offered maximum torque at a useable 4,200rpm, which gave driver satisfaction in a way few rivals can match with a build quality that can rival any car maker in the world.

Now, in the summer of 1992, came the the ultimate Ferrari. If anyone, anywhere, had any lingering doubts about the passion inspired by Ferrari, those doubts would have been totally dispelled at an event called FF40. The setting was Belgium's massive and ornate Parc Cinquantenaire: the time was August 1992: the occasion was the celebration of forty years collaboration between Ferrari and Pininfarina and forty years since the founding of the first overseas Ferrari agency (Belgium's Ecurie Francorchamps). Here was unveiled the most important new car since the death of Enzo Ferrari in 1989.

Against a glorious backdrop of earlier cars, a massive concours d'elegance and multi-million dollar parade around the Spa Francorchamps Grand

CHAPTER TWENTY-ONE

When the 348 arrived, it caused quite a stir, with its more compact aggressive looks, compared with the earlier 328. New owners would not be disappointed with the performance, either. But one point of particular interest is that, as we look at this shot of the 348tb, we see the origins of the lines of the next V-12 Ferrari - the 456.

Prix Circuit. Ferrari supremo Luca Montezemolo was spending an estimated three million dollars to launch the 456, the latest link in the chain of Ferrari evolution, stretching forward from the 212 Inter, via the 250GT 2 + 2, the 365GT/4 to the 412.

One glance was enough to know that the Ferrari design and production team had produced a great classic. The Pininfarina styling was a smoothly modern variation on the theme of the 365 Daytona complete with retractable headlights and a new interpretation of the classic Gran Turismo profile. The one aspect of the car which probably caused more favourable comment than any other among the gathered legends from the Ferrari pantheon, was that it carried its V-12 engine in the best possible place - at the front.

The beauty of this car was more than skin deep, too. Having experimented with various compound materials in the 1980s, the company had reverted to an aluminum body shell over a traditional tubular frame. However, to avoid the problem of catalytic corrosion inherent in such construction, the designers opted to use strips of Feran, an inert alloy to which steel can be welded on one side and alloy on the other. Maranello's own honeycomb and compound structure was reserved for the non-stressed components such as engine cover and trunk lid. The tremendously strong body was so rigid that, despite being a four-seater, the 456 felt and handled like a true two-seat sports car.

The new 65° Vee-Twelve engine was of light alloy construction, weighing just under 520 pounds and producing 442bhp at 6,250rpm. Drive to the rear-mounted 6-speed transaxle, with limited slip differential, came from a flywheel mounted clutch and an enclosed cardan shaft. In common with other current Ferraris, the Bosch Motronic M2.7 engine management system was used to supply and control the exact fuel/air mixture required to deliver optimum performance within worldwide pollution limits - amazingly on unleaded fuel.

Suspension on this new Ferrari marvel was a switchable three-mode system, achieved by using parallel wishbones, telescopic dampers and anti-roll bars, all electronically controlled and complemented with self-levelling at the rear. ZF's Servotronic power steering system is a standard feature for this 6 foot 3 inch wide Grand Tourer's 255/45-17 front wheels.

In keeping with stated Ferrari policy, the interior is little short of sumptuous. "We have tried to create an interior where the materials employed – Connolly hide for the seats and the metals for the controls and technical parts – played a contrasting role with the aseptic frigidity of today's average cars" announced Sergio Pininfarina. The result is a temple of muted good taste, reinforced by such creature comforts as air conditioning, CD player, electric multi-adjustable seats and steering wheel, central door locking and every other desirable comfort. Yet one of the most impressive features was grown from aerodynamic necessity, for when the doors are opened or shut, the windows automatically retract from their seals. A small touch, but a fine indication of the consideration

THE NEXT FIVE YEARS - 1988 TO 1993

When, in August 1992, the world was introduced to the magnificent new V-12 Ferrari (so the V-12 had not, after all, disappeared from the Ferrari menu), those who saw it marvelled at its sheer magnificence. Few observed the styling connection between the 348 and this beautiful new front engined Gran Turismo 2 + 2.

shown for the man who can afford the best and wants to travel in comfort at up to 188 miles per hour, while offering the opportunity for three other to share in the experience.

May Ferraris be for ever.

CHAPTER TWENTY-ONE

These styling drawings show how the 456 began to take shape - and how relatively close the finished car was to the early styling exercises. It is said that Enzo Ferrari did not like the original designs for the car, but he surely would have been proud of the final result.

Who said an engine could not be a work of art? Ferrari's latest underbonnet sculpture in the form of the 456 V-12 engine.

CHAPTER TWENTY-ONE

These early publicity shots of the 456 show its beautiful lines from all angles and the interior shot shows it to be a true "Lusso" Ferrari.

THE NEXT FIVE YEARS - 1988 TO 1993

CHAPTER TWENTY-ONE

So the Ferrari V-12 is not dead after all.

THE NEXT FIVE YEARS - 1988 TO 1993

SPECIFICATIONS

	MONDIAL T		348 ts/tb
Type	Mondial t	Type	348 ts/tb
Model	GT4 2 + 2	Model	2-seater
Years made	1989 -	Years made	1989 -
Chassis range		Chassis range	
Number produced		Number produced	
Coachbuiders	Pininfarina	Coachbuiders	Pininfarina
Body styles	Coupé/Cabriolet	Body styles	Coupé/Targa/Cabriolet
Body material	Aluminium on Steel	Body material	Alloy/composites on Steel
Seating capacity	2 + 2	Seating capacity	2
Engine type	V-8 90°	Engine type	V-8 90°
Displacement	3405cc	Displacement	3405cc
Bore and stroke	85mm x 75mm	Bore and stroke	85mm x 75mm
Cyl. head	DOHC four-valve single-plug	Cyl. head	DOHC four-valve single-plug
Ignition	Bosch twin coil	Ignition	Bosch twin coil
Compression	10.4 : 1	Compression	10.4 : 1
Carburation	Bosch Motronic M2.7	Carburation	Bosch Motronic M2.7
Lubrication	Dry sump	Lubrication	Dry sump
Horsepower	295 @ 7200rpm	Horsepower	295 @ 7200rpm
Chassis/Drivetrain	Mid engine/rear transaxle	Chassis/Drivetrain	Mid engine/rear transaxle
Frame	Tubular steel	Frame	Tubular steel
Transmission	5-speed transaxle	Transmission	5-speed transaxle
Axle ratio		Axle ratio	
Brakes	Vented discs all round with ABS	Brakes	Vented discs all round with ABS
Wheels	16" alloy bolt-on	Wheels	17" alloy bolt-on
Front suspension	Transverse arm/coil springs/telescopic dampers	Front suspension	Transverse arms/coil springs/telescopic dampers
Rear suspension	Transverse arm/coil springs/telescopic dampers	Rear suspension	Transverse arms/coil springs/telescopic dampers
Curb weight	Cpé = 3144lbs, Cabrio = 3236lbs	Curb weight	Cpé = 3153lbs, Spd = 3175lbs
Wheelbase	2650mm	Wheelbase	2450mm
Track front	1522mm	Track front	1502mm
Track rear	1560mm	Track rear	1578mm

SPECIFICATIONS

512 TR

Type	512 TR
Model	2-seater
Years made	1991 -
Chassis range	
Number produced	
Coachbuiders	Pininfarina
Body styles	Coupé
Body material	Alloy/composites on Steel
Seating capacity	2
Engine type	Flat-12 "Boxer"
Displacement	4943cc
Bore and stroke	82mm x 78mm
Cyl. head	DOHC four-valve single-plug
Ignition	Digiplex
Compression	10.1 : 1
Carburation	Bosch Motronic M2.7
Lubrication	Dry sump
Horsepower	428 @ 6750rpm
Chassis/Drivetrain	Mid engine/rear transaxle
Frame	Tubular steel
Transmission	5-speed transaxle
Axle ratio	
Brakes	Vented discs all round with ABS
Wheels	18" alloy bolt-on
Front suspension	Independent, "A"-arms
Rear suspension	Independent, "A"-arms
Curb weight	3593lbs
Wheelbase	2550mm
Track front	1532mm
Track rear	1644mm

456GT

Type	456 GT
Model	GT4 2 + 2
Years made	1992 -
Chassis range	
Number produced	
Coachbuiders	Pininfarina
Body styles	Coupé
Body material	Aluminium on Steel
Seating capacity	2 + 2
Engine type	V-12 65°
Displacement	5473.9cc
Bore and stroke	88mm x 75mm
Cyl. head	DOHC single-plug
Ignition	Bosch twin coil
Compression	10.6 : 1
Carburation	Bosch Motronic M2.7
Lubrication	Dry sump, twin pump
Horsepower	442 @ 6250rpm
Chassis/Drivetrain	Front engine/rear transaxle
Frame	Tubular steel
Transmission	6-speed transaxle
Axle ratio	
Brakes	Vented discs all round with ABS
Wheels	17" alloy bolt-on
Front suspension	Coil & wishbone/ telescopic dampers
Rear suspension	Coil & wishbone/ telescopic dampers
Curb weight	3718lbs
Wheelbase	2600mm
Track front	1585mm
Track rear	1606mm

APPENDIX (THE NUMBERS)

WARNING: Neither the author nor the publisher wish to take any responsibility for the accuracy of the information contained herein. We invite you, the reader, to submit to us new information to enable us to make corrections in future editions.

INTRODUCTION

A complete listing of all Ferraris by chassis number and engine number is impossible. No Ferrari 'expert' will agree on any specific presentation. The simple fact is that new information is being gathered at all times and new cars never cease to be discovered. I humbly submit this first-ever published list in the hope that all of you, the readers, will assist in producing a second edition, that will be more complete.

Where anomalies exist in our list there is in some cases no explanation. I believe that in a few cases the factory failed to build a car for a number in the sequence.

This list stops at chassis number 11,183. After that number Ferrari produced his road cars in greater volume and more consistency. For example, from 11,183 to 12,171 only 2+2s GTCs, and GTSs were built. That is almost 500 numbers that would make very monotonous reading. For models made after 11,183 we list a range of chassis numbers showing the lowest and highest known.

Picture References

In 'The Numbers' section that follows we refer frequently to photographs of specific cars that are illustrated in other books. The following is the 'Key' to these references. At the same time we highly recommend all of these books. If you want to know everything about Ferraris your library should include the latest edition of each of these books.

1	BG/page number		'Illustrated Ferrari Buyers Guide' by Dean Batchelor.
2	P1/page number		'The Ferrari Legend: The Road Cars' by Antoine Prunet.
3	P2/page number		'Ferrari - Sport et Prototypes' by Antoine Prunet.
4	CR/page number		'Ferrari-Catalogue Raisonnée' in two volumes boxed.
5	FT/page number		'Ferrari Tipo 166' by Angelo Tito Anselmi.
6	FM/page number		'Ferrari' by Warren Fitzgerald, Richard F. Merritt and Jon Thompson.
7	MM/page number		'Ferrari - The Man, The Machines' edited by Stan Grayson.
8	JP/page number		'Ferrari 250GT Competition Cars by Jess G. Pourret. 1987 edition in English.

Recommended Reading

In addition to the above we highly recommend the following publications: <u>Ferrari Market Letter</u>, a unique and authoritative publication issued twenty-six times a year by Gerald Roush, an acknowledged Ferrari expert, contact Roush Publications Inc., P.O.Box 1498, Stone Mountain, GA 30086-1498; <u>Cavallino Magazine</u>, a Ferrari enthusiasts' magazine famous for the quality of its content, published six times a year, Cavallino Inc., Box 323, Scarsdale, N.Y. 10583-0323; <u>Prancing Horse</u>, the quarterly magazine of the Ferrari Club of America, contact the club at 9632 S.E. City View Drive, Portland, OR 97266.

Chassis No.	Picture Ref.	Engine No.	Type	Model	Body Style	Coach-builder	First Owner	Original Location	Present Location
1947									
001S*	FT125,CR15.	001S	166	Sport	Spyder	Allemano?	Count Bruno Sterzi	Milan,Italy	

Believed built November 1947 and sold by factory on 4/2/48. Outright winner 1948 Targa Florio, Biondetti/Troubetzkoy. DNF in 1948 Mille Miglia, Righetti/Bruno Sterzi.2620mm WB.

1948									
003S*	P1/22,23,32.	003S	166	Sport	Coupé	Allemano	Factory	Italy	

Believed built April 1948 and sold by factory on 7/2/49.Outright winner of 1948 Mille Miglia, Biondetti/Navone. Sold 3/49 to Bianchetti. Was DNF 1949 Mille Miglia and 2nd OA 1949. Coppa Inter Europa.Comments: 2620mm WB.

| 005S* | FT 65 | 005S | 166 | Sport | Coupé (Notchback) | Touring | Count Bruno Sterzi | Milan,Italy | Italy. |

Built by factory in 8/48 and shown at 48 Turin Show. Sold by factory on 11/25/48 to Sterzi. Outright winner of 49 Inter Europa Cup. 2620 mm WB. First Touring bodied Ferrari. Aerlux sunroof.

1949									
007S*	FT 67	007S	166	Inter	Coupé(Notchback)	Touring	Cantiere Spa	Genoa,Italy	U.S.A.

Sold by factory on 2/7/49. Finished 3rd OA 49 Coppa Inter Europa.2420mm WB.First chassis designated Inter.

| 009S* | P1/30,FT74. | 009S | 166 | Inter | Berlinetta | Stabilimenti Farina | | Italy | In U.S.A. for many years. |

Built early in 49.First owner probably Franco Cornacchia.2420mm WB.

| 011S* | P1/33. | 011S | 166 | Inter | Convertible | Stabilimenti Farina | Roberto Rossellini? | Italy | In U.S.A. for many years. |

Likely built in January 1949 and first shown at 1949 Geneva Auto Show.

| 013S* | | 013S | F2 | | 166 | | | | See notes |

Possibly not built.Reported as a Touring coupé in Italian junkyard in 1970s.Also is reported to be in the Schlumpf Museum in France as a F2 Monoposto.

| 015S* | P1/27. | | 166 | Inter | Coupé(Notchback) | Touring | P.Castelnouvo | Milan,Italy | Last known in U.S.A. |

Sold by factory on 1/7/49.Touring Body No.3190.Fitted with "T" spoked steering wheel.

| 017S* | FT 69. | 017S | 166 | Inter | Berlinetta | Touring | Franco Cornacchia | Milan,Italy | |

Probably built in July 1949.First Touring body with smooth sides.

| 019S* | P1/28. | 019S | 166 | Inter | Coupé(Notchback) | Touring | J.Lodi | Paris,France | U.K. |

Sold on 6/7/49.Shown at 49 Paris Salon. Sold to Jean Renaldo, France,and raced by him e.g.52 Albi. Fitted "Aerlux" sunroof.Touring Body No.3392.

| 021S* | | 021S | 166 | Inter | Berlinetta | Stabilimenti Farina | | | U.K. |

Sold by factory on 27/7/49.

| 023S* | | 023S | 166 | Inter | Berlinetta | Touring | P.Nogara | Portugal | In U.S.A. since 1960s. |

Sold by factory on 12/11/49. Fitted with Aerlux sunroof.Fitted with Engine 075S.

| 025S* | | 025S | 166 | Inter | Coupé? | Touring | Rizzoli | Milan,Italy | Italy. |

Rebodied in 1970 by Fantuzzi,Modena as a Touring Barchetta replica.

| 027S* | | 027S | 166 | Inter | Coupé? | Touring | A.Caraceni | Rome, Italy | |

Raced in 1951 Mille Miglia as a 195 Sport.Possibly Bertone Conv rebodied as Touring Coupé. Advertised in Italy as SWB Touring Le Mans Coupé(?).

| 029S* | | 029S | 166 | Inter | Coupé(Notchback) | Touring | W.Defoe | NY U.S.A. | In U.S.A. since new. |

Sold by factory on 14/5/49.Touring Body No.3396.

| 031S* | | 031S | 166 | Inter | Berlinetta | Stabilimenti Farina | | Italy | U.S.A. |

Sold by the factory on 9/6/49.In Colorado,U.S.A. in 1960s with Buick engine. May have been rebodied with old Spyder body.

| 033S* | P1/34,FT 77. | 033S | 166 | Inter | Convertible | Stabilimenti Farina | Wax & Vitale | Genoa,Italy | CH in'70s |

Sold in 1949.Cabo disc wheels with Ferrari hub caps

| 035S* | | 035S | 166 | Inter | Coupé(Notchback) | Touring | V.Sampeli | Italy | Italy |

1950									
037S*		037S	166	Inter	Berlinetta	Stabilimenti Farina	Tamorri	Rome,Italy	U.S.A.

Built in 1950.

| 039S* | | 039S | 166 | Inter | Berlinetta | Touring | Angelo Biemmi | Brescia,Italy | U.S.A.. |

C of O dated 5/11/49.Sold by the factory on 20/6/50. Rebodied by Vignale in 1950 and listed by Vignale as '2-seat Type 51 Deluxe Coupé'. (Engine in seperate location.)

| 041S* | | 041S | 166 | Inter | Berlinetta | Stabilimenti Farina | | | U.S.A. |

Sold in 1950s to D.Cameron Peck in the U.S.A. as a Stabilimenti Farina Coupé.Was recently examined and is confirmed as a Stabilimenti Farina Coupé! Once believed to be a Touring Le Mans Berlinetta.

| 043S* | | 043S | 166 | Inter | Berlinetta | Touring | Aicar (Argentine Automobile Club) | Milan,Italy | Holland |

| 045S* | P1/37. | 045S | 166 | Inter | Berlinetta | Vignale | Nogara | Portugal | Italy |

Sold by the Ferrari factory on 13/10/50. Possibly driven by Raymond Sommer in 1950.Similar styling to 069S.

| 047S* | | 047S | 166 | Inter | Berlinetta(Fastback | Touring | Ing. L.Pomini | Milan,Italy | U.S.A. |

Sold by the factory on 1/7/50. Possibly the car shown at the 1950 Turin Motor Show. Fitted with "Aerlux" sunroof.

| 049S* | FT 89. | 049S | 166 | Inter | Berlinetta | Ghia | | | U.S.A. |

In U.S.A. for many years.Engine sold and believe reunited in recent years. Also reported as a Touring Berlinetta.

| 051S* | P1/37. | 051S | 166 | Inter | Berlinetta | Vignale | G.Vaccari | Milan,Italy | U.S.A. |

Sold by factory on 15/7/50. Reported converted to a Vignale Convertible.

| 053S* | | 053S | 166(195) | Inter | Berlinetta | Touring | Italian literary figure | Italy | U.S.A. |

Engine likely enlarged to 195. Touring Body No.3456.

| 055S* | | 055S | 166 | Inter | Coupé? | Touring | | Genoa,Italy | |
| 057S* | | 057S | 166(195) | Mille Miglia? | Berlinetta? | Touring? | | | U.S.A.? |

Reported in U.S.A. in early 1960s as a Touring Barchetta. Was likely rebodied from Berlinetta to Barchetta. Could be Ghia Coupé.

| 059S* | | 059S | 166 | Inter | Coupé | Vignale | F.Caimi | | Italy |

Sold by factory on 8/7/50.Recent owner reports it has 195 engine.

| 061S* | | 061S | 166 | Inter | Berlinetta | Vignale | A.Rosso | Turin,Italy | |

Sold by factory on 18/10/50. Also reported to be the 166 Bertone Convertible.

| 063S* | P1/35,FT 78. | 063S | 166 | Inter | Convertible | Stabilimenti Farina | P.Valee | Paris,France | U.K. |

Sold by the factory in September 1950 in Paris. Sold from Switzerland to U.K. in derelict condition without engine in 1960s. Rebodied as replica Corsa Spyder with 250GT engine. Originally exhibited in 1950 Paris Salon.

Chassis No.	Picture Ref.	Engine No.	Type	Model	Body Style	Coach-builder	First Owner	Original Location	Present Location
065S*	Like P1/41.	065S	166	Inter	Berlinetta	Vignale	L.Spinotti	Castello,Italy	Italy
	Sold by factory on 22/1/51.Possibly converted to 195.								
067S*		067S	166(195)	Mille Miglia	Barchetta Spyder	Touring	Charles Moran	U.S.A.	U.S.A..
	Finished 16th overall at LeMans 24 Hour Race in 1951 driven by Charles Moran.Another 067S was driven in the 1952 Mille Miglia: a 195S Vignale (or Touring?) Coupé!May have been renumbered from 0100M. Touring body No. 3479								
069S*	Like P1/36.	069S	166	Inter	Berlinetta	Vignale	I.Bernabei	Rome,Italy	U.S.A.
	Sold by factory on 22/1/51 but car was completed on 15/9/50. In U.S.A. since 1957								
071S*		071S	166	Inter	Berlinetta	Vignale	Fratelli Cerana	Italy	U.S.A.
	Engine converted to 195. Looks identical to 069S								
073S*		073S	166	Inter	Berlinetta	Touring			
	Also reported to be a Vignale Coupé like 069S								
075S*	P1/29.	075S	166	Inter	Berlinetta	Touring	Italesta Spa	Milan,Italy	
	Sold by factory on 16/9/50.to Giannino Marzotto. Chrome on hood air intake added later. Engine in 023S.								
077S*	FT 50,51	077S	166	Inter	Berlinetta	Touring	I.Bernabei	Rome,Italy	Italy
	Sold by factory on 29/9/50								
079S		079S	166	Inter	Berlinetta	Touring			U.S.A.
	In Switzerland in 1970 with Alfa 6C2500 engine. Last known with engine no.049S								
081S*		081S	195	Inter	Berlinetta(Fastback	Touring	J.C.Walsh?		U.S.A.
	Sold by the factory on 31/10/50. Imported to U.S.A. in 1959. Touring Body No.3463.								
083S*		083S	195	Inter	Coupé	Vignale ?	V.Boncalneri	Milan, Italy	Engine U.K..
085S*		085S	195	Inter	Berlinetta(Fastback	Touring	Automotonautica	Milan,Italy	U.S.A.
	Touring Body No. 3465 (3405 in error in Touring book). Fitted with Aerlux sunroof.								
087S*		087S	195	Inter	Coupé	Ghia			U.S.A. with Chevy engine.
089S*		089S	195	Inter	Coupé	Ghia	Probably Lion Sven in Belgium.		U.K.
091S*		091S	195	Inter	Coupé	Vignale?			Possibly in U.S.A.
	Engine in U.S.A..								
093S*		093S	195	Inter	Coupé	Ghia		Venezuela?	
095S*		095S	195	Inter	Coupé	Vignale?	Marchese Carega?	Turin,Italy	
097S*		097S	195	Inter	Berlinetta	Vignale			U.K.
	Burned out in U.S.A. in 1960s; chassis salvaged without engine. Fitted with Vignale Coupé body from 0024M in 1982. Probably with shortened chassis to fit body.								
099S*		099S	195	Inter	Coupé?	Vignale?	Paolo Tacchini	Turin/Florence Italy	
	Also reported to be a Touring Berlinetta.								
0101S*	FM40	0101S	195	Inter	Coupé 2+2	Ghia			U.S.A.
0103S*		0103S	195	Inter	Berlinetta	Vignale	Joao Gaspar?	Portugal	U.S.A.
	Stayed in Portugal until 1978.								
0105S*		0105S	212	Inter	Coupé	Ghia			U.S.A.
0106E*	P1/55.	0106E	212	Export	Convertible	Vignale			U.K.
	Imported into U.K. in early 1960s.								
0107S	FM 41?	0107S	212	?	Berlinetta	Stabilimenti Farina			U.S.A.
	Also reported to be with a body by Pinin Farina. Last Ferrari with body by Stabilimenti Farina.								
0108E*		0108E	212	Export	Berlinetta(Fastback	Touring	G.Fassio	Genoa,Italy	U.S.A.
	Imported into U.S.A. in late 1950s.No racing history known. Luxury exterior/interior indicates not built for racing.								
0109S*		0109S	195	Inter	Coupé	Ghia			U.S.A.
0110E*	P1/54.	0110E	212	Export	Convertible	Vignale	Portugese Ambassador to France	France	U.S.A.
	Imported into U.S.A. in 1960s. Similar to 0106E.								
0111S*		0111S	212	Inter	Berlinetta	Vignale			U.K.
	In U.S.A. for many years								
0113S*		0113S	195	Inter	Coupé	Ghia			U.S.A.
0115S*	P1/43.	0115S	195	Inter	Berlinetta	Vignale			U.K.
	Sold by the factory on 8/1/51								
0117S*		0117S	212? (195?)	Inter		195 Motto	Ammendola	Italy	
	A Motto bodied fastback coupé was raced by Salvatore Ammendola in 1951. His 1951 Mille Miglia entry was reported as a 195 Sport with berlinetta Vignale body.(?)								
0119S*		0119S	212(195)	Inter	Berlinetta	Vignale		Italy	
0121S*		0121S	195	Inter	Coupé 2 + 2	Ghia			Germany

1951

Chassis No.	Picture Ref.	Engine No.	Type	Model	Body Style	Coach-builder	First Owner	Original Location	Present Location
0123S*		0123S	195	Inter	Berlinetta	Touring	Cornacchia	Milan,Italy	
	Possibly raced by Scuderia Guastalla.								
0125 EL*		0125EL	212	Inter	Convertible	Vignale			Germany
	Similar coachwork to 0106E								
0127S*		0127S	212	Inter	Berlinetta	Vignale			
0128 EX*		0128EX	212	Export	Berlinetta	Vignale	Bob Wilke	U.S.A.	U.S.A.
	Imported into the U.S.A. from new.Competition chassis built for high speed touring.								
0129S*		0129S	195	Inter	Coupé	Ghia	Villoresi?	Italy	U.S.A.
0130 AL*	Like P1/79.	0130AL	340	America	Coupé	Ghia	David Brown	U.K.	U.K.
	First shown at the 1951 Paris Salon in October.								
0131 E*	FM39(No30)	0131E	212	Inter	Berlinetta	Vignale	Luigi Chinetti	U.S.A.	U.S.A.
	Raced by Phil Hill in 1952 Carrera Panamerican and finished 6th OA with Arnold Stubbs as co-driver. Did not run in the 1951 Carrera Panamericana.								
0132 A*	P1/75.	0132A	340	America	Berlinetta	Vignale	Johnny Ysmael	U.S.A.	U.S.A. ,with Chevy engine.
	Specially built for a young Philippine millionaire living in the U.S.A..								

Chassis No.	Picture Ref.	Engine No.	Type	Model	Body Style	Coach-builder	First Owner	Original Location	Present Location
0133 E*		0133E	195	Inter	Coupé	Ghia		Switzerland?	Last known Switzerland.
0135 E*	P1/52.	0135E	212	Export Lungo	Coupé	Vignale			U.S.A.
	Shown at 1951 Paris Salon.								
0137 E*		0137E	212	Export Lungo	Berlinetta	Ghia Aigle, Switzerland			U.K.
	Body is based on design by Michelotti.								
0138 A*		0138A	340	America	Convertible	Vignale			U.S.A.
	In U.S.A. for many years.								
0139 E		0139E	212	Export Lungo?	Coupé	Vignale			Netherlands
	Claimed to be 250. Car presently looks like Europa (may be rebody). LHD								
0141 T*	MM 63.	0141T	212	Tuboscocca	Berlinetta (Fastback)	Touring	Ferrari	Milan, Italy	Italy (original engine U.S.A.?
	May have been styling exercise: has one piece curved windshield and reshaped rear side windows. Tuboscocca chassis. Appears to be on SWB Mille Miglia WB.								
0142 A*		0142A	340	America	Coupé	Ghia	Juan Peron	Argentina	U.S.A.
	In U.S.A. for many years.								
0143 E*		0143E	212	Export Lungo	Berlinetta (Fastback)	Touring	La Piscina Spa	Gubbio, Italy	U.S.A.
	Sold on 22/9/51. Returned to factory and sold to Mike Hawthorn for his personal use. Imported by Hawthorn into U.K.. Aerlux sunroof.								
0144 A*		0144A	340	America	Coupé	Vignale			Italy
0145 E*		0145E	212	Inter	Coupé	Touring	Franco Cornacchia	Italy	U.S.A. (engine only).
	Possibly a Ghia Coupé.								
0147 E*		0147E	212	Export Lungo?	Convertible	Vignale			U.K.
	Rebodied in late 1950s with "California" Spider body by Scaglietti.								
0148 A*		0148A	340	America	Coupé	Ghia	Michel Paul Cavallier	France	
	Built for a director of Ferrari, the President of Pont-a-Mousson, France.								
0149 E*		0149E	212	Export Lungo	Coupé	Ghia			U.K. (parts only)
	Sold on 2/1/52. Imported into U.K. in early 1960s and eventually parted out. Engine with 0106E as spare.								
0150 A*		0150A	340	America	Coupé	Ghia	Tony Parravano	U.S.A.	U.S.A.
	Built as a touring car but converted to a race car by Parravano.								
0151 S*		0151S	195	Inter?	Berlinetta	Vignale		Portugal?	Italy
	Also reported as Vignale Spider - may be rebody.								
0153 EL*		0153EL	212	Export Lungo	Coupé	Ghia			U.K.
	Shown at the 1951 London Motor Show.								
0155 EL*		0155EL	212	Export Lungo	Coupé	Ghia		U.K.	U.K.
	Also reported as 250S(?).								
0157 EL*	P1/48.	0157EL	212	Export Lungo	Coupé 2+2	Vignale			U.S.A.
	2+2								
0159 E*		0159E	212	Export Lungo?	Convertible	Vignale	Scotti?		Switzerland
	Shown at the 1951 Brussels Motor Show. Reported as Viotti Convertible.								
0161 EL*	FM 51	0161EL	212	Export Lungo	Coupé	Vignale	Ferrari	Italy	Mexico.
	Finished 2nd OA in 1951 Carrera Panamericana driven by Ascari/Villoresi. Sold in Mexico after race.								
0163 EL*		0163 EL	212	Export Lungo	Coupé	Vignale			U.K. (engine).
	May be the car which finished 1st OA in the 1951 Carrera Panamericana driven by Taruffi/Chinetti. which was identical to 0161EL.								
0165 EL*		0165 EL	212	Export Lungo	D/H Coupé	Abbott (U.K.)	TT Garage	Farnham, U.K	U.K.
	Shown as show chassis only at 1951 Earl's Court Motor Show. Body built by Abbott for TT Garage since removed and junked. New body built.								
0167 EL*		0167 EL	212	Inter	Berlinetta	Touring			Italy?
	Reported in Uruguay some years ago.								
0169 E*		0169 E	212	Inter	Coupé	Ghia			U.S.A.
0171 EL*		0171 EL	212	Export Lungo	Berlinetta	Vignale	?	Mexico?	Mexico
	Remained in Mexico and since fitted with 340 Engine No.0212A.								
0173 E*		0173 E	212	Export Lungo?	Coupé	Vignale			U.K.?
0174 A*		0174A	340	America	Coupé	Vignale			U.S.A.
	Surfaced in U.S.A. in 1970s.								
0175 EL*		0175 EL	225	Export Lungo	Berlinetta	Vignale	Anna Magnani?	Italy	U.S.A.
	Brought to U.S.A. and Buick engine installed. Later original engine was reinstalled. Was possibly built as 212 and converted to 225. Monza cap thru rear window & convex grill.								
0177 E*	P1/61.	0177 E	212	Inter	Convertible	Pinin Farina	Filipinetti	Switzerland	Switzerland
	First convertible by PF and first Ferrari by PF. Sold in 1952.								
0179 EL*		0179 EL	212	Export Lungo	Berlinetta	Vignale	Cornacchia	Italy	U.S.A. (with 250GT engine)
	Variously reported as a 195 and a 225.								
0181 EL*	P1/56.	0181 EL	195	Export Lungo	Coupé	Vignale	Anna Magnani	Italy	Italy
	Sold on 19/1/52. Also reported to be a 212.								
0183 EL*		0183 EL	212	Export Lungo	Coupé	Ghia	Joao Gaspar	Portugal	Spain (with PF Coupé body)
	Rebodied as Pinin Farina Coupé. In U.K. in 1960s as chassis only.								
0185 EL*		0185 EL	212	Export Lungo	Coupé	Ghia			U.S.A.
0187 EL*		0187 EL	212	Export Lungo					Switzerland
	Possibly a Ghia Coupé. In Switzerland for many years.								
0189 EL*		0189 EL	212	Export Lungo	Coupé	Ghia	King Farouk	Egypt	U.S.A.
	Shown at the 1951 Paris Salon and probably sold afterwards. 2+2.								
0190 ED*		0190ED	212	Export	Coupé	Vignale			Africa?
1952									
0191 EL*		0191 EL	212	Export Lungo	Coupé	Ghia	Edit. Domus	Italy	Argentina
	Sold to South America many years ago.								
0193 EL		0193 EL	212	Export Lungo	Coupé	Ghia			Morocco
	In North Africa for many years. 2+2.								

Chassis No.	Picture Ref.	Engine No.	Type	Model	Body Style	Coach-builder	First Owner	Original Location	Present Location
0195 EL*		0195 EL	195	Export Lungo	Coupé	Ghia Aigle(Switzerlan	R.Bellorini	Switzerland	Australia
	Based on a design by Michelotti Owned in U.S.A. since late 1950s.								
0196 AM*		0196AM	340	America	Coupé	Vignale			U.S.A.
	Completed on 23/7/52.								
0197 EL*	P1 59	0197 EL	212	Export Lungo	Berlinetta	Vignale	M.Signoret	France	U.K.(with 250GT engine)
	Sold on 15/6/52.A unique fastback berlinetta with vestigal fins. Similar to 0104ED.In U.S.A. from late 1950s.								
0199 EL*		0199 EL	212	Export Lungo	Coupé	Ghia			U.S.A.
0201 EL*		0201 EL	212	Export Lungo	Coupé	Ghia			U.S.A.
	Once mistaken for 020I.								
0203 EL*		0203 EL	212	Export Lungo	Berlinetta	Vignale			Australia?
	Believed in Australia with supercharged GPV12 engine.								
0205 EL*		0205 EL	212	Export Lungo	Coupé	Ghia			
	Also listed by Touring "0205(?)"as Touring Coupé.								
0207 EL*		0207 EL	212	Export Lungo	Convertible	Vignale			France?
	Reported in France years ago.								
0209 EL*		0209 EL	212	Export Lungo?	Convertible	Vignale			U.K.
	Photo of car taken in U.K. shows what appears to be a competition style coupé on SWB. Engine reported in U.S.A..								
0211 EL*		0211 EL	212	Export Lungo	Berlinetta	Vignale	Riv Spa	Italy	U.S.A.
	Sold in 1951								
0212 EL		0212 EL	212	Export Lungo	Spyder	Vignale			U.S.A.
	(Engine 0212A with 0171EL in Mexico.)								
0213 EL	P1/57.	0213 EL	212	Export Lungo	Coupé	Ghia	Taruffi?	Italy?	U.S.A.
	Still with original owner in U.S.A.? Elegant 2 window coupé.								
0215 EL*		0215 EL	212	Export Lungo	Berlinetta	Touring		Belgium?	Italy
	Sold on 31/3/52. Curved 1 piece windshield.Touring Body No. 3714.								
0217 EL*	FM 42.	0217 EL	212	Export Lungo	Berlinetta	Vignale			U.S.A.
	Shown at 1952 Brussels Motor Show.In U.S.A. for many years.								
0219 EL*		0219 EL	212	Export Lungo	Berlinetta	Vignale			U.S.A.
0221 EL		0221 EL	212	Export Lungo	Berlinetta	Vignale			
0223 EL		0223 EL	212	Export Lungo?	Berlinetta	Vignale			France
	In U.S.A. for many years. Also reported as 225.								
0225 EL*		0225 EL	212	Export Lungo	Berlinetta	Vignale			
	Also reported as Touring Coupé.								
0227 EL	P1/61.	0227 EL	212	Export Lungo	Convertible	Vignale	Luigi Chinetti?	U.S.A.	U.S.A.
	In U.S.A. for very long time. LHD								
0229 EL	P1/66.	0229 EL	212	Export Lungo	Coupé	Pinin Farina	Chinetti Hess	U.S.A.?	U.S.A.
	PF date:28/7/52. Last reported with Chevy engine. LHD.								
0231 EL*		0231 EL	212	Export Lungo	Coupé	Ghia			Argentina
	Also reported as a Vignale Coupé.								
0232 AL		0232 AL	342	America	Convertible	Vignale	O.Wild	Switzerland	U.S.A.
	Special one-off body. LHD.								
0233 EL*		0233 EL	212	Export Lungo	Convertible	Ghia			U.S.A.
	Reported with Chevy engine installed. Also reported as 0233E.								
0234 AL	P1/99.	0234AL	342	America	Convertible	Pinin Farina	King Leopold	Belgium	U.S.A.
	In U.S.A. since late 1950s. Special one off body.								
0235 EU	P1/65.	0235 EU	212	Inter	Convertible	Pinin Farina	Roberto Rossellini	Italy	U.S.A.(Engine elsewhere
	Believed shown at 1952 Paris Salon.Later in U.S.A. for many years. Second PF Convertible. LHD.								
0237 EU	FM 36.	0237 EU	250	Export Lungo	Berlinetta	Vignale	Franco Cornacchia.	Italy	U.S.A..
	Raced by Cornacchia and Bruno Moroni. Competition car.Last known with engine 0269EU. LHD.								
0239 EU		0239EU		Europa	Coupé	Vignale	Echeverria?	Mexico	See 0292M.
	Raced by Echeverria in the 1952 Carrera Panamericana. Was returned to Italy and traded to Ferrari for 0352M a 250MM PF Competition Coupé which was renumbered as 0239EU. 0239EU was renumbered as 0292M.See 0352M for details.								
0240 AL		0240AL	342	America	Coupé	Pinin Farina	Comm.Monti	Italy	Sweden.
	Special one off body.								
0241 EU*		0241 EU	212	Inter	Berlinetta	Touring			U.S.A.
0242 AL	P1/102.	0242AL	342	America	Coupé	Pinin Farina	Enzo Ferrari?	Italy	U.S.A.
0243 EU*?		0243 EU	212	Export Lungo?	Coupé	Vignale			
	Also reported as PF coupé in Switzerland.								
0245 EL*?		0245EL	212	Export Lungo	Coupé	Pinin Farina	Fontanella?		U.K.?
	PF date:14/10/52.								
0246 AL	P1/102.	0246AL	342	America	Coupé	Pinin Farina			U.S.A.
	Shown at the 1953 Geneva Auto Show.								
0247 EL*		0247 EL	212	Export Lungo	Coupé	Pinin Farina	Fontanella		U.K. (likely as parts only).
	PF date: 24/10/52.In England later as chassis only.Believed parted out in U.K..								
0248 AL	P1/102.	0248AL	342	America	Convertible	Pinin Farina			U.S.A.
	Shown at the 1953 New York Auto Show.								
0249 EL		0249 EL	212	Export Lungo	Coupé	Pinin Farina	Bianchi		Germany
	PF date: 18/10/52. Later fitted with 3 36DCS/3 carbs. LHD.								
0251 EU*?		0251EU	212	Europa	Berlinetta	Touring			U.S.A.?
	Also reported as Vignale coupé ex-Emperor Boa-Dai.								
0253 EU		0253 EU	212	Europa	Barchetta	Touring	William Ford	Dearborn U.S	U.S.A.
	Sold in 1952. The last Barchetta made. LWB.								
0255 EU*		0255 EU	212	Lungo	Convertible	Vignale			U.S.A.
	Sold in 1952. Similar to 0227EL								

Chassis No.	Picture Ref.	Engine No.	Type	Model	Body Style	Coach-builder	First Owner	Original Location	Present Location
0257 EU	P1/71.	0257 EU	212	Lungo	Coupé	Vignale	L.Chinetti	U.S.A.	Belgium
	In U.S.A. for many years? LHD.								
0259 EL*?		0259 EL	212	Export Lungo	Coupé	Pinin Farina	Nocentini	Florence, Italy	U.S.A. Australia?
	Engine with 0112E as spare.								
0261 EU*		0261 EL	212	Export Lungo	Coupé	Pinin Farina	Ferrario		U.S.A.(Engine elsewhere in U
	PF date: 13/11/52.In U.S.A. for many years with Olds V8 engine.								
0263 EU		0263 EU	212	Europa	Coupé	Pinin Farina	Guichenne		U.S.A.
	PF date: 14/1/53.Believed to have been shown at 1953 Geneva Auto Show.In U.S.A. for many years. LHD.								
0265 EU*		0265EU	212	Europa	Coupé	Pinin Farina	Roberto Rossellini	Italy	U.S.A.
	PF date: 10/12/52.Wedding gift for Ingrid Bergman.Reputed to be a 3 liter V12 prototype 250 engine.								

1953

Chassis No.	Picture Ref.	Engine No.	Type	Model	Body Style	Coach-builder	First Owner	Original Location	Present Location
0267 EU	P1/71.	0267 EU	212	Lungo	Coupé	Vignale		France	U.K.?
	In U.S.A. for many years.								
0269 EU		0269 EU	212	Europa	Coupé	Pinin Farina	Prince Bernhard	Netherlands	U.K.
	Engine in 0237EU in U.S.A..								
0271 EU	P1/71.	0271 EU	212	Lungo	Coupé	Vignale	Alfred Ducato	U.S.A.	U.S.A.
	In U.S.A. since new. First shown at 1953 Geneva Auto Show. Similar to 0267EU.								
0273 EU		0273 EU	212	Europa?	Convertible	Vignale			U.S.A.?
	Also reported as 225 and as a 212 Vignale Coupé.								
0275 EU		0275 EU	212	Lungo	Coupé	Pinin Farina	Fontanella?		U.S.A.
	PF date: 10/3/53.In U.S.A. for many years.								
0277 EU		0277 EU	212	Lungo	Coupé	Pinin Farina	Ducros		France?
0279 EU*?		0279 EU	212	Lungo	Coupé	Pinin Farina	B.Ferrari	U.S.A.	U.S.A.
	PF date: 14/3/53.Also reported as first owned by Bruno Sterzi.								
0281 EU*		0281 EU	212	Lungo	Coupé	Pinin Farina		Rome, Italy	
	PF date: 18/3/53.								
0283 EU		0283 EU	212	Lungo	Coupé	Pinin Farina	Roucoroni		U.S.A.
	PF date: 14/3/53.								
0285 EU	P1/85.	0285 EU	212	Lungo	Coupé	Vignale	Luigi Chinetti	U.S.A.	U.S.A.
	Shown at 1953 New York Auto Show. Similar to 0267EU.								
0287 EU	P1/71.	0287 EU	212	Lungo	Coupé	Vignale			U.S.A.
	Sold in 1953. Similar to 0267EU. LHD?.								
0289 EU	P1/71.	0289 EU	212	Lungo	Coupé	Vignale			U.S.A.
	Similar to 0267EU								
0291 EU	P1/72.	0291 EU	212	Europa	Coupé	Pinin Farina	Landi		Australia
	PF date: 20/3/53.In U.S.A. for many years. Once thought to be the last 212 made.								
0292 MM		0292 MM	212	Europa	Coupé	Vignale			Italy
	Originally built as 0239EU ,a 212 Europa. Later rebuilt by Ferrari with a 250MM engine and other modifications and renumbered 0292MM.								
0293 AL	P1/104,105.	0293 AL	375	America	Coupé	Pinin Farina	Howard Keck	U.S.A.	U.S.A.
	PF date: 25/8/53.Same owner for 33 years!								
0295 EU		0295 EU	250GT?	Europa?	Coupé	Vignale			U.S.A.
	May be first 250 Europa. 110".Lampredi engine. LWB.								
0297 EU		0297 EU	212	Lungo	Coupé	Pinin Farina			U.S.A.
	Really the last 212 made.								
0299 EU	P1/104 & 105	0299 EU	375?	America?	Coupé	Pinin Farina	Roberto Rossellini	Italy	Switzerland
	PF show this to be 0299AL, a 375 America.This is the first of the first series Europa coupés and may have been fitted with a 375 engine specially for Rossellini. Likely a Europa converted to 375 America.								
0301 AL	P1/118.	0301 AL	250	Europa	Coupé	Vignale			
	Believed shown at the 1953 Paris Salon. Lampredi 3 litre engine.LWB.								
0303 AL		0303 AL	375	America	Coupé	Pinin Farina			U.K.
	Shown at the 1953 Brussels Motor Show. 110"WB								
0305 EU		0305 EU	250	Europa	Coupé	Pinin Farina	Magnolfi		
	PF date: 29/9/53.Lampredi 3 litre engine.LWB.								
0307 AL		0307 AL	375	America	Coupé	Pinin Farina	Fred Lip	Paris,France	U.S.A.
	PF date: 14/10/53								
0309 EU		0309EU	250	Europa	Coupé	Pinin Farina	Ferrari	Italy	U.S.A.
	Believed used as a demonstrator.May have been converted to 375 engine.								
0311EU	P1/119.	0311EU	250	Europa	Convertible	Pinin Farina	Ariowitch	U.S.A.	U.S.A.
	Shown at the 1954 New York Auto Show. LHD.Lampredi 3 litre engine.PF records show it as 0309AL a 375 America(?). Only PF Convertible on Europa chassis.								
0313 EU	P1/119.	0313 EU	250	Europa	Coupé	Vignale	Luigi Chinetti	U.S.A.	U.S.A.
	Shown at the 1954 New York Auto Show. Lampredi engine.All aluminum body.								
0315 EU		0315 EU	250	Europa	Coupé	Pinin Farina			U.S.A.
	PF date: 20/7/54. Also reported as 0315AL, a 375 America.Possibly a conversion.								
0317 AL	P1/108.	0317 AL	375	America	Coupé	Pinin Farina	Alois de Mencik	Belgium	Belgium
	PF date: 24/4/54.Finished 2nd OA in the 1954 Geneva Rally driven by de Mencik and J.Swaters.								
0319 AL		0319 AL	375	America	Coupé	Pinin Farina	Carpenter	U.S.A.	U.S.A.
	PF date: 7/4/54								
0321 EU		0321 EU	250	Europa	Coupé	Pinin Farina	Ferrari	Italy	U.S.A. (engine only).
	PF date: 1/12/53. In U.S.A. for many years. Lampredi 3 litre engine								
0323 EU*		0323 EU	250	Europa	Coupé	Pinin Farina			Probably Sweden.
	PF date: 9/12/53.Shown at the 1954 Stockholm Motor Show. Lampredi 3 litre engine.								

Chassis No.	Picture Ref.	Engine No.	Type	Model	Body Style	Coachbuilder	First Owner	Original Location	Present Location	Notes
0325 EU		0325 EU	250	Europa	Coupé	Pinin Farina	J.Murray		U.S.A.	PF date: 3/11/53. 5 window coupé. Lampredi 3 litre engine.
1954										
0327 AL	P1/108.	0327 AL	375	America	Coupé	Vignale			U.S.A.	Shown at the 1954 Geneva Auto Show.
0329 AL		0329AL	375	America	Coupé	Pinin Farina	Tony Parravano	U.S.A.	Switzerland	PF date: 21/4/54. Listed in error by PF as a 250MM - really refers to 0239EU.
0331 EU		0331 EU	250	Europa	Coupé	Pinin Farina	Count Somsky	Switzerland	U.S.A.	PF date: 5/2/54. Lampredi 3 litre engine.
0333 EU*		0333 EU	250	Europa	Coupé	Pinin Farina	Brinolf	Sweden	Sweden	PF date: 20/1/54. Shown at the 1954 Geneva Auto Show. Lampredi 3 litre engine.
0334 M		0334M	250MM	Mille Miglia	Coupé	Vignale			Holland	Appears to have been built as a road car. No known racing history.
0335 EU		0335 EU	250	Europa	Coupé	Pinin Farina	Castillon de Perron	France	U.S.A.	PF date: 25/1/54. Lampredi 3 litre engine.
0337 AL	P1 108.	0337 AL	375	America	Coupé	Vignale			U.S.A.	Believed shown at the 1954 Turin Motor Show.
0339 AL		0339 AL	375	America	Coupé	Pinin Farina	Franco Cornacchia	Italy	U.S.A.	PF date: 10/9/54
0341 EU		0341 EU	250	Europa	Coupé	Pinin Farina	Silvano Bianchi		Canada	PF date: 8/3/54. Lampredi 3 litre engine.
0343 EU		0343 EU	250	Europa	Coupé	Pinin Farina	Barge		U.S.A.	PF date: 5/3/54. 110" WB. Lampredi 3 litre engine.
0345 EU		0345 EU	250	Europa	Coupé	Pinin Farina	Stimson		U.S.A.	PF date: 7/4/54. Lampredi 3 litre engine.
0347 EU		0347 EU	250	Europa	Coupé	Vignale				Also reported as Ghia coupé. Engine in U.S.A.
0349 EU		0349 EU	250	Europa	Coupé	Pinin Farina			Mexico	PF date: 26/6/54. Lampredi 3 litre engine.
0351 EU		0351 EU	250	Europa	Coupé	Pinin Farina	Clarence Brown	France	U.S.A.	PF date: 25/5/54. Last of the First Series Europa Coupés. Lampredi 3 litre engine.
0353 EU	P1/109, MF44.	0353EU	375	America	Convertible	Vignale	B.Colizzi	Italy	U.S.A.	Built on 11/12/54 as a 250GT Europa with 250 Lampredi engine - rebuilt by the factory a year later as a 375 America with Engine No. 0353AL and Chassis Plate 0353EU.
0355 AL	P1/115, FM46.	0355 AL	375	America	Coupé	Pinin Farina	G.Agnelli	Italy	U.S.A.	PF date: 10/11/54. Shown at the 1955 Turin Motor Show. Later brought into U.S.A. by Luigi Chinetti. Special one off design. Last 375 America. Rectangular grill.
0357 EU	P1/150.	0357 EU	250	Europa GT	Coupé	Pinin Farina			U.K.	Shown at the 1954 Paris Salon. PF date: 17/7/54. Finished 3rdOA in the 1956 Tour de France driven by Gendebien/Ringoir. Can be considered the 1st prototype Tour de France. First of the 2nd Series SWB Europa 250GTs. WB:102.3".
0359 GT	P1/156, FM 44.0	0359 GT	250	Europa GT	Coupé	Vignale	Princess L de Rethy	Belgium	U.S.A.	Built by Vignale from a design of Michelotti for a very important customer. Wraparound windshield.
0361 GT		0361GT	250	Europa GT	Coupé	Pinin Farina	Laudini			PF date: 1/10/54.
0363 GT		0363GT	250	Europa GT	Coupé	Pinin Farina		Brussels		
0365 GT		0365 GT	250	Europa GT	Coupé	Pinin Farina	Ferrari	Italy		Believed to be factory demonstrator.
0367 GT		0367 GT	250	Europa GT	Coupé	Pinin Farina	Baron de Rothschild	France		PF date: 30/10/54.
0368 AM	P2/85.	0368AM	375	Mille Miglia	Berlinetta	PininFarina.	P.Cavallier	France	Europe	
0369 EU	P1/158.	0369 EU	250	Europa GT	Berlinetta	Pinin Farina	Charlie Chaplin?	Switzerland		PF date: 10/11/54. Sold on 3/5/55. 2nd prototype Tour de France.
0371 GT		0371 GT	250	Europa GT	Coupé	Pinin Farina	Roger Mitchell		U.S.A.(virtually totalled).	PF date: 5/11/54. Later shipped to U.S.A. and burned out.
0373 GT		0373 GT	250	Europa GT	Coupé	Pinin Farina	Washer			PF date: 15/11/54.
0375 GT*		0375 GT	250	Europa GT	Coupé	Pinin Farina	Sautet		U.K.	PF date: 8/11/54.
0377 GT		0377 GT	250	Europa GT	Coupé	Pinin Farina	Jan deVroom		U.S.A.	PF date: 26/11/54
0378 AM*	P2/86.	0378AM	375	Mille Miglia	Berlinetta	Pinin Farina	Wax & Vitale	Genoa,Italy		No racing history.
0379 GT		0379 GT	250	Europa GT	Coupé	Pinin Farina	Francois Ferrario		U.S.A.	PF date: 30/11/54
0381 GT		0381 GT	250	Europa GT	Coupé	Pinin Farina	Voos	Holland	Holland	PF date: 3/12/54.
1955										
0383 GT	P1/159, JP19	0383 GT	250	Europa GT	Berlinetta	Pinin Farina	Coulibeuf	France	U.S.A.	PF date:10/12/54. Believed shown at 1955 Paris Salon. Raced in 1955 Mille Miglia, 1956 Coppa Europa Monza, and Tour de France. Later raced in U.S.A. thru 1960. Considered first 'production' Tour de France.
0385 GT	JP 16,18.	0385 GT	250	Europa GT	Berlinetta	Pinin Farina	L.Bertett	Italy	Japan	PF date:14/2/55. Never raced. Imported into Greece, crashed, and eventually brought to U.S.A. after total restoration. Considered 2nd production Tour de France.

Chassis No.	Picture Ref.	Engine No.	Type	Model	Body Style	Coach-builder	First Owner	Original Location	Present Location
0387 GT		0387 GT	250	Europa GT	Coupé	Pinin Farina	Prince Bernhard	Netherlands	
	PF date:12/3/55.								
0389 GT		0389 GT	250	Europa GT	Coupé	Pinin Farina	Camai		U.S.A.
	PF date:15/3/55. All aluminum body.								
0391 GT		0391 GT	250	Europa GT	Coupé	Pinin Farina	Barilla		U.S.A.
	PF date:17/6/55								
0393 GT	P1/160	0393 GT	250GT	Tour de France	Berlinetta	Pinin Farina	Dubonne	France	U.S.A.
	PF date:20/6/55.Shown at 1955 Paris Salon.Never raced. One off 14 louvre styling prototype.								
0395 GT		0395GT	250	Europa GT	Coupé	Pinin Farina	D'Antona		U.S.A.
	PF date:22/6/55								
0397 GT		0397 GT	250	Europa GT	Coupé	Pinin Farina	Gotelli		
	PF date:6/7/55								
0399 GT		0399 GT	250	Europa GT	Coupé	Pinin Farina	Charlie Chaplin	Switzerland	
	PF date:6/7/55								
0401 GT		0401 GT	250	Europa GT	Coupé	Pinin Farina			U.S.A.
	PF date:13/7/55.Shown at 1955 Paris Salon. 102"WB.Flat elliptical grill.								
0402 AM*	P2/99,FM 46	0402AM	375	Mille Miglia	Coupé	Scaglietti	Roberto Rossellini	Italy	France
	Originally built as a PF spyder and then rebodied by Scaglietti as a special coupé for Rossellini. All aluminum body.								
0403 GT	P1/161	0403 GT	250	Europa GT	Coupé Speciale	Pinin Farina	Jean Murray		U.S.A.
	Sold on:15/10/55.Considered a special bodied Tour de France. One off all aluminum special body.								
0405 GT		0405 GT	250	Europa GT	Coupé	Pinin Farina	Paul Vallee	France	U.S.A.
	PF date:2/8/55.								
0407 GT	P1/162	0407 GT	250	Europa GT	Coupé	Pinin Farina	Comm.Ferrario	Italy	U.S.A.
	PF date:27/7/55. Extra instruments and fin-like rear fenders.								
0409 GT		0409 GT	250	Europa GT	Coupé	Pinin Farina			
	PF date:2/8/55.								
0411 GT		0411 GT	250	Europa GT	Coupé	Pinin Farina	Barale		France
	PF date:27/7/55								
0413 GT		0413 GT	250	Europa GT	Coupé	Pinin Farina			
	PF date:23/8/55.								
0415 GT	JP 12,21.	0415 GT	250GT	Tour de France	Berlinetta	Pinin Farina	Perdisa/dePortago	Italy	Germany
	Sold on 16/11/55. Raced by dePortago in Nassau and Portugal. Last reported with engine 0445GT. All aluminum body.								
0416 AM	P2/87.	0416AM	375	Mille Miglia	Berlinetta	Pinin Farina	Sebastiani		Europe.
	In U.S.A. since early 1960s. No racing history.								
0417 GT		0417 GT	250	Europa GT	Coupé	Pinin Farina			
	PF date:7/8/55								
0419 GT		0419GT	250	Europa GT	Coupé	Pinin Farina			Holland
	PF date:30/8/55.Believed to have been shown at the 1955 Brussels Motor show.								
0421 GT		0421 GT	250	Europa GT	Coupé	Pinin Farina	S.Maasland		U.K.
	PF date:21/9/55. LHD?								
0423 SA	P1/114	0423 SA	410	Superamerica I	Coupé	Ghia			U.S.A.
	Sold on :1/9/55.First Series I 410 Superamerica.A prototype one off design.Shown at the 1955 Turin Motor Show. 2.60m WB.								
0425 GT	P1/163	0425 GT	250	Tour de France	Berlinetta	Pinin Farina	Wax & Vitale	Genoa,Italy	U.S.A.
	Sold on 20/4/56.Shown at 1956 Geneva Auto Show.								
0427 GT		0427 GT	250	Europa GT	Coupé	Pinin Farina			
	PF date:26/9/55. Last of classic Europa style by PF.								
0429 GT		0429 GT	250GT	Boano	Coupé	Pinin Farina	Sisini		U.S.A.
	PF date:26/9/55. Prototype of "Boano/Ellena" series.First one.Low roof.								
0431 GT		0431GT	250GT	Boano?	Coupé	Pinin Farina?	Braunsweg		
	PF date:1/10/55. Maybe a "Boano/Ellena" prototype.Low roof.								
0433 GT		0433 GT	250	Boano	Coupé	Boano			Germany
	Also reputed to be a Pinin Farina prototype. Low roof.								
0435 GT		0435GT	250GT	Boano?	Coupé	Pinin Farina			
	PF date:8/10/55. Low roof.								
0437 GT		0437 GT	250GT	Boano	Coupé	Boano			
	Low roof.								
0439 GT		0439GT	250GT	Boano	Coupé	Boano			
	Low roof.								
0441 GT		0441 GT	250GT	Boano	Coupé	Boano			U.S.A.
	Renumbered 0525GT. Low roof.All aluminum body								
0443 GT	P1/167	0443 GT	250GT	Boano	Coupé	Boano	Jean Estager	France	U.S.A.
	Sold on 8/5/56.Finished 1st OA in 1956 Alpine Rally driven by Estager. All aluminum.Low roof.								
0445 GT		0445 GT	250GT	Boano	Coupé	Pinin Farina			U.S.A.
	PF date:9/11/55 Last 250GT produced by PF. Prototype of "Boano/Ellena" coupé. Low roof.Engine in 0415GT.								
0447 GT		0447 GT	250GT	Boano	Coupé	Pinin Farina	M.Cantelli		U.S.A.
	PF date:31/10/55.Penultimate 250GT by PF 0445GT was the last one. Low roof.All aluminum body.								
0449 GT		0449 GT	250GT	Boano	Coupé	Boano			
	Low roof.								
0450 AM*	P2/99.	0450AM	375	Mille Miglia	Spyder	Pinin Farina	Emperor Bao Dai	France	France
	Later rebodied by Scaglietti as a special coupé!								
0451 GT		0451 GT	250GT	Boano	Coupé	Boano			
	Low roof.								
0453 GT		0453 GT	250GT	Boano	Coupé	Boano			
	Low roof.								

Chassis No.	Picture Ref.	Engine No.	Type	Model	Body Style	Coach-builder	First Owner	Original Location	Present Location
0455 GT		0455 GT	250GT	Boano	Coupé	Boano			
	Low roof.								
0456 AM	P1/110,111	0456AM	375	Mille Miglia	Coupé Speciale	Pinin Farina	Roberto Rossellini	Italy	U.S.A.
	First shown at the Paris Salon 1954. Concave areas behind front wheels believed the inspiration for similar feature on the 57 Corvette. One off show car.								
0457 GT		0457 GT	250GT	Boano	Coupé	Boano			
0459 GT		0459 GT	Boano	250GT	Coupé	Boano			
	Low roof.								
0460 AM*		0460AM	375	Mille Miglia	Spyder	Pinin Farina	Robert Day	U.S.A.	U.S.A.
	Sold as a road car for the first owner. Never raced.								
0461 GT	P1/172	0461 GT	250GT	Boano	Convertible	Boano	L.Chinetti/R.Lee	U.S.A.	U.S.A.
	Shown at the 1956 Geneva Auto Show and the 1956 New York Auto Show. First 250GT convertible. One off prototype design.								
0463 GT		0463 GT	250GT	Boano	Coupé	Boano			
	Michael Kowertz reported as owner.								
0465 GT		0465 GT	250GT	Boano	Coupé	Boano			
0467 GT		0467 GT	250GT	Boano?	Coupé?	Boano?		U.S.A.	
0469 GT		0469 GT	250GT	Boano	Coupé	Boano		U.S.A.	
0471 SA		0471 SA	410	Superamerica I	Coupé	Pinin Farina	Count Somsky	Switzerland	
0473 SA	P1/128	0473 SA	410	Superamerica I	Coupé	Ghia	Wilke	U.S.A.	U.S.A.
	Also reported as a '510' with special larger engine. Special design exercise by Savanuzzi for Ghia with huge rear fins.								
0475 SA		0475 SA	410	Superamerica I	Coupé	Pinin Farina	Carpenter		U.S.A.
	May be the car shown at the 1956 Paris Salon. 2.80m WB.								
0476 AM	P1/114.	0476 AM	375	Mille Miglia	Coupé	Ghia		U.S.A.?	U.S.A.
	Shown at the 1955 Turin Motor Show. Special one off design with angular lines not typical of Ghia.								
0477 SA	P1 129	0477 SA	410	Superamerica I	Coupé	Boano	Sisini		U.S.A.
	One off special coachwork. Shown at the 1956 Brussels Motor Show.								
0479 SA		0479 SA	410	Superamerica I	Coupé	Pinin Farina			U.K.
	2.80m WB.								
0481 SA	P1/127	0481 SA	410	Superamerica I	Coupé	Pinin Farina	Fred Lip	France	U.S.A.
	2.80m WB. No fender vents.								
0483 SA	P1/130	0483 SA	410	Superfast	Coupé	Pinin Farina	William Doheny	U.S.A.	U.S.A.
	Shown at the 1956 Paris Salon. Except for a brief stay in the U.K. has remained in the U.S.A. all its life. One off prototype styling exercise. 2.60m WB.								
0485 SA		0485 SA	410	Superamerica I	Convertible	Boano			U.S.A.
	Shown at the 1956 Turin Motor Show. The only 410SA convertible. One off prototype body.								
0487 SA		0487 SA	410	Superamerica I	Coupé	Pinin Farina			
	2.80mWB.								
0488 AM	P1/112	0488 AM	375+	Mille Miglia	Convertible	Pinin Farina	King Leopold	Belgium	U.S.A.
	A special one off body that would influence the future designs of PF convertibles and spyders.								
0489 SA		0489 SA	410	Superamerica I	Coupé	Pinin Farina	Edgar Fronteras	US Ferrari agent	U.S.A.
	Ordered for Robert Lee, U.S.A. with hidden compartment for Baretta pistol! 2.80m WB.								
0490 AM*	P2/89	0490 AM	375	Mille Miglia	Coupé Speciale	Pinin Farina			U.S.A.
	First shown at the 1955 Turin Motor Show. A special prototype show car.								
0491 SA		0491 SA	410	Superamerica I	Coupé	Pinin Farina			
	2.80mWB.								
0493 SA		0493 SA	410	Superamerica I	Coupé	Pinin Farina	Emperor Bao Dai	France	Italy
	PF date:4/4/56 2.80mWB.								
0495 SA		0495 SA	410	Superamerica II	Coupé	Pinin Farina	P.Barilla	Italy	U.S.A.
	Eventually shipped to U.S.A.. Reported with Engine/Transmission missing. 2.60m WB.								
0497 SA		0497 SA	410	Superamerica II	Coupé	Pinin Farina			U.S.A.
	2.60mWB.								
0499 SA		0499 SA	410	Superamerica II	Coupé	Pinin Farina			
	PF date:3/8/56 SWB. 2nd Series 410 Superamericas. 2.60mWB.								
0501 SA		0501 SA	410	Superamerica II	Coupé	Pinin Farina	Damman	Belgium	U.S.A.
	SWB. 2.60mWB.								
1956									
0503 GT	JP 44.	0503 GT	250 GT	Tour de France	Berlinetta	Scaglietti	A.Caraceni	Italy	U.S.A.
	Sold 8/5/56. 1st in GT in Mille Miglia and Tour de Sicily in 1956 driven by Gendebien/Washer! Raced again in 1957 and 1959. Rebodied in 1958 with 1958 style TdeF body. All aluminum body.								
0505 GT		0505 GT	250 GT	Boano	Coupé	Boano			
	Low Roof.								
0507 GT	JP 46.	0507 GT	250 GT	Tour de France	Berlinetta	Scaglietti	O.Randaccio	Italy	Denmark
	Completed on 23/4/56. Raced in 1957,1958,& 1959 in Italy and France. All aluminum body. Rear of body modified.								
0509 GT	JP 46.	0509 GT	250 GT	Tour de France	Berlinetta	Scaglietti	G.Giovanardi	Italy	U.S.A.
	Sold 27/5/56. Raced in 1956,1957 & 1958. All aluminum body.								
0511 GT		0511 GT	250 GT	Boano	Coupé	Boano			
0513 GT	JP 42.	0513 GT	250 GT	Tour de France	Berlinetta	Scaglietti	V.Colocci	Italy	U.S.A.?
	Sold 27/3/56. Raced in 1956 & 1957 in Italy,France and the U.S.A.. All aluminum body.								
0515 GT	JP 47,48.	0515 GT	250 GT	Tour de France	Berlinetta	Zagato	C.Luglio	Italy	Japan
	Sold 6/4/56. Raced in Italy in 1956. Raced in 1958 in Italy. Sold to U.S.A. in 1960. All aluminum one-off body.								
0517 GT		0517 GT	250 GT	Boano	Coupé	Boano			
	Low roof.								
0519 GT		0519 GT	250 GT	Boano	Coupé	Boano			
	Low roof.								

Chassis No.	Picture Ref.	Engine No.	Type	Model	Body Style	Coach-builder	First Owner	Original Location	Present Location
0521 GT		0521 GT	250 GT	Boano	Coupé	Boano			U.K.
	Low roof.								
0523 GT		0523 GT	250 GT	Boano	Coupé	Boano			U.S.A.
	Believed to have been Mr.Ferrari's personal car.								
0525 GT		0525 GT	250 GT	Boano	Coupé	Boano			U.S.A.
	Originally numbered 0441GT. Low roof.All aluminum body.								
0527 GT		0527 GT	250 GT	Boano	Coupé	Boano			U.S.A.
	Sold in 1956. Low roof. All aluminum body.								
0529 GT		0529 GT	250 GT	Boano	Coupé	Boano			U.S.A.?
0531 GT	P1/169.	0531 GT	250 GT	Speciale	Coupé	Boano			
	Sold in 1957. One off special body.Last Ferrari designed by Boano.								
0533 GT		0533 GT	250 GT	Boano	Coupé	Boano			
	Low roof.								
0535 GT		0535 GT	250 GT	Boano	Coupé	Boano			U.S.A.
	Low roof.All aluminum body.								
0537 GT		0537 GT	250 GT	Tour de France	Berlinetta	Zagato	C.Luglio/Vassali	Italy	U.S.A.?
	Sold 4/6/56.Raced in 1956 and 1957 in Italy. Sold to U.S.A. in 1960. All aluminum body.Special one-off body.								
0539 GT		0539 GT	250 GT	Tour de France	Berlinetta	Scaglietti	E.Lualdi	Italy	
	Sold 28/6/56.Raced in Italy in 1956. All aluminum body. One-off special body.								
0541 GT		0541 GT	250 GT	Boano	Coupé	Boano			
	Low roof.								
0543 GT		0543 GT	250 GT	Boano	Coupé	Boano			Canada
	Low roof.								
0545 GT		0545 GT	250 GT	Boano	Coupé	Boano			U.S.A.?
	Went from Italy to the U.K. to U.S.A.. Low roof.								
0547 GT		0547 GT	250 GT	Boano	Coupé	Boano			
	Low roof								
0549 GT		0549 GT	250 GT	Boano	Coupé	Boano			
	Low roof								
0551 GT		0551 GT	250 GT	Boano	Coupé	Boano			
	Low roof.								
0553 GT		0553 GT	250 GT	Boano	Coupé	Boano			
	Low roof.								
0555 GT	JP 43.	0555 GT	250 GT	Tour de France	Berlinetta	Scaglietti	Ferraro	Italy	U.S.A.
	Sold on 8/9/56.Finished 7th OA in 1956 Mille Miglia. Sold to U.S.A. in 1960s.Also reported to be another Tde F in Sicily? All aluminum body.								
0557 GT		0557 GT	250 GT	Tour de France	Coupé	Scaglietti	A.de Portago	Italy	U.K.
	First OA in the 1957 Tour de France driven by DePortago/Nelson.Sold to U.K. in 1957. All aluminum body.								
0559 GT		0559 GT	250 GT	Boano	Coupé	Boano			
	Low roof.								
0561 GT		0561 GT	250 GT	Boano	Coupé	Boano			
	Low roof.								
0563 GT	JP 45.	0563 GT	250 GT	Tour de France	Berlinetta	Scaglietti	Jacques Peron	France	U.S.A.
	Sold 10/9/56.Finished 8th OA in 1956 Tour de France.Finished 5th OA in 1957 driven always by Peron.Also raced in 1958 and sold to U.S.A.. Crashed in 1973 and totally rebuilt.All aluminum body.								
0565 GT		0565 GT	250 GT	Boano	Coupé	Boano			U.S.A.
	Low roof.								
0567 GT		0567 GT	250 GT	Boano	Coupé	Boano			
	Low roof.								
0569 GT		0569 GT	250 GT	Boano	Coupé	Boano			U.S.A.
	Low roof.All aluminum body.Parts car.								
0571 GT		0571 GT	250 GT	Boano	Coupé	Boano			U.S.A.
	Low roof.								
0573 GT		0573 GT	250 GT	Boano	Coupé	Boano			
	Low roof.								
0575 GT		0575 GT	250 GT	Boano	Coupé	Boano			
	Low roof.								
0577 GT		0577 GT	250 GT	Boano	Coupé	Boano			U.S.A.
	In U.S.A. for many years. Low roof.								
0579 GT		0579 GT	250 GT	Boano	Coupé	Boano			U.K.
	Low roof.All aluminum body.								
0581 GT		0581 GT	250 GT	Boano	Coupé	Boano			U.S.A.
	Low roof.								
0583 GT		0583 GT	250 GT	Boano	Coupé	Boano			
	Low roof.								
0585 GT		0585 GT	250 GT	Tour de France	Berlinetta	Scaglietti	Tony Parravano	U.S.A.	U.S.A.
	Sold on 15/11/56.Possibly never raced.All aluminum. First 14 louvre TdeF.								
0587 GT		0587 GT	250 GT	Boano	Coupé	Boano			U.K.?
	Low roof.								
0589 GT		0589 GT	250 GT	Boano	Coupé	Boano			
	Low roof.								
0591 GT		0591 GT	250 GT	Boano	Coupé	Boano			U.S.A.
	In U.S.A. for many years.Low roof.								
0593 GT		0593 GT	250 GT	Boano	Coupé	Boano			South Africa
	Low roof.								

Chassis No.	Picture Ref.	Engine No.	Type	Model	Body Style	Coach-builder	First Owner	Original Location	Present Location
0594 CM*	P1 136.	0594 CM	410	Sport	Coupé	Scaglietti	Michel Paul-Cavallier	France	France
	Rebodied for the first owner for road use. It had been built as a true 410 Sport sports/racing car.								
0595 GT		0595 GT	250 GT	Boano	Coupé	Boano			
	Low roof.								
0597 GT		0597 GT	250 GT	Tour de France	Berlinetta	Scaglietti	E.Lubish	Italy	
	Sold on 2/1/57. Raced throughout 1957,1958,1959 in Italy and a race in South America in 1960. All aluminum body. 14 louvres.								
0599 GT		0599 GT	250 GT	Boano	Coupé	Boano			
	Low roof.								
0601 GT		0601 GT	250 GT	Boano	Coupé	Boano			Switzerland
	In Switzerland for many years. v								
0603 GT		0603 GT	250 GT	Boano	Coupé	Boano			U.S.A.
	Low roof. All aluminum body.								
0605 GT		0605 GT	250 GT	Boano	Coupé	Boano			U.S.A.
	In U.S.A. for many years. Low roof.								
0607 GT		0607 GT	250 GT	Tour de France	Berlinetta	Scaglietti	Cavazzoli/W.Seidel		France
	Sold on 2/2/57. Finished 4th OA in the 1957 Tour of Sicily. Finished 2nd OA in the 1957 12 Hours of Rheims driven by Seidel and Phil Hill. Sold to France and further raced in 1958 and 1959 by Jean Guichet..All aluminum 14 louvre.								
0609 GT		0609 GT	250 GT	Boano	Coupé	Boano			
	Low roof.								
0611 GT		0611 GT	250 GT	Boano	Coupé	Boano			
	Low roof.								
0613 GT		0613 GT	250 GT	Boano	Coupé	Boano			U.K.
	Low roof.								
0615 GT		0615 GT	250 GT	Boano	Coupé	Boano			
	Low roof.								
0617 GT		0617 GT	250 GT	Boano	Coupé	Boano			U.K.
	Low roof.								
0619 GT		0619 GT	250 GT	Tour de France	Berlinetta	Scaglietti	Motorval		U.S.A.
	Sold on 28/3/1957. Finished 8th OA in 1957 Tour de France. Sold to Venezuela, crashed, returned to factory and rebodied with early 1958 style TdeF body; also renumbered 0805GT by the factory.								
0621 GT		0621 GT	250 GT	Boano	Coupé	Boano			U.S.A.
	In U.S.A. for many years. Low roof.								
0623 GT		0623 GT	250 GT	Boano	Coupé	Boano	Luigi Chinetti?	U.S.A.	U.S.A.
	In U.S.A. for many years. Low roof.								
0625 GT		0625 GT	250 GT	Boano	Coupé	Boano	Luigi Chinetti?	U.S.A.	U.S.A.
	.Low roof.								
0627 GT		0627 GT	250 GT	Boano	Coupé	Boano			Italy
	In U.S.A. for many years having arrived as a rebody with a 195LWB California Spider body by Scaglietti.								
0629 GT		0629 GT	250 GT	Tour de France	Berlinetta	Scaglietti	P.Lena		U.S.A.
	Sold on 6/2/57. Raced in 1957,1958 & 1959. Sold to U.S.A. in 1960s..All aluminum 14 louvre.								
0631 GT		0631 GT	250 GT	Boano	Coupé	Boano			U.S.A.
	Low roof.								
0633 GT		0633 GT	250 GT	Boano	Coupé	Boano			U.S.A.
	Low roof.								
0635 GT		0635 GT	250 GT	Boano	Coupé	Boano			
	Low roof.								
0637 GT		0637 GT	250 GT	Boano	Coupé	Boano	Volteres		Engine only in U.S.A.
	Reported in Venezuela. Also, 1029GT was renumbered by the factory to 0637GT!! Low roof.								
0639 GT		0639 GT	250 GT	Boano	Coupé	Boano			U.K.
	Low roof.								
0641 GT		0641 GT	250 GT	Boano	Coupé	Boano			U.S.A.
	In U.S.A. for many years. Low roof.								
0643 GT		0643 GT	250 GT	Boano	Coupé	Boano			
	Low roof.								
0645 GT		0645 GT	250 GT	Boano	Coupé	Boano			
	Low roof.								
0647 GT		0647 GT	250 GT	Tour de France	Berlinetta	Scaglietti	Lualdi Gabardi	Italy	U.S.A. (spares only)
	Sold on 7/3/57. Raced in 1957,1958 and sold to U.S.A. in late 1958. 14 louvres. Badly crashed & broken up for spares.								

1957

Chassis No.	Picture Ref.	Engine No.	Type	Model	Body Style	Coach-builder	First Owner	Original Location	Present Location
0649 GT		0649 GT	250 GT	Boano	Coupé	Boano			
	Low roof.								
0651 GT		0651 GT	250 GT	Boano	Coupé	Boano			U.K.
	In U.K. for many years. Low roof.								
0653 GT		0653 GT	250 GT	Boano	Coupé	Boano			Switzerland?
	Sold from Switzerland years ago. Low roof.								
0655 GT	P1/173.	0655 GT	250 GT	Series I	Spyder	Pininfarina	Peter Collins	Italy	U.S.A.
	PF date: 28/12/56. Sold in 1957. Shown at the 1957 Geneva Motor Show. Used as personal transport by Peter Collins. Later sold to U.S.A..Special spyder body with left door cut down. Prototype Series I.								
0657 GT		0657 GT	250 GT	Boano	Coupé	Boano			
	Low roof.								
0659 GT		0659 GT	250 GT	Boano	Coupé	Boano			
	Low roof.								
0661 GT		0661 GT	250 GT	Boano	Coupé	Boano			
	Low roof.								

Chassis No.	Picture Ref.	Engine No.	Type	Model	Body Style	Coach-builder	First Owner	Original Location	Present Location
0663 GT	P1/174 ,175.	0663 GT	250 GT	Series I	Spyder	Pininfarina	Leon Dernier	Belgium	Holland
	Sold in 1957. Called 'Spyder Competizione' by PF. Prototype Series I.								
0665 GT	JP 53.	0665 GT	250 GT	Tour de France	Berlinetta	Zagato	Vassali/Luglio	Italy	Germany
	Sold on 10/6/57. Raced with great success in 1957 and 1958 in Italy. Sold to U.S.A. in 1959. Sold to Germany in 1979. All aluminum special body.								
0667 GT		0667 GT	250 GT	Boano	Coupé	Boano			U.S.A.
	Sold from U.K. to U.S.A.. Low roof.								
0669 GT		0669 GT	250 GT	Boano	Coupé	Boano			
	Reported also to be a Series I Pinin Farina Convertible but not confirmed.								
0671 SA	P1/134.	0671 SA	410	Superamerica	Berlinetta	Scaglietti	Dr. Wax	Geneva	U.S.A.
	Special one off design with untypical chrome trim and fins at the rear!								
0673 GT		0673 GT	250 GT	Boano	Coupé	Boano			
	Low roof.								
0675 GT		0675 GT	250 GT	Boano	Coupé	Boano			
	Believed last low roof Boano made.								
0677 GT		0677 GT	250 GT	Tour de France	Berlinetta	Scaglietti	Ferrari	Italy	U.S.A.
	Made available for O.Gendebien early in 1957. Finished 3rd OA in the 1957 Mille Miglia! Raced with success the rest of 1957 and 1958. Raced in 1959 and sold to U.S.A.. All aluminum 14 louvre. All aluminum 14 louvre.								
0679 GT		0679 GT	250 GT	Boano	Coupé	Ellena			Sweden
	In Sweden for many years. High roof.								
0681 GT		0681 GT	250 GT	Boano	Coupé	Ellena			Holland
	High roof.								
0683 GT	JP 49.	0683 GT	250 GT	Tour de France	Berlinetta	Scaglietti	O.Cappelli	Italy	Venezuela?
	Sold on 19/4/57. Raced during 1957 thru 1959 and sold to Venezuela. All aluminum 14 louvre.								
0685 GT		0685 GT	250 GT	Boano	Coupé	Ellena			
	High roof.								
0687 GT		0687 GT	250 GT	Boano	Coupé	Ellena			
	High roof.								
0689 GT	JP 54.	0689 GT	250 GT	Tour de France	Berlinetta	Zagato	Di Micheli	Italy	U.S.A.
	Sold on 29/3/57. Raced in 1958 and 1960 in Italy. Sold to U.S.A. in 1960s. All aluminum one off special body.								
0691 GT		0691 GT	250 GT	Boano	Coupé	Ellena			
	High roof.								
0693 GT		0693 GT	250 GT	Boano	Coupé	Ellena			U.S.A.
	Reported as 'Low roof' but not confirmed.								
0695 GT		0695 GT	250 GT	Boano	Coupé	Ellena			
	High roof.								
0697 GT		0697 GT	250 GT	Boano	Coupé	Ellena			
	High roof.								
0699 GT		0699 GT	250 GT	Boano	Coupé	Ellena			Switzerland
	Last reported in Switzerland. High roof.								
0701 GT		0701 GT	250 GT	Boano	Coupé	Ellena			
	High roof.								
0703 GT		0703 GT	250 GT	Tour de France	Berlinetta	Scaglietti	A.Buticchi	Italy	U.S.A.
	Sold on 7/5/57. Raced in Italy in 1957 and 1958. Sold to U.S.A. in 1960. All aluminum 14 louvre.								
0705 GT	P1/178.	0705 GT	250 GT	Series I	Spyder	Pininfarina	M.Meert	Belgium	Holland
	Sold on 2/5/57. Special body. Prototype Series I.								
0707 GT		0707 GT	250 GT	Tour de France	Berlinetta	Scaglietti	Garage Francorchamps	Belgium	U.K.
	Sold on 19/7/57. Raced in 1957,1958 & 1959 in Holland, Belgium and France. Sold to U.S.A. in late 1960s. Later sold to U.K.. All aluminum body. Last 14 louvre TdeF made.								
0709 GT	P1/176.	0709 GT	250 GT	Series I	Spyder	Pininfarina	Prince Aga Khan	Paris,France	
	Sold on 2/5/57. Special body. Prototype Series I.								
0711 GT		0711 GT	250 GT	Boano	Coupé	Ellena			
	High roof.								
0713 SA	P1/133.	0713 SA	410	Superamerica II	Coupé	Pininfarina	R.Wolfe	U.S.A.	U.S.A.
	Sold on 28/6/57. Special body. 2.60m WB.								
0715 SA		0715 SA	410	Superamerica II	Coupé	Pininfarina	Morgan	U.S.A.	U.S.A.
	Sold on 4/7/57. Special body. 2.60m WB.								
0717 SA		0717 SA	410	Superamerica II	Coupé	Pininfarina			U.S.A.
	Possibly shown at 1957 Paris Salon. Special body. 2.60m WB.								
0719 SA	P1/135.	0719 SA	410	Superamerica II	Coupé	Pininfarina	Jan DeVroom	U.S.A.	U.S.A.
	Shown at the 57 Turin Motor Show. Totally new styling using elements of the 1956 Superfast I. Specially built 4.9 litre Superfast. 2.60m WB.								
0721 SA	P1/132.	0721SA	410	Superamerica II	Coupé	Pininfarina			U.S.A.
	Sold on 10/10/57. Shown at the 1957 Turin Motor Show. Special body. 2.60m WB.								
0723 GT		0723 GT	250 GT	Tour de France	Berlinetta	Scaglietti	Curt Lincoln	Sweden	Finland?
	Sold on 6/8/57. Raced in Sweden and Finland in 1957,1958, and 1959. Finally in a museum in Helsinki. All aluminum body with 3 vents on each side.								
0725 GT	P1/171.	0725 GT	250 GT	Speciale	Coupé	Pininfarina	Prince Bernhard	Holland	U.S.A.
	Sold on 4/7/57. Special body.								
0727 GT		0727 GT	250 GT	Boano?	Coupé?	Ellena?			
	Also reported to be a Series I PF Convertible.								
0729 GT		0729 GT	250 GT	Series I	Convertible	Pininfarina	Oscar Olson	U.S.A.	U.S.A.
	Sold on 4/7/57. Special body.								
0731 GT		0731 GT	250 GT	Tour de France	Berlinetta	Scaglietti	Malle	France	France
	Sold on 4/4/57. Raced in France in 1957 and 1958. All aluminum body with 3 vents each side like 0723GT.								

Chassis No.	Picture Ref.	Engine No.	Type	Model	Body Style	Coach-builder	First Owner	Original Location	Present Location
0733 GT		0733 GT	250 GT	Tour de France	Berlinetta	Scaglietti	Trintignant/Shell	France	U.S.A.
		Sold on 23/7/57.Finished 2nd OA in the 1957 Tour De France. Raced in 1958.Sold to U.S.A. in 1968. All aluminum body like 0723GT.3 vents.							
0735 GT		0735 GT	250 GT	Series I	Convertible	Pininfarina	Munemann	Germany	U.S.A.
		PF date:31/7/57.Shown at 1957 Frankfurt Motor Show. Sold from U.K. to U.S.A. about 1980. Special body.							
0737 GT	P1/178.	0737 GT	250 GT	Series I	Convertible	Pininfarina	Willard	France	France
		Shown at 1957 Paris Salon.							
0739 GT		0739 GT	250 GT	Boano	Coupé	Ellena			
	High roof.								
0741 GT		0741 GT	250 GT	Boano	Coupé	Ellena			
	High roof.								
0743 GT		0743 GT	250 GT	Boano	Coupé	Ellena		South Africa?	Finland
	High roof.								
0745 GT		0745 GT	250 GT	Boano	Coupé	Ellena			U.S.A. (parts only)
	Scrapped in 1982.High roof.								
0747 GT		0747 GT	250 GT	Tour de France	Berlinetta	Scaglietti	Aumas	Switzerland	Italy
		Sold on 6/10/57.Raced in 1957 and 1958.All aluminum 3 louver body.							
0749 GT		0749 GT	250 GT	Tour de France	Berlinetta	Scaglietti	Estager	France	France?
		Sold on 20/7/57.Raced in 1957 and 1958. All aluminum 3 louvre body.							
0751 GT	P1/171.	0751 GT	250 GT	Speciale?	Coupé	Pininfarina	Princess L De Rethy	Belgium	U.S.A.
	One off special body.								
0753 GT		0753 GT	250 GT	Tour de France	Berlinetta	Scaglietti	R.Cowles	U.S.A.	U.S.A.
		Sold on 28/9/57.Raced briefly. All aluminum 3 louvre body.							
0755 GT		0755 GT	250 GT	Boano	Coupé	Ellena			U.S.A.?
	High roof.								
0757 GT		0757 GT	250 GT	Boano	Coupé	Ellena			
	High roof.								
0759 GT		0759 GT	250 GT	Series I	Cabriolet	Pininfarina			
		Sold on 9/9/57.Believed shown at 57 Turin Motor Show.							
0761 GT		0761 GT	250 GT	Boano	Coupé	Ellena			
	High roof.								
0763 GT		0763 GT	250 GT	Tour de France	Berlinetta	Scaglietti	L.Dernier	Belgium	France
		Sold on 21/10/57.Briefly raced in 1958 and 1959. All aluminum 3 louvre body.							
0765 GT		0765 GT	250 GT	Boano	Coupé	Ellena			
	High roof.								
0767 GT		0767 GT	250 GT	Tour de France	Berlinetta	Scaglietti	A.Caraceni	Italy	Italy
		Sold on 13/11/57.Raced in 1958. All aluminum 3 louvre body.							
0769 GT	P1/211	0769 GT	250 GTY	LWB California	Spyder	Pininfarina	George Arents	U.S.A.	U.S.A.
		Completed 16/12/57.Prototype California Spyder.Believed shown at the 1957 Paris Salon.Covered headlights. Steel body. Crisper lines than later production cars.							
0771 GT		0771 GT	250 GT	Tour de France	Berlinetta	Scaglietti	H.Schaub?	U.S.A.	U.S.A.
		Sold on 16/12/57. All aluminum 3 louvre body.							
0773 GT		0773 GT	250 GT	Tour de France	Berlinetta	Scaglietti	George Arents	U.S.A.	Italy
		Sold on 14/11/57.Raced in 1957 & 1958. All aluminum 3 louvre body.							
0775 GT		0775 GT	250 GT	Series I	Convertible	Pininfarina	George Arents	U.S.A.	U.S.A.
	Sold on 3/10/57.								
0777 GT		0777 GT	250 GT	Series I	Convertible	Pininfarina	G. Fassio	Italy	U.S.A.
	Sold on 14/10/57.								
0779 GT		0779 GT	250 GT	Series I	Convertible	Pininfarina	Max Hoffman	U.S.A.	U.S.A.?
	Sold on 14/10/57.								
0781 GT		0781 GT	250 GT	Tour de France	Berlinetta	Scaglietti	H. Dulles	Switzerland	Sweden
		Sold on 20/12/57.Never raced. All aluminum 3 louvre body.							
0783 GT		0783 GT	250 GT	Series I	Convertible	Pininfarina	P.Rubirosa	France	
	Sold on 14/10/57.								
0785 GT		0785 GT	250 GT	Boano	Coupé	Ellena	Luigi Chinetti	U.S.A.	U.S.A.
	High roof.								
0787 GT		0787 GT	250 GT	Tour de France	Berlinetta	Scaglietti	O.Papais	Italy	Italy
		Sold on 10/2/58.Raced in 1958 and 1959. All aluminum 3 louvre body.							
0789 GT	P1 180.	0789 GT	250 GT	Series I	Cabriolet	Pininfarina	Fassio A.	Italy	Italy
	Sold on 18/10/57.								
0791 GT		0791 GT	250 GT	Series I	Convertible	Pininfarina	Pauetto	Italy	U.S.A.
	Sold on 18/10/57.								
0793 GT		0793 GT	250 GT	Tour de France	Berlinetta	Scaglietti	Giovanardi	Italy	Italy
		Sold on 13/3/58.Raced in 1958 and 1959. All aluminum 3 louvre body.							
0795 GT		0795 GT	250 GT	Series I	Convertible	Pininfarina	Dauffe	Belgium	U.S.A.
	Sold on 19/10/57.								
0797 GT		0797 GT	250 GT	PF Notchback	Coupé	Pininfarina			U.S.A.?
	Believed first prototype of 250GT PF Notchback Coupé.								
0799 GT		0799 GT	250 GT	Series I	Convertible	Pininfarina	Fabbri	Italy	U.S.A.
	PF date: 5/11/57.								
0801 GT		0801 GT	250 GT	Series I	Convertible	Pininfarina	Di Stefano		U.S.A.
		Shown at the 1958 Geneva Motor Show. Modified over the years. Reported with non-original engine.							
0803 GT		0803 GT	250 GT	Boano	Coupé	Ellena			U.S.A.
	High roof.								

Chassis No.	Picture Ref.	Engine No.	Type	Model	Body Style	Coach-builder	First Owner	Original Location	Present Location
0805 GT		0805 GT	250 GT	Tour de France	Berlinetta	Scaglietti	Pierre Noblet	France	U.S.A.(both?)
	Sold in January 1958. Raced in 1958, 1959 and 1960. Badly crashed. The factory renumbered 0619GT as 0805GT. However the crashed 0805GT still exists with Chassis and Engine No.0805GT! All aluminum 3 louvre body.								
0807 GT		0807 GT	250 GT	Boano	Coupé	Ellena			
	High roof.								
0809 GT		0809 GT	250 GT	Series I	Convertible	Pininfarina	Rifferts		U.S.A.
	Sold on 16/11/57. Shown at the 1958 New York Auto Show.								
0811 GT*		0811 GT	250 GT	Series I	Convertible	Pininfarina	Ager Motors/Lupini	South Africa	South Africa
	Sold on 9/11/57.								
0813 GT		0813 GT	250 GT	Series I	Convertible	Pininfarina	Norman		U.S.A.
	Sold on 19/11/57.								
0815 GT		0815 GT	250 GT	Boano	Coupé	Ellena			U.S.A.
	High roof.								
0817 GT		0817 GT	250 GT	Boano	Coupé	Ellena			
	High roof.								
0819 GT		0819 GT	250 GT	Boano	Coupé	Pininfarina			U.S.A.
0821 GT		0821 GT	250 GT	Boano	Coupé	Pininfarina			
0823 GT		0823 GT	250 GT	Boano	Coupé	Ellena			
	High roof.								
0825 GT		0825 GT	250 GT	Boano	Coupé	Ellena			
	High roof.								
0827 GT		0827 GT	250 GT	Boano	Coupé	Ellena			
	High roof.								
0829 GT		0829 GT	250 GT	Series I	Convertible	Pininfarina	Du Pont	U.S.A.	U.S.A.
	Sold on 22/11/57.								
0831 GT		0831 GT	250 GT	Boano	Coupé	Ellena			
	High roof.								
0833 GT		0833 GT	250 GT	Boano	Coupé	Ellena			
	High roof.								
0835 GT		0835 GT	250 GT	Boano	Coupé	Ellena			
	High roof.								
0837 GT		0837 GT	250 GT	Boano	Coupé	Ellena			
	.High roof.								
0839 GT		0839 GT	250 GT	Boano	Coupé	Ellena	Luigi Chinetti	U.S.A.	U.S.A.
	In U.S.A. since new. High roof.								
0841 GT	P1/184.	0841 GT	250 GT	PF Notchback	Coupé	Pininfarina	J. C. Roussel	France	France?
	PF date:13/12/57. Prototype PF Notchback.								
0843 GT	P1/184.	0843 GT	250 GT	PF Notchback	Coupé	Pininfarina	H. Rousell	France	France?
	PF date:13/12/57. Prototype PF Notchback.								
				1958					
0845 GT		0845 GT	250 GT	Series I	Convertible	Pininfarina	Ferrari Reps of California	U.S.A.	U.S.A.?
	PF date:4/1/58.								
0847 GT		0847 GT	250 GT	Boano	Coupé	Ellena	Luigi Chinetti	U.S.A.	
	High roof.								
0849 GT		0849 GT	250 GT	Series I	Convertible	Pininfarina	Zacchirin	France	France
	PF date:13/1/58.								
0851 GT		0851 GT	250 GT	PF Notchback	Coupé	Pininfarina			U.S.A.
	Believed to be the first pre-production PF notchback coupé.								
0853 GT	P1 185.	0853 GT	250 GT	PF Notchback	Special Coupé	Pininfarina	Prince Bertil, Sweden	Sweden	
	PF completion date:13/12/57. Believed to be another pre-production prototype for the PF notchback coupé.								
0855 GT		0855 GT	250 GT	Boano	Coupé	Ellena	Luigi Chinetti	U.S.A.	U.S.A.
	Imported new to U.S.A.. High roof.								
0857 GT		0857 GT	250 GT	Boano	Coupé	Ellena	Luigi Chinetti?	U.S.A.?	U.S.A.
	Believed to be in U.S.A. since new. High roof.								
0859 GT		0859 GT	250 GT	Boano	Coupé	Ellena			
	High roof.								
0861 GT		0861 GT	250 GT	Boano	Coupé	Ellena			U.S.A.
	High roof.								
0863 GT		0863 GT	250 GT	Boano	Coupé	Ellena			
	High roof.								
0865 GT*		0865 GT	250 GT	Boano	Coupé	Ellena			
	High roof.								
0867 GT		0867 GT	250 GT	Boano	Coupé	Ellena			U.S.A.
	High roof.								
0869 GT		0869 GT	250 GT	Boano	Coupé	Ellena		U.S.A.?	U.S.A.
	High roof.								
0871 GT		0871 GT	250 GT	Boano	Coupé	Ellena	Pittsburg Plate Glass	U.S.A.	U.S.A.
	High roof.								
0873 GT		0873 GT	250 GT	Series I	Convertible	Pininfarina	L.Chinetti /R.Thompson	U.S.A.	U.S.A.
	PF date:18/1/58.								
0875 GT		0875 GT	250 GT	Boano	Coupé	Ellena	Luigi Chinetti	U.S.A.	U.S.A.
	High roof.								
0877 GT		0877 GT	250 GT	Boano	Coupé	Ellena			
	High roof.								

Chassis No.	Picture Ref.	Engine No.	Type	Model	Body Style	Coach-builder	First Owner	Original Location	Present Location
0879 GT		0879 GT	250 GT	Tour de France	Berlinetta	Scaglietti	W.Seidel	Austria	Sweden
		Raced in 1958 and 1959. All aluminum 3 louvre body.							
0881 GT		0881 GT	250 GT	Tour de France	Berlinetta	Scaglietti		Belgium	Belgium?
		Sold on 25/2/58.All aluminum 3 louvre body.							
0883 GT		0883 GT	250 GT	Boano	Coupé	Ellena			U.S.A. (with V Ford engine)
		High roof.							
0885 GT		0885 GT	250 GT	Boano	Coupé	Ellena			
		High roof.							
0887 GT		0887 GT	250 GT	Boano	Coupé	Ellena			U.S.A.?
		High roof.Last Boano style Ellena coupé made.							
0889 GT		0889 GT	250 GT	PF Notchback	Coupé	Pininfarina			
		Believed to be PF Notchback prototype.							
0891 GT		0891 GT	250 GT	PF Notchback	Coupé	Pininfarina			
0893 GT		0893 GT	250 GT	Tour de France	Berlinetta	Scaglietti	George Reed	U.S.A.	U.S.A.
		Sold in 1958.Raced from 1958 thru 1963. All aluminum 3 louvre body.							
0895 GT		0895 GT	250 GT	Tour de France	Berlinetta	Scaglietti	C.Marchi	Italy	U.S.A.
		Sold on 21/3/58.Probably not raced. All aluminum 3 louvre body.Last 3 louvre produced.							
0897 GT		0897 GT	250 GT	Tour de France	Berlinetta	Scaglietti	Steve Earle	U.S.A.	U.S.A.
		In U.S.A. since new.Never raced. All aluminum 1 louver body.Covered headlights.							
0899 GT		0899 GT	250 GT	Tour de France	Berlinetta	Scaglietti	Lualdi	Italy	France (parts only).
		Sold in March 1958.In 1960 crashed and parted out.All aluminum 1 louver body.Covered headlights.							
0901 GT		0901 GT	250 GT	Tour de France	Berlinetta	Scaglietti	F.Picard	France	Europe
		Raced in 1958 and shipped to U.S.A.. All aluminum body.Open headlights.							
0903 GT		0903 GT	250 GT	Tour de France	Berlinetta	Scaglietti	T.Bjorstrom/Nottorp	Sweden	Sweden?
		Raced in 1958. All aluminum 1 louver body.							
0905 GT		0905 GT	250 GT	Tour de France	Berlinetta	Scaglietti	Ferraro	Italy	U.S.A.
		Raced in Italy in 1958 and shipped to U.S.A.. All aluminum 1 louvre body.Covered headlights.							
0907 GT		0907 GT	250 GT	Tour de France	Berlinetta	Scaglietti	Derstefanian	Italy	Italy?
		Raced in 1958. All aluminum body with 1 louvre							
0909 GT	JP 62.	0909 GT	250 GT	Tour de France	Berlinetta	Scaglietti	Lambert	Switzerland	Switzerland
		Raced in Switzerland from 1958 to 1961. All aluminum body with 1 louvre.Covered headlights.							
0911 GT		0911 GT	250 GT	Tour de France	Berlinetta	Scaglietti	Taramazzo	Italy	U.K.
		Completed 27/5/58.Raced in 1958 and 1959.All aluminum body with 1 louver..							
0913 GT		0913 GT	250 GT	Series I	Convertible	Pininfarina	Lacloche		U.K.
		PF date :21/3/58.							
0915 GT		0915 GT	250 GT	Series I	Convertible	Pininfarina	Reggiani	Italy	U.S.A.
		PF date:21/3/58.							
0917 GT		0917 GT	250 GT	Series I	Convertible	Pininfarina	Longhi	Italy	U.S.A.
		PF date:21/3/58.							
0919 GT		0919 GT	250 GT	LWB California	Spyder	Scaglietti			U.S.A.
		Completed on June 1958. Covered headlight.							
0921 GT*		0921 GT	250 GT	Series I	Convertible	Pininfarina	I.S.C.Ltd.	Hong Kong	Sweden
0923 GT		0923 GT	250 GT	LWB California	Spyder	Scaglietti			U.S.A.
		Completed July 1958.Last reported with Engine 1855GT but may have original engine. Covered headlight.							
0925 GT		0925 GT	250 GT	Tour de France	Berlinetta	Scaglietti	William Harrah	U.S.A.	U.S.A.
		Sold on 26/7/58.In U.S.A. since new.Never raced. All aluminum body with 1 louvre.							
0927 GT		0927 GT	250 GT	LWB California	Spyder	Scaglietti			U.S.A.
		Covered headlights.							
0929 GT		0929 GT	250 GT	LWB California	Spyder	Scaglietti			U.S.A.
		Completed 2/8/58. Covered headlights.							
0931 GT		0931 GT	250 GT	Tour de France	Berlinetta	Scaglietti	Ghersi	Italy	Belgium?
		Sold on 26/5/58.Never raced. Crashed and modified in making repairs. All aluminum body.with 1 louvre.							
0933 GT		0933 GT	250 GT	Tour de France	Berlinetta	Scaglietti	Toselli	Italy	France
		Sold on 17/6/58.Raced in 1958 and 1959. All aluminum body with 1 louver.							
0935 GT		0935 GT	250 GT	LWB California	Spyder	Scaglietti			U.S.A.
		Covered headlights.							
0937 GT		0937 GT	250 GT	LWB California	Spyder	Scaglietti			Japan
		Completed on July 1958. Covered headlights.							
0939 GT		0939 GT	250 GT	LWB California	Spyder	Scaglietti			U.S.A.
		Covered headlights.							
0941 GT		0941 GT	250 GT	PF Notchback	Coupé	Pininfarina			U.S.A.
0943 GT		0943 GT	250 GT	PF Notchback	Coupé	Pininfarina			
0945 GT		0945 GT	250 GT	PF Notchback	Coupé	Pininfarina			
0947 GT		0947 GT	250 GT	PF Notchback	Coupé	Pininfarina			U.S.A.
0949 GT		0949 GT	250 GT	PF Notchback	Coupé	Pininfarina			France
0951 GT		0951 GT	250 GT	PF Notchback	Coupé	Pininfarina			
0953 GT		0953 GT	250 GT	PF Notchback	Coupé	Pininfarina			
0955 GT		0955 GT	250 GT	PF Notchback	Coupé	Pininfarina			U.S.A.
0957 GT		0957 GT	250 GT	Tour de France	Berlinetta	Scaglietti			
		Not on Jess Pourret's list. All aluminum body.							
0959 GT		0959 GT	250 GT	PF Notchback	Coupé	Pininfarina			
0961 GT		0961 GT	250 GT	Series I	Convertible	Pininfarina	Ben Rosenberg		
		PF date:17/5/58.							

Chassis No.	Picture Ref.	Engine No.	Type	Model	Body Style	Coach-builder	First Owner	Original Location	Present Location
0963 GT		0963 GT	250 GT	Series I	Convertible	Pininfarina	Count Volpi	Italy	U.S.A.
	PF date:17/5/58.								
0965 GT		0965 GT	250 GT	LWB California	Spyder	Scaglietti			U.S.A.
	Covered headlights.								
0967 GT		0967 GT	250 GT	Tour de France	Berlinetta	Scaglietti	Ferrari Reps of Hollywood	U.S.A.	France
	Sold on 31/7/58.Raced in 1958 & 1959. All aluminum body.with 1 louvre.								
0969 GT	JP 62.	0969 GT	250 GT	Tour de France	Berlinetta	Scaglietti	Mairesse	Belgium	U.S.A.
	Sold on 4/7/58.Raced in 1958 and 1959. All aluminum body.with 1 louvre.								
0971 GT		0971 GT	250 GT	Tour de France	Berlinetta	Scaglietti	P.Faure	Switzerland	Sweden
	Raced in 1958 and 1959. All aluminum body with 1 louvre.								
0973 GT	JP 61.	0973 GT	250 GT	Tour de France	Berlinetta	Scaglietti	Bourillot	France	France
	Sold on 30/8/58.Raced in 1958 thru 1960. All aluminum body with 1 louvre.								
0975 GT		0975 GT	250 GT	PF Notchback	Coupé	Pininfarina			
0977 GT		0977 GT	250 GT		Coupé	Drogo	Siebenthal?	Switzerland?	U.S.A.
	Probably built originally as a PF notchback. Special one off custom all aluminum body.								
0979 GT		0979 GT	250 GT	Series I	Convertible	Pininfarina	Count Portanova	Italy	
	PF date:26/6/58.								
0981 GT		0981 GT	250 GT	Series I	Convertible	Pininfarina	Chinetti/P.Norair	U.S.A.	U.S.A.
	Shown at the 1958 Paris Salon.								
0983 GT		0983 GT	250 GT	PF Notchback	Coupé	Pininfarina	Suzanna Agnelli	Italy	U.S.A.
	Shipped to U.S.A. in late 1960s. Fibreglass trunk panel.								
0985 GT		0985 GT	250 GT	PF Notchback	Coupé	Pininfarina			U.S.A.
	In U.S.A. from early 1960s. Single distributor.								
0987 GT		0987 GT	250 GT	PF Notchback	Coupé	Pininfarina			
0989 GT		0989 GT	250 GT	PF Notchback	Coupé	Pininfarina			
	Believed Shown at the 1958 Paris Salon.								
0991 GT		0991 GT	250 GT	PF Coupé	PF Notchback	Pininfarina			
0993 GT		0993 GT	250 GT	PF Notchback	Coupé	Pininfarina			U.S.A.
0995 GT		0995 GT	250 GT	PF Notchback	Coupé	Pininfarina			
0997 GT		0997 GT	250 GT	PF Notchback	Coupé	Pininfarina			U.S.A.
0999 GT		0999 GT	250 GT	Series I	Convertible	Pininfarina			Holland
	Renumbered by factory from 0663GT.See 0663GT for details.								
1001 GT*		1001 GT	250 GT	PF Notchback	Coupé	Pininfarina			U.K.?
1003 GT		1003 GT	250 GT	PF Notchback	Coupé	Pininfarina			
1005 GT		1005 GT	250 GT	PF Notchback	Coupé	Pininfarina			U.S.A.
1007 GT		1007 GT	250 GT	PF Notchback	Coupé	Pininfarina	Chinetti/W.J.Bryan	U.S.A.	U.S.A.
	Special instruments and trim from factory.								
1009 GT		1009 GT	250 GT	PF Notchback	Coupé	Pininfarina			
1011 GT		1011 GT	250 GT	LWB California	Spyder	Scaglietti			U.S.A.
	Covered headlights.								
1013 GT		1013 GT	250 GT	PF Notchback	Coupé	Pininfarina	Day	Paris	U.S.A.
	Sold on 11/7/58.								
1015 SA		1015 SA	410 Superamerica	Series III	Coupé	Pininfarina	Day	U.S.A.	U.S.A.
	Shown at the 1958 Paris Salon and Turin Motor Show.The prototype - the first Series III 410 Superamerica.								
1017 GT		1017 GT	250 GT	PF Notchback	Coupé	Pininfarina	Mr Agnelli	Italy	
1019 GT		1019 GT	250 GT	PF Notchback	Coupé	Pininfarina			
1021 GT		1021 GT	250 GT	PF Notchback	Coupé	Pininfarina			U.S.A. (Engine gearbox only)
1023 GT		1023 GT	250 GT	PF Notchback	Coupé	Pininfarina			
1025 GT		1025 GT	250 GT	PF Notchback	Coupé	Pininfarina			
1027 GT		1027 GT	250 GT	PF Notchback	Coupé	Pininfarina			U.S.A.
	Built in 1959								
1029 GT		1029 GT	250 GT	PF Notchback	Coupé	Pininfarina			
	Was renumbered by factory to 0637GT								
1031 GT		1031 GT	250 GT	Tour de France	Berlinetta	Scaglietti	J.Peron	France	U.S.A.
	Sold on 12/9/58. Raced in 1958 and 1959. All aluminium body.								
1033 GT	JP 63.	1033 GT	250 GT	Tour de France	Berlinetta	Scaglietti	Gendebien	Belgium	France?
	Raced in 1958 and 1959.All aluminium body.								
1035 GT		1035 GT	250 GT	Tour de France	Berlinetta	Scaglietti	Gomez-Mena	Cuba	U.K.?
	Sold on 23/2/59.Raced in 1958 thru 1960.								
1037 GT		1037 GT	250 GT	Tour de France	Berlinetta	Scaglietti	Chimeri	Venezuela	Venezuela?
	Sold on 21/11/58.Raced in 1959 and 1960.								
1039 GT		1039 GT	250 GT	Tour de France	Berlinetta	Scaglietti	Chinetti/H.Harcourt	U.S.A.	U.S.A.
	Sold on 26/11/58.Possibly raced at Sebring in 1959? All aluminium body.								
1041 GT		1041 GT	250 GT	PF Notchback	Coupé	Pininfarina			
1043 GT		1043 GT	250 GT	PF Notchback	Coupé	Pininfarina			
1045 GT		1045 GT	250 GT	PF Notchback	Coupé	Pininfarina			U.K.
1047 GT		1047 GT	250 GT	PF Notchback	Coupé	Pininfarina			U.S.A.(parted
1049 GT		1049 GT	250 GT	PF Notchback	Coupé	Pininfarina			
1051 GT		1051 GT	250 GT	PF Notchback	Coupé	Pininfarina			
1053 GT		1053 GT	250 GT	PF Notchback	Coupé	Pininfarina			
1055 GT		1055 GT	250 GT	LWB California	Spyder	Scaglietti			U.S.A.
	Covered headlights.								

Chassis No.	Picture Ref.	Engine No.	Type	Model	Body Style	Coach-builder	First Owner	Original Location	Present Location
1057 GT		1057 GT	250 GT	LWB California	Spyder	Scaglietti			U.S.A.
Completed on 19/11/58. Covered headlights.									
1059 GT		1059 GT	250 GT	PF Notchback	Coupé	Pininfarina			Italy
1061 GT		1061 GT	250 GT	PF Notchback	Coupé	Pininfarina			U.S.A.
1063 GT		1063 GT	250 GT	PF Notchback	Coupé	Pininfarina			U.S.A.
1065 GT		1065 GT	250 GT	PF Notchback	Coupé	Pininfarina			
1067 GT		1067 GT	250 GT	PF Notchback	Coupé	Pininfarina			
1069 GT		1069 GT	250 GT	PF Notchback	Coupé	Pininfarina			U.S.A.
1071 GT		1071 GT	250 GT	PF Notchback	Coupé	Pininfarina			
1073 GT		1073 GT	250 GT	LWB California	Spyder	Scaglietti			U.S.A.
Completed on 6/12/58.									
1075 GT		1075 GT	250 GT	Series I	Convertible	Pininfarina			
Shown at the 1958 London Motor Show.									
1077 GT		1077 GT	250 GT	LWB California	Spyder	Scaglietti			Italy
Completed on 3/12/58									
1079 GT		1079 GT	250 GT	Series I	Convertible	Pininfarina	Mohamed Al Faisal		U.S.A.
Shown at the 1958 London Motor Show.									
1081 GT		1081 GT	250 GT	PF Notchback	Coupé	Pininfarina			U.K.
Shown at the 1958 London Motor Show.									
1083 GT		1083 GT	250 GT	PF Notchback	Coupé	Pininfarina			U.K.?
Shown at the 1958 London Motor Show.									
1085 GT		1085 GT	250 GT	LWB California	Spyder	Scaglietti			U.S.A.
Reputed to be a competition car. All aluminium body.									
1087 GT		1087 GT	250 GT	PF Notchback	Coupé	Pininfarina			
1089 GT		1089 GT	250 GT	PF Notchback	Coupé	Pininfarina			
1091 GT		1091 GT	250 GT	PF Notchback	Coupé	Pininfarina			U.S.A.?
1093 GT		1093 GT	250 GT	PF Notchback	Coupé	Pininfarina			
1095 GT		1095 GT	250 GT	PF Notchback	Coupé	Pininfarina			
1097 GT		1097 GT	250 GT	PF Notchback	Coupé	Pininfarina			
1099 GT		1099 GT	250 GT	PF Notchback	Coupé	Pininfarina			
1101 GT		1101 GT	250 GT	PF Notchback	Coupé	Pininfarina			
1103 GT		1103 GT	250 GT	PF Notchback	Coupé	Pininfarina			
1105 GT		1105 GT	250 GT	PF Notchback	Coupé	Pininfarina			
1107 GT		1107 GT	250 GT	PF Notchback	Coupé	Pininfarina			U.S.A.
1109 GT		1109 GT	250 GT	PF Notchback	Coupé	Pininfarina	Comm.Enzo Ferrari?	Italy	
1111 GT		1111 GT	250 GT	PF Notchback	Coupé	Pininfarina	Comm.Pinin Farina	Italy	
1113 GT		1113 GT	250 GT	Tour de France	Berlinetta	Scaglietti	William Sturgis	U.S.A.	U.S.A.
Sold on 13/11/58. Raced in 1959.									
1115 GT		1115 GT	250 GT	PF Notchback	Coupé	Pininfarina			
1117 GT		1117 GT	250 GT	PF Notchback	Coupé	Pininfarina			
1119 GT		1119 GT	250 GT	PF Notchback	Coupé	Pininfarina			U.S.A.(parted
1121 GT		1121 GT	250 GT	PF Notchback	Coupé	Pininfarina			
1123 GT		1123 GT	250 GT	PF Notchback	Coupé	Pininfarina	Mr Agnelli	Italy	U.S.A.
1125 GT		1125 GT	250 GT	PF Notchback	Coupé	Pininfarina			U.S.A.
Sold in January 1959.									
1127 GT		1127 GT	250 GT	Tour de France	Berlinetta	Scaglietti	George Reed	U.S.A.	U.S.A.
Sold on 13/11/58. Raced in 1959. All Aluminium body.									
1129 GT		1129 GT	250 GT	PF Notchback	Coupé	Pininfarina			Switzerland?
1131 GT		1131 GT	250 GT	PF Notchback	Coupé	Pininfarina			Sweden
1133 GT		1133 GT	250 GT	PF Notchback	Coupé	Pininfarina			Sweden
1135 GT		1135 GT	250 GT	PF Notchback	Coupé	Pininfarina			
1137 GT		1137 GT	250 GT	PF Notchback	Coupé	Pininfarina			
1139 GT		1139 GT	250 GT	Tour de France	Berlinetta	Scaglietti	Ferrari Reps of Hollywood	U.S.A.	U.S.A.
Sold on 18/12/58. Never raced. All aluminium.									
1141 GT		1141 GT	250 GT	Tour de France	Berlinetta	Scaglietti	Chinetti/G.Arents	U.S.A.	U.S.A.
Sold on 30/12/58.									
1143 GT		1143 GT	250 GT	Tour de France	Berlinetta	Scaglietti	J.Aumas	Switzerland	Switzerland
Sold on 11/2/59. Raced in 1959.									
1145 GT		1145 GT	250 GT	PF Notchback	Coupé	Pininfarina			
1147 GT		1147 GT	250 GT	PF Notchback	Coupé	Pininfarina			Switzerland?
1149 GT		1149 GT	250 GT	PF Notchback	Coupé	Pininfarina			
1151 GT		1151 GT	250 GT	PF Notchback	Coupé	Pininfarina			U.S.A.
1153 GT		1153 GT	250 GT	PF Notchback	Coupé	Pininfarina			U.S.A.
1155 GT		1155 GT	250 GT	PF Notchback	Coupé	Pininfarina			
1157 GT		1157 GT	250 GT	PF Notchback	Coupé	Pininfarina			Switzerland?
1159 GT		1159 GT	250 GT	PF Notchback	Coupé	Pininfarina			
1161 GT		1161 GT	250 GT	Tour de France	Berlinetta	Scaglietti	Chinetti/W.Luftman	U.S.A.	U.S.A.
Sold on 11/3/59. Raced very little. All aluminium body.									
1163 GT		1163 GT	250 GT	PF Notchback	Coupé	Pininfarina			
1165 GT		1165 GT	250 GT	PF Notchback	Coupé	Pininfarina			
1167 GT		1167 GT	250 GT	PF Notchback	Coupé	Pininfarina			
1169 GT		1169 GT	250 GT	PF Notchback	Coupé	Pininfarina			U.S.A.
1171 GT		1171 GT	250 GT	PF Notchback	Coupé	Pininfarina			
1173 GT		1173 GT	250 GT	PF Notchback	Coupé	Pininfarina			U.K.

Chassis No.	Picture Ref.	Engine No.	Type	Model	Body Style	Coach-builder	First Owner	Original Location	Present Location
1175 GT		1175 GT	250 GT	PF Notchback	Coupé	Pininfarina			U.S.A.
1177 GT		1177 GT	250 GT	PF Notchback	Coupé	Pininfarina			
1179 GT		1179 GT	250 GT	Series I	Convertible	Pininfarina	Garage Francorchamps	Belgium	U.S.A.
1181 GT		1181 GT	250 GT	Series I	Convertible	Pininfarina			U.S.A.
1183 GT		1183 GT	250 GT	Tour de France	Berlinetta	Scaglietti			
	Reported to be a Tour de France Berlinetta but not yet confirmed.								
1185 GT		1185 GT	250 GT	PF Notchback	Coupé	Pininfarina			Sweden
1187 GT	P1 190	1187 GT	250 GT	PF Notchback	Coupé	Pininfarina			U.S.A.
	Shown at the 1959 Geneva Auto Show. Special body looking like the 410SA Series III!								
1189 GT		1189 GT	250 GT	PF Notchback	Coupé	Pininfarina			U.S.A.
1191 GT		1191 GT	250 GT	PF Notchback	Coupé	Pininfarina			U.S.A.
1193 GT		1193 GT	250GT	Series I	Convertible	Pininfarina		Italy	U.S.A.
	Open headlights. Hard-top.								
1195 GT		1195 GT	250 GT	PF Notchback	Coupé	Pininfarina			U.S.A.
1959									
1197 GT		1197 GT	250 GT	PF Notchback	Coupé	Pininfarina			
	Believed one of the first cars made in 1959.								
1199 GT		1199 GT	250 GT	PF Notchback	Coupé	Pininfarina			
1201 GT		1201 GT	250 GT	PF Notchback	Coupé	Pininfarina			
1203 GT		1203 GT	250 GT	LWB California	Spyder	Scaglietti			U.S.A.
	Completed on 29/1/59. Covered headlights.								
1205 GT		1205 GT	250 GT	PF Notchback	Coupé	Pininfarina			Switzerland
	Shown at the 1959 Geneva Auto Show.								
1207 GT		1207 GT	250 GT	PF Notchback	Coupé	Pininfarina			
1209 GT		1209 GT	250 GT	PF Notchback	Coupé	Pininfarina	W. VonTrips	Germany	Germany? (U.S engine only).
1211 GT		1211 GT	250 GT	Series I	Convertible	Pininfarina		Italy	U.S.A.
1213 GT		1213 GT	250 GT	Series II	Convertible	Pininfarina			
	First prototype Series II PF Convertible.								
1215 GT		1215 GT	250 GT	LWB California	Spyder	Scaglietti			U.S.A.
	Completed on 12/2/59. Last reported with Engine No.2083GT. Open headlights.								
1217 GT		1217 GT	250 GT	LWB California	Spyder	Scaglietti	Jo Siffert?	Switzerland	U.S.A.
	Completed 23/2/59. Last reported with Engine No.2507. (Engine No.1217GT in 0815GT). Open headlights.								
1219 GT		1219 GT	250 GT	PF Notchback	Coupé	Pininfarina	Carlo Abarth	Italy	Italy?
1221 GT		1221 GT	250 GT	PF Notchback	Coupé	Pininfarina			U.S.A.
1223 GT		1223 GT	250 GT	PF Notchback	Coupé	Pininfarina			U.S.A.
1225 GT		1225 GT	250 GT	PF Notchback	Coupé	Pininfarina			
1227 GT		1227 GT	250 GT	PF Notchback	Coupé	Pininfarina			Holland
1229 GT		1229 GT	250 GT	PF Notchback	Coupé	Pininfarina			
1231 GT		1231 GT	250 GT	PF Notchback	Coupé	Pininfarina			
1233 GT		1233 GT	250 GT	PF Notchback	Coupé	Pininfarina			
1235 GT		1235 GT	250 GT	LWB California	Spyder	Scaglietti			Italy?
	Completed 7/3/59.								
1237 GT		1237 GT	250 GT	PF Notchback	Coupé	Pininfarina			
1239 GT		1239 GT	250 GT	PF Notchback	Coupé	Pininfarina			
1241 GT		1241 GT	250 GT	PF Notchback	Coupé	Pininfarina			U.S.A.
1243 GT		1243 GT	250 GT	PF Notchback	Coupé	Pininfarina			
1245 GT		1245 GT	250 GT	PF Notchback	Coupé	Pininfarina			
1247 GT		1247 GT	250 GT	PF Notchback	Coupé	Pininfarina			
1249 GT		1249 GT	250 GT	PF Notchback	Coupé	Pininfarina			
1251 GT		1251 GT	250 GT	PF Notchback	Coupé	Pininfarina			U.K.
1253 GT		1253 GT	250 GT	LWB California	Spyder	Scaglietti			U.S.A.
	Last reported with Engine No.1713GT. Covered headlights.								
1255 GT		1255 GT	250 GT	PF Notchback	Coupé	Pininfarina			
1257 GT		1257 GT	250 GT	PF Notchback	Coupé	Pininfarina			Germany
1259 GT		1259 GT	250 GT	PF Notchback	Coupé	Pininfarina			U.S.A.
1261 GT		1261 GT	250 GT	PF Notchback	Coupé	Pininfarina			
1263 GT		1263 GT	250 GT	PF Notchback	Coupé	Pininfarina			
1265 GT		1265 GT	250 GT	PF Notchback	Coupé	Pininfarina			
	Also reported to be a 410SA Coupé shown at the Geneva Auto Show.								
1267 GT		1267 GT	250 GT	PF Notchback	Coupé	Pininfarina			
1269 GT		1269 GT	250 GT	PF Notchback	Coupé	Pininfarina			
1271 GT		1271 GT	250 GT	PF Notchback	Coupé	Pininfarina			
1273 GT		1273 GT	250 GT	PF Notchback	Coupé	Pininfarina			Switzerland?
1275 GT		1275 GT	250 GT	PF Notchback	Coupé	Pininfarina			
1277 GT		1277 GT	250 GT	PF Notchback	Coupé	Pininfarina			
1279 GT		1279 GT	250 GT	PF Notchback	Coupé	Pininfarina			
1281 GT		1281 GT	250 GT	PF Notchback	Coupé	Pininfarina			U.S.A.
1283 GT		1283 GT	250 GT	LWB California	Spyder	Scaglietti	Roger Vadim?	France	
	Completed 11/4/59.								
1285 SA		1285 SA	410 Superamerica	Series III	Coupé	Pininfarina	Stallings	U.S.A.	U.S.A.
	PF date: 3/2/59.								
1287 GT		1287 GT	250 GTE		2 + 2	Pininfarina			
	Completed 2/5/59. The first pre-production prototype of the yet unannounced 250GTE 2 + 2.								

Chassis No.	Picture Ref.	Engine No.	Type	Model	Body Style	Coach-builder	First Owner	Original Location	Present Location
1289 GT		1289 GT	250 GT	PF Notchback	Coupé	Pininfarina			U.S.A.
1291 GT		1291 GT	250 GT	PF Notchback	Coupé	Pininfarina			U.S.A.
1293 GT		1293 GT	250 GT	PF Notchback	Coupé	Pininfarina			
1295 GT		1295 GT	250 GT	PF Notchback	Coupé	Pininfarina			U.S.A.
1297 GT		1297 GT	250 GT	PF Notchback	Coupé	Pininfarina			U.S.A.
1299 GT		1299 GT	250 GT	PF Notchback	Coupé	Pininfarina			Switzerland?
1301 GT		1301 GT	250 GT	PF Notchback	Coupé	Pininfarina			
1303 GT		1303 GT	250 GT	PF Notchback	Coupé	Pininfarina			
1305 SA		1305 SA	410 Superamerica	Series III	Coupé	Pininfarina	Griffin	U.S.A.?	U.S.A.
1307 GT		1307 GT	250 GT	LWB California	Spyder	Scaglietti			U.S.A.
	Open headlights.								
1309 GT		1309 GT	250 GT	Tour de France	Berlinetta	Scaglietti	DeMicheli	Italy	U.S.A.
	Sold on 24/3/59.Raced in 1959. All aluminium body.Reported with Engine 3917GT.								
1311 SA		1311SA	410 Superamerica	Series III	Coupé	Pininfarina	Buck Fulp	U.S.A.	U.S.A.
1313 GT		1313 GT	250 GT	PF Notchback	Coupé	Pininfarina			
1315 GT		1315 GT	250 GT	PF Notchback	Coupé	Pininfarina			
	Also reported to be a Series III 410 Superamerica but not confirmed.								
1317 GT		1317 GT	250 GT	PF Notchback	Coupé	Pininfarina			
1319 GT		1319 GT	250 GT	PF Notchback	Coupé	Pininfarina			Switzerland?
1321 GT		1321 GT	250 GT	Tour de France	Berlinetta	Scaglietti	Beurlys (Jean Blaton)	Belgium	U.S.A.
	Sold on 27/3/59.Raced in 1959. All aluminium body.								
1323 SA		1323 SA	410 Superamerica	Series III	Coupé	Pininfarina	Gill	U.S.A.?	U.S.A.
	PF date:26/2/59.								
1325 GT		1325 GT	250 GT	PF Notchback	Coupé	Pininfarina			U.K.?
1327 GT		1327 GT	250 GT	PF Notchback	Coupé	Pininfarina			
1329 GT		1329 GT	250 GT	PF Notchback	Coupé	Pininfarina			
1331 GT		1331 GT	250 GT	PF Notchback	Coupé	Pininfarina			U.S.A.
1333 GT	JP 66.	1333 GT	250 GT	Tour de France	Berlinetta	Scaglietti	Abate?	Italy	Switzerland?
	Sold on 9/4/59.Raced in 1959 and 1960. All aluminium body.Modified.								
1335 GT		1335 GT	250 GT	Tour de France	Berlinetta	Scaglietti	C.Toselli	Italy	Italy
	Sold on 23/4/59. Raced in 1959 and 1960. All aluminium body.								
1337 GT		1337 GT	250 GT	PF Notchback	Coupé	Pininfarina			
1339 GT		1339 GT	250 GT	PF Notchback	Coupé	Pininfarina			U.S.A.
1341 GT		1341 GT	250 GT	PF Notchback	Coupé	Pininfarina			
1343 GT		1343 GT	250 GT	PF Notchback	Coupé	Pininfarina			
1345 GT		1345 GT	250 GT	PF Notchback	Coupé	Pininfarina			
1347 GT		1347 GT	250 GT	PF Notchback	Coupé	Pininfarina			U.S.A.
1349 GT		1349 GT	250 GT	PF Notchback	Coupé	Pininfarina			
1351 GT		1351 GT	250 GT	PF Notchback	Coupé	Pininfarina			
1353 GT		1353 GT	250 GT	Tour de France	Berlinetta	Scaglietti	Ferraro	Italy	U.K.
	Sold on 11/5/59. All aluminium body.								
1355 SA		1355 SA	410 Superamerica	Series III	Coupé	Pininfarina	Murray	U.S.A.?	
	PF date:18/3/59.								
1357 GT		1357 GT	250 GT	Tour de France	Berlinetta	Scaglietti	Dumay?	France	U.S.A.
	Sold on 23/4/59.Raced in 1959 and 1960. All aluminium body.								
1359 SA		1359 SA	410 Superamerica	Series III	Coupé	Pininfarina			U.S.A.
	Also reported to be a 250GT PF Notchback Coupé.								
1361 GT		1361 GT	250 GT	PF Notchback	Coupé	Pininfarina			
1363 GT		1363 GT	250 GT	PF Notchback	Coupé	Pininfarina			
1365 GT		1365 GT	250GT	PF Notchback	Coupé	Pininfarina			U.S.A.
1367 GT	JP 68.	1367 GT	250 GT	Tour de France	Berlinetta	Zagato	Luglio	Italy	Italy
	Sold on 26/7/59.Probably raced in Italy. All aluminium body.The last Zagato bodied TdeF.								
1369 GT		1369 GT	250 GT	PF Notchback	Coupé	Pininfarina			U.S.A.
1371 GT		1371 GT	250 GT	PF Notchback	Coupé	Pininfarina			
1373 GT		1373 GT	250 GT	PF Notchback	Coupé	Pininfarina			
	Also reported as a Series III 410 Superamerica.								
1375 GT		1375 GT	250 GT	PF Notchback	Coupé	Pininfarina			U.S.A.
1377 GT	JP 69.	1377 GT	250 GT	Interim	Berlinetta	Scaglietti	Kaufmann	Venezuela	U.S.A.
	Sold on 10/6/59.Raced in 1959 and 1960.Badly crashed and engine sold. Prototype for Interim all aluminium body.Being restored.								
1379 GT		1379 GT	250 GT	LWB California	Spyder	Scaglietti	Enzo Stuarti	U.S.A.	U.S.A.
	In U.S.A. since new. Covered headlights.								
1381 GT		1381 GT	250 GT	PF Notchback	Coupé	Pininfarina			U.S.A.
1383 GT		1383 GT	250 GT	PF Notchback	Coupé	Pininfarina			U.S.A.
1385 GT		1385 GT	250 GT	Tour de France	Berlinetta	Scaglietti	L.Piotti	Italy	U.S.A.
	Sold on 2/5/59.Raced in 1959. All aluminium body.								
1387 SA		1387 SA	410 Superamerica	Series III	Coupé	Pininfarina	Nogara	Portugal?	
1389 GT		1389 GT	250 GT	Tour de France	Berlinetta	Scaglietti	A.Thiele	Italy	U.S.A.
	Sold on 29/5/59.Raced in 1959.								
1391 GT		1391 GT	250 GT	PF Notchback	Coupé	Pininfarina			
1393 GT		1393 GT	250 GT	PF Notchback	Coupé	Pininfarina			
1395 GT		1395 GT	250 GT	PF Notchback	Coupé	Pininfarina			
1397 GT		1397 GT	250 GT	PF Notchback	Coupé	Pininfarina			
1399 GT		1399 GT	250 GT	Tour de France	Berlinetta	Scaglietti	C.Marquant	France	France?
	Sold on 22/5/59.Never raced.All aluminium body.								

Chassis No.	Picture Ref.	Engine No.	Type	Model	Body Style	Coach-builder	First Owner	Original Location	Present Location
1401 GT	JP 65.	1401 GT	250 GT	Tour de France	Berlinetta	Scaglietti	L.Taramazzo	Italy	Switzerland
	Sold on 23/5/59.Raced in 1959 and 1960All aluminium body.								
1403 GT		1403 GT	250 GT	PF Notchback	Coupé	Pininfarina			U.S.A.
1405 GT		1405 GT	250 GT	PF Notchback	Coupé	Pininfarina			
1407 GT		1407 GT	250 GT	PF Notchback	Coupé	Pininfarina			
1409 GT		1409 GT	250 GT	PF Notchback	Coupé	Pininfarina			U.S.A.
1411 GT		1411 GT	250 GT	LWB California	Spyder	Scaglietti			U.K.
	Was in the U.S.A. for many years.Engine and many parts missing.								
1413 GT		1413 GT	250 GT	LWB California	Spyder	Scaglietti			
1415 GT		1415 GT	250 GT	PF Notchback	Coupé	Pininfarina			
1417 GT*?		1417 GT	250 GT	PF Notchback	Coupé	Pininfarina			Australia
1419 GT		1419 GT	250 GT	PF Notchback	Coupé	Pininfarina			U.S.A.
1421 GT		1421 GT	250 GT	PF Notchback	Coupé	Pininfarina			U.S.A.
1423 SA	P1 143	1423 SA	410 Superamerica	Series III	Coupé	Pininfarina	W.Dulles	U.K.	U.K.
	Open headlights.								
1425 GT		1425 GT	250 GT	LWB California	Spyder	Scaglietti			U.S.A.
	Covered headlights.								
1427 GT		1427 GT	250 GT	PF Notchback	Coupé	Pininfarina			
1429 GT		1429 GT	250 GT	PF Notchback	Coupé	Pininfarina			
1431 GT		1431 GT	250 GT	LWB California	Spyder	Scaglietti			U.S.A.
	Covered headlights.								
1433 GT		1433 GT	250 GT	PF Notchback	Coupé	Pininfarina			
1435 GT		1435 GT	250 GT	PF Notchback	Coupé	Pininfarina			Switzerland?
1437 GT		1437 GT	250 GT	PF Notchback	Coupé	Pininfarina			
1439 GT		1439 GT	250 GT	Series I	Convertible	Pininfarina			U.S.A.
1441 GT		1441 GT	250 GT	PF Notchback	Coupé	Pininfarina			U.S.A.
1443 GT		1443 GT	250 GT	PF Notchback	Coupé	Pininfarina			U.S.A.
	Used as the basis for a 250TR replica.								
1445 GT		1445 GT	250 GT	PF Notchback	Coupé	Pininfarina			U.S.A.
1447 GT		1447 GT	250 GT	PF Notchback	Coupé	Pininfarina			
1449 SA		1449 SA	410 Superamerica	Series III	Coupé	Pininfarina	Chinetti/Fuller	U.S.A.	
	Open headlights.								
1451 GT	P1 215	1451 GT	250 GT	LWB California	Spyder	Scaglietti	Bob Grossman	U.S.A.	U.S.A.
	Sold on 15/6/59.Finished 5th OA LeMans 1959!Later raced in U.S.A.. Delivered with special engine to TR specs and other special modifications. Open headlights.Aluminium body.Outside filler cap.								
1453 GT		1453 GT	250 GT	PF Notchback	Coupé	Pininfarina			
1455 GT		1455 GT	250 GT	PF Notchback	Coupé	Pininfarina			
1457 GT		1457 GT	250 GT	PF Notchback	Coupé	Pininfarina			U.S.A.
1459 GT		1459 GT	250 GT	LWB California	Spyder	Scaglietti			
1461 GT	JP 70	1461 GT	250 GT	Interim	Berlinetta	Scaglietti	Chinetti	U.S.A.	U.S.A.?
	Sold on 17/6/59. Raced in 1959. All aluminium body.Special racing engine.								
1463 GT		1463 GT	250 GT	PF Notchback	Coupé	Pininfarina			
1465 GT		1465 GT	250 GT	Interim	Berlinetta	Scaglietti	U.Satori	Italy	Holland
	Sold on 2/9/59.Believe never raced. All aluminium body.								
1467 GT		1467 GT	250 GT	PF Notchback	Coupé	Pininfarina			
1469 GT		1469 GT	250 GT	PF Notchback	Coupé	Pininfarina			Switzerland?
1471 GT		1471 GT	250 GT	PF Notchback	Coupé	Pininfarina			U.S.A.
1473 GT		1473 GT	250 GT	PF Notchback	Coupé	Pininfarina			
1475 GT		1475 GT	250 GT	Series I	Convertible	Pininfarina	Ferrari Rep California	U.S.A.	U.S.A.
1477 SA		1477 SA	410 Superamerica	Series III	Coupé	Pininfarina	Ferrari Rep California	U.S.A.	U.S.A.
	Sold to first owner William Harrah.								
1479 GT		1479 GT	250 GT	PF Notchback	Coupé	Pininfarina			U.K.
1481 GT		1481 GT	250 GT	PF Notchback	Coupé	Pininfarina			
1483 GT		1483 GT	250 GT	PF Notchback	Coupé	Pininfarina			U.S.A.
1485 GT		1485 GT	250 GT	PF Notchback	Coupé	Pininfarina			
1487 GT		1487 GT	250 GT	LWB California	Spyder	Scaglietti			
	All aluminium body.								
1489 GT		1489 GT	250 GT	LWB California	Spyder	Scaglietti			
1491 GT		1491 GT	250 GT	PF Notchback	Coupé	Pininfarina			
1493 GT		1493 GT	250 GT	PF Notchback	Coupé	Pininfarina			
	Last PF Notchback with drum brakes.								
1495 SA		1495 SA	410 Superamerica	Series III	Coupé	Pininfarina	Chinetti	U.S.A.	U.S.A.
	Open headlights.								
1497 GT		1497 GT	250 GT	LWB California	Spyder	Scaglietti			U.S.A.
	Open headlights.								
1499 GT		1499 GT	250 GT	PF Notchback	Coupé	Pininfarina			
	First PF Notchback with disc brakes.								
1501 GT		1501 GT	250 GT	LWB California	Spyder	Scaglietti	Drogo/Chinetti?	Italy	U.S.A.?
	Completed 19/12/59. Covered headlight.								
1503 GT		1503 GT	250GT	LWB California	Spyder	Scaglietti			U.S.A.
1505 GT		1505 GT	250 GT	LWB California	Spyder	Scaglietti			U.S.A.
	Open headlights.								
1507GT		1507GT	250?	GTE?	2 + 2?	Pininfarina?			
	Reported as a prototype 250GTE 2+2.								

Chassis No.	Picture Ref.	Engine No.	Type	Model	Body Style	Coach-builder	First Owner	Original Location	Present Location
1509 GT	JP 71	1509 GT	250 GT	Interim	Berlinetta	Scaglietti	Jo Schlesser	France	France
	Sold on 8/9/59. Raced in 1959 and 1960. All aluminium body.								
1511 GT		1511 GT	250 GT	PF Notchback	Coupé	Pininfarina			
	Shown at the 1959 Paris Salon with disc brakes.								
1513 GT		1513 GT	250GT	PF Notchback	Coupé	Pininfarina			
1515 GT		1515 GT	250 GT	PF Notchback	Coupé	Pininfarina			
1517 SA	P1 246	1517 SA	400 Superamerica	Series I SWB	Coupé	Pininfarina	G. Agnelli	Italy	Italy
	Shown at the 1959 Turin Motor Show. Special one off design with wraparound windshield.								
1519 GT	JP 71	1519 GT	250 GT	Interim	Berlinetta	Scaglietti	Jean-Pierre Schild	Switzerland	U.S.A. (engine elsewhere U.S.
	Sold on 12/9/59. Raced in 1959 and 1960.								
1521 GT	JP 72.	1521 GT	250 GT	Interim	Berlinetta	Scaglietti	Pierre Dumay	France	U.S.A.
	Sold on 16/9/59. Raced in 1959 and 1960. All aluminium body.								
1523 GT	JP 72.	1523 GT	250 GT	Interim	Berlinetta	Scaglietti	Oliver Gendebien	Belgium	U.S.A.(engine
	Sold in September 1959. Raced in 1959, 1960 & 1961. Destroyed in 1961 except for engine. The last LWB.								
1525 GT		1525 GT	250 GT	LWB California	Spyder	Scaglietti			U.S.A.
1527 GT		1527 GT	250 GT	LWB California	Spyder	Scaglietti			U.S.A.
	Open headlights?								
1529 GT		1529 GT	250 GT	PF Notchback	Coupé	Pininfarina			U.S.A.
1531 GT		1531 GT	250 GT	PF Notchback	Coupé	Pininfarina			U.S.A.
1533 GT		1533 GT	250 GT	PF Notchback	Coupé	Pininfarina			
1535 GT		1535 GT	250 GT	PF Notchback	Coupé	Pininfarina			
1537 GT		1537 GT	250 GT	Series II	Convertible	Pininfarina			
	First production Series II PF Convertible.								
1539 GT	JP 82.	1539 GT	250 GT	Competition SWB	Berlinetta	Scaglietti	G. Pennington	U.S.A.	Belgium
	Sold on 4/3/60. Raced in 1960. Sold to U.K. and converted to RHD and back to LHD. Prototype SWB.								
1541 GT		1541 GT	250 GT	PF Notchback	Coupé	Pininfarina			
1543 GT		1543 GT	250 GT	PF Notchback	Coupé	Pininfarina			U.S.A.
1545 GT		1545 GT	250 GT	PF Notchback	Coupé	Pininfarina			
1547 GT		1547 GT	250 GT	PF Notchback	Coupé	Pininfarina			
1549 GT		1549 GT	250 GT	PF Notchback	Coupé	Pininfarina			U.S.A.
1551 GT		1551 GT	250 GT	PF Notchback	Coupé	Pininfarina			
1553 GT		1553 GT	250 GT	PF Notchback	Coupé	Pininfarina			
1555 GT		1555 GT	250 GT	PF Notchback	Coupé	Pininfarina			U.S.A. (engine & trans only)
1557 GT		1557 GT	250 GT	PF Notchback	Coupé	Pininfarina			
1559 GT		1559 GT	250 GT	Series II	Convertible	Pininfarina			
1561 GT		1561 GT	250 GT	Series II	Convertible	Pininfarina			
1563 GT		1563 GT	250 GT	PF Notchback	Coupé	Pininfarina			
1565 GT		1565 GT	250 GT	PF Notchback	Coupé	Pininfarina			
1567 GT		1567 GT	250 GT	PF Notchback	Coupé	Pininfarina			U.S.A.
1569 GT		1569 GT	250 GT	PF Notchback	Coupé	Pininfarina			
1571 GT		1571 GT	250 GT	PF Notchback	Coupé	Pininfarina			
1573 GT		1573 GT	250 GT	PF Notchback	Coupé	Pininfarina			
1575 GT		1575 GT	250 GT	LWB California	Spyder	Scaglietti			
1577 GT		1577 GT	250 GT	PF Notchback	Coupé	Pininfarina			
1579 GT		1579 GT	250 GT	PF Notchback	Coupé	Pininfarina			
1581 GT		1581 GT	250 GT	PF Notchback	Coupé	Pininfarina			
	Identity of this car not confirmed.								
1583 GT		1583 GT	250 GT	PF Notchback	Coupé	Pininfarina			Italy
1585 GT		1585 GT	250 GT	PF Notchback	Coupé	Pininfarina			
1587 GT		1587 GT	250 GT	PF Notchback	Coupé	Pininfarina			
1589 GT		1589 GT	250 GT	PF Notchback	Coupé	Pininfarina			
1591 GT		1591 GT	250 GT	PF Notchback	Coupé	Pininfarina			France
1593 GT		1593 GT	250 GT	PF Notchback	Coupé	Pininfarina			
1595 GT		1595 GT	250 GT	PF Notchback	Coupé	Pininfarina			
1597 GT		1597 GT	250 GT	PF Notchback	Coupé	Pininfarina			U.S.A.
1599 GT		1599 GT	250 GT	PF Notchback	Coupé	Pininfarina			
1601 GT		1601 GT	250 GT	PF Notchback	Coupé	Pininfarina			
1603 GT		1603 GT	250 GT	LWB California	Spyder	Scaglietti	George Reed	U.S.A.	U.S.A.
	Completed 23/11/59. Finished 5th OA in 1960 Sebring race. Covered headlights. All Aluminium body. Outside filler cap.								
1605 GT		1605 GT	250 GT	PF Notchback	Coupé	Pininfarina			
1607 GT		1607 GT	250 GT	PF Notchback	Coupé	Pininfarina			
1609 GT		1609 GT	250 GT	PF Notchback	Coupé	Pininfarina			
1611 SA	P1 248	1611 SA	400 Superamerica	Series I SWB	Convertible	Pininfarina	George Arents	U.S.A.	U.S.A.
	Shown at the Brussels and New York Auto Shows in 1960.								
1613 GT	JP 83.	1613 GT	250 GT	Competition SWB	Berlinetta	Scaglietti	J. DaSilva Marques Pinto	Angola	U.S.A..(Non original engine
	Sold on 23/2/60. Shown at the 1960 Turin Motor Show. Raced in 1961, 1962 & 1963. All aluminium body.								
1615 GT		1615 GT	250 GT	LWB California	Spyder	Scaglietti			U.S.A. (destroy in fire).
	Completed 24/12/59. Built as competition car but racing history. Original engine in 2163GT. Totally destroyed in fire. Covered headlights. All aluminium body.								

1960

Chassis No.	Picture Ref.	Engine No.	Type	Model	Body Style	Coach-builder	First Owner	Original Location	Present Location
1617 GT		1617 GT	250 GT	PF Notchback	Coupé	Pininfarina			
1619 GT		1619 GT	250 GT	PF Notchback	Coupé	Pininfarina			
1621 GT		1621 GT	250 GT	PF Notchback	Coupé	Pininfarina			

Chassis No.	Picture Ref.	Engine No.	Type	Model	Body Style	Coach-builder	First Owner	Original Location	Present Location
1623 GT		1623 GT	250 GT	PF Notchback	Coupé	Pininfarina			U.S.A.
		Rebodied in 1964 by Neri & Bonaccini with an all aluminium spyder body for Tom Meade. Chassis shortened.							
1625 GT		1625 GT	250 GT	PF Notchback	Coupé	Pininfarina			
1627 GT		1627 GT	250 GT	LWB California	Spyder	Scaglietti			U.S.A.
		Believed built as competition car. Racing history. Covered headlights. All aluminium body.							
1629 GT		1629 GT	250 GT	PF Notchback	Coupé	Pininfarina			U.S.A.
1631 GT		1631 GT	250 GT	PF Notchback	Coupé	Pininfarina			U.S.A.
1633 GT		1633 GT	250 GT	PF Notchback	Coupé	Pininfarina			U.S.A.
1635 GT		1635 GT	250 GT	PF Notchback	Coupé	Pininfarina	Chinetti/Bob Wilke	U.S.A.	U.S.A.
		Shown at 1960 New York Auto Show							
1637 GT		1637 GT	250 GT	PF Notchback	Coupé	Pininfarina			
1639 GT		1639 GT	250 GT	LWB California	Spyder	Scaglietti	Ed Hugus	U.S.A.	U.S.A.
		Completed 9/1/60. Covered headlights.							
1641 GT		1641 GT	250 GT	LWB California	Spyder	Scaglietti			U.S.A.
		Completed on 29/1/60. Possibly built as competition car. No racing history known. Covered headlights. All aluminium body.							
1643 GT		1643 GT	250 GT	PF Notchback	Coupé	Pininfarina			U.S.A.
1645 GT		1645 GT	250 GT	PF Notchback	Coupé	Pininfarina			Canada
1647 GT		1647 GT	250 GT	PF Notchback	Coupé	Pininfarina			
1649 GT		1649 GT	250 GT	PF Notchback	Coupé	Pininfarina			Switzerland?
1651 GT		1651 GT	250 GT	PF Notchback	Coupé	Pininfarina			
1653 GT		1653 GT	250 GT	PF Notchback	Coupé	Pininfarina			
1655 GT		1655 GT	250 GT	PF Notchback	Coupé	Pininfarina			
1657 GT		1657 GT	250 GT	PF Notchback	Coupé	Pininfarina			U.S.A.
1659 GT		1659 GT	250 GT	PF Notchback	Coupé	Pininfarina			U.S.A.
1661 GT		1661 GT	250 GT	PF Notchback	Coupé	Pininfarina			
1663 GT		1663 GT	250 GT	LWB California	Spyder	Scaglietti			U.S.A.?
		Covered headlights.							
1665 GT		1665 GT	250 GT	PF Notchback	Coupé	Pininfarina			
1667 GT		1667 GT	250 GT	PF Notchback	Coupé	Pininfarina			
1669 GT		1669 GT	250 GT	PF Notchback	Coupé	Pininfarina			U.S.A.?
1671 GT		1671 GT	250 GT	PF Notchback	Coupé	Pininfarina			U.S.A.
1673 GT		1673 GT	250 GT	PF Notchback	Coupé	Pininfarina			U.S.A.
1675 GT		1675 GT	250 GT	PF Notchback	Coupé	Pininfarina			
1677 GT*?		1677 GT	250 GT	PF Notchback	Coupé	Pininfarina			Australia
1679 GT		1679 GT	250 GT	PF Notchback	Coupé	Pininfarina			U.S.A.
1681 GT		1681 GT	250 GT	PF Notchback	Coupé	Pininfarina			
1683 GT		1683 GT	250 GT	PF Notchback	Coupé	Pininfarina			
1685 SA		1685 SA	400 Superamerica	Series I SWB?	Convertible?	Pininfarina			
		Also reported to be a 250GT PF Notchback Coupé in the U.S.A..							
1687 GT		1687 GT	250 GT	PF Notchback	Coupé	Pininfarina			
1689 GT		1689 GT	250 GT	PF Notchback	Coupé	Pininfarina			
1691 GT		1691 GT	250 GT	PF Notchback	Coupé	Pininfarina			
1693 GT		1693 GT	250 GT	PF Notchback	Coupé	Pininfarina			
1695 GT		1695 GT	250 GT	Series II	Convertible	Pininfarina			U.S.A.
1697 GT		1697 GT	250GT	LWB California	Spyder	Scaglietti			U.S.A.
1699 GT		1699 GT	250 GT	LWB California	Spyder	Scaglietti			U.S.A.
		Completed 15/2/60. Covered headlights. All aluminium body.							
1701 GT		1701 GT	250 GT	PF Notchback	Coupé	Pininfarina			
1703 GT		1703 GT	250 GT	PF Notchback	Coupé	Pininfarina			
1705 GT		1705 GT	250 GT	PF Notchback	Coupé	Pininfarina			
1707 GT		1707 GT	250 GT	PF Notchback	Coupé	Pininfarina			U.S.A.
1709 GT		1709 GT	250 GT	PF Notchback	Coupé	Pininfarina			
1711 GT		1711 GT	250 GT	PF Notchback	Coupé	Pininfarina			
1713 GT		1713 GT	250 GT	LWB California	Spyder	Scaglietti			
1715 GT		1715 GT	250 GT	LWB California	Spyder	Scaglietti			U.S.A.
		Completed 27/2/60. Covered headlights. Disc brakes. Last LWB California made.							
1717 GT		1717 GT	250 GT	PF Notchback	Coupé	Pininfarina			
1719 GT		1719 GT	250 GT	PF Notchback	Coupé	Pininfarina			Holland
1721 GT		1721 GT	250 GT	PF Notchback	Coupé	Pininfarina			
1723 GT		1723 GT	250 GT	Series II	Convertible	Pininfarina			U.S.A.
1725 GT		1725 GT	250 GT	PF Notchback	Coupé	Pininfarina			
1727 GT		1727 GT	250 GT	Series II	Convertible	Pininfarina			France
1729 GT		1729 GT	250 GT	PF Notchback	Coupé	Pininfarina			Switzerland
1731 GT		1731 GT	250 GT	PF Notchback	Coupé	Pininfarina			
1733 GT		1733 GT	250 GT	PF Notchback	Coupé	Pininfarina			U.S.A.
1735 GT		1735 GT	250 GT	PF Notchback	Coupé	Pininfarina			
1737 GT	P1 225	1737 GT	250GT	Series II	Convertible	Pininfarina			
		Special one off body with covered headlights & hardtop.							
1739 GT	JP 111	1739 GT	250 GT	Alloy SWB	Berlinetta	Bertone	Wax & Vitale	Genoa, Italy	U.S.A.
		Sold on 8/1/60. Never raced. 1959 Competition model. All aluminium body. One off show model.							
1741 GT		1741 GT	250 GT	Competition SWB Berlinetta		Scaglietti	Chinetti/B.Schur	U.S.A.	U.S.A.
		Sold on 7/3/60. Shown at the 1960 New York Auto Show. Raced in 1960 by NART. All aluminium body.							
1743 GT		1743 GT	250 GT	PF Notchback	Coupé	Pininfarina			U.S.A.
1745 GT		1745 GT	250 GT	PF Notchback	Coupé	Pininfarina			

Chassis No.	Picture Ref	Engine No.	Type	Model	Body Style	Coach-builder	First Owner	Original Location	Present Location
1747 GT		1747 GT	250 GT	PF Notchback	Coupé	Pininfarina			
1749 GT		1749 GT	250 GT	PF Notchback	Coupé	Pininfarina			
1751 GT		1751 GT	250 GT	PF Notchback	Coupe	Pininfarina			U.S.A.
1753 GT		1753 GT	250 GT	Series II	Convertible	Pininfarina			Switzerland?
1755 GT		1755 GT	250 GT	Series II	Convertible	Pininfarina			
1757 GT		1757 GT	250 GT	Competition SWB	Berlinetta	Scaglietti	Chinetti/B.Schur	U.S.A.	U.S.A.
Sold on 7/3/60.Shown at the 1960 New York Auto Show. Raced in 1960. All aluminium 1960 competition car.									
1759 GT		1759 GT	250 GT	Competition SWB	Berlinetta	Scaglietti	Chinetti/B.Schur	U.S.A..	U.S.A.
Sold on 18 June 1960.Raced in 1960. All aluminium competition car.									
1761 GT		1761 GT	250 GT	Series II	Convertible	Pininfarina			
1763 GT		1763 GT	250 GT	PF Notchback	Coupe	Pininfarina			
1765 GT		1765 GT	250 GT	PF Notchback	Coupe	Pininfarina			
1767 GT		1767 GT	250 GT	PF Notchback	Coupe	Pininfarina			
1769 GT		1769 GT	250 GT	PF Notchback	Coupe	Pininfarina			
1771 GT		1771 GT	250 GT	Competition SWB	Berlinetta	Scaglietti	Monteverdi	Switzerland	Switzerland?
Sold on 25/3/60.Raced from 1960 thru 1963. All aluminium competition car.									
1773 GT		1773 GT	250 GT	Competition SWB	Berlinetta	Scaglietti	Chinetti/Arents	U.S.A.	Germany
Sold on 16/3/60.Raced in 1960 and 1961. All aluminium competition body. All aluminium competition body.									
1775 GT		1775 GT	250 GT	PF Notchback	Coupe	Pininfarina			U.S.A.
1777 GT	JP/146.	1777 GT	250 GT	PF Notchback	Coupe	Pininfarina		Italy	U.S.A.
Chassis shortened and rebodied as special one off Berlinetta by Neri & Bonaccini for Tom Meade.									
1779 GT		1779 GT	250 GT	Series II	Convertible	Pininfarina			
1781 GT		1781 GT	250 GT	Series II	Convertible	Pininfarina			U.S.A.
1783 GT		1783 GT	250 GT	Series II	Convertible	Pininfarina			
1785 GT		1785 GT	250 GT	Alloy SWB	Berlinetta	Scaglietti	C.Kreisler	U.S.A.	U.S.A. (engine 1931GT Eng o
Sold on 16/3/60.Raced in 1960. All aluminium competition car.									
1787 GT		1787 GT	250 GT	Series II	Convertible	Pininfarina			
1789 GT		1789 GT	250 GT	PF Notchback	Coupe	Pininfarina			Unkown
1791 GT		1791 GT	250 GT	Competition SWB	Berlinetta	Scaglietti	G.Lombardi	Italy	Italy?
Sold on 4/4/60.Raced 1960 thru 1964. All aluminium competition car.									
1793 GT		1793 GT	250 GT	PF Notchback	Coupe	Pininfarina			
1795 GT		1795 GT	250 GT	SWB California	Spyder	Scaglietti			U.S.A.
Completed 5/5/60. Covered headlights.First SWB California.									
1797 GT		1797 GT	250 GT	Series II	Convertible	Pininfarina			
1799 GT		1799 GT	250 GT	PF Notchback	Coupe	Pininfarina			
1801 GT		1801 GT	250 GT	Series II	Convertible	Pininfarina			U.S.A.
1803 GT		1803 GT	250 GT	Series II	Convertible	Pininfarina			U.S.A.
1805 GT		1805 GT	250 GT	Series II	Convertible	Pininfarina			
1807 GT		1807 GT	250 GT	Competition SWB	Berlinetta	Scaglietti	W.Seidel	Germany	U.S.A.(with Er No.1953GT)
Sold on 29/4/60.Raced in 1960 thru 1962. All aluminium competition car.									
1809 GT		1809 GT	250 GT	PF Notchback	Coupe	Pininfarina			
1811 GT		1811 GT	250 GT	Competition SWB	Berlinetta	Scaglietti	Garage Francorchamps	Belgium	U.S.A.
Sold on 10/5/60.Raced in 1960 thru 1962. All aluminium competition car.									
1813 GT		1813 GT	250 GT	Competition SWB	Berlinetta	Scaglietti	Ferraro	Italy	U.S.A.
Sold on 2/5/60.Raced in 1960 thru 1962. All aluminium competition car.									
1815 GT		1815 GT	250 GT	Series II	Convertible	Pininfarina			
1817 GT		1817 GT	250 GT	Series II	Convertible	Pininfarina			U.S.A.
Special side vents similar to 410SA Series III Coupes.									
1819 GT		1819 GT	250 GT	Series II	Coupe	Pininfarina			
1821 GT		1821 GT	250 GT	Series II	Convertible	Pininfarina			
1823 GT		1823 GT	250 GT	PF Notchback	Coupe	Pininfarina			
1825 GT		1825 GT	250 GT	PF Notchback	Coupe	Pininfarina			
1827 GT		1827 GT	250 GT	PF Notchback	Coupe	Pininfarina			
1829 GT		1829 GT	250 GT	PF Notchback	Coupe	Pininfarina			U.S.A.
1831 GT		1831 GT	250 GT	PF Notchback	Coupé	Pininfarina			
1833 GT		1833 GT	250 GT	PF Notchback	Convertible	Pininfarina			U.S.A.
1835 GT		1835 GT	250 GT	Series II	Convertible	Pininfarina			
1837 GT		1837 GT	250 GT	PF Notchback	Coupe	Pininfarina			
1839 GT		1839 GT	250 GT	PF Notchback	Coupe	Pininfarina			France
1841 GT		1841 GT	250 GT	Series II	Convertible	Pininfarina			U.S.A.
1843 GT		1843 GT	250 GT	Series II	Convertible	Pininfarina			
1845 GT		1845 GT	250 GT	PF Notchback	Coupe	Pininfarina			
1847 GT		1847 GT	250 GT	PF Notchback	Coupe	Pininfarina			
1849 GT		1849 GT	250 GT	Competition SWB	Berlinetta	Scaglietti	G.Billi	Italy	U.S.A.
Sold on 9/5/60.Never raced. All aluminium competition car.									
1851 GT		1851 GT	250 GT	PF Notchback	Coupe	Pininfarina			
1853 GT		1853 GT	250 GT	PF Notchback	Coupe	Pininfarina			
1855 GT		1855 GT	250 GT	Series II	Convertible	Pininfarina			
1857 GT		1857 GT	250 GT	PF Notchback	Coupe	Pininfarina			
1859 GT		1859 GT	250 GT	PF Notchback	Coupe	Pininfarina			U.S.A.
1861 GT		1861 GT	250 GT	PF Notchback	Coupe	Pininfarina			U.S.A.
1863 GT		1863 GT	250 GT	Series II	Convertible	Pininfarina			
1865 GT		1865 GT	250 GT	Series II	Convertible	Pininfarina			
1867 GT		1867 GT	250 GT	Series II	Convertible	Pininfarina			

Chassis No.	Picture Ref	Engine No.	Type	Model	Body Style	Coach-builder	First Owner	Original Location	Present Location
1869 GT		1869 GT	250 GT	Series II	Convertible	Pininfarina			U.S.A.
1871 GT		1871 GT	250 GT	PF Notchback	Coupe	Pininfarina			U.S.A.
1873 GT		1873 GT	250 GT	PF Notchback	Coupe	Pininfarina			
1875 GT		1875 GT	250 GT	Alloy SWB	Berlinetta	Scaglietti	Gerini/Volpi	Italy	Switzerland(w incorrect engir
		Sold on 4/4/60.Raced 1960 thru 1965.Eventually restored with a new body and parts from a GTE. All aluminium competition car.							
1877 GT		1877 GT	250 GT	PF Notchback	Coupe	Pininfarina			
1879 GT		1879 GT	250 GT	Series II	Convertible	Pininfarina			
1881 GT		1881 GT	250 GT	Series II	Convertible	Pininfarina			
1883 GT		1883 GT	250 GT	SWB California	Spyder	Scaglietti			U.S.A.
		Completed 9/8/60.							
1885 SA		1885 SA	400 Superamerica	Series I SWB	Convertible	Pininfarina	Mouzino	Italy?	U.S.A.
		PF date:23/3/60.							
1887 GT		1887 GT	250 GT	Competition SWB	Berlinetta	Scaglietti	Jean Guichet	France	Sweden
		Sold on 21/5/60.Raced in 1960 and 1961. All aluminium competition car.							
1889 GT		1889 GT	250 GT	PF Notchback	Coupe	Pininfarina			
1891 GT		1891 GT	250 GT	Series II	Convertible	Pininfarina			
1893 GT		1893 GT	250 GT	Series II	Convertible	Pininfarina			U.K.
1895 GTE		1895 GTE	250	GTE	2 + 2	Pininfarina			
		Believed to be the second 250GTE 2+2 prototype. Completed in June 1960.							
1897 GT		1897 GT	250 GT	PF Notchback	Coupe	Pininfarina			
1899 GT		1899 GT	250 GT	PF Notchback	Coupe	Pininfarina			U.S.A.
1901 GT		1901 GT	250 GT	PF Notchback	Coupe	Pininfarina			Switzerland
1903 GTE		1903 GTE	250	GTE	2 + 2	Pininfarina			
		Completed June 1960.Believed to be the third prototype 250GTE 2+2.							
1905 GT		1905 GT	250 GT	Competition SWB	Berlinetta	Scaglietti	R.Bialetti	Italy	U.S.A.
		Sold on 24/4/60.Raced briefly in Italy. All aluminium competition car.							
1907 GT		1907 GT	250 GT	PF Notchback	Coupe	Pininfarina			
1909 GT		1909 GT	250 GT	PF Notchback	Coupe	Pininfarina			
1911 GT		1911 GT	250 GT	Series II	Convertible	Pininfarina			
1913 GT		1913 GT	250 GT	PF Notchback	Coupe	Pininfarina			
1915 GT		1915 GT	250 GT	SWB California	Spyder	Scaglietti			
1917 GT		1917 GT	250 GT	Competition SWB	Berlinetta	Scaglietti	German Agent	Germany	Germany
		Sold on 18/5/60.Raced 1960 thru 1964. All aluminium competition car.							
1919 GT		1919 GT	250 GT	PF Notchback	Coupe	Pininfarina			
1921 GT		1921 GT	250 GT	PF Notchback	Coupe	Pininfarina			U.S.A.
1923 GT		1923 GT	250 GT	PF Notchback	Coupe	Pininfarina			
1925 GT		1925 GT	250 GT	Series II	Convertible	Pininfarina	King of Morocco	Morocco	
		Special coachwork including hardtop in brushed aluminium!							
1927 GT		1927 GT	250 GT	PF Notchback	Coupe	Pininfarina			U.S.A./Switzer
1929 GT		1929 GT	250 GT	PF Notchback	Coupe	Pininfarina			U.S.A.
1931 GT		1931 GT	250 GT	Competition SWB	Berlinetta	Scaglietti	George Arents	U.S.A.	U.S.A.
		Sold on 18/6/60.Raced in 1960 & 1961. All aluminium competition car.							
1933 GT		1933 GT	250 GT	PF Notchback	Coupe	Pininfarina			
1935 GT		1935 GT	250 GT	PF Notchback	Coupe	Pininfarina			
1937 GT		1937 GT	250 GT	Series II	Convertible	Pininfarina			U.S.A.(Lusso engine in '87)
1939 GT		1939 GT	250 GT	Series II	Convertible	Pininfarina			
1941 GT		1941 GT	250 GT	Series II	Convertible	Pininfarina			U.S.A.
1943 GT		1943 GT	250 GT	PF Notchback	Coupe	Pininfarina			U.S.A.
1945 SA		1945 SA	400 Superamerica	Series I SWB	Convertible	Pininfarina	Horten		U.S.A.
1947 GT		1947 GT	250 GT	Series II	Convertible	Pininfarina			
1949 GT		1949 GT	250 GT	Series II	Convertible	Pininfarina			
1951 GT		1951 GT	250 GT	SWB California	Spyder	Scaglietti			
		Completed 19/9/60.							
1953 GT		1953 GT	250 GT	Competition SWB	Berlinetta	Scaglietti	C.Marchi	Italy	U.S.A.?
		Sold on 28/6/60.Probably never raced. All aluminium competition car.							
1955 GT		1955 GT	250 GT	Series II	Convertible	Pininfarina			
1957 GT		1957 GT	250 GT	SWB California	Spyder	Scaglietti			
				Not confirmed as a California.					
1959 GT		1959 GT	250 GT	Series II	Convertible	Pininfarina			
1961 GT		1961 GT	250 GT	Series II	Convertible	Pininfarina			U.S.A.
		Covered headlights which may not be original.							
1963 GT		1963 GT	250 GT	SWB California	Spyder	Scaglietti			
		Not confirmed as a California.							
1965 GT		1965 GT	250 GT	Competition SWB	Berlinetta	Scaglietti	Francorchamps	Belgium	U.S.A.
		Sold on 13/6/60.Raced in 1960 thru 1962.Crashed and totally destroyed. Reappeared in 1964 with special Drogo body and stamped 1965GT. All aluminium body.							
1967 GT		1967 GT	250 GT	Series II	Convertible	Pininfarina			U.S.A.
1969 GT		1969 GT	250 GT	Series II	Convertible	Pininfarina			U.S.A.
1971 GT		1971 GT	250 GT	PF Notchback	Coupe	Pininfarina			
1973 GT		1973 GT	250 GT	PF Notchback	Coupe	Pininfarina			
1975 GT*?		1975 GT	250 GT	PF Notchback	Coupe	Pininfarina			U.K.?
1977 GT		1977 GT	250 GT	PF Notchback	Coupe	Pininfarina			
1979 GT		1979 GT	250 GT	Series II	Convertible	Pininfarina			
1981 GT		1981 GT	250 GT	Series II	Convertible	Pininfarina			

Chassis No.	Picture Ref	Engine No.	Type	Model	Body Style	Coach-builder	First Owner	Original Location	Present Location
1983 GT		1983 GT	250 GT	Series II	Convertible	Pininfarina			
1985 GT		1985 GT	250 GT	PF Notchback	Coupe	Pininfarina			U.S.A.
1987 GT		1987 GT	250 GT	PF Notchback	Coupe	Pininfarina			U.S.A.
1989 GT		1989 GT	250 GT	PF Notchback	Coupe	Pininfarina			
1991 GT		1991 GT	250 GT	Series II	Convertible	Pininfarina			
1993 GT*		1993 GT*	250 GT	Steel SWB	Berlinetta	Scaglietti	Ronnie Hoare/David Cl	U.K.	U.K.
	Sold on 25/7/60.Never raced.								
1995 GT*		1995 GT*	250 GT	Steel SWB	Berlinetta	Scaglietti	M.Eyre	U.K.	U.K.
	Sold on 3/9/60.Never raced.								
1997 GT		1997 GT	250 GT	Competition SWB	Berlinetta	Scaglietti			U.S.A.
	Sold on 15/6/60.Also reported to be a SWB California Spyder! All aluminium body.								
1999 GT		1999 GT	250 GT	Competition SWB	Berlinetta	Scaglietti	C.-M. Abate	Italy	Italy
	Sold on 20/6/60.Raced in1960.Crashed and completely destroyed.In 1978 a new car was being constructed using the same number.All aluminium competition coupé.								
2001 GT		2001 GT	250 GT	Competition SWB	Berlinetta	Scaglietti	F.Tavano	France	Germany?
	Sold on 20/6/60.Raced in 1960,1961,1964 & 1965. All aluminium competition car.								
2003 GT		2003 GT	250 GT	PF Notchback	Coupe	Pininfarina			
2005 GT		2005 GT	250 GT	Series II	Convertible	Pininfarina			
2007 SA	P1/250,251,25!	2007 SA	400 Superamerica	Series I	Coupe	Pininfarina	N. De Nora	Italy	U.S.A.
	Shown at the 1960 Turin Motor Show as Superfast II and later became Superfast IV.Believed based on a Series II PF Convertible chassis.								
2009 GT		2009 GT	250 GT	Competition SWB	Berlinetta	Scaglietti	G.Whitehead	U.K.	Italy
	Sold on 21/6/60.Raced in 1960 and 1961. All aluminium body.								
2011 GT		2011 GT	250 GT	Series II	Convertible	Pininfarina			
2013 GT		2013 GT	250 GT	Series II	Convertible	Pininfarina			
2015 GT		2015 GT	250 GT	SWB California	Spyder	Scaglietti	Sturgis?	U.S.A.	U.S.A.
	Completed on 20/6/60.DNFd in 1960 LeMans driven by Sturgis & Schlesser. Covered headlights.All aluminium body.Outside filler cap.								
2017 GT		2017 GT	250 GT	PF Notchback	Coupe	Pininfarina			
2019 GT		2019 GT	250 GT	PF Notchback	Coupe	Pininfarina			
2021 GT		2021 GT	250 GT	Competition SWB	Berlinetta	Scaglietti	O.Benedetti/Noblet	France	France
	Sold on 7/6/60.Raced in 1960,1961,1964,1965,& 1966. All aluminium competition car.								
2023 GT		2023 GT	250 GT	PF Notchback	Coupe	Pininfarina			
2025 GT		2025 GT	250 GT	Competition SWB	Berlinetta	Scaglietti	A.Colombo/Lualdi	Italy	Italy.(Not original engine
	Sold on 22/7/60.Raced in 1960 & 1961.Later in an accident. All aluminium body.								
2027 GT		2027 GT	250 GT	PF Notchback	Coupe	Pininfarina			
2029 GT		2029 GT	250 GT	Series II	Convertible	Pininfarina			Switzerland?
2031 GTE		2031 GTE	250	GTE	2 + 2	Pininfarina			
	Shown at the 1961 Turin Motor Show.Belived to be the fourth prototype 250GTE 2 + 2 and the first production version.								
2033 GT		2033 GT	250 GT	Competition SWB	Berlinetta	Scaglietti	Luglio	Italy	U.S.A.
	Sold on 5/8/60. All aluminium body.								
2035 GT		2035 GT	250 GT	Competition SWB	Berlinetta	Scaglietti	J.Gaspar/H.Macedo	Portugal	U.S.A.
	Sold on 13/7/60.Raced from 1960 thru 1964. All aluminium body.								
2037 GT		2037 GT	250 GT	Series II	Convertible	Pininfarina			
2039 GT		2039 GT	250 GT	Series II	Convertible	Pininfarina			U.S.A.
2041 GT		2041 GT	250 GT	Series II	Convertible	Pininfarina			
2043 GTE	P1/230	2043 GTE	250	GTE	2 + 2	Pininfarina			France
	Shown at the 1960 Paris Salon .Believed to be the second production version of this new model.								
2045 GT		2045 GT	250 GT	Series II	Convertible	Pininfarina			
2047 GT		2047 GT	250 GT	Series II	Convertible	Pininfarina			
2049 GT		2049 GT	250 GT	PF Notchback	Coupe	Pininfarina			
2051 GT		2051 GT	250 GT	PF Notchback	Coupe	Pininfarina			
2053 GT		2053 GT	250 GT	Competition SWB	Berlinetta	Scaglietti	C.Toselli	Italy	Destroyed
	Sold on 2/8/60.Raced 1960 thru 1964.Destroyed in accident. Used by the factory as an early study for the GTO. All aluminium body.								
2055 GT		2055 GT	250 GT	Steel SWB	Berlinetta	Scaglietti	M.Attilio	Italy	U.S.A.
	Sold on 12/8/60.Never raced.								
2057 GT		2057 GT	250 GT	Series II	Convertible	Pininfarina			U.S.A.
	Rebuilt as replica 250GTR for Count Volpi.								
2059 GT		2059 GT	250 GT	Series II	Convertible	Pininfarina			
2061 GT		2061 GT	250 GT	Series II	Convertible	Pininfarina			
2063 GT		2063 GT	250 GT	Series II	Convertible	Pininfarina			
2065 GT		2065 GT	250 GT	PF Notchback	Coupe	Pininfarina			U.K.
	Rebodied in the 1960s with Drogo body - body removed in late 1970s.In 1980s another Drogo coupé body fitted.								
2067 GT		2067 GT	250 GT	Steel SWB	Berlinetta	Scaglietti	F.Caimi	Italy	U.K.
	Sold on 11/8/60.Never raced.Later rebodied by Drogo.Recently rebodied again with a GTO style body.								
2069 GT		2069 GT	250 GT	Steel SWB	Berlinetta	Scaglietti	Francorchamps/ De Feirland	Belgium	Switzerland?
	Sold on 23/10/60.Never raced.								
2071 GT		2071 GT	250 GT	Series II	Convertible	Pininfarina			
2073 GT		2073 GT	250 GT	Series II	Convertible	Pininfarina			
2075 GT		2075 GT	250 GT	Series II	Convertible	Pininfarina			
2077 GT		2077 GT	250 GT	Series II	Convertible	Pininfarina			
2079 GT		2079 GT	250 GT	Series II	Convertible	Pininfarina			
2081 GT		2081 GT	250 GT	PF Notchback	Coupe	Pininfarina			
	Last one built.								
2083 GT		2083 GT	250 GT	Competition SWB	Berlinetta	Scaglietti	A.Recordati/Volpi	Italy	U.S.A.
	Sold on 9/9/60.Raced in 1960. All aluminium body.								
2085 GT		2085 GT	250 GT	Series II	Convertible	Pininfarina			

Chassis No.	Picture Ref	Engine No.	Type	Model	Body Style	Coach-builder	First Owner	Original Location	Present Location
2087 GT		2087 GT	250 GT	Series II	Convertible	Pininfarina			
2089 GT		2089 GT	250 GT	Series II	Convertible	Pininfarina			
2091 GT		2091 GT	250 GT	Series II	Convertible	Pininfarina			
2093 GT		2093 GT	250 GT	Series II	Convertible	Pininfarina			
2095 GT		2095 GT	250 GT	Competition SWB	Berlinetta	Scaglietti	A.Cacciari	Italy	U.S.A.
	Sold on 13/8/60. Raced 1960 thru 1962.								
2097 GT		2097 GT	250 GT	Series II	Convertible	Pininfarina			
2099 GT		2099 GT	250 GT	Series II	Convertible	Pininfarina			
2101 GT		2101 GT	250 GT	Series II	Convertible	Pininfarina			
2103 GT		2103 GT	250 GT	Series II	Convertible	Pininfarina			
2105 GT		2105 GT	250 GT	Series II	Convertible	Pininfarina			
2107 GT		2107 GT	250 GT	Series II	Convertible	Pininfarina			
2109 GT		2109 GT	250 GT	Series II	Convertible	Pininfarina			
2111 GT		2111 GT	250 GT	Steel SWB	Berlinetta	Scaglietti	A.Roma	Italy	U.S.A.
	Sold in September 1961.								
2113 GT		2113 GT	250 GT	Series II	Convertible	Pininfarina			
2115 GT		2115 GT	250 GT	Series II	Convertible	Pininfarina			
2117 GT*		2117 GT	250 GT	Series II	Convertible	Pininfarina			
2119 GT*		2119 GT	250 GT	Competition SWB	Berlinetta	Scaglietti	G.Piccinini/S.Moss/ R.Walker	U.K.	U.K.
	Sold on 11/8/60. Raced in 1960 and 1961. All aluminium competition car.								
2121 GT		2121 GT	250 GT	Series II	Convertible	Pininfarina			
2123 GT		2123 GT	250 GT	Series II	Convertible	Pininfarina			
2125 GT		2125 GT	250 GT	Series II	Convertible	Pininfarina			
2127 GT		2127 GT	250 GT	Competition SWB	Berlinetta	Scaglietti	Pierre Dumay	France	France
	Sold on 12/9/60. Raced 1960 thru 1964. All aluminium competition car.								
2129 GT	JP/84,85.	2129 GT	250 GT	Competition SWB	Berlinetta	Scaglietti	Willie Mairesse	Belgium	U.K.
	Sold on 12/9/60. Raced 1960 & 1961. All aluminium body.								
2131 GT		2131 GT	250 GT	Series II	Convertible	Pininfarina			
2133 GT		2133 GT	250 GT	Series II	Convertible	Pininfarina			
2135 GT		2135 GT	250 GT	Series II	Convertible	Pininfarina			
2137 GT		2137 GT	250 GT	Series II	Convertible	Pininfarina			
2139 GT		2139 GT	250 GT	Series II	Cabriolet	Pininfarina			
2141 GT		2141 GT	250 GT	Competition SWB	Berlinetta	Scaglietti	Zambrini/Volpi	Italy	Italy (parts only)
	Sold on 12/9/60. Raced in 1960. Destroyed but motor saved. All aluminium body.								
2143 GT		2143 GT	250 GT	Series II	Convertible	Pininfarina			
2145 GT		2145 GT	250 GT	Series II	Convertible	Pininfarina			
2147 GT		2147 GT	250 GT	Series II	Convertible	Pininfarina			
2149 GT		2149 GT	250 GT	Competition SWB	Berlinetta	Scaglietti	Olivier Gendebien	Belgium	Switzerland
	Sold on 12/9/60. Raced in 1960. All aluminium body.								
2151 GT		2151 GT	250 GT	Series II	Convertible	Pininfarina			
2153 GT		2153 GT	250 GT	Series II	Convertible	Pininfarina			
2155 GT		2155 GT	250 GT	Series II	Convertible	Pininfarina			
2157 GT		2157 GT	250 GT	Series II	Convertible	Pininfarina			
2159 GT		2159 GT	250 GT	Competition SWB	Berlinetta	Scaglietti	Spinedi	Switzerland	Holland
	Sold on 28/9/60. Raced in 1961 thru 1964.								
2161 GT		2161 GT	250 GT	SWB California	Spyder	Scaglietti			
2163 GT		2163 GT	250 GT	Competition SWB	Berlinetta	Scaglietti	V.Malago/Volpi	Italy	U.K.
	Raced in 1960 & 1961. All aluminium body.						(with Engine 1615GT from competition California.)		
2165 GT		2165 GT	250 GT	Competition SWB	Berlinetta	Scaglietti	Andre Simon	France	France
	Sold on 14/9/60. Raced 1960 thru 1962. All aluminium body.								
2167 GT		2167 GT	250 GT	SWB California	Spyder	Scaglietti		Italy	U.S.A.
	Completed in December 1960. Remained in Italy until 1985.								
2169 GTE		2169 GTE	250	GTE	2 + 2	Pininfarina			
	Shown at the 1960 Paris Salon.								
2171 GTE		2171 GTE	250	GTE	2 + 2	Pininfarina			
2173 GTE		2173 GTE	250	GTE	2 + 2	Pininfarina			
2175 GT		2175 GT	250 GT	SWB California	Spyder	Scaglietti	Roger Vadim	France	France
	Remained in France throughout its life. Believed special engine.								
2177 GT		2177 GT	250 GT	Steel SWB	Berlinetta	Scaglietti	DeGraffenried/Zimmer	Switzerland	U.S.A.
	Sold on 29/10/60. Never raced. Competition gearbox.								
2179 GT		2179 GT	250 GT	Competition SWB	Berlinetta	Scaglietti	M.Vandelli	Belgium	Holland
	Sold on 17/10/60. Raced in 1961. All aluminium body.								
2181 GTE		2181 GTE	250	GTE	2 + 2	Pininfarina			
2183 GTE		2183 GTE	250	GTE	2 + 2	Pininfarina			
2185 GTE*		2185 GTE	250	GTE	2 + 2	Pininfarina			
	Believed shown at the 1960 London Motor Show. The first RHD version.								
2187 GTE		2187 GTE	250	GTE	2 + 2	Pininfarina			
2189 GTE		2189 GTE	250	GTE	2 + 2	Pininfarina			U.K.
2191 GTE		2191 GTE	250	GTE	2 + 2	Pininfarina			
2193 GTE		2193 GTE	250	GTE	2 + 2	Pininfarina			
2195 GTE		2195 GTE	250	GTE	2 + 2	Pininfarina			
2197 GTE		2197 GTE	250	GTE	2 + 2	Pininfarina			
2199 GTE		2199 GTE	250	GTE	2 + 2	Pininfarina			U.K.
2201 GTE		2201 GTE	250	GTE	2 + 2	Pininfarina			

Chassis No.	Picture Ref	Engine No.	Type	Model	Body Style	Coach-builder	First Owner	Original Location	Present Location
2203 GTE		2203 GTE	250	GTE	2 + 2	Pininfarina			
2205 GTE		2205 GTE	250	GTE	2 + 2	Pininfarina			Switzerland
2207 SA	P1/250,255	2207 SA	400 Superamerica	Series I SWB	Coupe	Pininfarina	N.de Nora	Italy	U.S.A.
	Shown at the 1960 Turin Motor Show as Superfast II. Later revised and became Superfast IV. Special one off show car.								
2209 GT		2209 GT	250 GT	Competition SWB Berlinetta		Scaglietti	Jo Schlesser	France	U.K.(Non-original engine
	Sold on 19/10/60. Raced in 1960, 1961 & 1963. Rebodied by Drogo. Later rebodied back to standard in U.K..(Drogo body used on 2065GT.)								
2211 GT		2211 GT	250 GT	Series II	Convertible	Pininfarina			
	First of the second 100 Series II Convertibles.								
2213 GTE		2213 GTE	250	GTE	2 + 2	Pininfarina			
2215 GTE		2215 GTE	250	GTE	2 + 2	Pininfarina			
2217 GTE		2217 GTE	250	GTE	2 + 2	Pininfarina			
2219 GTE		2219 GTE	250	GTE	2 + 2	Pininfarina			
2221 GT*		2221 GT	250 GT	Competition SWB Berlinetta		Scaglietti	Ron Fry	U.K.	Italy
	Sold on 5/10/60. All aluminium body.								
2223 GTE		2223 GTE	250	GTE	2 + 2	Pininfarina			
2225 GTE		2225 GTE	250	GTE	2 + 2	Pininfarina			
2227 GTE		2227 GTE	250	GTE	2 + 2	Pininfarina			
2229 GTE		2229 GTE	250	GTE	2 + 2	Pininfarina			
2231 GT		2231 GT	250 GT	Competition SWB Berlinetta		Scaglietti	Adrian Conan Doyle	Switzerland	U.K.
	Sold on 9/11/60. Later modified with Chiti nose. All aluminium body.								
2233 GTE		2233 GTE	250	GTE	2 + 2	Pininfarina			
2235 GTE	FM/159.	2235 GTE	250	GTE	2 + 2	Pininfarina			U.S.A.
	Rebodied by Fantuzzi for Luigi Chinetti with 'basket handle' body like a 250P and fitted with a TR specification engine.								
2237 GT		2237 GT	250 GT	Competition SWB Berlinetta		Scaglietti	Chinetti/C.Hayes	U.S.A.	Germany
	Sold on 14/11/60. Raced in 1961 & 1962. All aluminium body.								
2239 GTE		2239 GTE	250	GTE	2 + 2	Pininfarina			
2241 GTE		2241 GTE	250	GTE	2 + 2	Pininfarina			
2243 GT		2243 GT	250 GT	Steel SWB	Berlinetta	Scaglietti	Chinetti/R.Gray	U.S.A.	U.S.A.
	Sold on 29/11/60. Never raced.								
2245 GTE*		2245 GTE	250	GTE	2 + 2	Pininfarina			U.K.?
2247 GTE		2247 GTE	250	GTE	2 + 2	Pininfarina			
2249 GT		2249 GT	250 GT	SWB California	Spyder	Scaglietti			
2251 GT		2251 GT	250 GT	Steel SWB	Berlinetta	Scaglietti	F.Mosters		Holland
	Sold on 12/12/60. Never raced.								
2253 GTE*?		2253 GTE	250	GTE	2 + 2	Pininfarina			Australia
2255 GTE		2255 GTE	250	GTE	2 + 2	Pininfarina			Germany
2257 SA		2257 SA	400 Superamerica	Speciale	2 + 2	Pininfarina	M.Paul Cavallier	France	U.S.A.
	400SA engine installed in a 250GTE 2+2 body.								
2259 GTE		2259 GTE	250	GTE	2 + 2	Pininfarina			
2261 GTE		2261 GTE	250	GTE	2 + 2	Pininfarina			France
2263 GTE		2263 GTE	250	GTE	2 + 2	Pininfarina			
2265 GT		2265 GT	250 GT	Steel SWB	Berlinetta	Scaglietti	Don Marsh	U.S.A.	Mexico
	Sold 12/12/60. Never raced.								
2267 GTE		2267 GTE	250	GTE	2 + 2	Pininfarina			
2269 GT		2269 GT	250 GT	Steel SWB	Coupe	Scaglietti	Robert Fergus	U.S.A.	Germany?
	Sold on 29/12/60. Sold to Germany without engine/gearbox.								
2271 GTE		2271 GTE	250	GTE	2 + 2	Pininfarina			
2273 GTE		2273 GTE	250	GTE	2 + 2	Pininfarina			
2275 GT		2275 GT	250 GT	Series II	Convertible	Pininfarina			
	Believed shown at the 1960 Brussels Motor Show.								
1961									
2277 GT		2277 GT	250 GT	SWB California	Spyder	Scaglietti			U.S.A.
	Shown at Brussels Motor Show 1961.								
2279 GTE		2279 GTE	250	GTE	2 + 2	Pininfarina			
2281 GTE		2281 GTE	250	GTE	2 + 2	Pininfarina			
2283 GT		2283 GT	250 GT	Steel SWB	Berlinetta	Scaglietti	Foussier	France	France
	Sold on 20/1/61. Never raced.								
2285 GTE*		2285 GTE	250	GTE	2 + 2	Pininfarina			U.K.?
2287 GTE*		2287 GTE	250	GTE	2 + 2	Pininfarina			U.K.?
2289 GT		2289 GT	250 GT	Steel SWB	Berlinetta	Scaglietti	Pozzi/Martin	France	France
	Sold on 8/2/61. Never raced.								
2291 GT		2291 GT	250 GT	Steel SWB	Berlinetta	Scaglietti	Francorchamps/L.Dernier	Belgium	U.S.A.
	Sold on 1/1/61. Raced in 1961.								
2293 GTE		2293 GTE	250	GTE	2 + 2	Pininfarina			
2295 GTE		2295 GTE	250	GTE	2 + 2	Pininfarina			
2297 GTE		2297 GTE	250	GTE	2 + 2	Pininfarina			
2299 GTE*		2299 GTE	250	GTE	2 + 2	Pininfarina			U.K.?
2301 ??		2301 ??		??	??				
2303 GTE		2303 GTE	250	GTE	2 + 2	Pininfarina			France
2305 GT		2305 GT	250 GT	Series II	Convertible	Pininfarina			
2307 GT		2307 GT	250 GT	Series II	Convertible	Pininfarina			
2309 GTE		2309 GTE	250	GTE	2 + 2	Pininfarina			
2311 SA*	P1/256	2311 SA	400 Superamerica	Series I SWB	Spyder California	Scaglietti	F.Gosce	Italy	U.S.A.
	Completed 5/5/61. In U.K. for many years. Covered headlights. Outside filler cap.								

Chassis No.	Picture Ref	Engine No.	Type	Model	Body Style	Coach-builder	First Owner	Original Location	Present Location
2313 GTE		2313 GTE	250	GTE	2 + 2	Pininfarina			
2315 GTE		2315 GTE	250	GTE	2 + 2	Pininfarina			
2317 GTE		2317 GTE	250	GTE	2 + 2	Pininfarina			
2319 GT		2319 GT	250 GT	Series II	Convertible	Pininfarina			
2321 GT		2321 GT	250 GT	Competition SWB	Berlinetta	Scaglietti		Italy	France
Sold on 2/2/61. Sold to France. All aluminium body.									
2323 GTE*?		2323 GTE	250	GTE	2 + 2	Pininfarina			Australia
2325 GTE		2325 GTE	250	GTE	2 + 2	Pininfarina			
2327 GT		2327 GT	250 GT	Series II	Convertible	Pininfarina			U.K.
2329 GT		2329 GT	250 GT	Series II	Cabriolet	Pininfarina			
2331 SA		2331 SA	400 Superamerica	Series I SWB	Convertible	Pininfarina		Italy	U.S.A.
Delivered on 13/2/60. Shown at the 1960 Geneva Motor Show.									
2333 GTE		2333 GTE	250	GTE	2 + 2	Pininfarina			
2335 GT		2335 GT	250 GT	Steel SWB	Berlinetta	Scaglietti	Pozzi/L.Gamet	France	France
Sold on 1/1/61. Never raced.									
2337 GTE		2337 GTE	250	GTE	2 + 2	Pininfarina			
2339 GTE		2339 GTE	250	GTE	2 + 2	Pininfarina			
2341 GT		2341 GT	250 GT	Series II	Cabriolet	Pininfarina			
2343 GT		2343 GT	250 GT	Series II	Convertible	Pininfarina			
2345 GTE		2345 GTE	250	GTE	2 + 2	Pininfarina			U.S.A.
2347 GT		2347 GT	250 GT	Steel SWB	Berlinetta	Scaglietti	Ferrari Rep of Hollywood	U.S.A.	U.K.(with Engi No.1903GT).
Sold on 11/2/61. Never raced.									
2349 GTE		2349 GTE	250	GTE	2 + 2	Pininfarina			Sweden
2351 GTE*?		2351 GTE	250	GTE	2 + 2	Pininfarina			Australia
2353 GTE		2353 GTE	250	GTE	2 + 2	Pininfarina			
2355 GTE		2355 GTE	250	GTE	2 + 2	Pininfarina			
2357 GTE		2357 GTE	250	GTE	2 + 2	Pininfarina			
2359 GT		2359 GT	250 GT	Series II	Convertible	Pininfarina			
2361 GT		2361 GT	250 GT	Series II	Convertible	Pininfarina			U.S.A.
2363 GTE		2363 GTE	250	GTE	2 + 2	Pininfarina			
2365 GT		2365 GT	250 GT	Steel SWB	Berlinetta	Scaglietti			Holland
(Not on Jess Pourretr's list.)									
2367 GTE		2367 GTE	250	GTE	2 + 2	Pininfarina			
2369 GTE		2369 GTE	250	GTE	2 + 2	Pininfarina			
2371 GTE		2371 GTE	250	GTE	2 + 2	Pininfarina			
2373 SA		2373 SA	400 Superamerica	Series I SWB	Coupe	Pininfarina	O.de Nora	Italy	U.S.A.
Delivered on 3/3/61.									
2375 GTE		2375 GTE	250	GTE	2 + 2	Pininfarina			U.S.A.
2377 GT		2377 GT	250 GT	SWB California	Spyder	Scaglietti			U.S.A.
Completed 3/3/61. Once owned by actor James Coburn. Covered headlights.									
2379 GTE		2379 GTE	250	GTE	2 + 2	Pininfarina			
2381 GT		2381 GT	250 GT	Series II	Convertible	Pininfarina			
2383 GT		2383 GT	250 GT	SWB California	Spyder	Scaglietti			U.S.A.
May have been built as a competition car but no racing history known. Covered headlights. All aluminium body.									
2385 GT		2385 GT	250 GT	Series II	Convertible	Pininfarina			
2387 GTE		2387 GTE	250	GTE	2 + 2	Pininfarina			
2389 GT		2389 GT	250 GT	Steel SWB	Berlinetta	Scaglietti	Roussel	France	U.S.A.
Sold March 1961. Raced briefly. (Last 1960 model)									
2391 GTE		2391 GTE	250	GTE	2 + 2	Pininfarina			
2393 GT		2393 GT	250 GT	Series II	Convertible	Pininfarina			
2395 GT		2395 GT	250 GT	Series II	Convertible	Pininfarina			
Converted to covered headlights?									
2397 GTE		2397 GTE	250	GTE	2 + 2	Pininfarina			Holland
2399 GT		2399 GT	250 GT	Steel SWB	Berlinetta	Scaglietti	Montchoisy	Switzerland	Italy
Sold on 9/3/61. Never raced.									
2401 GTE		2401 GTE	250	GTE	2 + 2	Pininfarina			
2403 GTE		2403 GTE	250	GTE	2 + 2	Pininfarina			
2405 GT		2405 GT	250	GTE	2 + 2	Pininfarina			
2407 SA*	P1/249	2407 SA	400 SA	Superamerica	Convertible	Pininfarina	F.Rivetti	Italy	U.S.A.
Delivered on 29/4/61. Special body with hardtop.									
2409 GTE		2409 GTE	250	GTE	2 + 2	Pininfarina			
2411 GTE		2411 GTE	250	GTE	2 + 2	Pininfarina			
2413 GT		2413 GT	250 GT	Series II	Convertible	Pininfarina			
2415 GT		2415 GT	250 GT	Series II	Convertible	Pininfarina			U.S.A.
2417 GT		2417 GT	250 GT	Competition SWB	Berlinetta	Scaglietti	Ronnie Hoare	U.K.	France
Sold on 31/7/61. Raced by the factory in 1961 and Maranello Concessionnaires in 1961. All aluminium body.									
2419 GT		2419 GT	250 GT	Steel SWB	Berlinetta	Scaglietti	Blondet	France	France
Sold on 28/4/61. Last heard of crashed and being restored.									
2421 GTE		2421 GTE	250	GTE	2 + 2	Pininfarina			
2423 GTE		2423 GTE	250	GTE	2 + 2	Pininfarina			
2425 GTE		2425 GTE	250	GTE	2 + 2	Pininfarina			
2427 GTE		2427 GTE	250	GTE	2 + 2	Pininfarina			Switzerland
2429 GT	P1/259	2429 GT	250 GT	Competition SWB	Berlinetta	Pininfarina	Villard	France	France.
Sold on 16/5/61. One-off prototype for the GTO. All aluminium body.									

Chassis No.	Picture Ref	Engine No.	Type	Model	Body Style	Coach-builder	First Owner	Original Location	Present Location
2431 GTE		2431 GTE	250	GTE	2 + 2	Pininfarina			
2433 GTE		2433 GTE	250	GTE	2 + 2	Pininfarina			
2435 GTE		2435 GTE	250	GTE	2 + 2	Pininfarina			
2437 GTE*		2437 GTE	250	GTE	2 + 2	Pininfarina			
2439 GT		2439 GT	250 GT	Alloy SWB	Berlinetta	Scaglietti	G.Andersson	Sweden	Sweden
		Sold on 16/5/61. Raced in 1961. All Aluminium competion car.							
2441 GT		2441 GT	250 GT	Series II	Convertible	Pininfarina			
2443 GT		2443 GT	250 GT	Steel SWB	Berlinetta	Scaglietti	Zweidler	Switzerland	Italy.
		Sold on 4/5/61. Never raced.							
2445 GT		2445 GT	250 GT	Alloy SWB	Berlinetta	Scaglietti	Adrian/Crevits	Belgium	Switzerland (parts only).
		Sold on 16 May 1961. Raced in 1961 and 1962. Crashed and parted out. All aluminium competition car.							
2447 GT		2447 GT	250 GT	Series II	Convertible	Pininfarina			
2449 GT		2449 GT	250 GT	Series II	Convertible	Pininfarina			
2451 GTE		2451 GTE	250	GTE	2 + 2	Pininfarina			
2453 GTE		2453 GTE	250	GTE	2 + 2	Pininfarina			
2455 GT		2455 GT	250 GT	Competition SWB	Berlinetta	Scaglietti	Chinetti/Price	U.S.A.	U.S.A.
		Sold in March 1961. Raced in 1961. All aluminium body.							
2457 GTE		2457 GTE	250	GTE	2 + 2	Pininfarina			
2459 GTE		2459 GTE	250	GTE	2 + 2	Pininfarina			
2461 GTE		2461 GTE	250	GTE	2 + 2	Pininfarina			
2463 GTE		2463 GTE	250	GTE	2 + 2	Pininfarina			
2465 GT		2465 GT	250 GT	Series II	Convertible	Pininfarina			
2467 GT		2467 GT	250 GT	SWB California	Spyder	Scaglietti			U.S.A.
		Completed 21/4/61.							
2469 GT		2469 GT	250 GT	SWB California	Spyder	Scaglietti			U.S.A.
2471 GT		2471 GT	250 GT	Series II	Convertible	Pininfarina			
2473 GT		2473 GT	250 GT	Series II	Convertible	Pininfarina			
2475 GTE		2475 GTE	250	GTE	2 + 2	Pininfarina			
2477 GTE		2477 GTE	250	GTE	2 + 2	Pininfarina			
2479 GTE		2479 GTE	250	GTE	2 + 2	Pininfarina			
2481 GTE		2481 GTE	250	GTE	2 + 2	Pininfarina			
2483 GTE		2483 GTE	250	GTE	2 + 2	Pininfarina			
		Shown at the 1961 Geneva Motor Show.							
2485 GTE		2485 GTE	250	GTE	2 + 2	Pininfarina			
2487 GTE		2487 GTE	250	GTE	2 + 2	Pininfarina			
2489 GT		2489 GT	250 GT	Series II	Convertible	Pininfarina			Switzerland?
2491 GT		2491 GT	250 GT	SWB	Berlinetta	Scaglietti			U.S.A.
		Rebodied by Zagato in 1971. as the '3Z' Convertible for Chinetti's NART and shown at the 1971 Turin Motor Show.							
2493 GTE		2493 GTE	250	GTE	2 + 2	Pininfarina			
2495 GTE		2495 GTE	250	GTE	2 + 2	Pininfarina			U.S.A.
2497 GTE		2497 GTE	250	GTE	2 + 2	Pininfarina			
2499 GTE		2499 GTE	250	GTE	2 + 2	Pininfarina			
2501 GT		2501 GT	250 GT	Steel SWB	Berlinetta	Scaglietti	Chenetti/Price	U.S.A.	U.S.A.
2503 GTE		2503 GTE	250	GTE	2 +2	Pininfarina			
2505 GT		2505 GT	250 GT	SWB California	Spyder	Scaglietti			
2507 GTE		2507 GTE	250	GTE	2 + 2	Pininfarina			Switzerland
2509 GTE		2509 GTE	250	GTE	2 + 2	Pininfarina			
2511 GTE		2511 GTE	250	GTE	2 + 2	Pininfarina			
2513 GTE		2513 GTE	250	GTE	2 + 2	Pininfarina			
2515 GT		2515 GT	250	GTE	2 + 2	Pininfarina			Switzerland
2517 GT		2517 GT	250 GT	Comp. SWB	Berlinetta	Scaglietti	FBA	France	France
		Raced in 1961 and 1962. All aluminium body.							
2519 GT		2519 GT	250 GTE	Series II	Convertible	Pininfarina			
2521 GT		2521 GT	250 GT	Steel SWB	Berlinetta	Scaglietti	R. Ceschina	Italy	U.S.A.
		Sold on 8/8/61. In U.S.A. since early 1960's							
2523 GTE		2523 GTE	250	GTE	2 + 2	Pininfarina			
		Rebodied in 1986 with all aluminium replica body based on 250TR 0666GT.							
2525 GTE		2525 GTE	250	GTE	2 + 2	Pininfarina			
2527 GTE		2527 GTE	250	GTE	2 + 2	Pininfarina			
2529 GTE		2529 GTE	250	GTE	2 + 2	Pininfarina			U.S.A.
2531 GTE		2531 GTE	250	GTE	2 + 2	Pininfarina			
2533 GT		2533 GT	250 GTF	Series II	Convertible	Pininfarina			
2535 GT		2535 GT	250 GTF	Series II	Convertible	Pininfarina			
2537 GT		2537 GT	250 GT	SWB California	Spyder	Scaglietti	W.VonTrips?	Italy	U.S.A.
		In U.S.A. for many years. Open headlights.							
2539 GTE		2539 GTE	250	GTE	2 + 2	Pininfarina			
2541 GTE		2541 GTE	250	GTE	2 + 2	Pininfarina			
2543 GTE		2543 GTE	250	GTE	2 + 2	Pininfarina			
2545 GTE		2545 GTE	250	GTE	2 + 2	Pininfarina			
2547 GTE		2547 GTE	250	GTE	2 + 2	Pininfarina			
2549 GT		2549 GT	250 GT	Steel SWB	Berlinetta	Scaglietti	Dave Garraway	U.S.A.	U.S.A.
		In U.S.A. from new.							
2551 GT		2551 GT	250 GT	Steel SWB	Berlinetta	Scaglietti	L.Canavese	Italy	U.S.A.
		Sold on 13/5/61.							
2553 GTE		2553 GTE	250	GTE	2 + 2	Pininfarina			
2555 GTE		2555 GTE	250	GTE	2 + 2	Pininfarina			Switzerland
2557 GTE		2557 GTE	250	GTE	2 + 2	Pininfarina			

Chassis No.	Picture Ref	Engine No.	Type	Model	Body Style	Coach-builder	First Owner	Original Location	Present Location
2559 GTE		2559 GTE	250	GTE	2 + 2	Pininfarina			
2561 GT		2561 GT	250 GT	SWB California	Spyder	Scaglietti			
2563 GT		2563 GT	250 GT	Steel SWB	Berlinetta	Scaglietti	A.Demetriadi	Italy	Switzerland
	Sold on 15/5/61.								
2565 GTE		2565 GTE	250	GTE	2 + 2	Pininfarina			
2567 GTE		2567 GTE	250	GTE	2 + 2	Pininfarina			
2569 GTE		2569 GTE	250	GTE	2 + 2	Pininfarina			
2571 GTE		2571 GTE	250	GTE	2 + 2	Pininfarina			
2573 GTE		2573 GTE	250	GTE	2 + 2	Pininfarina			
2575 GTE		2575 GTE	250	GTE	2 + 2	Pininfarina			
2577 GTE		2577 GTE	250	GTE	2 + 2	Pininfarina			
2579 GTE		2579 GTE	250	GTE	2 + 2	Pininfarina			
2581 GTE		2581 GTE	250	GTE	2 + 2	Pininfarina			
2583 GTE		2583 GTE	250	GTE	2 + 2	Pininfarina			
2585 GT		2585 GT	250 GTF	Series II	Convertible	Pininfarina			
2587 GT		2587 GT	250 GTF	Series II	Convertible	Pininfarina			
2589 GT		2589 GT	250 GT	Steel SWB	Berlinetta	Scaglietti	Livanos	France	U.K.
	Sold on 17/7/61.								
2591 GT		2591 GT	250	SWB California	Spyder	Scaglietti			
2593 GT		2593 GT	250 GTF	Series II	Convertible	Pininfarina			
2595 GT		2595 GT	250 GT	Steel SWB	Berlinetta	Scaglietti	M.Attilio	Italy	Germany
	Sold on 23/6/61. Raced in 1963.								
2597 GTE		2597 GTE	250	GTE	2 + 2	Pininfarina			
2599 GTE		2599 GTE	250	GTE	2 + 2	Pininfarina			
2601 GTE		2601 GTE	250	GTE	2 + 2	Pininfarina			
2603 GTE		2603 GTE	250	GTE	2 + 2	Pininfarina			
2605 GTE		2605 GTE	250	GTE	2 + 2	Pininfarina			
2607 GTE		2607 GTE	250	GTE	2 + 2	Pininfarina			
2609 GTE*		2609 GTE	250	GTE	2 + 2	Pininfarina			U.K.
2611 GT		2611 GT	250 GTF	Series II	Convertible	Pininfarina			U.S.A.
2613 GT	P1/260,JP/144	2613 GT	250 GT	Steel SWB	Berlinetta	Pininfarina	Prince Bernhard	Holland	Holland.
	Sold in August 1961. Body design based on 400SA Coupé Aerodinamico. Special one off prototype body.								
2615 GTE*		2615 GTE	250	GTE	2 + 2	Pininfarina			U.K.
2617 GT		2617 GT	250 GT	Steel SWB	Berlinetta	Scaglietti	Charles Rezzaghi	U.S.A.	U.S.A.
	Sold on 9/6/61.								
2619 GTE		2619 GTE	250	GTE	2 + 2	Pininfarina			
2621 GT		2621 GT	250 GTF	Series II	Convertible	Pininfarina			
2623 GTE		2623 GTE	250	GTE	2 + 2	Pininfarina			
2625 GTE		2625 GTE	250	GTE	2 + 2	Pininfarina			Switzerland
2627 GTE		2627 GTE	250	GTE	2 + 2	Pininfarina			
2629 GT		2629 GT	250 GTF	Series II	Convertible	Pininfarina			
2631 SA		2631 SA	400	Superamerica	Coupé	Pinifarina	Count Volpi	Italy	U.S.A.
	Delivered on 15/6/61. Coupé Aerodinamico.								
2633 GTE		2633 GTE	250	GTE	2 + 2	Pininfarina			
2635 GTE		2635 GTE	250	GTE	2 + 2	Pininfarina			
2637 GTE		2637 GTE	250	GTE	2 + 2	Pininfarina			
2639 GT		2639 GT	250 GT	Steel SWB	Berlinetta	Scaglietti	M.DallOrso	Italy	U.S.A.
	Sold on 21/7/61.								
2641 GTE*		2641 GTE	250	GTE	2 + 2	Pininfarina			Switzerland
2643 GT	P1/261	2643 GT	250 GT	Comp. SWB	Berlinetta	Scaglietti	Luigi Chinetti	U.S.A.	Italy
	Sold in January 1962. Raced by Ferrari at LeMans 1961 and at Daytona with NART. In U.S.A. for most of its life. Styling based on 400SA Coupé Aerodinamico. All aluminium body. One off prototype for the GTO.								
2645 GTE		2645 GTE	250	GTE	2 + 2	Pininfarina			Switzerland
2647 GTE		2647 GTE	250	GTE	2 + 2	Pininfarina			
2649 GT		2649 GT	250 GT	Steel SWB	Berlinetta	Scaglietti	R.Ricceri	Italy	Switzerland?
	Sold on 24/7/61.								
2651 GTE		2651 GTE	250	GTE	2 + 2	Pininfarina			
2653 GTE		2653 GTE	250	GTE	2 + 2	Pininfarina			
2655 GTE		2655 GTE	250	GTE	2 + 2	Pininfarina			
2657 GTE		2657 GTE	250	GTE	2 + 2	Pininfarina			
2659 GTE		2659 GTE	250	GTE	2 + 2	Pininfarina			
2661 GTE		2661 GTE	250	GTE	2 + 2	Pininfarina			
2663 GTE		2663 GTE	250	GTE	2 + 2	Pininfarina			
2665 GTE		2665 GTE	250	GTE	2 + 2	Pininfarina			
2667 GT		2667 GT	250 GT	Comp. SWB	Berlinetta	Scaglietti	C.Marchi	Italy	U.S.A.
	Sold on 14/7/61. All aluminium body.								
2669 GT		2669 GT	250 GT	Steel SWB	Berlinetta	Scaglietti	Mariotti	Switzerland	France
	Sold on 24/1/62.								
2671 GTE*		2671 GTE	250	GTE	2 + 2	Pininfarina			U.K.
2673 GTE		2673 GTE	250	GTE	2 + 2	Pininfarina			
2675 GTE		2675 GTE	250	GTE	2 + 2	Pininfarina			
2677 GTE*		2677 GTE	250	GTE	2 + 2	Pininfarina		U.K.	U.K.
	Believed to be the prototype for the 1962 version.								
2679 GTE		2679 GTE	250	GTE	2 + 2	Pininfarina			
2681 GTE		2681 GTE	250	GTE	2 + 2	Pininfarina			

Chassis No.	Picture Ref	Engine No.	Type	Model	Body Style	Coach-builder	First Owner	Original Location	Present Location
2683 GT		2683 GT	250 GTF	Series II	Convertible	Pininfarina			
2685 GTE		2685 GTE	250	GTE	2 + 2	Pininfarina			
2687 GT		2687 GT	250 GT	Comp. SWB	Berlinetta	Scaglietti	CAG/Lualdi	Italy	
Sold on 21 June 1961. Raced in Italy by Lualdi in 1961 and 1962. All aluminium body.									
2689 GT		2689 GT	250 GT	Comp. SWB	Berlinetta	Scaglietti	Pierre Noblet	France	U.S.A.
Sold on 3 June 1961. Finished 1st in GT class and 3rd OA at 1961 LeMans! Raced with further success in 1961 and 1962. All aluminium body.									
2691 GTE		2691 GTE	250	GTE	2 + 2	Pininfarina			
2693 GTE		2693 GTE	250	GTE	2 + 2	Pininfarina			
2695 GTE		2695 GTE	250	GTE	2 + 2	Pininfarina			
2697 GTE		2697 GTE	250	GTE	2 + 2	Pininfarina			
2699 GT		2699 GT	250 GTF	Series II	Convertible	Pininfarina			
2701 GT		2701 GT	250 GT	Comp. SWB	Berlinetta	Scaglietti	Leto diPriolo	Italy	U.S.A.
Sold in July 1961. Raced in 1961 and 1962. Last reported with non-original engine. All aluminium body.									
2703 GT		2703 GT	250 GTF	Series II	Convertible	Pininfarina			
2705 GTE		2705 GTE	250	GTE	2 + 2	Pininfarina			
2707 GTE		2707 GTE	250	GTE	2 + 2	Pininfarina			
2709 GTE		2709 GTE	250	GTE	2 + 2	Pininfarina			
2711 GTE		2711 GTE	250	GTE	2 + 2	Pininfarina		U.K.	U.K.
Believed to be a prototype for the 1962 version.									
2713 GTE		2713 GTE	250	GTE	2 + 2	Pininfarina			
Believed to be another 1962 version prototype.									
2715 GTE		2715 GTE	250	GTE	2 + 2	Pininfarina			Switzerland
2717 GTE		2717 GTE	250	GTE	2 + 2	Pininfarina			
2719 GTE		2719 GTE	250	GTE	2 + 2	Pininfarina			
2721 GTE		2721 GTE	250	GTE	2 + 2	Pininfarina			
2723 GTE		2723 GTE	250	GTE	2 + 2	Pininfarina			
2725 GT		2725 GT	250 GT	Comp. SWB	Berlinetta	Scaglietti	Chinetti/Arents	U.S.A.	U.S.A.
Sold in June 1961. Raced in 1961 and 1962. In recent years fitted with Engine No.2469GT. All aluminium body.									
2727 GTE		2727 GTE	250	GTE	2 + 2	Pininfarina			
2729 GT		2729 GT	250 GT	Comp. SWB	Berlinetta	Scaglietti	Pierre Dumay	France	Germany
Sold on 5/5/61. Raced in 1961 and 1962. All aluminium body.									
2731 GT		2731 GT	250 GT	Comp. SWB	Berlinetta	Scaglietti	L.Chinetti/R.Grossman	U.S.A.	Switzerland
Sold on 26/7/61. Raced in 1961 and 1962. Restored with new body made in England. All aluminium body.									
2733 GT		2733 GT	250 GT	Comp. SWB	Berlinetta	Scaglietti	Count Volpi Team	Italy	U.S.A.
Sold on 3/6/61. Raced in 1960. Sold to U.S.A. in early 1960s. Acquired Engine No.1733GT. All aluminium body.									
2735 GT*		2735 GT	250 GT	Comp. SWB	Berlinetta	Scaglietti	Stirling Moss/ Rob Walker	U.K.	U.K.
Sold on 30/5/61. Raced 1961 through 1965. Crashed in 1962 and rebodied with low Drogo body. Rebodied in 1983 with original style alloy body. All aluminium body.									
2737 GT		2737 GT	250 GTF	Series II	Convertible	Pininfarina			
2739 GTE		2739 GTE	250	GTE	2 + 2	Pininfarina			
2741 GTE		2741 GTE	250	GTE	2 + 2	Pininfarina			
2743 GTE		2743 GTE	250	GTE	2 + 2	Pininfarina			
2745 GTE		2745 GTE	250	GTE	2 + 2	Pininfarina			
2747 GTE		2747 GTE	250	GTE	2 + 2	Pininfarina			
2749 GTE		2749 GTE	250	GTE	2 + 2	Pininfarina			
2751 GTE		2751 GTE	250	GTE	2 + 2	Pininfarina			
2753 GTE		2753 GTE	250	GTE	2 + 2	Pininfarina			
2755 GTE		2755 GTE	250	GTE	2 + 2	Pininfarina			
2757 GTE		2757 GTE	250	GTE	2 + 2	Pininfarina			
2759 GTE		2759 GTE	250	GTE	2 + 2	Pininfarina			
2761 GTE		2761 GTE	250	GTE	2 + 2	Pininfarina			
2763 GTE		2763 GTE	250	GTE	2 + 2	Pininfarina			U.S.A.
2765 GT		2765 GT	250 GT	Steel SWB	Berlinetta	Scaglietti	M.Recordati/ Volpi Team	Italy	Italy
Sold on 24/8/61. Never raced. 'Lusso' trim.									
2767 GT		2767 GT	250 GT	Comp. SWB	Berlinetta	Scaglietti	S.Bettoja	Italy	Italy
Sold on 15/6/61. Raced in 1961. All aluminium body.									
2769 GTE		2769 GTE	250	GTE	2 + 2	Pininfarina			
2771 GTE		2771 GTE	250	GTE	2 + 2	Pininfarina			
2773 GTE		2773 GTE	250	GTE	2 + 2	Pininfarina			
2775 GTE		2775 GTE	250	GTE	2 + 2	Pininfarina			
2777 GTE		2777 GTE	250	GTE	2 + 2	Pininfarina			
2779 GTE		2779 GTE	250	GTE	2 + 2	Pininfarina			U.S.A.
2781 GTE		2781 GTE	250	GTE	2 + 2	Pininfarina			
2783 GTE		2783 GTE	250	GTE	2 + 2	Pininfarina			
2785 GTE		2785 GTE	250	GTE	2 + 2	Pininfarina			
2787 GT		2787 GT	250 GT	Comp. SWB	Berlinetta	Scaglietti	H.Oreiller	France	
Sold on 28/7/61. Raced in 1961 and 1962. All aluminium body.									
2789 GTE		2789 GTE	250	GTE	2 + 2	Pininfarina			
2791 GTE		2791 GTE	250	GTE	2 + 2	Pininfarina			
2793 GTE		2793 GTE	250	GTE	2 + 2	Pininfarina			
2795 GTE		2795 GTE	250	GTE	2 + 2	Pininfarina			
2797 GTE		2797 GTE	250	GTE	2 + 2	Pininfarina			
2799 GTE		2799 GTE	250	GTE	2 + 2	Pininfarina			
2801 GTE		2801 GTE	250	GTE	2 + 2	Pininfarina			
2803 GTE		2803 GTE	250	GTE	2 + 2	Pininfarina			
2805 GT		2805 GT	250 GTF	Series II	Convertible	Pininfarina			

Chassis No.	Picture Ref	Engine No.	Type	Model	Body Style	Coach-builder	First Owner	Original Location	Present Location
2807 GT		2807 GT	250 GT	Comp. SWB	Berlinetta	Scaglietti	De La Geneste	France	Sweden
	\multicolumn{9}{l}{Sold on 31/7/61. Raced 1961 through 1963. All aluminium body.}								
2809 SA		2809 SA	400	Superamerica	Coupé	Pininfarina	Count Somsky	Switzerland	Italy
	\multicolumn{9}{l}{Delivered on 27/7/61.}								
2811 GTE		2811 GTE	250	GTE	2 + 2	Pininfarina			
2813 GTE		2813 GTE	250	GTE	2 + 2	Pininfarina			
2815 GTE		2815 GTE	250	GTE	2 + 2	Pininfarina			
2817 GTE		2817 GTE	250	GTE	2 + 2	Pininfarina			
2819 GT		2819 GT	250 GT	Comp. SWB	Berlinetta	Scaglietti	Olivier Gendebien	Belgium	U.S.A.
	Sold on 11/9/61. Raced in 1961 and 1962. At the end of 1961 it was bought by Count Volpi and rebodied as the 'Breadvan' with low engine/drive train with performance equal to a GTO! All aluminium body.								
2821 GT	P1/224	2821 GT	250 GT	Steel SWB	Coupé	Pininfarina	Maranello Concessionaires, U.K.		Mexico
	Sold on 5/10/61. Shown at the 1961 London Motor Show. Show car with special body based on lines of 400SA and 250GTE.								
2823 GTE		2823 GTE	250	GTE	2 + 2	Pininfarina			
2825 GTE		2825 GTE	250	GTE	2 + 2	Pininfarina			
2827 GTE		2827 GTE	250	GTE	2 + 2	Pininfarina			
2829 GTE		2829 GTE	250	GTE	2 + 2	Pininfarina			
2831 GTE		2831 GTE	250	GTE	2 + 2	Pininfarina			
2833 GT		2833 GT	250 GTF	Series II	Convertible	Pininfarina			
2835 GTE		2835 GTE	250	GTE	2 + 2	Pininfarina			
2837 GTE		2837 GTE	250	GTE	2 + 2	Pininfarina			
2839 GT		2839 GT	250 GT	Comp. SWB	Berlinetta	Scaglietti	G.P.Philip	Austria	Holland
	Sold on 2/9/61. Raced a bit, badly crashed and rebodied a la 275GTB. In 1980 restored with new English body and new motor built up from a Lusso. All aluminium body.								
2841 SA		2841 SA	400	Superamerica	Coupé	Pininfarina			U.S.A.
	Delivered on 4/8/61. Shown at the 1961 Paris Salon.								
2843 GTE		2843 GTE	250	GTE	2 + 2	Pininfarina			
2845 GT		2845 GT	250 GT	Comp. SWB	Berlinetta	Scaglietti	P.Ferraro/ Count Volpi Team	Italy	Germany
	All aluminium body.								
2847 GTE		2847 GTE	250	GTE	2 + 2	Pininfarina			
2849 GTE		2849 GTE	250	GTE	2 + 2	Pininfarina			
2851 GTE		2851 GTE	250	GTE	2 + 2	Pininfarina			Switzerland
2853 GTE		2853 GTE	250	GTE	2 + 2	Pininfarina			
	Believed shown at Frankfurt Motor Show in 1961.								
2855 GTE		2855 GTE	250	GTE	2 + 2	Pininfarina			
2857 GTE		2857 GTE	250	GTE	2 + 2	Pininfarina			
2859 GT		2859 GT	250 GTF	Series II	Convertible	Pininfarina			
	Believed shown at the 1961 Frankfurt Motor Show.								
2861 SA		2861 SA	400	Superamerica	Coupé	Pininfarina	William Harrah	U.S.A.	U.S.A.
	Shown at the 1961 Turin Motor Show.								
2863 GT		2863 GT	250 GT	Steel SWB	Berlinetta	Scaglietti	Montchoisy Co./ Filipinetti	Switzerland	U.K.
	Sold on 27/7/61.								
2865 GT		2865 GT	250 GTF	Series II	Convertible	Pininfarina			
2867 GT		2867 GT	250 GTF	Series II	Convertible	Pininfarina			
2869 GTE		2869 GTE	250	GTE	2 + 2	Pininfarina			
2871 GT		2871 GT	250 GT	Steel SWB	Berlinetta	Scaglietti	Frattini	Italy	Italy
	Reported in 1987 in Italy as a SWB California Spyder! This must be considered a rebody.								
2873 GTE		2873 GTE	250	GTE	2 + 2	Pininfarina			
2875 GTE		2875 GTE	250	GTE	2 + 2	Pininfarina			
	Believe shown at Paris Salon.								
2877 GTE		2877 GTE	250	GTE	2 + 2	Pininfarina			
2879 SA		2879 SA	400	Superamerica	Coupé	Pininfarina	Benelli	Italy	U.S.A.
	Delivered on 16/10/61. Coupé Aerodinamico.								
2881 GTE		2881 GTE	250	GTE	2 + 2	Pininfarina			
2883 GTE		2883 GTE	250	GTE	2 + 2	Pininfarina			
2885 GTE		2885 GTE	250	GTE	2 + 2	Pininfarina			
2887 GTE		2887 GTE	250	GTE	2 + 2	Pininfarina			
2889 GTE		2889 GTE	250	GTE	2 + 2	Pininfarina			
2891 GT		2891 GT	250 GT	SWB California	Spyder	Scaglietti			Switzerland
	Covered headlights.								
2893 SA		2893 SA	400	Superamerica	Coupé	Pininfarina	Enzo Ferrari?	Italy	U.S.A.
	Delivered on 8/11/61. Coupé Aerodinamico.								
2895 GTE		2895 GTE	250	GTE	2 + 2	Pininfarina			Switzerland
2897 GTE		2897 GTE	250	GTE	2 + 2	Pininfarina			
2899 GTE		2899 GTE	250	GTE	2 + 2	Pininfarina			
2901 GTE		2901 GTE	250	GTE	2 + 2	Pininfarina			
2903 GT		2903 GT	250 GT	SWB California	Spyder	Scaglietti			U.S.A.
	Completed on 20/9/61. Covered headlights.								
2905 GTE		2905 GTE	250	GTE	2 + 2	Pininfarina			
2907 GTE		2907 GTE	250	GTE	2 + 2	Pininfarina			
2909 GT		2909 GT	250 GT	Steel SWB	Berlinetta	Scaglietti	Auto-Becker/H.Cordes	Germany	U.K.(Engine o
	Sold on 16/9/61. Totally wrecked in 1962.								
2911 GTE		2911 GTE	250	GTE	2 + 2	Pininfarina			
2913 GTE		2913 GTE	250	GTE	2 + 2	Pininfarina			
2915 GTE		2915 GTE	250	GTE	2 + 2	Pininfarina			
2917 GT		2917 GT	250 GT	Steel SWB	Berlinetta	Scaglietti	Franco-Britannic/Fildi	France	France

Chassis No.	Picture Ref	Engine No.	Type	Model	Body Style	Coach-builder	First Owner	Original Location	Present Location
2919 GTE		2919 GTE	250	GTE	2 + 2	Pininfarina			
2921 GTE		2921 GTE	250	GTE	2 + 2	Pininfarina			
2923 GTE		2923 GTE	250	GTE	2 + 2	Pininfarina			
2925 GTE		2925 GTE	250	GTE	2 + 2	Pininfarina			
2927 GTE		2927 GTE	250	GTE	2 + 2	Pininfarina			
2929 GTE		2929 GTE	250	GTE	2 + 2	Pininfarina			
	Believe third prototype of 1962 series.								
2931 GT		2931 GT	250 GTF	Series II	Convertible	Pininfarina			
2933 GT		2933 GT	250 GTF	Series II	Convertible	Pininfarina			
2935 GT		2935 GT	250 GT	Steel SWB	Berlinetta	Scaglietti	Franco-Brittanic	France	U.S.A.
	Sold on 27/9/61.'Lusso' trim.								
2937 GT		2937 GT	250 GT	Comp. SWB	Berlinetta	Scaglietti	Willy Mairesse	Belgium	France
	Raced in 1961 through 1965. All aluminium body.								
2939 GT		2939 GT	250 GT	Comp. SWB	Berlinetta	Scaglietti	Montchoisy Co./Berney	Switzerland	Holland
	Sold on 7/9/61.Raced in 1961 and 1962. All aluminium body.								
2941 GT		2941 GT	250 GTF	Series II	Convertible	Pininfarina			
2943 GT		2943 GT	250 GTF	Series II	Convertible	Pininfarina			
2945 GT		2945 GT	250 GTF	Series II	Convertible	Pininfarina			
	Believe shown at 1961 Paris Salon.								
2947 GT		2947 GT	330	America	2 + 2	Pinifarina	Enzo Ferrari?	Italy	
	Believed to be prototype for the 330 America.								
2949 GTE		2949 GTE	250	GTE	2 + 2	Pininfarina			
2951 GTE		2951 GTE	250	GTE	2 + 2	Pininfarina			
2953 GTE		2953 GTE	250	GTE	2 + 2	Pininfarina			
2955 GT		2955 GT	250 GT	SWB California	Spyder	Scaglietti			
	Covered headlights.								
2957 GTE		2957 GTE	250	GTE	2 + 2	Pininfarina			
2959 GTE		2959 GTE	250	GTE	2 + 2	Pininfarina			
2961 GTE		2961 GTE	250	GTE	2 + 2	Pininfarina			
2963 GTE		2963 GTE	250	GTE	2 + 2	Pininfarina			
2965 GTE		2965 GTE	250	GTE	2 + 2	Pininfarina			Switzerland
2967 GTE		2967 GTE	250	GTE	2 + 2	Pininfarina			
2969 GTE		2969 GTE	250	GTE	2 + 2	Pininfarina			
2971 GTE		2971 GTE	250	GTE	2 + 2	Pininfarina			
2973 GT		2973 GT	250 GT	Comp. SWB	Berlinetta	Scaglietti	Andre Simon	France	France
	Sold on 11/9/61.Raced in 1961 and 1962. All aluminium body.								
2975 GTE		2975 GTE	250	GTE	2 + 2	Pininfarina			U.S.A.
2977 GTE		2977 GTE	250	GTE	2 + 2	Pininfarina			
2979 GTE		2979 GTE	250	GTE	2 + 2	Pininfarina			
2981 GTE		2981 GTE	250	GTE	2 + 2	Pininfarina			
2983 GTE		2983 GTE	250	GTE	2 + 2	Pininfarina			
2985 GT		2985 GT	250 GT	Steel SWB	Berlinetta	Scaglietti	A.Bossa	Italy	U.S.A.
	Sold on 29/11/61.'Lusso trim.								
2987 GT		2987 GT	250 GT	SWB California	Spyder	Scaglietti			Switzerland.
	Believed to have been built as a competition car but no racing history known. All aluminium body.								
2989 GT		2989 GT	250 GT	Steel SWB	Berlinetta	Scaglietti	Pastorelli	Italy	
	Sold on 10/11/61.'Lusso' trim. Also reported as 250 GTE 2 + 2.								
2991 GTE		2991 GTE	250	GTE	2 + 2	Pininfarina			
2993 GTE		2993 GTE	250	GTE	2 + 2	Pininfarina			
2995 GTE		2995 GTE	250	GTE	2 + 2	Pininfarina			
2997 GTE		2997 GTE	250	GTE	2 + 2	Pininfarina			Switzerland
2999 GTE		2999 GTE	250	GTE	2 + 2	Pininfarina			
3001 GTE		3001 GTE	250	GTE	2 + 2	Pininfarina			
3003 GTE		3003 GTE	250	GTE	2 + 2	Pininfarina			
3005 GT		3005 GT	250 GT	Comp. SWB	Berlinetta	Scaglietti	Luigi Chinetti	U.S.A.	Italy
	Sold on 18/11/61.Raced in 1961 and 1962. All aluminium body.								
3007 GT		3007 GT	250 GT	SWB California	Spyder	Scaglietti			Italy
	Covered headlights.								
3009 GT		3009 GT	250 GTE	Series II	Convertible	Pininfarina			
3011 GTE		3011 GTE	250	GTE	2 + 2	Pininfarina			
3013 GTE		3013 GTE	250	GTE	2 + 2	Pininfarina			
3015 GTE		3015 GTE	250	GTE	2 + 2	Pininfarina			
3017 GTE		3017 GTE	250	GTE	2 + 2	Pininfarina			
3019 GTE		3019 GTE	250	GTE	2 + 2	Pininfarina			
3021 GT		3021 GT	250 GT	SWB California	Spyder	Scaglietti	Francois Sagan	France	U.S.A.
3023 GTE		3023 GTE	250	GTE	2 + 2	Pininfarina			
3025 GTE		3025 GTE	250	GTE	2 + 2	Pininfarina			
3027 GTE		3027 GTE	250	GTE	2 + 2	Pininfarina			
3029 GTE		3029 GTE	250	GTE	2 + 2	Pininfarina			
3031 GTE		3031 GTE	250	GTE	2 + 2	Pininfarina			
3033 GT		3033 GT	250 GTF	Series II	Convertible	Pininfarina			
3035 GT		3035 GT	250 GT	Steel SWB	Berlinetta	Scaglietti	Fred Ducato	U.S.A.	U.S.A.
	Sold on 22/11/61.'Lusso' trim.								
3037 GT*		3037 GT	250 GT	Steel SWB	Berlinetta	Scaglietti	Maranello Conc.	U.K.	U.K.
	Sold on 13/10/61. 'Lusso' trim.Outside filler cap.								
3039 GT		3039 GT	250 GT	Steel SWB	Berlinetta	Scaglietti	Garage Francorchamps	Belgium	U.S.A.
	Sold on 29/11/61.'Lusso' trim.								

Chassis No.	Picture Ref	Engine No.	Type	Model	Body Style	Coach-builder	First Owner	Original Location	Present Location
3041 GTE		3041 GTE	250	GTE	2 + 2	Pininfarina			
3043 GTE		3043 GTE	250	GTE	2 + 2	Pininfarina			
3045 GTE		3945 GTE	250	GTE	2 + 2	Pininfarina			U.S.A.
3047 GTE		3047 GTE	250	GTE	2 + 2	Pininfarina			
3049 GTE		3049 GTE	250	GTE	2 + 2	Pininfarina			
3051 GT		3051 GT	250 GTF	Series II	Convertible	Pininfarina			
3053 GT		3053 GT	250 GT	SWB California	Spyder	Scaglietti			
	Covered headlights.								
3055 GT		3055 GT	250 GTF	Series II	Convertible	Pininfarina			
3057 GT		3057 GT	250 GTF	Series II	Convertible	Pininfarina			
3059 GT		3059GT	250GT	SWB California	Spyder	Scaglietti			
3061 GTE		3061 GTE	250	GTE	2 + 2	Pininfarina			
3063 GTE		3063 GTE	250	GTE	2 + 2	Pininfarina			
3065 GTE		3065 GTE	250	GTE	2 + 2	Pininfarina			
3067 GT*		3067 GT*	250 GT	Comp. SWB	Berlinetta	Scaglietti	Maranello Conc.	U.K.	U.K.
	Sold on 14/12/61. 'Lusso' trim. All aluminium?								
3069 GTE		3069 GTE	250	GTE	2 + 2	Pininfarina			
3071 GTE		3071 GTE	250	GTE	2 + 2	Pininfarina			
3073 GT		3073 GT	250 GT	Steel SWB	Berlinetta	Scaglietti	T.Bjorstrom,H.Pehrsson	Sweden	Sweden
	Sold on 14/12/61.'Lusso' trim.								
3075 GTE		3075 GTE	250	GTE	2 + 2	Pininfarina			
3077 GT		3077 GT	250 GT	SWB California	Spyder	Scaglietti			U.K.
	Covered headlights.								
3079 GTE		3079 GTE	250	GTE	2 + 2	Pininfarina			Switzerland
3081 GTE		3081 GTE	250	GTE	2 + 2	Pininfarina			
3083 GTE		3083 GTE	250	GTE	2 + 2	Pininfarina			
	Believed to be a 1962 model.								
3085 GT		3085 GT	250 GTF	Series II	Convertible	Pininfarina			
3087 GT		3087 GT	250 GT	Steel SWB	Berlinetta	Scaglietti	O.Feretti	Italy	U.S.A.
	'Lusso' trim.								
3089 GT		3089 GT	250 GTF	Series II	Convertible	Pininfarina			U.S.A.
3091 GT		3091 GT	250 GTF	Series II	Convertible	Pininfarina			
3093 GT		3093 GT	250 GTF	Series II	Convertible	Pininfarina			
3095 GT		3095 GT	250 GT	SWB California	Spyder	Scaglietti			U.S.A.
	In France many years ago. Covered headlights.								
3097 SA		3097 SA	400	Superamerica	Coupé	Pinifarina	Charpentier	France	U.S.A.
	Delivered on 12/12/61.								
3099 GT		3099 GT	250 GT	SWB California	Spyder	Scaglietti			U.S.A.
	In U.S.A. for many years.								

1962

Chassis No.	Picture Ref	Engine No.	Type	Model	Body Style	Coach-builder	First Owner	Original Location	Present Location
3101 GT		3101 GT	250 GTF	Series II	Convertible	Pininfarina			
3103 GTE		3103 GTE	250	GTE	2 + 2	Pininfarina			
3105 GTE		3105 GTE	330	GT	2 + 2	Pininfarina			
	Believed to be prototype 330GT.								
3107 GT		3107 GT	250 GT	Steel SWB	Berlinetta	Scaglietti	Auregli	Italy	U.S.A.
	Sold on 19/1/62.Never raced. 'Lusso'trim.Electric windows.								
3109 GTE		3109 GTE	250	GTE	2 + 2	Pininfarina			
3111 GTE		3111 GTE	250	GTE	2 + 2	Pininfarina			
3113 GT		3113 GT	250 GT	Steel SWB	Berlinetta	Scaglietti	Franco-Britannic/ Mrs.Blackwood	France	France
	Sold on 13/2/62.Never raced. 'Lusso' trim								
3115 GTE		3115 GTE	250	GTE	2 + 2	Pininfarina			
3117 GTE		3117 GTE	250	GTE	2 + 2	Pininfarina			
3119 GT		3119 GT	250 GT	SWB California	Spyder	Scaglietti			U.S.A.
	Covered headlights.								
3121 GTE		3121 GTE	250	GTE	2 + 2	Pininfarina			U.S.A.
3123 GTE		3123 GTE	250	GTE	2 + 2	Pininfarina			
3125 GTE		3125 GTE	250	GTE	2 + 2	Pininfarina			
3127 GTE		3127 GTE	250	GTE	2 + 2	Pininfarina			
3129 GT		3129 GT	250 GT	Steel SWB	Berlinetta	Scaglietti	D.S.Gross	U.S.A.	U.S.A.
	Sold on 2/2/62.Never raced. 'Lusso' trim								
3131 GTE		3131 GTE	250	GTE	2 + 2	Pininfarina			
3133 GTE		3133 GTE	250	GTE	2 + 2	Pininfarina			
3135 GTE		3135 GTE	250	GTE	2 + 2	Pininfarina			
3137 GTE		3137 GTE	250	GTE	2 + 2	Pininfarina			
3139 GTE		3139 GTE	250	GTE	2 + 2	Pininfarina			
3141 GTE		3141 GTE	250	GTE	2 + 2	Pininfarina			
3143 GT		3143 GT	250 GT	Steel SWB	Berlinetta	Scaglietti	C.G.Hale	U.S.A.	U.S.A.
	Sold January/February 1962?Never raced. Outside filler cap.								
3145 GTE		3145 GTE	250	GTE	2 + 2	Pininfarina			
3147 GTE		3147 GTE	250	GTE	2 + 2	Pininfarina			
3149 GTE		3149 GTE	250	GTE	2 + 2	Pininfarina			
3151 GTE		3151 GTE	250	GTE	2 + 2	Pininfarina			U.S.A.
3153 GTE		3153 GTE	250	GTE	2 + 2	Pininfarina			
3155 GTE		3155 GTE	250	GTE	2 + 2	Pininfarina			
3157 GTE		3157 GTE	250	GTE	2 + 2	Pininfarina			
3159 GTE		3159 GTE	250	GTE	2 + 2	Pininfarina			
3161 GTE		3161 GTE	250	GTE	2 + 2	Pininfarina			

Chassis No.	Picture Ref	Engine No.	Type	Model	Body Style	Coach-builder	First Owner	Original Location	Present Location
3163 GT		3163 GT	250 GT	SWB California	Spyder	Scaglietti			U.S.A.
	Completed on 12/1/62. Covered headlights and hard-top.								
3165 GTE		3165 GTE	250	GTE	2 + 2	Pininfarina			
3167 GTE		3167 GTE	250	GTE	2 + 2	Pininfarina			
3169 GT		3169 GT	250 GT	Steel SWB	Berlinetta	Scaglietti	Chinetti/ Brumos Porsche	U.S.A.	U.S.A.
	Sold on February 1962. Never raced. 'Lusso' trim.								
3171 GTE		3171 GTE	250	GTE	2 + 2	Pininfarina			
3173 GTE		3173 GTE	250	GTE	2 + 2	Pininfarina			
3175 GT		3175 GT	250 GT	Steel SWB	Berlinetta	Scaglietti	E. Dibos	Peru	Italy
	Sold on 8/1/62. Used for GTO engine tests. 'Lusso' trim.								
3177 GTE		3177 GTE	250	GTE	2 + 2	Pininfarina			Canada
3179 GT		3179 GT	250 GTF	Series II	Convertible	Pininfarina			
3181 GTE		3181 GTE	250	GTE	2 + 2	Pininfarina			
3183 GTE		3183 GTE	250	GTE	2 + 2	Pininfarina			
3185 GT		3185 GT	250 GT	SWB California	Spyder	Scaglietti			U.S.A.
	Covered headlights and hard-top.								
3187 GTE		3187 GTE	250	GTE	2 + 2	Pininfarina			
3189 GTE		3189 GTE	250	GTE	2 + 2	Pininfarina			
3191 GTE		3191 GTE	250	GTE	2 + 2	Pininfarina			
3193 GTE		3193 GTE	250	GTE	2 + 2	Pininfarina			
3195 GT		3195 GT	250 GT	SWB California	Spyder	Scaglietti	Jan DeVroom		U.S.A.
3197 GTE		3197 GTE	250	GTE	2 + 2	Pininfarina			
3199 GTE		3199 GTE	250	GTE	2 + 2	Pininfarina			
3201 GTE		3201 GTE	250	GTE	2 + 2	Pininfarina			
3203 GTE		3203 GTE	250	GTE	2 + 2	Pininfarina			
3205 GTE		3205 GTE	250	GTE	2 + 2	Pininfarina			
3207 GTE		3207 GTE	250	GTE	2 + 2	Pininfarina			
3209 GTE		3209 GTE	250	GTE	2 + 2	Pininfarina			
3211 GTE		3211 GTE	250	GTE	2 + 2	Pininfarina			
3213 GTE		3213 GTE	250	GTE	2 + 2	Pininfarina			
3215 GTE		3215 GTE	250	GTE	2 + 2	Pininfarina			
3217 GT		3217 GT	250 GTF	Series II	Convertible	Pininfarina			U.S.A.
3219 GTE		3219 GTE	250	GTE	2 + 2	Pininfarina			
3221 SA		3221 SA	400	Superamerica	Coupé	Pinifarina			France
	Delivered on 30/1/62. Shown at the 1962 Geneva Motor Show. Coupé Aerodinamico.								
3223 GT		3223 GT	250 GTO	GTO	Berlinetta	Scaglietti	Factory/NART/McKelv	U.S.A.	U.S.A.
	Sold on 19/6/62. The first GTO! The 1962 factory press conference car. Raced in 1962 through 1964 and 1966. All aluminium body.								
3225 GTE		3225 GTE	250	GTE	2 + 2	Pininfarina			
3227 GTE		3227 GTE	250	GTE	2 + 2	Pininfarina			
3229 GTE		3229 GTE	250	GTE	2 + 2	Pininfarina			
3231 GTE		3231 GTE	250	GTE	2 + 2	Pininfarina			
3233 GT		3233 GT	250 GT	Steel SWB	Berlinetta	Scaglietti	Bulgari	Italy	U.S.A.
	Sold on 22/2/62. Never raced. Outside filler cap.								
3235 GTE		3235 GTE	250	GTE	2 + 2	Pininfarina			
3237 GTE		3237 GTE	250	GTE	2 + 2	Pininfarina			
3239 GT		3239 GT	250 GTF	Series II	Convertible	Pininfarina			
3241 GTE		3241 GTE	250	GTE	2 + 2	Pininfarina			Italy
	Converted to a replica GTO in 1986.								
3243 GTE		3243 GTE	250	GTE	2 + 2	Pininfarina			
3245 GT		3245 GT	250 GT	SWB California	Spyder	Scaglietti			U.S.A.
3247 GTE		3247 GTE	250	GTE	2 + 2	Pininfarina			U.K.?
3249 GTE		3249 GTE	250	GTE	2 + 2	Pininfarina			
3251 GTE		3251 GTE	250	GTE	2 + 2	Pininfarina			
3253 GTE		3253 GTE	250	GTE	2 + 2	Pininfarina			
3255 GTE		3255 GTE	250	GTE	2 + 2	Pininfarina			
3257 GTE*		3257 GTE	250	GTE	2 + 2	Pininfarina			
3259 GTE*		3259 GTE	250	GTE	2 + 2	Pininfarina			
3261 GTE		3261 GTE	250	GTE	2 + 2	Pininfarina			Switzerland
3263 GTE		3263 GTE	250	GTE	2 + 2	Pininfarina			
3265 GTE		3265 GTE	250	GTE	2 + 2	Pininfarina			
3267 GTE		3267 GTE	250	GTE	2 + 2	Pininfarina			
3269 GT	FM 148.	3269 GT	250 GT	Steel SWB	Berlinetta	Bertone	Nuccio Bertone	Italy	U.S.A.
	Completed in May 1962. Built as one-off special prototype body with Chiti nose. The last of two Bertone 250s.								
3271 GTE		3271 GTE	250	GTE	2 + 2	Pininfarina			
3273 GTE		3273 GTE	250	GTE	2 + 2	Pininfarina			
3275 GTE		3275 GTE	250	GTE	2 + 2	Pininfarina			
3277 GTE		3277 GTE	250	GTE	2 + 2	Pininfarina			
3279 GTE		3279 GTE	250	GTE	2 + 2	Pininfarina			
3281 GT*		3281 GT	250 GT	Steel SWB	Berlinetta	Scaglietti	Loewe	Australia	Australia?
3283 GTE		3283 GTE	250	GTE	2 + 2	Pininfarina			
3285 GTE		3285 GTE	250	GTE	2 + 2	Pininfarina			
3287 GT*		3287 GT	250 GT	Steel SWB	Berlinetta	Scaglietti	Maranello Conc.	U.K.	U.K.
	Sold on 3/3/62. Never raced.								
3289 GTE		3289 GTE	250	GTE	2 + 2	Pininfarina			
3291 GTE		3291 GTE	250	GTE	2 + 2	Pininfarina			
3293 GT		3293 GT	250 GT	SWB California	Spyder	Scaglietti			U.S.A.
3295 GTE		3295 GTE	250	GTE	2 + 2	Pininfarina			

Chassis No.	Picture Ref	Engine No.	Type	Model	Body Style	Coach-builder	First Owner	Original Location	Present Location
3297 GTE		3297 GTE	250	GTE	2 + 2	Pininfarina			
3299 GTE		3299 GTE	250	GTE	2 + 2	Pininfarina			
3301 GT		3301 GT	250 GT	SWB California	Spyder	Scaglietti			Italy
	Reported as a 250GT Pininfarina Convertible in 1970.								
3303 GTE		3303 GTE	250	GTE	2 + 2	Pininfarina			
3305 GTE		3305 GTE	250	GTE	2 + 2	Pininfarina			
3307 GTE		3307 GTE	250	GTE	2 + 2	Pininfarina			
3309 SA	P1/249	3309 SA	400	Superamerica	Convertible	Pininfarina			France
	Delivered on 6/3/62. Shown at the 1962 Geneva Show.								
3311 GT		3311 GT	250 GTF	Series II	Convertible	Pininfarina			
3313 GTE		3313 GTE	250	GTE	2 + 2	Pininfarina			
3315 GT		3315 GT	250 GT	Steel SWB	Berlinetta	Scaglietti	Paleocapa	Italy	Italy
	Sold on 30/3/62. Never raced.								
3317 GTE		3317 GTE	250	GTE	2 + 2	Pininfarina			
3319 GTE		3319 GTE	250	GTE	2 + 2	Pininfarina			
3321 GTE		3321 GTE	250	GTE	2 + 2	Pininfarina			
3323 GTE		3323 GTE	250	GTE	2 + 2	Pininfarina			
3325 GTE		3325 GTE	250	GTE	2 + 2	Pininfarina			
3327 GT		3327 GT	250 GT	Comp. SWB	Berlinetta	Scaglietti	Chinetti/Baxter	U.S.A.	U.S.A.
	Sold on 5/3/62. Raced in 1962 through 1963. All aluminium body.								
3329 GTE		3329 GTE	250	GTE	2 + 2	Pininfarina			
3331 GT		3331 GT	250 GT	Steel SWB	Berlinetta	Scaglietti		Switzerland	Italy
	Sold in March 1962.								
3333 GTE		3333 GTE	250	GTE	2 + 2	Pininfarina			
3335 GTE		3335 GTE	250	GTE	2 + 2	Pininfarina			
3337 GT		3337 GT	250 GT	Steel SWB	Berlinetta	Scaglietti	Ferrari Rep of Hollywood	U.S.A.	Canada
	Sold on 14/3/62. Never raced. 'Lusso' trim.								
3339 GTE		3339 GTE	250	GTE	2 + 2	Pininfarina			
3341 GTE		3341 GTE	250	GTE	2 + 2	Pininfarina			
3343 GTE		3343 GTE	250	GTE	2 + 2	Pininfarina			
3345 GTE		3345 GTE	250	GTE	2+2	Pininfarina			Italy
	Reported to be a SWB California. May have been given a replica body. Also reported as SWB Berlinetta!								
3347 GTE		3347 GTE	250	GTE	2 + 2	Pininfarina			
3349 GTE		3349 GTE	250	GTE	2 + 2	Pininfarina			
3351 GTE		3351 GTE	250	GTE	2 + 2	Pininfarina			
3353 GTE		3353 GTE	250	GTE	2 + 2	Pininfarina			
3355 GTE		3355 GTE	250	GTE	2 + 2	Pininfarina			
3357 GTE		3357 GTE	250	GTE	2 + 2	Pininfarina			
3359 GT		3359 GT	250 GT	Steel SWB	Berlinetta	Scaglietti	G. Chiusolo	Italy	U.S.A.
	Sold on 12/4/62. Never raced. 'Lusso' trim.								
3361 SA	P1/253	3361 SA	400	Superamerica	Coupé	Pininfarina	Brainovitch/Lauro	Switzerland/ Italy	Italy
	Delivered on 10/3/62.								
3363 GTE		3363 GTE	250	GTE	2 + 2	Pininfarina			
3365 GTE		3365 GTE	250	GTE	2 + 2	Pininfarina			
3367 GT		3367 GT	250 GT	Steel SWB	Berlinetta	Scaglietti	Martinelli & Sonvico	Switzerland	U.K.
	Sold on 9/3/62. 'Lusso' trim.								
3369 GTE		3369 GTE	250	GTE	2 + 2	Pininfarina			
3371 GT		3371 GT	250 GTF	Series II	Convertible	Pininfarina			
3373 GTE		3373 GTE	250	GTE	2 + 2	Pininfarina			
3375 GTE		3375 GTE	250 GTE	GTE	2 + 2	Pininfarina			
3377 GTE		3377 GTE	250 GTE	GTE	2 +2	Pininfarina			
3379 GT		3379 GT	250 GT	Steel SWB	Berlinetta	Scaglietti	Perruchetti	Italy	Italy?
	Sold on 21/4/62. 'Lusso trim.								
3381 GTE		3381 GTE	250	GTE	2 + 2	Pininfarina			U.S.A.
	Shown at the 1962 New York Auto Show.								
3383 GTE		3383 GTE	250	GTE	2 + 2	Pininfarina			
	Shown at the Geneva Motor Show 1962.								
3385 GT		3385 GT	250 GTF	Series II	Convertible	Pininfarina			
3387 GT		3387 GT	250 GT0	GTO	Berlinetta	Scaglietti	Chinetti/Grossman	U.S.A.	U.S.A.
	Sold on 16/3/62. Raced in 1962 through 1964. The second GTO. All aluminium body.								
3389 GTE		3389 GTE	250	GTE	2 + 2	Pininfarina			
3391 GTE		3391 GTE	250	GTE	2 + 2	Pininfarina			
3393 GTE		3393 GTE	250	GTE	2 + 2	Pininfarina			
3395 GT		3395 GT	250 GT	SWB California	Spyder	Scaglietti			
	Covered headlights. Also reported as 250GTE 2+2.								
3397 GT		3397 GT	250 GTF	Series II	Convertible	Pininfarina			
3399 GTE		3399 GTE	250	GTE	2 + 2	Pininfarina			
3401 GT		3401 GT	250 GT	Steel SWB	Berlinetta	Scaglietti	Molgara	Italy	Switzerland
	Sold on 21/4/62.								
3403 GTE		3403 GTE	250	GTE	2 + 2	Pininfarina			
3405 GTE		3405 GTE	250	GTE	2 + 2	Pininfarina			
3407 GT		3407 GT	250 GTF	Series II	Convertible	Scaglietti			

Chassis No.	Picture Ref	Engine No.	Type	Model	Body Style	Coach-builder	First Owner	Original Location	Present Location
3409 GT		3409 GT	250 GT	Steel SWB	Berlinetta	Scaglietti	DellaSerra	Italy	U.S.A.
	Sold on 14/5/62.								
3411 GTE		3411 GTE	250	GTE	2 + 2	Pininfarina			
3413 GT		3413 GT	250 GTO	GTO	Berlinetta	Scaglietti	Colombo/Lualdi	Italy	U.K.
	Sold on 30/4/62. Raced in 1962 through 1965. Rebodied by factory with 1964 'tunnel back' body.								
3415 GTE		3415 GTE	250	GTE	2 + 2	Pininfarina			
3417 GTE		3417 GTE	250	GTE	2 + 2	Pininfarina			
3419 GTE		3419 GTE	250	GTE	2 + 2	Pininfarina			
3421 GTE		3421 GTE	250	GTE	2 + 2	Pininfarina			
3423 GTE		3423 GTE	250	GTE	2 + 2	Pininfarina			
3425 GT		3425 GT	250 GT	Steel SWB	Berlinetta	Scaglietti		Switzerland	France
	Sold in May 1962.								
3427 GT		3427 GT	250 GTF	Series II	Convertible	Pininfarina			
3429 GTE		3429 GTE	250	GTE	2 + 2	Pininfarina			
3431 GT		3431 GT	250 GT	Steel SWB	Berlinetta	Scaglietti	Allazetta	Italy	Italy
	Sold on 27/4/62.								
3433 GTE		3433 GTE	250	GTE	2 + 2	Pininfarina			
3425 GTE		3425 GTE	250	GTE	2 + 2	Pininfarina			
3437 GTE		3437 GTE	250	GTE	2 + 2	Pininfarina			
3439 GTE		3439 GTE	250	GTE	2 + 2	Pininfarina			
3441 GTE		3441 GTE	250	GTE	2 + 2	Pininfarina			
3443 GT		3443 GT	250 GTF	Series II	Convertible	Pininfarina			
3445 GT		3445 GT	250 GTO	GTO	Berlinetta	Scaglietti	Conti/Bettoja/Volpi	Italy	U.K.
	Sold on 30/4/62. Raced in 1962 through 1964. Rebodied in 1982 with original style body in Italy. Drogo body put on 2067GT. All aluminium body.								
3447 GTE		3447 GTE	250	GTE	2 + 2	Pininfarina			
3449 GT		3449 GT	250 GTF	Series II	Convertible	Pininfarina			
3451 GT		3451 GT	250 GTO	GTO	Berlinetta	Scaglietti	San Guisto Ferraro	Italy	France
	Sold on 20/4/62. Raced 1962 through 1967. All aluminium body.								
3453 GT		3453 GT	250 GTF	Series II	Convertible	Pininfarina			
3455 GTE		3455 GTE	250	GTE	2 + 2	Pininfarina			
3457 GTE*		3457 GTE	250	GTE	2 + 2	Pininfarina			U.K.?
3459 GT		3459 GT	250 GTF	Series II	Convertible	Pininfarina			
3461 GTE		3461 GTE	250	GTE	2 + 2	Pininfarina			
3463 GT		3463 GT	250 GT	Steel SWB	Berlinetta	Scaglietti	Chinetti	U.S.A.	U.S.A.
	Sold on 22/5/62. The first 1962 with "Lusso" trim.								
3465 GTE*		3465 GTE	250	GTE	2 + 2	Pininfarina			U.K.?
3467 GT		3467 GT	250 GTF	Series II	Convertible	Pininfarina			
3469 SA?		3469 SA?	400SA?	Series I SWB?	Convertible?	Pininfarina			
	Sold on 21/4/62.								
3471 GTE		3471 GTE	250	GTE	2 + 2	Pininfarina			
3473 GTE		3473 GTE	250	GTE	2 + 2	Pininfarina			
3475 GT		3475 GT	250 GTF	Series II	Convertible	Pininfarina			
3477 GT		3477 GT	250 GT	Steel SWB	Berlinetta	Scaglietti	G.Galassini	Italy	Switzerland
	Sold on 25/5/62. Wrecked and motor gone to 1321GT. Totally rebuilt in 1975.								
3479 GTE		3479 GTE	250	GTE	2 + 2	Pininfarina			
3481 GTE*		3481 GTE	250	GTE	2 + 2	Pininfarina			
3483 GTE		3483 GTE	250	GTE	2 + 2	Pininfarina			
3485 GTE		3485 GTE	250	GTE	2 + 2	Pininfarina			U.S.A.
3487 GT		3487 GT	250 GT	Steel SWB	Berlinetta	Scaglietti	Chinetti	U.S.A.	U.S.A.
	Sold on 4/6/62.								
3489 GTE		3489 GTE	250	GTE	2 + 2	Pininfarina			
3491 GT		3491 GT	250 GTF	Series II	Convertible	Pininfarina			
3493 GTE		3493 GTE	250	GTE	2 + 2	Pininfarina			
3495 GTE		3495 GTE	250	GTE	2 + 2	Pininfarina			
3497 GTE*		3497 GTE	250	GTE	2 + 2	Pininfarina			U.K.?
3499 GT		3499 GT	250 GTF	Series II	Convertible	Pininfarina			
3501 GTE		3501 GTE	250	GTE	2 + 2	Pininfarina			
3503 GTE		3503 GTE	250	GTE	2 + 2	Pininfarina			
3505 GT*		3505 GT	250 GTO	GTO	Berlinetta	Scaglietti	UDT/Laystall/S.Moss	U.K.	U.K.
	Sold on 20/4/62. Raced in 1962 through 1964.								
3507 GT		3507 GT	250 GT	Steel SWB	Berlinetta	Scaglietti	R.Scalabrin	Italy	Italy
	Sold on 9/6/62.								
3509 GTE		3509 GTE	250	GTE	2 + 2	Pininfarina			
3511 GTE		3511 GTE	250	GTE	2 + 2	Pininfarina			
3513 SA		3513 SA	400	Superamerica	Coupé	Pininfarina	Marshall	U.S.A.	
	Delivered on 5/5/62. Coupé Aerodinamico.								
3515 GTE		3515 GTE	250	GTE	2 + 2	Pininfarina			
3517 GT		3517 GT	250 GTF	Series II	Convertible	Pininfarina			
3519 GTE		3519 GTE	250	GTE	2 + 2	Pininfarina			
3521 GTE		3521 GTE	250	GTE	2 + 2	Pininfarina			
3523 GTE		3523 GTE	250	GTE	2 + 2	Pininfarina			
3525 GTE		3525 GTE	250	GTE	2 + 2	Pininfarina			
3527 GT		3527 GT	250 GTO	GTO	Berlinetta	Scaglietti	Koechert	Austria	U.K.
	Sold on 22/5/62. Raced 1962 through 1964.								

Chassis No.	Picture Ref	Engine No.	Type	Model	Body Style	Coach-builder	First Owner	Original Location	Present Location
3529 GTE		3529 GTE	250	GTE	2 + 2	Pininfarina			
3531 GT		3531 GT	250 GTF	Series II	Convertible	Pininfarina			
3533 GTE		3533 GTE	250	GTE	2 + 2	Pininfarina			
3535 GTE		3535 GTE	250	GTE	2 + 2	Pininfarina			
3537 GTE		3537 GTE	250	GTE	2 + 2	Pininfarina			
3539 GT		3539 GT	250 GT	Competition SWB	Berlinetta	Scaglietti	Ted Marlia	U.S.A.	Italy (a 'recreation'!)

Sold on 4/6/62. Totally destroyed in 1960s. Has been reported reconstructed with a new alloy body.

Chassis No.	Picture Ref	Engine No.	Type	Model	Body Style	Coach-builder	First Owner	Original Location	Present Location
3541 GTE		3541 GTE	250	GTE	2 + 2	Pininfarina			
3543 GTE		3543 GTE	250	GTE	2 + 2	Pininfarina			
3545 GTE		3545 GTE	250	GTE	2 + 2	Pininfarina			
3547 GTE		3547 GTE	250	GTE	2 + 2	Pininfarina			
3549 GT		3549 GT	250 GTF	Series II	Convertible	Pininfarina			Switzerland
3551 GT*		3551 GT	250 GT	Steel SWB	Berlinetta	Scaglietti	W.Lowe	Australia	Australia

Sold on 24/6/62.

Chassis No.	Picture Ref	Engine No.	Type	Model	Body Style	Coach-builder	First Owner	Original Location	Present Location
3553 GT		3553 GT	250 GTF	Series II?	Convertible?	Pininfarina			
3555 GTE		3555 GTE	250	GTE	2 + 2	Pininfarina			
3557 GT		3557 GT	250 GTF	Series II	Convertible	Pininfarina			
3559 SA		3559 SA	400	Superamerica	Coupé	Pininfarina	U.Colombo	Italy	U.S.A.

Delivered on 11/6/62. Coupé Aerodinamico.

Chassis No.	Picture Ref	Engine No.	Type	Model	Body Style	Coach-builder	First Owner	Original Location	Present Location
3561 GTE		3561 GTE	250	GTE	2 + 2	Pininfarina			
3563 GTE		3563 GTE	250	GTE	2 + 2	Pininfarina			
3565 GT		3565 GT	250 GT	Competition SWB	Berlinetta	Scaglietti	Franco Brittanic/ Bertoldi	France	France

Sold on 28/5/62. All aluminium body.

Chassis No.	Picture Ref	Engine No.	Type	Model	Body Style	Coach-builder	First Owner	Original Location	Present Location
3567 GTE		3567 GTE	250	GTE	2 + 2	Pininfarina			
3569 GTE		3569 GTE	250	GTE	2 + 2	Pininfarina			
3571 GTE		3571 GTE	250	GTE	2 + 2	Pininfarina			
3573 GTE		3573 GTE	250	GTE	2 + 2	Pininfarina			
3575 GT		3575 GT	250 GT	Steel SWB?	Berlinetta?	Scaglietti?			

Not confirmed as a SWB Berlinetta.

Chassis No.	Picture Ref	Engine No.	Type	Model	Body Style	Coach-builder	First Owner	Original Location	Present Location
3577 GT		3577 GT	250 GT	Steel SWB	Berlinetta	Scaglietti	S.Buzetti	Italy	Switzerland

Sold on 18/7/62.

Chassis No.	Picture Ref	Engine No.	Type	Model	Body Style	Coach-builder	First Owner	Original Location	Present Location
3579 GTE		3579 GTE	250	GTE	2 + 2	Pininfarina			Switzerland
3581 GT		3581 GT	250 GTF	Series II	Convertible	Pininfarina			
3583 GTE		3583 GTE	250	GTE	2 + 2	Pininfarina			
3585 GTE		3585 GTE	250	GTE	2 + 2	Pininfarina			
3587 GTE		3587 GTE	250	GTE	2 + 2	Pininfarina			
3589 GT*		3589 GT	250 GTO	GTO	Berlinetta	Scaglietti	Hoare/T.Sopwith	U.K.	U.S.A.

Sold on 20/4/62. Raced in 1962 through 1963. "Stored" in a field from 1972 to 1987! Finally rescued to be restored. All aluminium body.

Chassis No.	Picture Ref	Engine No.	Type	Model	Body Style	Coach-builder	First Owner	Original Location	Present Location
3591 GTE		3591 GTE	250	GTE	2 + 2	Pininfarina			
3593 GTE		3593 GTE	250	GTE	2 + 2	Pininfarina			
3595 GTE		3595 GTE	250	GTE	2 + 2	Pininfarina			
3597 GTE		3597 GTE	250	GTE	2 + 2	Pininfarina			
3599 GT		3599 GT	250 GTF	Series II	Convertible	Pininfarina			
3601 GTE		3601 GTE	250	GTE	2 + 2	Pininfarina			
3603 GTE		3603 GTE	250	GTE	2 + 2	Pininfarina			
3605 GT*		3605 GT	250 GT	Steel SWB	Berlinetta	Scaglietti	Maranello Conc./ Lord Portman	U.K.	Japan

Sold on 3/6/62.

Chassis No.	Picture Ref	Engine No.	Type	Model	Body Style	Coach-builder	First Owner	Original Location	Present Location
3607 GT		3607 GT	250 GTO	GTO	Berlinetta	Scaglietti	Comp Ital Petroli	Italy	U.S.A.

Sold on 5/6/62. Raced 1962 through 1965. All aluminium body.

Chassis No.	Picture Ref	Engine No.	Type	Model	Body Style	Coach-builder	First Owner	Original Location	Present Location
3609 GTE		3609 GTE	250	GTE	2 + 2	Pininfarina			
3611 GTE*		3611 GTE	250	GTE	2 + 2	Pininfarina	Maranello Conc.	U.K.	U.K.
3613 GT		3613 GT	250 GTF	Series II	Convertible	Pininfarina			
3615 GT		3615 GT	250 GT	SWB Speciale	Berlinetta	Pinifarina	F.Gatta	Italy	U.S.A.

Sold on 23/7/62. 400SA body like 2613GT.

Chassis No.	Picture Ref	Engine No.	Type	Model	Body Style	Coach-builder	First Owner	Original Location	Present Location
3617 GTE		3617 GTE	250	GTE	2 + 2	Pininfarina			
3619 GTE		3619 GTE	250	GTE	2 + 2	Pininfarina			
3621 SA		3621 SA	400	Superamerica	Coupé	Pininfarina	FIMA	Italy	Australia

Delivered on 16/7/62. Coupé Aerodinamico

Chassis No.	Picture Ref	Engine No.	Type	Model	Body Style	Coach-builder	First Owner	Original Location	Present Location
3623 GTE		3623 GTE	250	GTE	2 + 2	Pininfarina			
3625 GT		3625 GT	250 GTF	Series II	Convertible	Pininfarina			
3627 GTE		3627 GTE	250	GTE	2 + 2	Pininfarina			
3629 GTE		3629 GTE	250	GTE	2 + 2	Pininfarina			U.S.A.
3631 GTE		3631 GTE	250	GTE	2 + 2	Pininfarina			
3633 GT		3633 GT	250 GTF	Series II	Convertible	Pininfarina			
3635 GTE		3635 GTE	250	GTE	2 + 2	Pininfarina			
3637 GTE		3637 GTE	250	GTE	2 + 2	Pininfarina			
3639 GT		3639 GT	250 GT	Steel SWB	Berlinetta	Scaglietti	G.Galbani	Italy	U.S.A.

Sold on 8/9/62.

Chassis No.	Picture Ref	Engine No.	Type	Model	Body Style	Coach-builder	First Owner	Original Location	Present Location
3641 GTE		3641 GTE	250	GTE	2 + 2	Pininfarina			
3643 GTE*		3643 GTE	250	GTE	2 + 2	Pininfarina	Maranello Conc.	U.K.	
3645 GT		3645 GT	250 GTF	Series II	Convertible	Pininfarina			
3647 GT*		3647 GT	250 GTO	GTO	Berlinetta	Scaglietti	Maranello Conc./ Bowmaker/Surtees	U.K.	U.S.A.

Sold on 6/6/62. Raced 1962 through 1965. Same owner since 1967. All aluminium body.

Chassis No.	Picture Ref	Engine No.	Type	Model	Body Style	Coach-builder	First Owner	Original Location	Present Location
3649 GTE		3649 GTE	250	GTE	2 + 2	Pininfarina			
3651 GTE		3651 GTE	250	GTE	2 + 2	Pininfarina			
3653 GTE		3653 GTE	250	GTE	2 + 2	Pininfarina			
3655 GT		3655 GT	250 GTF	Series II	Convertible	Pininfarina			
3657 GT		3657 GT	250 GT	Steel SWB	Berlinetta	Scaglietti	Chinetti	U.S.A.	U.S.A.
		Sold on 27/9/62.							
3659 GTE		3659 GTE	250	GTE	2 + 2	Pininfarina			
3661 GTE		3661 GTE	250	GTE	2 + 2	Pininfarina			
3663 GTE		3663 GTE	250	GTE	2 + 2	Pininfarina			
3665 GT		3665 GT	250 GT	SWB California	Spyder	Scaglietti			France
3667 GTE*		3667 GTE	250	GTE	2 + 2	Pininfarina	Maranello Conc.	U.K.	U.K.?
3669 GT		3669 GT	250 GTF	Series II	Convertible	Pininfarina			
3671 GTE		3671 GTE	250	GTE	2 + 2	Pininfarina			Germany
		Rebodied as a replica GTO.							
3673 SA		3673 SA	400	GTO	Berlinetta	Scaglietti			U.K.
		Sold on 19/11/62.Built as a 4 litre GTO with a 400SA engine. Believed crashed and rebuilt by factory with SWB Berlinetta body. In 1987 being rebuilt with a GTO-style body. All aluminium body.							
3675 GTE*		3675 GTE	250	GTE	2 + 2	Pininfarina	Maranello Conc.	U.K.	U.K.?
3677 GT		3677 GT	250 GT	SWB California	Spyder	Scaglietti			U.S.A.
		Open headlights.							
3679 GTE		3679 GTE	250	GTE	2 + 2	Pininfarina			
3681 GTE		3681 GTE	250	GTE	2 + 2	Pininfarina			
3683 GT		3683 GT	250 GT	Series II	Convertible	Pininfarina			
3685 GTE		3685 GTE	250	GTE	2 + 2	Pininfarina			
3687 GTE		3687 GTE	250	GTE	2 + 2	Pininfarina			
3689 GTE		3689 GTE	250	GTE	2 + 2	Pininfarina			
3691 GTE		3691 GTE	250	GTE	2 + 2	Pininfarina			
3693 GTE		3693 GTE	250	GTE	2 + 2	Pininfarina			
3695 GT		3695 GT	250 GT	Steel SWB	Berlinetta	Scaglietti	M.L.Caccia	Italy	U.S.A.?
		Sold on 28/7/62.							
3697 GTE		3697 GTE	250	GTE	2 + 2	Pininfarina			
3699 GT		3699 GT	250 GT	Series II	Convertible	Pininfarina			
3701 GTE		3701 GTE	250	GTE	2 + 2	Pininfarina			
3703 GTE		3703 GTE	250	GTE	2 + 2	Pininfarina			
3705 GT		3705 GT	250 GTO	GTO	Berlinetta	Scaglietti	Jean Guichet	France	Japan
		Sold on 14/6/62.Raced 1962 through 1965. All aluminium body.							
3707 GTE		3707 GTE	250	GTE	2 + 2	Pininfarina			
3709 GT		3709 GT	250 GT	Steel SWB	Berlinetta	Scaglietti	Buzzi	Italy	Italy
		Sold on 31/7/62.Same owner since new.							
3711 GTE		3711 GTE	250	GTE	2 + 2	Pininfarina			
3713 GTE		3713 GTE	250	GTE	2 + 2	Pininfarina			
3715 GT		3715 GT	250 GT	Series II	Convertible	Pininfarina			
3717 GTE		3717 GTE	250	GTE	2 + 2	Pininfarina			
3719 GTE		3719 GTE	250	GTE	2 + 2	Pininfarina			
3721 GTE		3721 GTE	250	GTE	2 + 2	Pininfarina			
3723 GTE		3723 GTE	250	GTE	2 + 2	Pininfarina			
3725 GTE		3725 GTE	250	GTE	2 + 2	Pininfarina			
3727 GT		3727 GT	250 GT	Series II	Convertible	Pininfarina			
3729 GT*		3729 GT	250 GT0	GTO	Berlinetta	Scaglietti	Maranello Conc./ Salvadori/Coombs	U.K.	U.K.
		Sold on 28/7/62.Raced 1962 through 1964.							
3731 GTE		3731 GTE	250	GTE	2 + 2	Pininfarina			
3733 GTE		3733 GTE	250	GTE	2 + 2	Pininfarina			
3735 GT		3735 GT	250 GT	Steel SWB	Berlinetta	Scaglietti	Chinetti/Rezzaghi/ DiGrazia	U.S.A.	U.S.A.
		Sold on 30/8/62.							
3737 GTE		3737 GTE	250	GTE	2 + 2	Pininfarina			
3739 GTE		3739 GTE	250	GTE	2 + 2	Pininfarina			U.S.A.
3741 GTE		3741 GTE	250	GTE	2 + 2	Pininfarina			
3743 GTE		3743 GTE	250	GTE	2 + 2	Pininfarina			
3745 GTE		3745 GTE	250	GTE	2 + 2	Pininfarina			
3747 SA		3747 SA	400	Superamerica	Coupé	Pininfarina		U.S.A.	U.S.A.
		Delivered on 16/8/62. Coupé Aerodinamico.Last Series I SWB.							
3749 GTE		3749 GTE	250	GTE	2 + 2	Pininfarina			
3751 GT		3751 GT	250 GT	Series II	Convertible	Pininfarina			
3753 GTE		3753 GTE	250	GTE	2 + 2	Pininfarina			
3755 GTE		3755 GTE	250	GTE	2 + 2	Pininfarina			
3757 GT		3757 GT	250 GTO	GTO	Berlinetta	Scaglietti	Francorchamps/ Dernier	Belgium	U.K.
		Sold on 14/6/62.Raced 1962 through 1965.							
3759 GTE		3759 GTE	250	GTE	2 + 2	Pininfarina			
3761 GTE		3761 GTE	250	GTE	2 + 2	Pininfarina			
3763 GT		3763 GT	250 GT	Series II	Convertible	Pininfarina			
3765 LM		3765 LM	4 Litre GTO		Berlinetta	Scaglietti	del Timava P.Ferraro	Italy	U.S.A.
		Sold on 11/9/62.Raced 1962 through 1966. All aluminium body.Built with 4 litre engine.							
3767 GT*		3767 GT	250 GTO	GTO	Berlinetta	Scaglietti	David Piper	U.K.	U.K.
		Sold on 28/7/62.Raced 1962 through 1964.Restored with new all aluminium body.							

Chassis No.	Picture Ref	Engine No.	Type	Model	Body Style	Coach-builder	First Owner	Original Location	Present Location
3769 GT		3769 GT	250 GTO	GTO	Berlinetta	Scaglietti	R.Tavano	France	U.S.A.
	Sold on 13/6/62. Raced 1962 through 1966. Received engine from 3451GT in 1967.								
3771 GT	FM 160	3771 GT	250 GT	Steel SWB	Berlinetta	Scaglietti	E.Melozzi	Italy	U.S.A.
	Sold on 26/7/62. Rebodied in 1966 for Tom Meade as "Nembo" Spyder by Neri & Bonaccini, Modena.								
3773 GT		3773 GT	250GT	Series II	Convertible	Pininfarina			
3775 GT		3775 GT	250 GT	Series II	Convertible	Pininfarina			
3777 GTE		3777 GTE	250	GTE	2 + 2	Pininfarina			
3779 GTE		3779 GTE	250	GTE	2 + 2	Pininfarina			
3781 GTE		3781 GTE	250	GTE	2 + 2	Pininfarina			
3783 GT		3783 GT	250 GT	Series II	Convertible	Pininfarina			
3785 GTE		3785 GTE	250	GTE	2 + 2	Pininfarina			U.S.A.
3787 GTE		3787 GTE	250	GTE	2 + 2	Pininfarina			
3789 GTE		3789 GTE	250	GTE	2 + 2	Pininfarina			
3791 GTE		3791 GTE	250	GTE	2 + 2	Pininfarina			
3793 GTE		3793 GTE	250	GTE	2 + 2	Pininfarina			
3795 GTE		3795 GTE	250	GTE	2 + 2	Pininfarina			
3797 GTE		3797 GTE	250	GTE	2 + 2	Pininfarina			
3799 GTE		3799 GTE	250	GTE	2 + 2	Pininfarina			
3801 GTE*		3801 GTE	250	GTE	2 + 2	Pininfarina	Maranello Conc.	U.K.	U.K.
3803 GT		3803 GT	250 GT	Series II	Convertible	Pininfarina			
3805 GTE		3805 GTE	250	GTE	2 + 2	Pininfarina			
3807 GT		3807 GT	250 GT	Series II	Convertible	Pininfarina			
	Last Series II Convertible built.								
3809 GT		3809 GT	250 GTO	GTO	Berlinetta	Scaglietti	K.von Czazy	Switzerland	Germany
	Sold on 9/7/62. Raced 1962 through 1964. All aluminium body.								
3811 GTE		3811 GTE	250	GTE	2 + 2	Pininfarina			
3813 GTE		3813 GTE	250	GTE	2 + 2	Pininfarina			
3815 GT		3815 GT	250 GT	Steel SWB	Berlinetta	Scaglietti	G.Gedda	Italy	Italy
	Sold in July 1962.								
3817 GTE		3817 GTE	250	GTE	2 + 2	Pininfarina			
3819 GTE		3819 GTE	250	GTE	2 + 2	Pininfarina			
3821 GTE		3821 GTE	250	GTE	2 + 2	Pininfarina			
3823 GTE		3823 GTE	250	GTE	2 + 2	Pininfarina			
3825 GTE		3825 GTE	250	GTE	2 + 2	Pininfarina			
3827 GTE		3827 GTE	250	GTE	2 + 2	Pininfarina			
3829 GT		3829 GT	250 GT	Steel SWB	Berlinetta	Scaglietti	Frigerio	Italy	France
	Sold on 27/10/62.								
3831 GTE		3831 GTE	250	GTE	2 + 2	Pininfarina			
3833 GTE		3833 GTE	250	GTE	2 + 2	Pininfarina			
3835 GTE		3835 GTE	250	GTE	2 + 2	Pininfarina			
3837 GTE		3837 GTE	250	GTE	2 + 2	Pininfarina			
3839 GTE		3839 GTE	250	GTE	2 + 2	Pininfarina			
3841 GTE		3841 GTE	250	GTE	2 + 2	Pininfarina			
3843 GTE		3843 GTE	250	GTE	2 + 2	Pininfarina			
3845 GTE		3845 GTE	250	GTE	2 + 2	Pininfarina			
3847 GT		3847 GT	250 GT	Steel SWB	Berlinetta	Scaglietti	Sopefim	Italy	Switzerland
	Sold on 11/11/62.								
3849 GT		3849 GT	250 GT	Lusso	Berlinetta	Pininfarina			
	Prototype Lusso Berlinetta. 3.78 to 1 rear axle.								
3851 GT		3851 GT	250 GTO	GTO	Berlinetta	Scaglietti	Jo Schlesser	France	Italy
	Sold on 11/9/62. Raced 1962 through 1964. All aluminium body.								
3853 GTE		3853 GTE	250	GTE	2 + 2	Pininfarina			
3855 GTE		3855 GTE	250	GTE	2 + 2	Pininfarina			
3857 GTE		3857 GTE	250	GTE	2 + 2	Pininfarina			Switzerland
3859 GTE		3859 GTE	250	GTE	2 + 2	Pininfarina			
3861 GTE		3861 GTE	250	GTE	2 + 2	Pininfarina			
3863 GT		3863 GT	250 GT	Steel SWB	Berlinetta	Scaglietti	Chinetti/Collins	U.S.A.	U.S.A.
	Sold on 27/11/62.								
3865 GTE		3865 GTE	250	GTE	2 + 2	Pininfarina			
3867 GT		3867 GT	250 GT	SWB California	Spyder	Scaglietti			Holland
	Last reported fitted with correct type but non original engine.								
3869 GT*		3869 GT	250 GTO	GTO	Berlinetta	Scaglietti	Maranello Conc.	U.K.	Switzerland
	Sold on 8/10/62. Shown at 1962 London Motor Show. Raced 1963 through 1965. All aluminium body.								
3871 GTE*		3871 GTE	250	GTE	2 + 2	Pininfarina	Maranello Conc.	U.K.	U.K.
3873 GTE*		3873 GTE	250	GTE	2 + 2	Pininfarina	Maranello Conc.	U.K.	U.K.
3875 GTE		3875 GTE	250	GTE	2 + 2	Pininfarina			
3877 GT		3877 GT	250 GT	Steel SWB	Berlinetta	Scaglietti	Chinetti/Don Fong	U.S.A.	U.S.A.
	Sold on 16/10/62.								
3879 GTE*		3879 GTE	250	GTE	2 + 2	Pininfarina			
3881 GTE		3881 GTE	250	GTE	2 + 2	Pininfarina			
3883 GTE*		3883 GTE	250	GTE	2 + 2	Pininfarina	Maranello Conc.	U.K.	U.K.
3885 GTE		3885 GTE	250	GTE	2 + 2	Pininfarina			
3887 GTE*		3887 GTE	250	GTE	2 + 2	Pininfarina	Maranello Conc.	U.K.	U.K.
3889 GTE		3889 GTE	250	GTE	2 + 2	Pininfarina			

Chassis No.	Picture Ref	Engine No.	Type	Model	Body Style	Coach-builder	First Owner	Original Location	Present Location
3891 GTE		3891 GTE	250	GTE	2 + 2	Pininfarina			
3893 GTE		3893 GTE	250	GTE	2 + 2	Pininfarina			
3895 GTE		3895 GTE	250	GTE	2 + 2	Pininfarina			Switzerland
3897 GTE		3897 GTE	250	GTE	2 + 2	Pininfarina			
3899 GTE		3899 GTE	250	GTE	2 + 2	Pininfarina			
3901 GTE*		3901 GTE	250	GTE	2 + 2	Pininfarina	Maranello Conc.	U.K.	U.K.
3903 GTE		3903 GTE	250	GTE	2 + 2	Pininfarina			
3905 GTE		3905 GTE	250	GTE	2 + 2	Pininfarina			
3907 GTE		3907 GTE	250	GTE	2 + 2	Pininfarina			
3909 GT		3909 GT	250 GTO	GTO	Berlinetta	Scaglietti	Berney/Filipinetti/Volpi	Switzerland	U.K.
	Sold on 10/9/62. Raced 1962 through 1967. English body in 1983. All aluminium body.								
3911 GT		3911 GT	250 GT	Steel SWB	Berlinetta	Scaglietti	Chinetti/C.Rezzaghi	U.S.A.	U.S.A.
	Sold on 8/11/62.								
3913 GTE		3913 GTE	250	GTE	2 + 2	Pininfarina			
3915 GTE*		3915 GTE	250	GTE	2 + 2	Pininfarina	Maranello Conc.	U.K.	U.K.?
	Also reported as a SWB California Spyder.								
3917 GTE		3917 GTE	250	GTE	2 + 2	Pininfarina			
3919 GTE		3919 GTE	250	GTE	2 + 2	Pininfarina			
3921 GTE		3921 GTE	250	GTE	2 + 2	Pininfarina			
3923 GT		3923 GT	250 GT	SWB California	Spyder	Scaglietti			U.S.A.
	Open headlights.								
3925 GTE		3925 GTE	250	GTE	2 + 2	Pininfarina			
3927 GTE		3927 GTE	250	GTE	2 + 2	Pininfarina			
3929 GTE		3929 GTE	250	GTE	2 + 2	Pininfarina			
3931 SA		3931 SA	400 II	Superamerica	Coupé	Pininfarina			
	Shown at the London Motor Show 1962. Coupé Aerodinamica. The first Series II LWB.								
3933 GTE*		3933 GTE	250	GTE	2 + 2	Pininfarina			U.K.
3935 GTE		3935 GTE	250	GTE	2 + 2	Pininfarina			
3937 GTE		3937 GTE	250	GTE	2 + 2	Pininfarina			
3939 GTE		3939 GTE	250	GTE	2 + 2	Pininfarina			
3941 GTE		3941 GTE	250	GTE	2 + 2	Pininfarina			
3943 GT		3943 GT	250 GTO	GTO	Berlinetta	Scaglietti	Pierre Noblet	France	U.S.A.
	Sold on 16/10/62. Raced 1962 through 1967.								
3945 GTE		3945 GTE	250	GTE	2 + 2	Pininfarina			
3947 GTE		3947 GTE	250	GTE	2 + 2	Pininfarina			
3949 SA		3949 SA	400 II	Superamerica	Coupé	Pininfarina	Erwin Goldschmidt	U.S.A.	U.S.A.
	Delivered on 29/9/62. Shown at the 1962 Turin Motor Show. Coupé Aerodinamico.								
3951 GTE		3951 GTE	250	GTE	2 + 2	Pininfarina			
3953 GTE		3953 GTE	250	GTE	2 + 2	Pininfarina			
3955 GTE		3955 GTE	250	GTE	2 + 2	Pininfarina			
3957 GTE*		3957 GTE	250	GTE	2 + 2	Pininfarina	Maranello Conc.	U.K.	U.K.
3959 GTE*		3959 GTE	250	GTE	2 + 2	Pininfarina	Maranello Conc.	U.K.	U.K.
3961 GTE		3961 GTE	250	GTE	2 + 2	Pininfarina			U.S.A.
3963 GT		3963 GT	250 GT	Steel SWB	Berlinetta	Scaglietti	Petruzzelli	Italy	U.S.A.
	Sold on 17/12/62.								
3965 GTE		3965 GTE	250	GTE	2 + 2	Pininfarina			
3967 GTE		3967 GTE	250	GTE	2 + 2	Pininfarina			
3969 GTE		3969 GTE	250	GTE	2 + 2	Pininfarina			
3971 GTE		3971 GTE	250	GTE	2 + 2	Pininfarina			
3973 GTE		3973 GTE	250	GTE	2 + 2	Pininfarina			
3975 GTE		3975 GTE	250	GTE	2 + 2	Pininfarina			
3977 GTE		3977 GTE	250	GTE	2 + 2	Pininfarina			
3979 GTE		3979 GTE	250	GTE	2 + 2	Pininfarina			
3981 GTE		3981 GTE	250	GTE	2 + 2	Pininfarina			
3983 GTE		3983 GTE	250	GTE	2 + 2	Pininfarina			
3985 GTE		3985 GTE	250	GTE	2 + 2	Pininfarina			
3987 GT		3987 GT	250 GTO	GTO	Berlinetta	Scaglietti	Chinetti/NART	U.S.A.	U.S.A.
	Sold on 11/10/62. Raced 1962 through 1964.								
3989 GTE		3989 GTE	250	GTE	2 + 2	Pininfarina			U.S.A.
3991 GTE		3991 GTE	250	GTE	2 + 2	Pininfarina			
3993 GTE		3993 GTE	250	GTE	2 + 2	Pininfarina			
3995 GT		3995 GT	250 GT	SWB California	Spyder	Scaglietti			U.S.A.
	Covered headlights.								
3997 GTE		3997 GTE	250	GTE	2 + 2	Pininfarina			
3999 GTE		3999 GTE	250	GTE	2 + 2	Pininfarina			
4001 GTE		4001 GTE	250	GTE	2 + 2	Pininfarina			
4003 GTE		4003 GTE	250	GTE	2 + 2	Pininfarina			
4005 GTE		4005 GTE	250	GTE	2 + 2	Pininfarina			
4007 GTE		4007 GTE	250	GTE	2 + 2	Pininfarina			
4009 GTE		4009 GTE	250	GTE	2 + 2	Pininfarina			Switzerland
4011 GTE		4011 GTE	250	GTE	2 + 2	Pininfarina			
4013 GT		4013 GT	250 GT	SWB California	Spyder	Scaglietti			U.S.A.
4015 GTE		4015 GTE	250	GTE	2 + 2	Pininfarina			U.S.A.
4017 GTE		4017 GTE	250	GTE	2 + 2	Pininfarina			

Chassis No.	Picture Ref	Engine No.	Type	Model	Body Style	Coach-builder	First Owner	Original Location	Present Location
4019 GTE		4019 GTE	250	GTE	2 + 2	Pininfarina			
4021 GTE		4021 GTE	250	GTE	2 + 2	Pininfarina			
4023 GTE		4023 GTE	250	GTE	2 + 2	Pininfarina			
4025 GTE		4025 GTE	250	GTE	2 + 2	Pininfarina			
4027 GTE		4027 GTE	250	GTE	2 + 2	Pininfarina			
4029 GTE		4029 GTE	250	GTE	2 + 2	Pininfarina			
4031 SA		4031 SA	400 II	Superamerica	Coupé	Pininfarina			U.S.A.
	Coupé Aerodinamico. Built on SWB!								
4033 GTE		4033 GTE	250	GTE	2 + 2	Pininfarina			
4035 GTE		4035 GTE	250	GTE	2 + 2	Pininfarina			
4037 GT		4037 GT	250 GT	Steel SWB	Berlinetta	Scaglietti	Chinetti/Sheppard	U.S.A.	Italy
	Sold on 30/3/63.								
4039 GTE		4039 GTE	250	GTE	2 + 2	Pininfarina			
4041 GTE		4041 GTE	250	GTE	2 + 2	Pininfarina			
4043 GTE		4043 GTE	250	GTE	2 + 2	Pininfarina			
4045 GTE		4045 GTE	250	GTE	2 + 2	Pininfarina			U.S.A.(Parted
4047 GTE		4047 GTE	250	GTE	2 + 2	Pininfarina			
4049 GTE		4049 GTE	250	GTE	2 + 2	Pininfarina			
4051 GT		4051 GT	250 GT	Steel SWB	Berlinetta	Scaglietti	Chinetti/Zipper	U.S.A.	U.S.A.
	Sold in February 1963.								
4053 GT	P1 237	4053 GT	250 GT	Lusso	Berlinetta	Scaglietti			
	A prototype Lusso Berlinetta - probably the second one.								
4055 GTE		4055 GTE	250	GTE	2 + 2	Pininfarina			
4057 GT		4057 GT	250 GT	Steel SWB	Berlinetta	Scaglietti	L.Caccia	Italy	
	Sold on 11/1/63.								
4059 SA		4059 SA	400 II	Superamerica	Coupé	Pininfarina	Franzozi	Belgium	U.S.A.
	Delivered on 10/12/62. Coupé Aerodinamico.								
4061 GTE		4061 GTE	250	GTE	2 + 2	Pininfarina			
4063 GTE		4063 GTE	250	GTE	2 + 2	Pininfarina			
4065 GT		4065 GT	250 GT	Steel SWB	Berlinetta	Scaglietti	Chinetti/Zipper/ C.Cord	U.S.A.	U.S.A.
	Sold February 1963. The last SWB Berlinetta made.								
4067 GTE		4067 GTE	250	GTE	2 + 2	Pininfarina		U.S.A.	
4069 GTE		4069 GTE	250	GTE	2 + 2	Pininfarina			U.S.A.
4071 GTE		4071 GTE	250	GTE	2 + 2	Pininfarina			
4073 GTE		4073 GTE	250	GTE	2 + 2	Pininfarina			
4075 GTE		4075 GTE	250	GTE	2 + 2	Pininfarina			
4077 GTE		4077 GTE	250	GTE	2 + 2	Pininfarina			U.S.A.
4079 GTE		4079 GTE	250	GTE	2 + 2	Pininfarina			Switzerland
4081 GTE		4081 GTE	250	GTE	2 + 2	Pininfarina			
4083 GT		4083 GT	250 GT	SWB California	Spyder	Scaglietti			
	Open headlights.								
4085 GT		4085 GT	330	GT	2 + 2	Pininfarina			
	Sold on 21/9/62. Believe prototype 330GT.								
4087 GTE		4087 GTE	250	GTE	2 + 2	Pininfarina			
4089 GTE		4089 GTE	250	GTE	2 + 2	Pininfarina			
4091 GT		4091 GT	250 GTO	GTO	Berlinetta	Scaglietti	Bettoja	Italy	U.S.A.
	Sold on 17/11/62. Rebodied in 1963 with 64 "tunnel back" body. Raced 1963 through 1966.								
4093 GTE		4093 GTE	250	GTE	2 + 2	Pininfarina			
4095 GT		4095 GT	250 GT	SWB California	Spyder	Scaglietti	Saddrudine Aga Khan	France	France?
	Open headlights.								
4097 GTE		4097 GTE	250	GTE	2 + 2	Pininfarina			Switzerland
4099 GTE		4099 GTE	250	GTE	2 + 2	Pininfarina			U.S.A.
4101 GTE		4101 GTE	250	GTE	2 + 2	Pininfarina			
4103 GT		4103 GT	250 GT	SWB California	Spyder	Scaglietti			
	Once reported as the first production Lusso Berlinetta.								
4105 GTE		4105 GTE	250	GTE	2 + 2	Pininfarina			
4107 GT		4107 GT	250 GT	SWB California	Spyder	Scaglietti			
4109 SA		4109 SA	400 II	Superamerica	Coupé	Pininfarina	Alessio	Italy	
	Sold on 15/1/63.								
4111 SA		4111 SA	400 II	Superamerica	Coupé	Pininfarina	Filipinetti	Switzerland	U.K.
	Shown at 1963 Geneva Motor Show. Coupé Aerodinamico.								
4113 SA		4113 SA	400 II	Superamerica	Coupé	Pininfarina	Faina	Italy	U.S.A.
	Delivered on 13/4/63. Coupé Aerodinamico.								
4115 GT		4115 GT	250 GTO	GTO	Berlinetta	Scaglietti	Auto-Becker/Cordes	Germany	U.K.
	Sold on 7/12/62. Raced 1963 through 1965.								
4117 GTE		4117 GTE	250	GTE	2 + 2	Pininfarina			
4119 GTE		4119 GTE	250	GTE	2 + 2	Pininfarina			
4121 GT		4121 GT	250 GT	SWB California	Spyder	Scaglietti			U.S.A.
	Completed on 15/1/63. Open headlights. Hard-top.								
4123 GTE		4123 GTE	250	GTE	2 + 2	Pininfarina			
4125 GT		4125 GT	250 GT	SWB California	Spyder	Scaglietti	Movie star	Venezuela	U.S.A.
	In Venezuela until shipped to U.S.A. in 1979. Open headlights.								
4127 GTE		4127 GTE	250	GTE	2 + 2	Pininfarina			
4129 GTE		4129 GTE	250	GTE	2 + 2	Pininfarina			

Chassis No.	Picture Ref	Engine No.	Type	Model	Body Style	Coach-builder	First Owner	Original Location	Present Location
4131 GT		4131 GT	250 GT	SWB California	Spyder	Scaglietti			U.S.A.
	Completed 28/12/62. In Switzerland than U.S.A. many years ago.								
				1963					
4133 GTE		4133 GTE	250	GTE	2 + 2	Pininfarina			
4135 GTE		4135 GTE	250	GTE	2 + 2	Pininfarina			
4137 GT		4137 GT	250 GT	SWB California	Spyder	Scaglietti			
	Completed 6/2/63. Covered headlights. Last SWB California made.								
4139 GTE		4139 GTE	250	GTE	2 + 2	Pininfarina			
4141 GTE		4141 GTE	250	GTE	2 + 2	Pininfarina			
4143 GTE		4143 GTE	250	GTE	2 + 2	Pininfarina			
4145 GTE		4145 GTE	250	GTE	2 + 2	Pininfarina			
4147 GTE		4147 GTE	250	GTE	2 + 2	Pininfarina			
4149 GTE		4149 GTE	250	GTE	2 + 2	Pininfarina			
4151 GTE		4151 GTE	250	GTE	2 + 2	Pininfarina			
4153 GT		4153 GT	250 GTO	GTO	Berlinetta	Scaglietti	Francorchamps/ P.Dumay	France	France
	Sold on 2/6/63. All aluminium body.								
4155 GTE		4155 GTE	250	GTE	2 + 2	Pininfarina			
4157 GTE		4157 GTE	250	GTE	2 + 2	Pininfarina			
4159 GTE		4159 GTE	250	GTE	2 + 2	Pininfarina			
4161 GTE		4161 GTE	250	GTE	2 + 2	Pininfarina			
4163 GTE		4163 GTE	250	GTE	2 + 2	Pininfarina			
4165 GTE		4165 GTE	250	GTE	2 + 2	Pininfarina			
4167 GTE		4167 GTE	250	GTE	2 + 2	Pininfarina			
4169 GTE		4169 GTE	250	GTE	2 + 2	Pininfarina			
4171 GTE		4171 GTE	250	GTE	2 + 2	Pininfarina			
4173 GTE		4173 GTE	250	GTE	2 + 2	Pininfarina			
4175 GTE		4175 GTE	250	GTE	2 + 2	Pininfarina			
4177 GTE		4177 GTE	250	GTE	2 + 2	Pininfarina			
4179 GTE		4179 GTE	250	GTE	2 + 2	Pininfarina			
4181 GTE		4181 GTE	250	GTE	2 + 2	Pininfarina			
4183 GTE		4183 GTE	250	GTE	2 + 2	Pininfarina			
4185 GTE		4185 GTE	250	GTE	2 + 2	Pininfarina			
4187 GTE		4187 GTE	250	GTE	2 + 2	Pininfarina			
4189 GTE		4189 GTE	250	GTE	2 + 2	Pininfarina			
4191 GTE		4191 GTE	250	GTE	2 + 2	Pininfarina			
4193 GTE		4193 GTE	250	GTE	2 + 2	Pininfarina			
4195 GTE		4195 GTE	250	GTE	2 + 2	Pininfarina			
4197 GTE		4197 GTE	250	GTE	2 + 2	Pininfarina			
4199 GTE		4199 GTE	250	GTE	2 + 2	Pininfarina			
4201 GTE		4201 GTE	250	GTE	2 + 2	Pininfarina			U.S.A.
4203 GTE		4203 GTE	250	GTE	2 + 2	Pininfarina			
4205 GTE		4205 GTE	250	GTE	2 + 2	Pininfarina			
4207 GTE		4207 GTE	250	GTE	2 + 2	Pininfarina			
4209 GTE		4209 GTE	250	GTE	2 + 2	Pininfarina			
4211 GTE		4211 GTE	250	GTE	2 + 2	Pininfarina			
4213 GT		4213 GT	250 GT	Lusso	Berlinetta	Scaglietti			
4215 GTE		4215 GTE	250	GTE	2 + 2	Pininfarina			
4217 GTE		4217 GTE	250	GTE	2 + 2	Pininfarina			
4219 GT		4219 GT	250 GTO	GTO	Berlinetta	Scaglietti	Chinetti/ Mamie Reynolds	U.S.A.	U.S.A.
	Sold on 5/2/63. Raced in 1963 and 1964.								
4221 GTE		4221 GTE	250	GTE	2 + 2	Pininfarina			
4223 GTE		4223 GTE	250	GTE	2 + 2	Pininfarina			
4225 GTE		4225 GTE	250	GTE	2 + 2	Pininfarina			
4227 GTE		4227 GTE	250	GTE	2 + 2	Pininfarina			
4229 GTE		4229 GTE	250	GTE	2 + 2	Pininfarina			
4231 GTE		4231 GTE	250	GTE	2 + 2	Pininfarina			
4233 GTE		4233 GTE	250	GTE	2 + 2	Pininfarina			
4235 GTE		4235 GTE	250	GTE	2 + 2	Pininfarina			
4237 GT		4237 GT	250 GT	Lusso	Berlinetta	Scaglietti			
4239 GTE*		4239 GTE	250	GTE	2 + 2	Pininfarina			
4241 SA		4241 SA	400 II	Superamerica	Convertible	Pininfarina	Henry	France	France
	Delivered on 21/5/63.								
4243 GTE*		4243 GTE	250	GTE	2 + 2	Pininfarina			
4245 GTE		4245 GTE	250	GTE	2 + 2	Pininfarina			
4247 GTE		4247 GTE	250	GTE	2 + 2	Pininfarina			
4249 GTE		4249 GTE	250	GTE	2 + 2	Pininfarina			
4251 SA		4251 SA	400 II	Superamerica	Coupé	Pininfarina	Bolt	U.S.A.	U.S.A.
	Delivered on 7/2/63. Coupé Aerodinamico.								
4253 GTE*		4253 GTE	250	GTE	2 + 2	Pininfarina			
4255 GTE*		4255 GTE	250	GTE	2 + 2	Pininfarina			
4257 GTE*		4257 GTE	250	GTE	2 + 2	Pininfarina			U.S.A.
4259 GTE		4259 GTE	250	GTE	2 + 2	Pininfarina			
4261 GT		4261 GT	250GT	Lusso	Berlinetta	Scaglietti			
4263 GTE		4263 GTE	250	GTE	2 + 2	Pininfarina			

Chassis No.	Picture Ref	Engine No.	Type	Model	Body Style	Coach-builder	First Owner	Original Location	Present Location
4265 GTE		4265 GTE	250	GTE	2 + 2	Pininfarina			
4267 GT		4267 GT	250 GT	Lusso	Berlinetta	Scaglietti			
4269 GTE		4269 GTE	250	GTE	2 + 2	Pininfarina			
4271 SA		4271 SA	400 II	Superamerica	Coupé	Pininfarina	Riva	Switzerland	U.S.A.
	Coupé Aerodinamico.								
4273 GTE		4273 GTE	250	GTE	2 + 2	Pininfarina			
4275 GTE		4275 GTE	250	GTE	2 + 2	Pininfarina			
4277 GTE		4277 GTE	250	GTE	2 + 2	Pininfarina			
4279 SA		4279 SA	400 II	Superamerica	Coupé	Pininfarina	Mereghetti	Italy	U.S.A.
	Delivered on 24/5/63.								
4281 GTE		4281 GTE	250	GTE	2 + 2	Pininfarina			
4283 GTE		4283 GTE	250	GTE	2 + 2	Pininfarina			
4285 GTE		4285 GTE	250	GTE	2 + 2	Pininfarina			
4287 GTE		4287 GTE	250	GTE	2 + 2	Pininfarina			
4289 GTE		4289 GTE	250	GTE	2 + 2	Pininfarina			
4291 GTE		4291 GTE	250	GTE	2 + 2	Pininfarina			
4293 GT		4293 GT	250 GTO	GTO	Berlinetta	Scaglietti	SC San Ambreus	Italy	Japan
	Sold on 22/4/63. Raced in 1963. All aluminium body.								
4295 GTE		4295 GTE	250	GTE	2 + 2	Pininfarina			
4297 GT		4297 GT	250 GT	Lusso	Berlinetta	Scaglietti			
	Acquired Engine No.5661GT.								
4299 GTE		4299 GTE	250	GTE	2 + 2	Pininfarina			
4301 GTE		4301 GTE	250	GTE	2 + 2	Pininfarina			
4303 GTE		4303 GTE	250	GTE	2 + 2	Pininfarina			
4305 GTE		4305 GTE	250	GTE	2 + 2	Pininfarina			
4307 GT		4307 GT	250 GT	Lusso	Berlinetta	Scaglietti			
4309 GTE*		4309 GTE	250	GTE	2 + 2	Pininfarina			
4311 GTE		4311 GTE	250	GTE	2 + 2	Pininfarina			
4313 GTE		4313 GTE	250	GTE	2 + 2	Pininfarina			
4315 GTE		4315 GTE	250	GTE	2 + 2	Pininfarina			
4317 GTE		4317 GTE	250	GTE	2 + 2	Pininfarina			
4319 GTE		4319 GTE	250 GTE	Lusso	Berlinetta	Scaglietti			
4321 GTE		4321 GTE	250	GTE	2 + 2	Pininfarina			
4323 GTE		4323 GTE	250	GTE	2 + 2	Pininfarina			
4325 GTE		4325 GTE	250	GTE	2 + 2	Pininfarina			
4327 GTE		4327 GTE	250	GTE	2 + 2	Pininfarina			
4329 GTE		4329 GTE	250	GTE	2 + 2	Pininfarina			
4331 GTE		4331 GTE	250	GTE	2 + 2	Pininfarina			
4333 GTE		4333 GTE	250	GTE	2 + 2	Pininfarina			
4335 GT	P1 139	4335 GT	250 GT	Lusso	Berlinetta	Pininfarina			
	Shown at the 1964 London Motor Show with covered headlights.								
4337 GTE		4337 GTE	250	GTE	2 + 2	Pininfarina			
4339 GTE		4339 GTE	250	GTE	2 + 2	Pininfarina			
4341 GTE		4341 GTE	250	GTE	2 + 2	Pininfarina			
4343 GTE		4343 GTE	250	GTE	2 + 2	Pininfarina			
4345 GTE		4345 GTE	250	GTE	2 + 2	Pininfarina			
4347 GTE		4347 GTE	250	GTE	2 + 2	Pininfarina			
4349 GTE		4349 GTE	250	GTE	2 + 2	Pininfarina			
4351 GTE		4351 GTE	250	GTE	2 + 2	Pininfarina			
4353 GTE		4353 GTE	250	GTE	2 + 2	Pininfarina			
4355 GTE*		4355 GTE	250	GTE	2 + 2	Pininfarina	Maranello Conc.	U.K.	U.K.
4357 GTE		4357 GTE	250	GTE	2 + 2	Pininfarina			
4359 GT		4359 GT	250 GT	Lusso	Berlinetta	Scaglietti			U.S.A.
	First Lusso built in 1963.								
4361 GTE		4361 GTE	250	GTE	2 + 2	Pininfarina			
4363 GT		4363 GT	250 GT	Lusso	Berlinetta	Scaglietti			
	Acquired Engine No.2025GT.								
4365 GT		4365 GT	250 GT	Lusso	Berlinetta	Scaglietti			
4367 GTE		4367 GTE	250	GTE	2 + 2	Pininfarina			
4369 GTE		4369 GTE	250	GTE	2 + 2	Pininfarina			
4371 GTE		4371 GTE	250	GTE	2 + 2	Pininfarina			
4373 GT		4373 GT	250 GT	Lusso	Berlinetta	Scaglietti			
4375 GT		4375 GT	250 GT	Lusso	Berlinetta	Scaglietti			
4377 GT		4377 GT	250 GT	Lusso	Berlinetta	Scaglietti			
4379 GT		4379 GT	250 GT	Lusso	Berlinetta	Scaglietti			
4381 GT		4381 GT	330 LMB	LMB	Berlinetta	Scaglietti			
	All aluminium body.								
4383 GT		4383 GT	250 GT	Lusso	Berlinetta	Scaglietti			
	Acquired revised GTO-like nose and Engine No.5193GT.								
4385 GT		4385 GT	250 GT	Lusso	Berlinetta	Scaglietti			
	Nose like GTO. Engine with 6 carbs. 3.78 to 1 axle.								
4387 GT		4387 GT	250 GT	Lusso	Berlinetta	Scaglietti			

Chassis No.	Picture Ref	Engine No.	Type	Model	Body Style	Coach-builder	First Owner	Original Location	Present Location
4389 GT		4389 GT	250 GT	Lusso	Berlinetta	Scaglietti			
4391 GT		4391 GT	250 GT	Lusso	Berlinetta	Scaglietti			
	Reported with 330 engine and 5 speed gearbox.								
4393 GT		4393 GT	250 GT	Lusso	Berlinetta	Scaglietti			
4395 GTE		4395 GTE	250	GTE	2 + 2	Pininfarina			
4397 GTE		4397 GTE	250	GTE	2 + 2	Pininfarina			
4399 GT		4399 GT	250 GTO	GTO	Berlinetta	Scaglietti	Hoare	U.K.	U.K.
	Sold on 29/5/63. Built as a 'fast back' and rebodied as a 'tunnel back' with roof spoiler. First GTO to be equipped with the 1964 style 'tunnel back' body. Raced in 1963 through 1965.								
4401 GT		4401 GT	250 GT	Lusso	Berlinetta	Scaglietti			
4403 GT		4403 GT	250 GT	Lusso	Berlinetta	Scaglietti			
4405 GT		4405 GT	250 GT	Lusso	Berlinetta	Scaglietti			
4407 GT		4407 GT	250 GT	Lusso	Berlinetta	Scaglietti			
	Reported with 5 speed gearbox.								
4409 GT		4409 GT	250 GT	Lusso	Berlinetta	Scaglietti			
	Reported using 40DCZ carbs.								
4411 GT		4411 GT	250 GT	Lusso	Berlinetta	Scaglietti			
4413 GT*		4413 GT	250 GT	Lusso	Berlinetta	Scaglietti	Maranello Conc.	U.K.	U.K.
4415 GT		4415 GT	250 GT	Lusso	Berlinetta	Scaglietti			
4417 GT		4417 GT	250 GT	Lusso	Berlinetta	Scaglietti			
4419 GT		4419 GT	250 GT	Lusso	Berlinetta	Scaglietti			
4421 GT		4421 GT	250 GT	Lusso	Berlinetta	Scaglietti			
4423 SA		4423 SA	400 S.2	Superamerica	Convertible	Pininfarina	Maggiore	Italy	
4425 GT		4425 GT	250 GT	Lusso	Berlinetta	Scaglietti			
	Acquired Engine No.3213GT.								
4427 GT		4427 GT	250 GT	Lusso	Berlinetta	Scaglietti			
4429 GT		4429 GT	250 GT	Lusso	Berlinetta	Scaglietti			
4431 GT		4431 GT	250 GT	Lusso	Berlinetta	Scaglietti			
4433GT		4433GT	250 GT	Lusso	Berlinetta	Scaglietti			
4435 GT*		4435 GT	250 GT	Lusso	Berlinetta	Scaglietti			U.K.
4437 GT		4437 GT	250 GT	Lusso	Berlinetta	Scaglietti			
	Uses 40DCZ carbs.								
4439 GT		4439 GT	250 GT	Lusso	Berlinetta	Scaglietti			
4441 GT		4441 GT	250 GT	Lusso	Berlinetta	Scaglietti			
	Reported wrecked and being parted out.								
4443 SA		4443 SA	400 S.2	Superamerica	Coupé	Pininfarina	Count Chandon	France	France
	Coupé Aerodinamico								
4445 GT		4445 GT	250 GT	Lusso	Berlinetta	Scaglietti			
4447 GT		4447 GT	250 GT	Lusso	Berlinetta	Scaglietti			
4449 GT		4449 GT	250 GT	Lusso	Berlinetta	Scaglietti			
4451 GT		4451 GT	250 GT	Lusso	Berlinetta	Scaglietti			
4453 GT		4453 GT	330 LMB	LMB	Berlinetta	Scaglietti			
	All aluminium body. Styling like Lusso Berlinetta.								
4455 GTE		4455 GTE	250	GTE	2 + 2	Pininfarina			
4457 GT		4457 GT	250 GT	Lusso	Berlinetta	Scaglietti			
4459 GT		4459 GT	250 GT	Lusso	Berlinetta	Scaglietti			
4461 GT		4461 GT	250 GT	Lusso	Berlinetta	Scaglietti			
4463 GTE		4463 GTE	250	GTE	2 + 2	Pininfarina			
4465 SA		4465 SA	400 S.2	Superamerica	Coupé	Pininfarina			
	Coupé Aerodinamico								
4467 GT		4467 GT	250 GT	Lusso	Berlinetta	Scaglietti			
4469 GT		4469 GT	250 GT	Lusso	Berlinetta	Scaglietti			
4471 GT		4471 GT	250 GT	Lusso	Berlinetta	Scaglietti			
4473 GTE		4473 GTE	250	GTE	2 + 2	Pininfarina			
4475 GTE		4475 GTE	250	GTE	2 + 2	Pininfarina			
4477 GTE		4477 GTE	250	GTE	2 + 2	Pininfarina			
4479 GTE		4479 GTE	250	GTE	2 + 2	Pininfarina			
4481 GT		4481 GT	250 GT	Lusso	Berlinetta	Scaglietti			
4483 GTE		4483 GTE	250	GTE	2 + 2	Pininfarina			
4485 GTE		4485 GTE	250	GTE	2 + 2	Pininfarina			
4487 GTE		4487 GTE	250	GTE	2 + 2	Pininfarina			
4489 GTE		4489 GTE	250	GTE	2 + 2	Pininfarina			
4491 GT*		4491 GT	250 GTO	GTO	Berlinetta	Scaglietti	David Piper	U.K.	Italy
	Sold on 7/6/63. Raced 1963 through 1965. All aluminium body. Modified body by Piper.								
4493 GT		4493 GT	250 GT	Lusso	Berlinetta	Scaglietti			
4495 GTE		4495 GTE	250	GTE	2 + 2	Pininfarina			
4497 GT		4497 GT	250 GT	Lusso	Berlinetta	Scaglietti			
	U.S.A. instruments.								
4499 GTE		4499 GTE	250	GTE	2 + 2	Pininfarina			
4501 GTE		4501 GTE	250	GTE	2 + 2	Pininfarina			
4503 GT		4503 GT	250 GT	Lusso	Berlinetta	Scaglietti			
4505 GTE		4505 GTE	250	GTE	2 + 2	Pininfarina			
4507 GTE		4507 GTE	250	GTE	2 + 2	Pininfarina			
4509 GT		4509 GT	250 GT	Lusso	Berlinetta	Scaglietti			

Chassis No.	Picture Ref	Engine No.	Type	Model	Body Style	Coach-builder	First Owner	Original Location	Present Location
4511 GTE		4511 GTE	250	GTE	2 + 2	Pininfarina			
4513 GT		4513 GT	250 GT	Lusso	Berlinetta	Scaglietti			
4515 GTE		4515 GTE	250	GTE	2 + 2	Pininfarina			
4517 GTE		4517 GTE	250	GTE	2 + 2	Pininfarina			
4519 GT		4519 GT	250 GT	Lusso	Berlinetta	Scaglietti			
4521 GT		4521 GT	250 GT	Lusso	Berlinetta	Scaglietti			
4523 GTE		4523 GTE	250	GTE	2 + 2	Pininfarina			
4525 GTE		4525 GTE	250	GTE	2 + 2	Pininfarina			
4527 GT		4527 GT	250 GT	Lusso	Berlinetta	Scaglietti			
4529 GTE		4529 GTE	250	GTE	2 + 2	Pininfarina			
4531 GTE		4531 GTE	250	GTE	2 + 2	Pininfarina			
4533 GTE		4533 GTE	250	GTE	2 + 2	Pininfarina			
4535 GTE		4535 GTE	250	GTE	2 + 2	Pininfarina			
4537 GT		4537 GT	250 GT	Lusso	Berlinetta	Scaglietti			
	3.78 to 1 axle ratio.								
4539 GT		4539 GT	250 GT	Lusso	Berlinetta	Scaglietti			
4541 GTE		4541 GTE	250	GTE	2 + 2	Pininfarina			
4543 GTE		4543 GTE	250	GTE	2 + 2	Pininfarina			
4545 GTE		4545 GTE	250	GTE	2 + 2	Pininfarina			
4547 GTE		4547 GTE	250	GTE	2 + 2	Pininfarina			
4549 GT		4549 GT	250 GT	Lusso	Berlinetta	Scaglietti			
4551 GTE		4551 GTE	250	GTE	2 + 2	Pininfarina			
4553 GTE?		4553 GTE?	250	GTE	2 + 2	Pininfarina			
	Might be Lusso.								
4555 GT		4555 GT	250 GT	Lusso	Berlinetta	Scaglietti			U.S.A.
4557 GTE		4557 GTE	250	GTE	2 + 2	Pininfarina			Italy
4559 GTE		4559 GTE	250	GTE	2 + 2	Pininfarina			
4561 SA		4561 SA	400 GTO	GTO	Berlinetta	Scaglietti	M. Paul-Cavallier	France	Switzerland
	Sold on 23/9/63. Never raced. Specially built for the first owner, a director of Ferrari. All aluminium body. WB:2450mm.								
4563 GT		4563 GT	250 GT	Lusso	Berlinetta	Scaglietti			
4565 GTE		4565 GTE	250	GTE	2 + 2	Pininfarina			
4567 GT		4567 GT	250 GT	Lusso	Berlinetta	Scaglietti			
4569 GTE		4569 GTE	250	GTE	2 + 2	Pininfarina			
4571 GTE		4571 GTE	250	GTE	2 + 2	Pininfarina			
4573 GTE		4573 GTE	250	GTE	2 + 2	Pininfarina			
4575 GT		4575 GT	250 GT	Lusso	Berlinetta	Scaglietti			
4577 GT		4577 GT	250 GT	Lusso	Berlinetta	Scaglietti			
4579 GTE		4579 GTE	250	GTE	2 + 2	Pininfarina			
4581 GT		4581 GT	250 GT	Lusso	Berlinetta	Scaglietti			U.S.A.
4583 GTE		4583 GTE	250	GTE	2 + 2	Pininfarina			
4585 GTE		4585 GTE	250	GTE	2 + 2	Pininfarina			
4587 GT		4587 GT	250 GT	Lusso	Berlinetta	Scaglietti			
	Converted to covered headlights.								
4589 GTE		4589 GTE	250	GTE	2 + 2	Pininfarina			
4591 GT		4591 GT	250 GT	Lusso	Berlinetta	Scaglietti			
4593 GTE		4593 GTE	250	GTE	2 + 2	Pininfarina			
4595 GT		4595 GT	250 GT	Lusso	Berlinetta	Scaglietti			
4597 GTE		4597 GTE	250	GTE	2 + 2	Pininfarina			
4599 GTE		4599 GTE	250	GTE	2 + 2	Pininfarina			
4601 GTE		4601 GTE	250	GTE	2 + 2	Pininfarina			
4603 GTE		4603 GTE	250	GTE	2 + 2	Pininfarina			
4065 GTE		4065 GTE	250	GTE	2 + 2	Pininfarina			
4607 GT		4607 GT	250 GT	Lusso	Berlinetta	Scaglietti			
4609 GTE		4609 GTE	250	GTE	2 + 2	Pininfarina			
4611 GTE		4611 GTE	250	GTE	2 + 2	Pininfarina			
4613 GT		4613 GT	250 GT	Lusso	Berlinetta	Scaglietti			
4615 GTE		4615 GTE	250	GTE	2 + 2	Pininfarina			
4617 GTE		4617 GTE	250	GTE	2 + 2	Pininfarina			
4619 GT		4619 GT	330 LMB	LMB	Berlinetta	Scaglietti			
	All aluminium body.								
4621 GT		4621 GT	250 GT	Lusso	Berlinetta	Scaglietti			
4623 GT		4623 GT	250 GT	Lusso	Berlinetta	Scaglietti			
4625 GT		4625 GT	250 GT	Lusso	Berlinetta	Scaglietti			
4627 GT		4627 GT	250 GT	Lusso	Berlinetta	Scaglietti			
4629 GTE		4629 GTE	250	GTE	2 + 2	Pininfarina			
4631 GT		4631 GT	250 GT	Lusso	Berlinetta	Scaglietti			
4633 GTE		4633 GTE	250	GTE	2 + 2	Pininfarina			
4635 GT		4635 GT	250 GT	Lusso	Berlinetta	Scaglietti			
4637 GTE		4637 GTE	250	GTE	2 + 2	Pininfarina			
4639 GTE		4639 GTE	250	GTE	2 + 2	Pininfarina			
4641 GTE		4641 GTE	250	GTE	2 + 2	Pininfarina			
4643 GTE		4643 GTE	250	GTE	2 + 2	Pininfarina			U.S.A.
4645 GTE*		4645 GTE	250	GTE	2 + 2	Pininfarina	Maranello Conc.	U.K.	U.K.
4647 GTE		4647 GTE	250	GTE	2 + 2	Pininfarina			

Chassis No.	Picture Ref	Engine No.	Type	Model	Body Style	Coach-builder	First Owner	Original Location	Present Location
4649 GTE		4649 GTE	250	GTE	2 + 2	Pininfarina			
4651 SA		4651 SA	400 S.2	Superamerica	Coupé	Pininfarina	Horath		
4653 GTE		4653 GTE	250	GTE	2 + 2	Pininfarina			
4655 GT*		4655 GT	250 GT	Lusso	Berlinetta	Scaglietti			
4657 GTE		4657 GTE	250	GTE	2 + 2	Pininfarina			
4659 GTE		4659 GTE	250	GTE	2 + 2	Pininfarina			
4661 GTE		4661 GTE	250	GTE	2 + 2	Pininfarina			
4663 GTE		4663 GTE	250	GTE	2 + 2	Pininfarina			
4665 GTE		4665 GTE	250	GTE	2 + 2	Pininfarina			
4667 GTE		4667 GTE	250	GTE	2 + 2	Pininfarina			
4669 GTE		4669 GTE	250	GTE	2 + 2	Pininfarina			
4671 GTE		4671 GTE	250	GTE	2 + 2	Pininfarina			
4673 GTE		4673 GTE	250	GTE	2 + 2	Pininfarina			
4675 GT		4675 GT	250 GTO	GTO	Berlinetta	Scaglietti	Vecar/Annunziata	Italy	U.S.A.
		Sold on 23/4/63. Raced 1963 through 1966. All aluminium body. Rebodied at end of 1963 w/'tunnel back' body.							
4677 GTE		4677 GTE	250	GTE	2 + 2	Pininfarina			
4679 SA		4679 SA	400 S.2	Superamerica	Coupé	Pininfarina	W.David		
		Coupé Aerodinamico.							
4681 GTE		4681 GTE	250	GTE	2 + 2	Pininfarina			
4683 GTE		4683 GTE	250	GTE	2 + 2	Pininfarina			
4685 GTE		4685 GTE	250	GTE	2 + 2	Pininfarina			
4687 GTE		4687 GTE	250	GTE	2 + 2	Pininfarina			
4689 GTE		4689 GTE	250	GTE	2 + 2	Pininfarina			
4691 GTE		4691 GTE	250	GTE	2 + 2	Pininfarina			
4693 GTE		4693 GTE	250	GTE	2 + 2	Pininfarina			
4695 GTE		4695 GTE	250	GTE	2 + 2	Pininfarina			
4697 GTE		4697 GTE	250	GTE	2 + 2	Pininfarina			
4699 GTE		4699 GTE	250	GTE	2 + 2	Pininfarina			
4701 GTE		4701 GTE	250	GTE	2 + 2	Pininfarina			
4703 GTE		4703 GTE	250	GTE	2 + 2	Pininfarina			
4705 GT		4705 GT	250 GT	Lusso	Berlinetta	Scaglietti			U.S.A.
4707 GTE		4707 GTE	250	GTE	2 + 2	Pininfarina			
4709 GTE		4709 GTE	250	GTE	2 + 2	Pininfarina			
4711 GTE		4711 GTE	250	GTE	2 + 2	Pininfarina			
4713 GT		4713 GT	250 GTO	GTO	Berlinetta	Scaglietti	Chinetti/de Vroom	U.S.A.	U.S.A.
		Sold on 5/6/63. Raced 1963 and 1964. All aluminium body. Design similar to Lusso Berlinetta.							
4715 GT		4715 GT	250 GT	Lusso	Berlinetta	Scaglietti			
		No hood air inlet.							
4717 GTE		4717 GTE	250	GTE	2 + 2	Pininfarina			
4719 GTE		4719 GTE	250	GTE	2 + 2	Pininfarina			
4721 GTE		4721 GTE	250	GTE	2 + 2	Pininfarina			
4723 GTE?		4723 GTE?	250	GTE	2 + 2	Pininfarina			
		Might be a Lusso.							
4725 GT?		4725 GT?	250 GT	Lusso	Berlinetta	Scaglietti			
		Also reported as a 330LMB.							
4727 GT		4727 GT	250 GT	Lusso	Berlinetta	Scaglietti			
4729 SA		4729 SA	400 S.2	Superamerica	Coupé	Pininfarina	Mereghetti	Italy	U.S.A.
		Coupé Aerodinamico							
4731 GTE		4731 GTE	250	GTE	2 + 2	Pininfarina			
4733 GTE		4733 GTE	250	GTE	2 + 2	Pininfarina			
4735 GT		4735 GT	250 GT	Lusso	Berlinetta	Scaglietti			
4737 GTE		4737 GTE	250	GTE	2 + 2	Pininfarina			
4739 GTE		4739 GTE	250	GTE	2 + 2	Pininfarina			
4741 GTE		4741 GTE	250	GTE	2 + 2	Pininfarina			
4743 GTE		4743 GTE	250	GTE	2 + 2	Pininfarina			
4745 GTE		4745 GTE	250	GTE	2 + 2	Pininfarina			
4747 GTE		4747 GTE	250	GTE	2 + 2	Pininfarina			
4749 GTE		4749 GTE	250	GTE	2 + 2	Pininfarina			
4751 GTE		4751 GTE	250	GTE	2 + 2	Pininfarina			
4753 GTE		4753 GTE	250	GTE	2 + 2	Pininfarina			U.S.A.
4755 GTE		4755 GTE	250	GTE	2 + 2	Pininfarina			
4757 GT		4757 GT	250 GTO	GTO	Berlinetta	Scaglietti	Count Volpi	Italy	U.S.A.
		Sold on 5/6/63. Raced 1963 through 1965. All aluminium body.							
4759 GT		4759 GT	250 GT	Lusso	Berlinetta	Scaglietti			
4761 GTE		4761 GTE	250	GTE	2 + 2	Pininfarina			
4763 GTE		4763 GTE	250	GTE	2 + 2	Pininfarina			
4765 GTE		4765 GTE	250	GTE	2 + 2	Pininfarina			
4767 GTE		4767 GTE	250	GTE	2 + 2	Pininfarina			
4769 GTE		4769 GTE	250	GTE	2 + 2	Pininfarina			
4771 GTE		4771 GTE	250	GTE	2 + 2	Pininfarina			
4773 GTE		4773 GTE	250	GTE	2 + 2	Pininfarina			
4775 GTE?		4775 GTE?	250	GTE	2 + 2	Pininfarina			
		Also reported to be a Lusso.							
4777 GTE		4777 GTE	250	GTE	2 + 2	Pininfarina			

Chassis No.	Picture Ref	Engine No.	Type	Model	Body Style	Coach-builder	First Owner	Original Location	Present Location
4779 GT		4779 GT	250 GT	Lusso	Berlinetta	Scaglietti			
	Reported wrecked and parted out.								
4781 SA		4781 SA	400 S.2	Superamerica	Convertible	Pininfarina	Shapiro	U.S.A.	U.S.A.
4783 GTE		4783 GTE	250	GTE	2 + 2	Pininfarina			
4785 GT*		4785 GT	250 GT	Lusso	Berlinetta	Scaglietti			
4787 GTE		4787 GTE	250	GTE	2 + 2	Pininfarina			
4789 GT		4789 GT	250 GT	Lusso	Berlinetta	Scaglietti			
4791 GTE		4791 GTE	250	GTE	2 + 2	Pininfarina			
4793 GTE		4793 GTE	250	GTE	2 + 2	Pininfarina			
4795 GTE		4795 GTE	250	GTE	2 + 2	Pininfarina			
4797 GTE		4797 GTE	250	GTE	2 + 2	Pininfarina			
4799 GTE?		4799 GTE?	250	GTE	2 + 2	Pininfarina			
	Also reported to be a Lusso.								
4801 GTE		4801 GTE	250	GTE	2 + 2	Pininfarina			
4803 GTE		4803 GTE	250	GTE	2 + 2	Pininfarina			
4805 GTE		4805 GTE	250	GTE	2 + 2	Pininfarina			
4807 GTE		4807 GTE	250	GTE	2 + 2	Pininfarina			
4809 GTE		4809 GTE	250	GTE	2 + 2	Pininfarina			
4811 GTE		4811 GTE	250	GTE	2 + 2	Pininfarina			
4813 GTE		4813 GTE	250	GTE	2 + 2	Pininfarina			
4815 GT		4815 GT	250 GT	Lusso	Berlinetta	Scaglietti			
	Uses 40DCL carbs.								
4817 GTE		4817 GTE	250	GTE	2 + 2	Pininfarina			
4819 GTE		4819 GTE	250	GTE	2 + 2	Pininfarina			
4821 GTE		4821 GTE	250	GTE	2 + 2	Pininfarina			
4823 GTE		4823 GTE	250	GTE	2 + 2	Pininfarina			
4825 GT		4825 GT	250 GT	Lusso	Berlinetta	Scaglietti			
	Wrecked.								
4827 GTE		4827 GTE	250	GTE	2 + 2	Pininfarina			
4829 GTE		4829 GTE	250	GTE	2 + 2	Pininfarina			
4831 GTE		4831 GTE	250	GTE	2 + 2	Pininfarina			
4833 GTE		4833 GTE	250	GTE	2 + 2	Pininfarina			
4835 GTE		4835 GTE	250	GTE	2 + 2	Pininfarina			
4837 GT		4837 GT	250 GT	Lusso	Berlinetta	Scaglietti			U.S.A.
4839 GTE		4839 GTE	250	GTE	2 + 2	Pininfarina			
4841 GTE		4841 GTE	250	GTE	2 + 2	Pininfarina			
4843 GTE		4843 GTE	250	GTE	2 + 2	Pininfarina			
4845 GT*		4845 GT*	250 GT	Lusso	Berlinetta	Scaglietti			
	Uses 36DCZ carbs and factory installed ammeter in place of clock.								
4847 GTE		4847 GTE	250	GTE	2 + 2	Pininfarina			
4849 GT		4849 GT	250 GT	Lusso	Berlinetta	Scaglietti			
4851 GT		4851 GT	250 GT	Lusso	Berlinetta	Scaglietti			
	3.78 to 1 axle ratio.								
4853 GTE*		4853 GTE	250	GTE	2 + 2	Pininfarina			
4855 GTE		4855 GTE	250	GTE	2 + 2	Pininfarina			
4857 GTE		4857 GTE	250	GTE	2 + 2	Pininfarina			
4859 GTE		4859 GTE	250	GTE	2 + 2	Pininfarina			
4861 GTE		4861 GTE	250	GTE	2 + 2	Pininfarina			
4863 GT		4863 GT	250 GT	Lusso	Berlinetta	Scaglietti			
4865 GTE		4865 GTE	250	GTE	2 + 2	Pininfarina			
4867 GT		4867 GT	250 GT	Lusso	Berlinetta	Scaglietti			
	Modified nose. May be special body.								
4869 GTE		4869 GTE	250	GTE	2 + 2	Pininfarina			
4871 GTE		4871 GTE	250	GTE	2 + 2	Pininfarina			
4873 GTE*		4873 GTE	250	GTE	2 + 2	Pininfarina			
4875 GTE		4875 GTE	250	GTE	2 + 2	Pininfarina			
4877 GT		4877 GT	250 GT	Lusso	Berlinetta	Scaglietti			
4879 GTE		4879 GTE	250	GTE	2 + 2	Pininfarina			
4881 GTE		4881 GTE	250	GTE	2 + 2	Pininfarina			
4883 GTE		4883 GTE	250	GTE	2 + 2	Pininfarina			
4885 GTE		4885 GTE	250	GTE	2 + 2	Pininfarina			
4887 GTE*		4887 GTE	250	GTE	2 + 2	Pininfarina			U.K.
4889 GTE		4889 GTE	250	GTE	2 + 2	Pininfarina			
4891 GT		4891 GT	250 GT	Lusso	Berlinetta	Scaglietti			
4893 GTE		4893 GTE	250	GTE	2 + 2	Pininfarina			
4895 GTE		4895 GTE	250	GTE	2 + 2	Pininfarina			
4897 GTE		4897 GTE	250	GTE	2 + 2	Pininfarina			
4899 GTE		4899 GTE	250	GTE	2 + 2	Pininfarina			
4901 GTE		4901 GTE	250	GTE	2 + 2	Pininfarina			
4903 GT		4903 GT	250 GT	Lusso	Berlinetta	Scaglietti			U.S.A.
4905 GTE		4905 GTE	250	GTE	2 + 2	Pininfarina			
4907 GTE*		4907 GTE	250	GTE	2 + 2	Pininfarina			
4909 GTE		4909 GTE	250	GTE	2 + 2	Pininfarina			
4911 GTE		4911 GTE	250	GTE	2 + 2	Pininfarina			

Chassis No.	Picture Ref	Engine No.	Type	Model	Body Style	Coach-builder	First Owner	Original Location	Present Location
4913 GTE		4913 GTE	250	GTE	2 + 2	Pininfarina			
4915 GTE		4915 GTE	250	GTE	2 + 2	Pininfarina			
4917 GTE		4917 GTE	250	GTE	2 + 2	Pininfarina			
4919 GTE		4919 GTE	250	GTE	2 + 2	Pininfarina			
4921 GTE		4921 GTE	250	GTE	2 + 2	Pininfarina			
4923 GTE		4923 GTE	250	GTE	2 + 2	Pininfarina			
4925 GTE		4925 GTE	250	GTE	2 + 2	Pininfarina			
4927 GTE		4927 GTE	250	GTE	2 + 2	Pininfarina			
4929 GTE		4929 GTE	250	GTE	2 + 2	Pininfarina			
4931 GTE		4931 GTE	250	GTE	2 + 2	Pininfarina			
4933 GTE		4933 GTE	250	GTE	2 + 2	Pininfarina			
4935 GT		4935 GT	250 GT	Lusso	Berlinetta	Scaglietti			
	Destroyed.								
4937 GTE		4937 GTE	250	GTE	2 + 2	Pininfarina			
4939 GTE		4939 GTE	250	GTE	2 + 2	Pininfarina			
4941 GTE		4941 GTE	250	GTE	2 + 2	Pininfarina			
4943 GTE		4943 GTE	250	GTE	2 + 2	Pininfarina			
4945 GT*		4945 GT	250 GT	Lusso	Berlinetta	Scaglietti			
4947 GTE		4947 GTE	250	GTE	2 + 2	Pininfarina			
4949 GTE		4949 GTE	250	GTE	2 + 2	Pininfarina			U.S.A.
4951 GTE		4951 GTE	250	GTE	2 + 2	Pininfarina			
4953 GT		4953 GT	330	America	2 + 2	Pininfarina			
4955 GT		4955 GT	250 GT	Lusso	Berlinetta	Scaglietti			
4957 GTE		4957 GTE	250	GTE	2 + 2	Pininfarina			
4959 GTE		4959 GTE	250	GTE	2 + 2	Pininfarina			
4961 GTE		4961 GTE	250	GTE	2 + 2	Pininfarina			
	Reported to be the last 250GTE 2+2 made.								
4963 GT		4963 GT	330	GT	2 + 2	Pininfarina			
	Believed first production 330GT.Four headlight version with 4-speed plus overdrive gearbox.Used by Enzo Ferrari.								
4965 GT		4965 GT	250 GT	Lusso	Berlinetta	Scaglietti			
	Raced in 1964 and 1965.								
4967 GT		4967 GT	330	GT	2 + 2	Pininfarina			
4969 GT		4969 GT	330	America	2 + 2	Pininfarina			
4971 GT		4971 GT	250 GT	Lusso	Berlinetta	Scaglietti			
4973 GT		4973 GT	330	America	2 + 2	Pininfarina			
4975 GT		4975 GT	330	America	2 + 2	Pininfarina			
4977 GT		4977 GT	250 GT	Lusso	Berlinetta	Scaglietti			
4979 GT		4979 GT	250 GT	Lusso	Berlinetta	Scaglietti			
4981 GT		4981 GT	330	America	2 + 2	Pininfarina			
4983 GT		4983 GT	250 GT	Lusso	Berlinetta	Scaglietti			
	4.57 to 1 rear axle.								
4985 GT		4985 GT	250 GT	Lusso	Berlinetta	Scaglietti			
4987 GT		4987 GT	330	America	2 + 2	Pininfarina			
4989 GT		4989 GT	330	America	2 + 2	Pininfarina			
4991 GT		4991 GT	330	America	2 + 2	Pininfarina			U.S.A.
4993 GT		4993 GT	330	America	2 + 2	Pininfarina			U.S.A.
4995 GT		4995 GT	330	America	2 + 2	Pininfarina			
4997 GT		4997 GT	330	GT	2 + 2	Pininfarina			U.S.A.
4999 GT		4999 GT	330	America	2 + 2	Pininfarina			
5001 GT*		5001 GT	330	America	2 + 2	Pininfarina	Maranello Conc.	U.K.	U.K.
5003 GT		5003 GT	250 GT/L	Lusso	Berlinetta	Scaglietti			
5005 GT		5005 GT	330	America	2 + 2	Pininfarina			
5007 GT		5007 GT	330	America	2 + 2	Pininfarina			
5009 GT		5009 GT	330	America	2 + 2	Pininfarina			
5011 GT		5011 GT	330	America	2 + 2	Pininfarina			
5013 GT		5013 GT	330	America	2 + 2	Pininfarina			
5015 GT		5015 GT	330	America	2 + 2	Pininfarina			
5017 GT		5017 GT	250 GT/L	Lusso	Berlinetta	Scaglietti			
	Converted to 5-speed transmission.								
5019 GT		5019 GT	330	America	2 + 2	Pininfarina			
5021 SA		5021 SA	400	Superamerica	Coupé	Pininfarina			U.S.A.
	Shown at the 1963 Turin Motor Show.Coupé Aerodinamico.								
5023 GT		5023 GT	330	America	2 + 2	Pininfarina			
5025 GT		5025 GT	330	America	2 + 2	Pininfarina			
5027 GT		5027 GT	330	America	2 + 2	Pininfarina			Canada
5029 SA		5029 SA	400	Superamerica	Coupé	Pininfarina	Maggiore	Italy	
	Coupé Aerodinamico.								
5031 GT*		5031 GT	250 GT/L	Lusso	Berlinetta	Scaglietti			U.K.
	3.78 to 1 rear axle.								
5033 GT		5033 GT	330	America	2 + 2	Pininfarina			
5035 GT		5035 GT	330	America	2 + 2	Pininfarina			
5037 GT		5037 GT	330	America	2 + 2	Pininfarina			
5039 GT		5039 GT	330	America	2 + 2	Pininfarina			

Chassis No.	Picture Ref	Engine No.	Type	Model	Body Style	Coach-builder	First Owner	Original Location	Present Location
5041 GT		5041 GT	330	America	2 + 2	Pininfarina			
5043 GT		5043 GT	250 GT/L	Lusso	Berlinetta	Scaglietti			
5045 GT		5045 GT	250 GT/L	Lusso	Berlinetta	Scaglietti			
5047 GT		5047 GT	330	America	2 + 2	Pininfarina			
5049 GT		5049 GT	330	America	2 + 2	Pininfarina			
5051 GT		5051 GT	330	America	2 + 2	Pininfarina			
5053 GT		5053 GT	330	America	2 + 2	Pininfarina			
5055 GT		5055 GT	330	America	2 + 2	Pininfarina			
5057 GT		5057 GT	250 GT/L	Lusso	Berlinetta	Scaglietti			
5059 GT*?		5059 GT	330	America	2 + 2	Pininfarina			U.K.
	Rebuilt in 1980s as TR look-alike.								
5061 GT		5061 GT	330	America	2 + 2	Pininfarina			U.S.A.
5063 GT		5063 GT	250 GT/L	Lusso	Berlinetta	Scaglietti			
	Pronounced rear spoiler & side vents.								
5065 GT		5065 GT	330	America	2 + 2	Pininfarina			
5067 GT		5067 GT	250 GT/L	Lusso	Berlinetta	Scaglietti			U.S.A.
5069 GT		5069 GT	330	America	2 + 2	Pininfarina			
5071 GT		5071 GT	330	America	2 + 2	Pininfarina			
5073 GT		5073 GT	250 GT/L	Lusso	Berlinetta	Scaglietti			U.S.A.
5075 GT		5075 GT	330	America	2 + 2	Pininfarina			
5077 GT		5077 GT	330	America	2 + 2	Pininfarina			
5079 GT		5079 GT	330	America	2 + 2	Pininfarina			
5081 GT		5081 GT	250 GT/L	Lusso	Berlinetta	Scaglietti			South Africa
5083 GT		5083 GT	330	America	2 + 2	Pininfarina			
5085 GT		5085 GT	250 GT/L	Lusso	Berlinetta	Scaglietti			
5087 GT		5087 GT	250 GT/L	Lusso	Berlinetta	Scaglietti			
5089 GT		5089 GT	250 GT/L	Lusso	Berlinetta	Scaglietti			
5091 GT		5091 GT	250 GT/L	Lusso	Berlinetta	Scaglietti			
1964									
5093 SA		5093 SA	400	Superamerica	Convertible	Pininfarina	Bloomingdale	U.S.A.	U.S.A.?
5095 GT		5095 GT	250 GTO	GTO	Berlinetta	Scaglietti	SSR(Volpi)	Italy	France
	Sold on 6/9/63. Raced in 1963 and 1964. All aluminium body.								
5097 GT		5097 GT	250 GT/L	Lusso	Berlinetta	Scaglietti			
5099 GT		5099 GT	250 GT/L	Lusso	Berlinetta	Scaglietti			
5101 GT		5101 GT	250 GT/L	Lusso	Berlinetta	Scaglietti			
5103 GT		5103 GT	330	America	2 + 2	Pininfarina			
5105 GT		5105 GT	330	America	2 + 2	Pininfarina			
5107 GT		5107 GT	330	America	2 + 2	Pininfarina			
5109 GT		5109 GT	330	America	2 + 2	Pininfarina			
5111 GT		5111 GT	250 GTO	GTO	Berlinetta	Scaglietti	J.Guichet	France	U.S.A.
	Sold on 6/9/63. Raced in 1963 thru 1965. All aluminium body.								
5113 GT		5113 GT	330	America	2 + 2	Pininfarina			
5115 SA		5115 SA	400	Superamerica	Coupé	Pininfarina	Nelson Rockefeller	U.S.A.	U.S.A.
	Coupé Aerodynamico.								
5117 GT		5117 GT	250 GT/L	Lusso	Berlinetta	Scaglietti			
5119 GT		5119 GT	250 GT/L	Lusso	Berlinetta	Scaglietti			
5121 GT		5121 GT	330	America	2 + 2	Pininfarina			
5123 GT		5123 GT	250 GT/L	Lusso	Berlinetta	Scaglietti			U.S.A.
5125 GT		5125 GT	330	America	2 + 2	Pininfarina			
	Believed to be the last 330 America.								
5127 GT		5127 GT	250 GT/L	Lusso	Berlinetta	Scaglietti			
5129 GT		5129 GT	250 GT/L	Lusso	Berlinetta	Scaglietti			
5131 SA		5131 SA	400 SUPER	Superamerica	Coupé	Pininfarina	Reiss	Germany	U.S.A.
	Coupé Aerodinamico.								
5133 GT		5133 GT	250 GT/L	Lusso	Berlinetta	Scaglietti			
5135 GT		5135 GT	250 GT/L	Lusso	Berlinetta	Scaglietti			
5137 GT		5137 GT	250 GT/L	Lusso	Berlinetta	Scaglietti			
5139 SA		5139 SA	400 SUPER	Superamerica	Coupé	Pininfarina	Rolando	Italy	
	Coupé Aerodinamico. Last Series II LWB.								
5141 GT		5141 GT	250 GT/L	Lusso	Berlinetta	Scaglietti			Canada
5143 GT*		5143 GT	250 GT/L	Lusso	Berlinetta	Scaglietti			U.K.
5145 GT		5145 GT	250 GT/L	Lusso	Berlinetta	Scaglietti			
5147 GT		5147 GT	250 GT/L	Lusso	Berlinetta	Scaglietti			
5149 GT*		5149 GT	250 LM	LM	Berlinetta	Scaglietti	NART	U.S.A.	U.S.A.
	Completed in 1963. Shown at the 1963 Paris Salon. Damaged by fire and is to be restored. Homologation chassis. The only 250LM with a true 250 3-litre engine. Prototype. All aluminium body.								
5151 GT		5151 GT	250 GT/L	Lusso	Berlinetta	Scaglietti			
5153 GT		5153 GT	250 GT/L	Lusso	Berlinetta	Scaglietti			
5155 GT		5155 GT	250 GT/L	Lusso	Berlinetta	Scaglietti			
5157 GT		5157 GT	250 GT/L	Lusso	Berlinetta	Scaglietti			
5159 GT		5159 GT	250 GT/L	Lusso	Berlinetta	Scaglietti			U.S.A.
5161 GT		5161 GT	250 GT/L	Lusso	Berlinetta	Scaglietti			
5163 GT		5163 GT	250 GT/L	Lusso	Berlinetta	Scaglietti			
5165 GT		5165 GT	250 GT/L	Lusso	Berlinetta	Scaglietti			

Chassis No.	Picture Ref	Engine No.	Type	Model	Body Style	Coach-builder	First Owner	Original Location	Present Location
5167 GT		5167 GT	250 GT/L	Lusso	Berlinetta	Scaglietti			
5169 GT		5169 GT	250 GT/L	Lusso	Berlinetta	Scaglietti			
5171 GT		5171 GT	250 GT/L	Lusso	Berlinetta	Scaglietti			
5173 GT		5173 GT	250 GT/L	Lusso	Berlinetta	Scaglietti			
5175 GT		5175 GT	250 GT/L	Lusso	Berlinetta	Scaglietti			
5177 GT		5177 GT	250 GT/L	Lusso	Berlinetta	Scaglietti			
5179 GT		5179 GT	250 GT/L	Lusso	Berlinetta	Scaglietti			
5181 GT		5181 GT	250 GT/L	Lusso	Berlinetta	Scaglietti			
5183 GT		5183 GT	250 GT/L	Lusso	Berlinetta	Scaglietti			U.S.A.
5185 GT		5185 GT	250 GT/L	Lusso	Berlinetta	Scaglietti			U.S.A.
5187 GT		5187 GT	250 GT/L	Lusso	Berlinetta	Scaglietti			
5189 GT		5189 GT	250 GT/L	Lusso	Berlinetta	Scaglietti			
5191 GT		5191 GT	250 GT/L	Lusso	Berlinetta	Scaglietti			Switzerland
5193 GT		5193 GT	250 GT/L	Lusso	Berlinetta	Scaglietti			U.S.A.
5195 GT		5195 GT	250 GT/L	Lusso	Berlinetta	Scaglietti			
5197 GT		5197 GT	250 GT/L	Lusso	Berlinetta	Scaglietti			
5199 GT		5199 GT	250 GT/L	Lusso	Berlinetta	Scaglietti			
5201 GT		5201 GT	250 GT/L	Lusso	Berlinetta	Scaglietti			
5203 GT		5203 GT	250 GT/L	Lusso	Berlinetta	Scaglietti			
5205 GT		5205 GT	250 GT/L	Lusso	Berlinetta	Scaglietti			
5207 GT		5207 GT	250 GT/L	Lusso	Berlinetta	Scaglietti			U.S.A.
5209 GT		5209 GT	250 GT/L	Lusso	Berlinetta	Scaglietti			
5211 GT		5211 GT	250 GT/L	Lusso	Berlinetta	Scaglietti			
5213 GT		5213 GT	250 GT/L	Lusso	Berlinetta	Scaglietti			
5215 GT		5215 GT	250 GT/L	Lusso	Berlinetta	Scaglietti			
5217 GT		5217 GT	250 GT/L	Lusso	Berlinetta	Scaglietti			
5219 GT		5219 GT	250 GT/L	Lusso	Berlinetta	Scaglietti			
5221 GT		5221 GT	250 GT/L	Lusso	Berlinetta	Scaglietti			
5223 GT		5223 GT	250 GT/L	Lusso	Berlinetta	Scaglietti			
	3.78 to 1 rear axle.								
5225 GT		5225 GT	250 GT/L	Lusso	Berlinetta	Scaglietti			U.S.A.
5227 GT		5227 GT	250 GT/L	Lusso	Berlinetta	Scaglietti			U.S.A.
5229 GT*		5229 GT	250 GT/L	Lusso	Berlinetta	Scaglietti			
5231 GT		5231 GT	250 GT/L	Lusso	Berlinetta	Scaglietti			
	3.78 to 1 rear axle.								
5233 GT		5233 GT	250 GT/L	Lusso	Berlinetta	Scaglietti			
5235 GT		5235 GT	250 GT/L	Lusso	Berlinetta	Scaglietti			
5237 GT		5237 GT	250 GT/L	Lusso	Berlinetta	Scaglietti			
5239 GT		5239 GT	250 GT/L	Lusso	Berlinetta	Scaglietti			
5241 GT		5241 GT	250 GT/L	Lusso	Berlinetta	Scaglietti			
5243 GT		5243 GT	250 GT/L	Lusso	Berlinetta	Scaglietti			
5245 GT		5245 GT	250 GT/L	Lusso	Berlinetta	Scaglietti			
5247 GT		5247 GT	250 GT/L	Lusso	Berlinetta	Scaglietti			
5249 GT		5249 GT	250 GT/L	Lusso	Berlinetta	Scaglietti			
5251 GT		5251 GT	250 GT/L	Lusso	Berlinetta	Scaglietti			
5253 GT		5253 GT	250 GT/L	Lusso	Berlinetta	Scaglietti			
5255 GT		5255 GT	250 GT/L	Lusso	Berlinetta	Scaglietti			
	First 1964 Lusso.								
5257 GT		5257 GT	250 GT/L	Lusso	Berlinetta	Scaglietti			
5259 GT		5259 GT	250 GT/L	Lusso	Berlinetta	Scaglietti			
5261 GT		5261 GT	250 GT/L	Lusso	Berlinetta	Scaglietti			
	No air inlet in hood.								
5263 GT		5263 GT	330	GT	2 + 2	Pininfarina			
5265 GT		5265 GT	330	GT	2 + 2	Pininfarina			
5267 GT		5267 GT	330	GT	2 + 2	Pininfarina			
5269 GT		5269 GT	250 GT/L	Lusso	Berlinetta	Scaglietti			U.S.A.
5271 GT		5271 GT	330 GT	330	2 + 2	Pininfarina			
5273 GT		5273 GT	330 GT	330	2 + 2	Pininfarina			
5275 GT		5275 GT	250 GT/L	Lusso	Berlinetta	Scaglietti			
5257 GT		5257 GT	250 GT/L	Lusso Berlinetta	Berlinetta	Scaglietti			Switzerland
5259 GT		5259 GT	250 GT/L	Lusso	Berlinetta	Scaglietti			
5281 GT		5281 GT	250 GT/L	Lusso	Berlinetta	Scaglietti			
5283 GT		5283 GT	250 GT/L	Lusso	Berlinetta	Scaglietti			
5285 GT		5285 GT	250 GT/L	Lusso	Berlinetta	Scaglietti			
5287 GT		5287 GT	250 GT/L	Lusso	Berlinetta	Scaglietti			
5289 GT		5289 GT	250 GT/L	Lusso	Berlinetta	Scaglietti			
5291 GT		5291 GT	250 GT/L	Lusso	Berlinetta	Scaglietti			
5293 GT		5293 GT	330 GT	330	2 + 2	Pininfarina			
5295 GT		5295 GT	250 GT/L	Lusso	Berlinetta	Scaglietti			
5297 GT		5297 GT	250 GT/L	Lusso	Berlinetta	Scaglietti			
5299 GT		5299 GT	250 GT/L	Lusso	Berlinetta	Scaglietti			U.S.A.
5301 GT		5301 GT	250 GT/L	Lusso	Berlinetta	Scaglietti			
5303 GT		5303 GT	250 GT/L	Lusso	Berlinetta	Scaglietti			
5305 GT		5305 GT	250 GT/L	Lusso	Berlinetta	Scaglietti			

Chassis No.	Picture Ref	Engine No.	Type	Model	Body Style	Coach-builder	First Owner	Original Location	Present Location
5307 GT		5307 GT	250 GT/L	Lusso	Berlinetta	Scaglietti			France
5309 GT		5309 GT	250 GT/L	Lusso	Berlinetta	Scaglietti			
5311 GT		5311 GT	250 GT/L	Lusso	Berlinetta	Scaglietti			
5313 GT		5313 GT	250 GT/L	Lusso	Berlinetta	Scaglietti			Australia
5315 GT		5315 GT	250 GT/L	Lusso	Berlinetta	Scaglietti			Austria
5317 GT		5317 GT	250 GT/L	Lusso	Berlinetta	Scaglietti			U.S.A.
5319 GT		5319 GT	250 GT/L	Lusso	Berlinetta	Scaglietti			
5321 GT		5321 GT	250 GT/L	Lusso	Berlinetta	Scaglietti			
5323 GT		5323 GT	250 GT/L	Lusso	Berlinetta	Scaglietti			
5325 GT		5325 GT	250 GT/L	Lusso	Berlinetta	Scaglietti			
5327 GT		5327 GT	330	GT	2 + 2	Pininfarina			
5329 GT		5329 GT	250 GT	Lusso	Berlinetta	Scaglietti			
5331 GT		5331 GT	330 GT	330	2 + 2	Pininfarina			
5333 GT		5333 GT	330 GT	330	2 + 2	Pininfarina			
5335 GT		5335 GT	250 GT/L	Lusso	Berlinetta	Scaglietti			U.S.A.
5337 GT		5337 GT	250 GT/L	Lusso	Berlinetta	Scaglietti			
5339 GT		5339 GT	250 GT/L	Lusso	Berlinetta	Scaglietti			U.S.A.
5341 GT		5341 GT	250 GT/L	Lusso	Berlinetta	Scaglietti			
5343 GT		5343 GT	330 GT	330	2 + 2	Pininfarina			
5345 GT		5345 GT	250 GT/L	Lusso	Berlinetta	Scaglietti			
5347 GT		5347 GT	330 GT	330	2 + 2	Pininfarina			
5349 GT		5349 GT	330 GT	330	2 + 2	Pininfarina			
5351 GT		5351 GT	250 GT/L	Lusso	Berlinetta	Scaglietti			
5353 GT		5353 GT	250 GT/L	Lusso	Berlinetta	Scaglietti			
5355 GT		5355 GT	330 GT	330	2 + 2	Pininfarina			
5357 GT		5357 GT	250 GT/L	Lusso	Berlinetta	Scaglietti			
5359 GT		5359 GT	250 GT/L	Lusso	Berlinetta	Scaglietti			
5361 GT		5361 GT	250 GT/L	Lusso	Berlinetta	Scaglietti			
5363 GT		5363 GT	250 GT/L	Lusso	Berlinetta	Scaglietti			
5365 GT		5365 GT	330 GT	330	2 + 2	Pininfarina			
5367 GT		5367 GT	250 GT/L	Lusso	Berlinetta	Scaglietti			
5369 GT		5369 GT	250 GT/L	Lusso	Berlinetta	Scaglietti			
5371 GT		5371 GT	250 GT/L	Lusso	Berlinetta	Scaglietti			U.S.A.
5373 GT		5373 GT	250 GT/L	Lusso	Berlinetta	Scaglietti			
5375 GT		5375 GT	250 GT/L	Lusso	Berlinetta	Scaglietti			Germany
5377 GT		5377 GT	250 GT/L	Lusso	Berlinetta	Scaglietti			France
5379 GT		5379 GT	250 GT/L	Lusso	Berlinetta	Scaglietti			
5381 GT		5381 GT	250 GT/L	Lusso	Berlinetta	Scaglietti			
5383 GT		5383 GT	250 GT/L	Lusso	Berlinetta	Scaglietti			
5385 GT		5385 GT	250 GT/L	Lusso	Berlinetta	Scaglietti			
5387 GT		5387 GT	250 GT/L	Lusso	Berlinetta	Scaglietti			
5389 GT		5389 GT	250 GT/L	Lusso	Berlinetta	Scaglietti			
5391 GT		5391 GT	250 GT/L	Lusso	Berlinetta	Scaglietti			U.S.A.
5393 GT		5393 GT	330 GT	330	2 + 2	Pininfarina			
5395 GT		5395 GT	250 GT/L	Lusso	Berlinetta	Scaglietti			
5397 GT		5397 GT	250 GT/L	Lusso	Berlinetta	Scaglietti			Canada
5399 GT		5399 GT	250 GT/L	Lusso	Berlinetta	Scaglietti			U.S.A.
5401 GT		5401 GT	330 GT	330	2 + 2	Pininfarina			
5403 GT		5403 GT	330 GT	330	2 + 2	Pininfarina			
5405 GT		5405 GT	330 GT	330	2 + 2	Pininfarina			U.S.A.
5407 GT		5407 GT	330 GT	330	2 + 2	Pininfarina			
5409 GT		5409 GT	330 GT	330	2 + 2	Pininfarina			
5411 GT		5411 GT	330 GT	330	2 + 2	Pininfarina			U.S.A.
5413 GT		5413 GT	330 GT	330	2 + 2	Pininfarina			
5415 GT		5415 GT	330 GT	330	2 + 2	Pininfarina			
5417 GT		5417 GT	250 GT/L	Lusso	Berlinetta	Scaglietti			U.K.
5419 GT		5419 GT	250 GT/L	Lusso	Berlinetta	Scaglietti			
5421 GT		5421 GT	330 GT	330	2 + 2	Pininfarina			
5423 GT		5423 GT	330 GT	330	2 + 2	Pininfarina			
5425 GT		5425 GT	250 GT/L	Lusso	Berlinetta	Scaglietti			
5427 GT		5427 GT	250 GT/L	Lusso	Berlinetta	Scaglietti			Italy
5429 GT		5429 GT	330 GT	330	2 + 2	Pininfarina			
5431 GT		5431 GT	330 GT	330	2 + 2	Pininfarina			
5433 GT		5433 GT	250 GT/L	Lusso	Berlinetta	Scaglietti			
5435 GT		5435 GT	330 GT	330	2 + 2	Pininfarina			
5437 GT		5437 GT	330 GT	330	2 + 2	Pininfarina			
5439 GT		5439 GT	250 GT/L	Lusso	Berlinetta	Scaglietti			France
5441 GT*		5441 GT	250 GT/L	Lusso	Berlinetta	Scaglietti			
5443 GT*		5443 GT	250 GT/L	Lusso	Berlinetta	Scaglietti			U.K.
5445 GT		5445 GT	330 GT	330	2 + 2	Pininfarina			
5447 GT		5447 GT	330 GT	330	2 + 2	Pininfarina			
5449 GT		5449 GT	250 GT/L	Lusso	Berlinetta	Scaglietti			
5451 GT		5451 GT	250 GT/L	Lusso	Berlinetta	Scaglietti			U.S.A.
5453 GT		5453 GT	330 GT	330	2 + 2	Pininfarina			

Chassis No.	Picture Ref	Engine No.	Type	Model	Body Style	Coach-builder	First Owner	Original Location	Present Location
5455 GT		5455 GT	330 GT	330	2 + 2	Pininfarina			
5457 GT		5457 GT	330 GT	330	2 + 2	Pininfarina			
5459 GT		5459 GT	330 GT	330	2 + 2	Pininfarina			
5461 GT*		5461 GT	250 GT/L	Lusso	Berlinetta	Scaglietti	Maranello Conc.	U.K.	U.K.
5463 GT*		5463 GT	250 GT/L	Lusso	Berlinetta	Scaglietti	Maranello Conc.	U.K.	South Africa
5465 GT*		5465 GT	330 GT	330	2 + 2	Pininfarina	Maranello Conc.	U.K.	
5467 GT*		5467 GT	250 GT/L	Lusso	Berlinetta	Scaglietti	Maranello Conc.	U.K.	U.S.A.
5469 GT*		5469 GT	250 GT/L	Lusso	Berlinetta	Scaglietti	Maranello Conc.	U.K.	
5471 GT		5471 GT	250 GT/L	Lusso	Berlinetta	Scaglietti			
5473 GT		5473 GT	250 GT/L	Lusso	Berlinetta	Scaglietti			
5475 GT		5475 GT	250 GT/L	Lusso	Berlinetta	Scaglietti			
5477 GT		5477 GT	250 GT/L	Lusso	Berlinetta	Scaglietti			
5479 GT		5479 GT	330 GT	330	2 + 2	Pininfarina			
5481 GT*		5481 GT	330 GT	330	2 + 2	Pininfarina	Maranello Conc.	U.K.	
5483 GT		5483 GT	250 GT/L	Lusso	Berlinetta	Scaglietti			
5485 GT		5485 GT	250 GT/L	Lusso	Berlinetta	Scaglietti			
5487 GT		5487 GT	250 GT/L	Lusso	Berlinetta	Scaglietti			
5489 GT		5489 GT	330 GT	330	2 + 2	Pininfarina			
5491 GT		5491 GT	330 GT	330	2 + 2	Pininfarina			
5493 GT		5493 GT	330 GT	330	2 + 2	Pininfarina			
5495 GT		5495 GT	330 GT	330	2 + 2	Pininfarina			
5497 GT		5497 GT	250 GT/L	Lusso	Berlinetta	Scaglietti			
5499 GT		5499 GT	250 GT/L	Lusso	Berlinetta	Scaglietti			U.S.A.
5501 GT		5501 GT	330 GT	330	2 + 2	Pininfarina			U.S.A.
5503 GT		5503 GT	330 GT	330	2 + 2	Pininfarina			
5505 GT		5505 GT	250 GT/L	Lusso	Berlinetta	Scagliettî			U.S.A.
5507 GT		5507 GT	330 GT	330	2 + 2	Pininfarina			U.S.A.
5509 GT		5509 GT	250 GT/L	Lusso	Berlinetta	Scaglietti			
5511 GT		5511 GT	250 GT/L	Lusso	Berlinetta	Scaglietti			
5513 GT		5513 GT	330 GT	330	2 + 2	Pininfarina			
5515 GT		5515 GT	250 GT/L	Lusso	Berlinetta	Scaglietti			
5517 GT		5517 GT	330 GT	330	2 + 2	Pininfarina			
5519 GT		5519 GT	330 GT	330	2 + 2	Pininfarina			
5521 GT*?		5521 GT	250 GT/L	Lusso	Berlinetta	Scaglietti			U.K.
	Modified for competition.								
5523 GT		5523 GT	330 GT	330	2 + 2	Pininfarina			
5525 GT		5525 GT	250 GT/L	Lusso	Berlinetta	Scaglietti			
5527 GT		5527 GT	330 GT	330	2 + 2	Pininfarina			
5529 GT		5529 GT	250 GT/L	Lusso	Berlinetta	Scaglietti			
5531 GT		5531 GT	250 GT/L	Lusso	Berlinetta	Scaglietti			
5533 GT		5533 GT	250 GT/L	Lusso	Berlinetta	Scaglietti			
5535 GT		5535 GT	250 GT/L	Lusso	Berlinetta	Scaglietti			U.S.A.
5537 GT		5537 GT	250 GT/L	Lusso	Berlinetta	Scaglietti			
5539 GT		5539 GT	330 GT	330	2 + 2	Pininfarina			
5541 GT		5541 GT	250 GT/L	Lusso	Berlinetta	Scaglietti			
5543 GT		5543 GT	250 GT/L	Lusso	Berlinetta	Scaglietti			U.S.A.
5545 GT		5545 GT	250 GT/L	Lusso	Berlinetta	Scaglietti			
5547 GT		5547 GT	250 GT/L	Lusso	Berlinetta	Scaglietti			
5549 GT		5549 GT	250 GT/L	Lusso	Berlinetta	Scaglietti			
5551 GT		5551 GT	330 GT	330	2 + 2	Pininfarina			
5553 GT		5553 GT	250 GT/L	Lusso	Berlinetta	Scaglietti			
5555 GT		5555 GT	330 GT	330	2 + 2	Pininfarina			
5557 GT		5557 GT	250 GT/L	Lusso	Berlinetta	Scaglietti			U.S.A.
	GTO front end.								
5559 GT		5559 GT	330 GT	330	2 + 2	Pininfarina			
5561 GT		5561 GT	330 GT	330	2 + 2	Pininfarina			
5563 GT		5563 GT	330 GT	330	2 + 2	Pininfarina			Switzerland
5565 GT		5565 GT	250 GT/L	Lusso	Berlinetta	Scaglietti			U.K.
5567 GT		5567 GT	250 GT/L	Lusso	Berlinetta	Scaglietti			
5569 GT		5569 GT	330 GT	330	2 + 2	Pininfarina			
5571 GT		5571 GT	250 GTO	GTO	Berlinetta	Scaglietti	NART	U.S.A.	Switzerland
	Sold on 6/2/64. Raced in 1964. All aluminium body.								
5573 GT		5573 GT	250 GTO	GTO	Berlinetta	Scaglietti	NART	U.S.A.	France
	Sold on 11/6/64. Raced in 1964 and 1965. All aluminium body.								
5575 GT		5575 GT	250 GTO	GTO	Berlinetta	Scaglietti	Ecurie Francorchamps	Belgium	U.S.A.
	Sold on 11/5/64. Raced in 1964. All aluminium body. 'Tunnel back' LM-type top.								
5577 GT		5577 GT	330 GT	330	2 + 2	Pininfarina			U.K.
5579 GT		5579 GT	330 GT	330	2 + 2	Pininfarina			
5581 GT		5581 GT	330 GT	330	2 + 2	Pininfarina			Geneva 1964
5583 GT		5583 GT	330 GT	330	2 + 2	Pininfarina			
5585 GT		5585 GT	250 GT/L	Lusso	Berlinetta	Scaglietti			
5587 GT		5587 GT	250 GT/L	Lusso	Berlinetta	Scaglietti			
5589 GT		5589 GT	250 GT/L	Lusso	Berlinetta	Scaglietti			
5591 GT		5591 GT	250 GT/L	Lusso	Berlinetta	Scaglietti			

Chassis No.	Picture Ref	Engine No.	Type	Model	Body Style	Coach-builder	First Owner	Original Location	Present Location
5593 GT		5593 GT	250 GT/L	Lusso	Berlinetta	Scaglietti			U.S.A.
5595 GT		5595 GT	250 GT/L	Lusso	Berlinetta	Scaglietti			Switzerland
5597 GT		5597 GT	250 GT/L	Lusso	Berlinetta	Scaglietti			
5599 GT		5599 GT	250 GT/L	Lusso	Berlinetta	Scaglietti			
5601 GT		5601 GT	330 GT	330	2 + 2	Pininfarina			
5603 GT		5603 GT	330 GT	330	2 + 2	Pininfarina			
5605 GT		5605 GT	330 GT	330	2 + 2	Pininfarina			
5607 GT		5607 GT	250 GT/L	Lusso	Berlinetta	Scaglietti			
5609 GT		5609 GT	250 GT/L	Lusso	Berlinetta	Scaglietti			
5611 GT		5611 GT	250 GT/L	Lusso	Berlinetta	Scaglietti			U.K.
5613 GT		5613 GT	330 GT	330	2 + 2	Pininfarina			
5615 GT		5615 GT	330 GT	330	2 + 2	Pininfarina			
5617 GT		5617 GT	330 GT	330	2 + 2	Pininfarina			
5619 GT		5619 GT	330 GT	330	2 + 2	Pininfarina			
5621 GT		5621 GT	330 GT	330	2 + 2	Pininfarina			
5623 GT		5623 GT	330 GT	330	2 + 2	Pininfarina			
5625 GT		5625 GT	330 GT	330	2 + 2	Pininfarina			
5627 GT		5627 GT	250 GT/L	Lusso	Berlinetta	Scaglietti			
5629 GT		5629 GT	330 GT	330	2 + 2	Pininfarina			U.S.A.
5631 GT		5631 GT	330 GT	330	2 + 2	Pininfarina			
5633 GT		5633 GT	330 GT	330	2 + 2	Pininfarina			
5635 GT		5635 GT	330 GT	330	2 + 2	Pininfarina			
5637 GT		5637 GT	250 GT/L	Lusso	Berlinetta	Scaglietti			France
5639 GT		5639 GT	250 GT/L	Lusso	Berlinetta	Scaglietti			Sweden
5641 GT		5641 GT	330 GT	330	2 + 2	Pininfarina			
5643 GT		5643 GT	330 GT	330	2 + 2	Pininfarina			France
5645 GT		5645 GT	330 GT	330	2 + 2	Pininfarina			
5647 GT		5647 GT	330 GT	330	2 + 2	Pininfarina			
5649 GT		5649 GT	330 GT	330	2 + 2	Pininfarina			
5651 GT		5651 GT	250 GT/L	Lusso	Berlinetta	Scaglietti			
5653 GT		5653 GT	250 GT/L	Lusso	Berlinetta	Scaglietti			
5655 GT		5655 GT	250 GT/L	Lusso	Berlinetta	Scaglietti			
5657 GT		5657 GT	330 GT	330	2 + 2	Pininfarina			
5659 GT		5659 GT	330 GT	330	2 + 2	Pininfarina			
5661 GT		5661 GT	250 GT/L	Lusso	Berlinetta	Scaglietti			
5663 GT		5663 GT	330 GT	330	2 + 2	Pininfarina			
5665 GT		5665 GT	330 GT	330	2 + 2	Pininfarina			
5667 GT		5667 GT	250 GT/L	Lusso	Berlinetta	Scaglietti			
5669 GT		5669 GT	330 GT	330	2 + 2	Pininfarina			
5671 GT		5671 GT	250 GT/L	Lusso	Berlinetta	Scaglietti			
5673 GT		5673 GT	250 GT/L	Lusso	Berlinetta	Scaglietti			
5675 GT		5675 GT	250 GT/L	Lusso	Berlinetta	Scaglietti			Switzerland
5677 GT*		5677 GT	250 GT/L	Lusso	Berlinetta	Scaglietti	Maranello Conc.	U.K.	U.K.
5679 GT		5679 GT	250 GT/L	Lusso	Berlinetta	Scaglietti			
5681 GT		5681 GT	250 GT/L	Lusso	Berlinetta	Scaglietti			
5683 GT		5683 GT	250 GT/L	Lusso	Berlinetta	Scaglietti			
5685 GT*		5685 GT	250 GT/L	Lusso	Berlinetta	Scaglietti	Maranello Conc.	U.K.	U.K.
5687 GT*		5687 GT	250 GT/L	Lusso	Berlinetta	Scaglietti	Maranello Conc.	U.K.	
5689 GT		5689 GT	250 GT/L	Lusso	Berlinetta	Scaglietti			France
5691 GT		5691 GT	250 GT/L	Lusso	Berlinetta	Scaglietti			
5693 GT*		5693 GT	250 GT/L	Lusso	Berlinetta	Scaglietti	Maranello Conc.	U.K.	U.K.
5695 GT		5695 GT	250 GT/L	Lusso	Berlinetta	Scaglietti			
5697 GT*		5697 GT	250 GT/L	Lusso	Berlinetta	Scaglietti	Maranello Conc.	U.K.	U.S.A.
5699 GT		5699 GT	330 GT	330	2 + 2	Pininfarina			
5701 GT		5701 GT	330 GT	330	2 + 2	Pininfarina			
5703 GT		5703 GT	330 GT	330	2 + 2	Pininfarina			
5705 GT		5705 GT	330 GT	330	2 + 2	Pininfarina			
5707 GT		5707 GT	330 GT	330	2 + 2	Pininfarina			
5709 GT		5709 GT	250 GT/L	Lusso	Berlinetta	Scaglietti			

Plate says 330GTL but engine is Type 168. Speedo in miles.

Chassis No.	Picture Ref	Engine No.	Type	Model	Body Style	Coach-builder	First Owner	Original Location	Present Location
5711 GT*		5711 GT	250 GT/L	Lusso	Berlinetta	Scaglietti	Maranello Conc.	U.K.	U.K.
5713 GT		5713 GT	250 GT/L	Lusso	Berlinetta	Scaglietti			U.S.A.
5715 GT*		5715 GT	250 GT/L	Lusso	Berlinetta	Scaglietti	Maranello Conc.	U.K.	U.K.
5717 GT		5717 GT	330 GT	330	2 + 2	Pininfarina			
5719 GT		5719 GT	330 GT	330	2 + 2	Pininfarina			
5721 GT		5721 GT	330 GT	330	2 + 2	Pininfarina			
5723 GT		5723 GT	330 GT	330	2 + 2	Pininfarina			
5725 GT		5725 GT	330 GT	330	2 + 2	Pininfarina			
5727 GT		5727 GT	330 GT	330	2 + 2	Pininfarina			Switzerland
5729 GT*		5729 GT	250 GT/L	Lusso	Berlinetta	Scaglietti	Maranello Conc.	U.K.	U.S.A.
5731 GT		5731 GT	330 GT	330	2 + 2	Pininfarina			
5733 GT*		5733 GT	250 GT/L	Lusso	Berlinetta	Scaglietti	Maranello Conc.	U.K.	U.K.
5735 GT*		5735 GT	250 GT/L	Lusso	Berlinetta	Scaglietti	Maranello Conc.	U.K.	U.K.

3.78 to 1 rear axle. 40mm carburettors.

Chassis No.	Picture Ref	Engine No.	Type	Model	Body Style	Coach-builder	First Owner	Original Location	Present Location
5737 GT		5737 GT	330 GT	330	2 + 2	Pininfarina			
5739 GT		5739 GT	330 GT	330	2 + 2	Pininfarina			
5741 GT		5741 GT	330 GT	330	2 + 2	Pininfarina			
5743 GT		5743 GT	330 GT	330	2 + 2	Pininfarina			
5745 GT		5745 GT	330 GT	330	2 + 2	Pininfarina			
5747 GT		5747 GT	330 GT	330	2 + 2	Pininfarina			
5749 GT		5749 GT	330 GT	330	2 + 2	Pininfarina			
5751 GT		5751 GT	330 GT	330	2 + 2	Pininfarina			
5753 GT		5753 GT	330 GT	330	2 + 2	Pininfarina			
5755 GT		5755 GT	330 GT	330	2 + 2	Pininfarina			
5757 GT		5757 GT	330 GT	330	2 + 2	Pininfarina			
5759 GT		5759 GT	330 GT	330	2 + 2	Pininfarina			
5761 GT		5761 GT	330 GT	330	2 + 2	Pininfarina			
5763 GT		5763 GT	330 GT	330	2 + 2	Pininfarina			
5765 GT		5765 GT	330 GT	330	2 + 2	Pininfarina			
5767 GT		5767 GT	330 GT	330	2 + 2	Pininfarina			U.S.A.
5769 GT		5769 GT	330 GT	330	2 + 2	Pininfarina			
5771 GT		5771 GT	330 GT	330	2 + 2	Pininfarina			
5773 GT		5773 GT	330 GT	330	2 + 2	Pininfarina			
5775 GT		5775 GT	330 GT	330	2 + 2	Pininfarina			U.S.A.
5777 GT		5777 GT	330 GT	330	2 + 2	Pininfarina			
5779 GT		5779 GT	330 GT	330	2 + 2	Pininfarina			France
5781 GT		5781 GT	330 GT	330	2 + 2	Pininfarina			
5783 GT		5783 GT	250 GT/L	Lusso	Berlinetta	Scaglietti			U.S.A.
5785 GT		5785 GT	250 GT/L	Lusso	Berlinetta	Scaglietti			
5787 GT		5787 GT	330 GT	330	2 + 2	Pininfarina			
5789 GT		5789 GT	330 GT	330	2 + 2	Pininfarina			
5791 GT		5791 GT	250 GT/L	Lusso	Berlinetta	Scaglietti			
5793 GT		5793 GT	330 GT	330	2 + 2	Pininfarina			
5795 GT		5795 GT	250 GT/L	Lusso	Berlinetta	Scaglietti			
5797 GT		5797 GT	330 GT	330	2 + 2	Pininfarina			
5799 GT		5799 GT	330 GT	330	2 + 2	Pininfarina			
5801 GT		5801 GT	330 GT	330	2 + 2	Pininfarina			
5803 GT		5803 GT	330 GT	330	2 + 2	Pininfarina			
5805 GT*		5805 GT	330 GT	330	2 + 2	Pininfarina	Maranello Conc.	U.K.	
5807 GT*		5807 GT	330 GT	330	2 + 2	Pininfarina	Maranello Conc.	U.K.	U.K.
5809 GT		5809 GT	330 GT	330	2 + 2	Pininfarina			Holland
5811 GT		5811 GT	330 GT	330	2 + 2	Pininfarina			
5813 GT		5813 GT	330 GT	330	2 + 2	Pininfarina			
5815 GT		5815 GT	330 GT	330	2 + 2	Pininfarina			
5817 GT		5817 GT	250 GT/L	Lusso	Berlinetta	Scaglietti			
5819 GT*		5819 GT	330 GT	330	2 + 2	Pininfarina	Maranello Conc.	U.K.	
5821 GT		5821 GT	330 GT	330	2 + 2	Pininfarina			
5823 GT		5823 GT	330 GT	330	2 + 2	Pininfarina			
5825 GT		5825 GT	330 GT	330	2 + 2	Pininfarina			
5827 GT		5827 GT	330 GT	330	2 + 2	Pininfarina			
5829 GT*		5829 GT	330 GT	330	2 + 2	Pininfarina	Maranello Conc.		
5831 GT		5831 GT	330 GT	330	2 + 2	Pininfarina			
5833 GT		5833 GT	330 GT	330	2 + 2	Pininfarina			
5835 GT		5835 GT	330 GT	330	2 + 2	Pininfarina			
5837 GT		5837 GT	330 GT	330	2 + 2	Pininfarina			
5839 GT*		5839 GT	330 GT	330	2 + 2	Pininfarina	Maranello Conc.	U.K.	U.K.
5841 GT*		5841 GT	250 LM	LM	Berlinetta	Scaglietti	Filipinetti	Switzerland	France
		Completed in 1964. Raced once in 1965. Gear change on RH side. All aluminium body.							
5843 GT*		5843 GT	250 LM	LM	Berlinetta	Scaglietti	Ecurie Francorchamps	Belgium	U.S.A.
		Sold on 28/5/64. Raced 1964 thru 1966. All aluminium body.							
5845 GT*		5845 GT	250 LM	LM	Berlinetta	Scaglietti	Arthur Swanson?	Italy	U.S.A.
		Completed in 1965. Raced in 1966 and 1967. Special long Drogo nose with power operated headlight covers.							
5847 GT		5847 GT	250 GT/L	Lusso	Berlinetta	Scaglietti			
		Locking steering column. Ammeter in place of clock.							
5849 GT		5849 GT	250 GT/L	Lusso	Berlinetta	Scaglietti			U.S.A.
5851 GT		5851 GT	250 GT/L	Lusso	Berlinetta	Scaglietti			
5853 GT*				330	2 + 2	Pininfarina	Maranello Conc.	U.K.	
5855 GT		5855 GT	330 GT	330	2 + 2	Pininfarina			
5857 GT		5857 GT	330 GT	330	2 + 2	Pininfarina			
5859 GT		5859 GT		330					
5861 GT		5861 GT	250 GT/L	Lusso	Berlinetta	Scaglietti			
5863 GT*		5863 GT	330 GT	330	2 + 2	Pininfarina	Maranello Conc.	U.K.	
5865 GT		5865 GT	330 GT	330	2 + 2	Pininfarina			Australia
5867 GT		5867 GT	250 GT/L	Lusso	Berlinetta	Scaglietti			
5869 GT		5869 GT	250 GT/L	Lusso	Berlinetta	Scaglietti			
5871 GT		5871 GT	250 GT/L	Lusso	Berlinetta	Scaglietti			
5873 GT		5873 GT	250 GT/L	Lusso	Berlinetta	Scaglietti			

Chassis No.	Picture Ref	Engine No.	Type	Model	Body Style	Coach-builder	First Owner	Original Location	Present Location
5875 GT		5875 GT	250 GT/L	Lusso	Berlinetta	Scaglietti			
Air conditioning.Speedometer in miles.									
5877 GT		5877 GT	330 GT	330	2 + 2	Pininfarina			
5879 GT		5879 GT	330 GT	330	2 + 2	Pininfarina			France
5881 GT		5881 GT	330 GT	330	2 + 2	Pininfarina			
5883 GT		5883 GT	250 GT/L	Lusso	Berlinetta	Scaglietti			
5885 GT		5885 GT	250 GT/L	Lusso	Berlinetta	Scaglietti			France
5887 GT		5887 GT	330 GT	330	2 + 2	Pininfarina			
5889 GT		5889 GT	330 GT	330	2 + 2	Pininfarina			
5891 GT		5891 GT	250 LM	LM	Berlinetta	Scaglietti	Filipinetti	Switzerland	France(believe with Engine N
Completed on 6/4/65.Raced 1967 thru 1969. All aluminium body.									
5893 GT*		5893 GT	250 LM	LM	Berlinetta	Scaglietti	NART	U.S.A.	U.S.A.
Completed in 1964.Finished 1st OA at 1965 LeMans driven by Rindt/Gregory. All aluminium body.									
5895 GT*		5895 GT	250 LM	LM	Berlinetta	Scaglietti	Maranello Conc.	U.K.	Italy
Completed on 30/4/64.Raced 1964 thru 1967. All aluminium body.									
5897 GT*		5897 GT	250 LM	LM	Berlinetta	Scaglietti	Piper	U.K.	U.S.A.
Sold on 13/7/64.Raced 1964 thru 1966.Another '250LM' was built up in England and was given chassis no.5897GT! All aluminium body.									
5899 GT*	M19	5899 GT	250 LM	LM	Berlinetta	Scaglietti	Filipinetti	Switzerland	U.S.A. /Monac
Completed on 16/5/64. Raced in 1964 thru 1967.Car destroyed.New car with new frame and body built up in England with original engine. 'The chassis and other remains'are in Monaco.									
5901 GT*		5901 GT	250 LM	LM	Berlinetta	Scaglietti	NART	U.S.A.	U.S.A.
Completed on 24/9/64.Raced in 1966. All aluminium body.									
5903 GT		5903 GT	250 LM	LM	Berlinetta	Scaglietti	Gaessly	Italy	Italy
Completed on 30/1/65.Raced in 1968. Second of three LHD 250LMs.All aluminium body.									
5905 GT*		5905 GT	250 LM	LM	Berlinetta	Scaglietti	Filipinetti	Switzerland	U.S.A.
Sold on 24/3/65.Raced 1964 thru 1967. All aluminium body.									
5907 GT*		5907 GT	250 LM	LM	Berlinetta	Scaglietti	Maranello Conc.	U.K.	U.K.
Sold on 1/7/64.Raced in 1964,1965,& 1966. All aluminium body.									
5909 GT*		5909 GT	250 LM	LM	Berlinetta	Scaglietti	NART/Chinetti	U.S.A.	Switzerland
Completed on 27/5/64.Raced by NART in 1964. All aluminium body.									
5911 GT		5911 GT	330 GT	330	2 + 2	Pininfarina			
5913 GT		5913 GT	250 GT/L	Lusso	Berlinetta	Scaglietti			
5915 GT		5915 GT	250 GT/L	Lusso	Berlinetta	Scaglietti			U.S.A.
5917 GT		5917 GT	330 GT	330	2 + 2	Pininfarina			
5919 GT		5919 GT	330 GT	330	2 + 2	Pininfarina			
5921 GT		5921 GT	330 GT	330	2 + 2	Pininfarina			
5923 GT		5923 GT	330 GT	330	2 + 2	Pininfarina			
5925 GT		5925 GT	330 GT	330	2 + 2	Pininfarina			
5927 GT		5927 GT	330 GT	330	2 + 2	Pininfarina			
5929 GT		5929 GT	330 GT	330	2 + 2	Pininfarina			
5931 GT		5931 GT	250 GT/L	Lusso	Berlinetta	Scaglietti			
5933 GT		5933 GT	330 GT	330	2 + 2	Pininfarina			
5935 GT		5935 GT	330 GT	330	2 + 2	Pininfarina			
5937 GT		5937 GT	250 GT/L	Lusso	Berlinetta	Scaglietti			
5939 GT		5939 GT	250 GT/L	Lusso	Berlinetta	Scaglietti			France
5941 GT		5941 GT	250 GT/L	Lusso	Berlinetta	Scaglietti			
5943 GT		5943 GT	250 GT/L	Lusso	Berlinetta	Scaglietti			U.S.A.
5945 GT		5945 GT	250 GT/L	Lusso	Berlinetta	Scaglietti			
5947 GT		5947 GT	250 GT/L	Lusso	Berlinetta	Scaglietti			Germany
5949 GT		5949 GT	250 GT/L	Lusso	Berlinetta	Scaglietti			
5951 SF		5951 SF	500	Superfast	Coupé	Pinifarina	Autobecker	Germany	
Delivered on 4/3/64.Shown at the 1964 Geneva Motor Show. Prototype.First 500 Superfast Series I.									
5953 GT		5953 GT	250 GT/L	Lusso	Berlinetta	Scaglietti			U.K.
5955 GT		5955 GT	250 GT/L	Lusso	Berlinetta	Scaglietti			
Last Lusso.									
5957 GT		5957 GT	330 GT	330	2 + 2	Pininfarina			
5959 GT		5959 GT	330 GT	330	2 + 2	Pininfarina			
5961 GT		5961 GT	330 GT	330	2 + 2	Pininfarina			
5963 GT		5963 GT	330 GT	330	2 + 2	Pininfarina			
5965 GT		5965 GT	330 GT	330	2 + 2	Pininfarina			
5967 GT		5967 GT	330 GT	330	2 + 2	Pininfarina			
5969 GT		5969 GT	330 GT	330	2 + 2	Pininfarina			
5971 GT		5971 GT	330 GT	330	2 + 2	Pininfarina			
5973 GT		5973 GT	330 GT	330	2 + 2	Pininfarina			
1965									
5975 GT*		5975 GT	250 LM	LM	Berlinetta	Scaglietti	Helge Pehrsson	Sweden	France
Completed in 1965. All aluminium body.									
5977SF		5977SF	500	Superfast	Coupé	Pininfarina	Simons		Switzerland
5979 SF		5979 SF	500	Superfast	Coupé	Pininfarina	Zaffaroni	U.S.A.	U.S.A.
5981 SF		5981 SF	500	Superfast	Coupé	Pininfarina			U.S.A.
Shown at the 1964 Turin Motor Show.									
5983 SA		5983 SA	500	Superfast	Coupé	Pininfarina			
Shown at the 1964 Brussels Show.									

Chassis No.	Picture Ref	Engine No.	Type	Model	Body Style	Coach-builder	First Owner	Original Location	Present Location
5985 SA		5985 SA	500	Superfast	Coupé	Pininfarina			
Delivered on 23/12/64. Shown at the 1965 Chicago Auto Show.									
5987 GT*		5987 GT	330 GT	330	2 + 2	Pininfarina	Maranello Conc.	U.K.	U.K.
5989 SF		5989 SF	500	Superfast	Coupé	Pininfarina	Porta	U.S.A.	U.S.A.
5991 GT*		5991 GT	330 GT	330	2 + 2	Pininfarina	Maranello Conc.	U.K.	
5993 GT*		5993 GT	330 GT	330	2 + 2	Pininfarina	Maranello Conc.	U.K.	U.K.
5995 GT		5995 GT	250 LM	LM	Berlinetta	Scaglietti	Count Volpi	Italy	U.K.?
Completed in 1965. Raced only briefly in Italy. Third and last 250LM with LHD.									
5997 GT		5997 GT	330 GT	330	2 + 2	Pininfarina			
5999 GT		5999 GT	330 GT	330	2 + 2	Pininfarina			
6001 GT		6001 GT	275	GTS	Spyder	Pininfarina			
Prototype 275GTS. Shown at the Paris Salon in 1964.									
6003 GT		6003 GT	275 GTB	GTS Alloy	Berlinetta	Pininfarina			
Prototype. Shown at the 1964 Paris Salon.									
6005 GT		6005 GT	275 GTS	GTS	Spyder	Pininfarina			U.S.A.
Believed to be the first production 275GTS.									
6007 GT		6007 GT	330 GT	330	2 + 2	Pininfarina			
6009 GT*		6009 GT	330 GT	330	2 + 2	Pininfarina	Maranello Conc.	U.K.	U.K.
6011 GT		6011 GT	330 GT	330	2 + 2	Pininfarina			
6013 GT		6013 GT	330 GT	330	2 + 2	Pininfarina			
6015 GT*		6015 GT	330 GT	330	2 + 2	Pininfarina	Maranello Conc.	U.K.	U.K.
6017 GT*		6017 GT	330 GT	330	2 + 2	Pininfarina	Maranello Conc.	U.K.	U.K.
6019 GT*		6019 GT	330 GT	330	2 + 2	Pininfarina	Maranello Conc.	U.K.	U.K.
6021 GT		6021 GT	275 GTB	275 Alloy	Berlinetta	Scaglietti			
6023 GT*		6023 GT	250 LM	LM	Berlinetta	Scaglietti	Ecurie Francorchamps	Belgium	U.S.A.
Completed on 30/8/64. Raced in 1964, 1965 & 1966. All aluminium body.									
6025 GT*	M/18	6025 GT	250 LM	LM	Berlinetta	Pininfarina	Chinetti	U.S.A.	U.S.A.?
Shown at the 1965 Geneva Motor Show and the 1965 New York Auto Show. Never raced. Special prototype car by Pininfarina. All aluminium body.									
6027 GT*		6027 GT	330 GT	330	2 + 2	Pininfarina	Maranello Conc.	U.K.	
6029 GT		6029 GT	330 GT	330	2 + 2	Pininfarina			
6031 GT		6031 GT	330 GT	330	2 + 2	Pininfarina			
6033 SF		6033 SF	500	Superfast	Coupé	Pininfarina	Reiss	Germany	U.S.A.
Delivered on 26/1/65.									
6035 GT		6035 GT	330 GT	330	2 + 2	Pininfarina			
6037 GT		6037 GT	330 GT	330	2 + 2	Pininfarina			
6039 SA		6039 SA	500	Superfast	Coupé	Pininfarina			U.S.A.
Delivered on 25/2/65. Shown at the 1965 Geneva Motor Show.									
6041 SF		6041 SF	500	Superfast	Coupé	Pininfarina			U.S.A.
Delivered on 16/3/65. Shown at the 1965 New York Auto Show.									
6043 SF*		6043 SF	500	Superfast	Coupé	Pininfarina	Hanson	U.K.	
6045 GT*		6045 SF	250 LM	LM	Berlinetta	Scaglietti	William Harrah	U.S.A.	Japan
Cluxton									
6047 GT*		6047 GT	250 LM	LM	Berlinetta	Scaglietti	Mecom	U.S.A.	U.S.A.
Sold in 1964. Raced in 1964 and 1965. All aluminium body.									
6049 SF		6049 SF	500	Superfast	Coupé	Pininfarina	S. Aga Khan	France	
Delivered on 16/4/65.									
6051 GT*		6051 GT	250 LM	LM	Berlinetta	Scaglietti	Viscount Portman	U.K.	Holland
Sold on 8/9/64. Raced in 1965, 1966 & 1967. All aluminium body.									
6053 GT*		6053 GT	250 LM	LM	Berlinetta	Scaglietti	George Drummond	U.K.	U.S.A.
Completed 30/6/64. Raced in 1965, 1966 & 1967. All aluminium body.									
6055 GT		6055 GT	330 GT	330	2 + 2	Pininfarina			
6057 GT		6057 GT	330 GT	330	2 + 2	Pininfarina			
6059 GT		6059 GT	330 GT	330	2 + 2	Pininfarina			
6061 GT		6061 GT	330 GT	330	2 + 2	Pininfarina			
6063 GT		6063 GT	330 GT	330	2 + 2	Pininfarina			
6065 GT		6065 GT	330 GT	330	2 + 2	Pininfarina			
6067 GT		6067 GT	330 GT	330	2 + 2	Pininfarina			
6069 GT		6069 GT	330 GT	330	2 + 2	Pininfarina			
6071 GT		6071 GT	330 GT	330	2 + 2	Pininfarina			
6073 GT		6073 GT	330 GT	330	2 + 2	Pininfarina			
6075 GT		6075 GT	330 GT	330	2 + 2	Pininfarina			
6077 GT		6077 GT	330 GT	330	2 + 2	Pininfarina			
6079 GT		6079 GT	330 GT	330	2 + 2	Pininfarina			
6081 GT		6081 GT	330 GT	330	2 + 2	Pininfarina			
6083 GT		6083 GT	330 GT	330	2 + 2	Pininfarina			U.K.
6085 GT		6085 GT	330 GT	330	2 + 2	Pininfarina			
6087 GT		6087 GT	330 GT	330	2 + 2	Pininfarina			
6089 GT		6089 GT	330 GT	330	2 + 2	Pininfarina			
6091 GT		6091 GT	330 GT	330	2 + 2	Pininfarina			
6093 GT		6093 GT	330 GT	330	2 + 2	Pininfarina			
6095 GT		6095 GT	330 GT	330	2 + 2	Pininfarina			
6097 GT		6097 GT	330 GT	330	2 + 2	Pininfarina			

Chassis No.	Picture Ref	Engine No.	Type	Model	Body Style	Coach-builder	First Owner	Original Location	Present Location
6099 GT		6099 GT	330 GT	330	2 + 2	Pininfarina			
6101 GT		6101 GT	330 GT	330	2 + 2	Pininfarina			U.S.A.
6103 GT		6103 GT	330 GT	330	2 + 2	Pininfarina			
6105 GT*		6105 GT	250 LM	LM	Berlinetta	Scaglietti	Ron Fry	U.K.	U.K.
		Completed on 8/9/64.Raced in 1964,1965,& 1966.With other owners it was raced off and on through 1977. All aluminium body.							
6107 GT*		6107 GT	250 LM	LM	Berlinetta	Scaglietti	Steve Earle	U.S.A.	Japan
		Completed on 23/7/65.Raced in 1968 & 1969. All aluminium body.							
6109 GT		6109 GT	330		Convertible	Michelotti	Luigi Chinetti	U.S.A.	U.S.A.
		Designed and built by Giovanni Michelotti to the order of Luigi Chinetti. Built on a 330GT 2+2 chassis.							
6111 GT		6111 GT	330 GT	GT	2 + 2	Pininfarina			
6113 GT		6113 GT	330 GT	GT	2 + 2	Pininfarina			
6115 GT		6115 GT	330 GT	GT	2 + 2	Pininfarina			
6117 GT		6117 GT	330 GT	GT	2 + 2	Pininfarina			
6119 GT*		6119 GT	250 LM	LM	Berlinetta	Scaglietti	Filipinetti	Switzerland	U.K.
		Completed in 1964.Raced in 1964,1965,1966 & 1967. RHD.Believed to have fibreglass body.							
6121 GT		6121 GT	330 GT	330	2 + 2	Pininfarina			
6123 GT		6123 GT	330 GT	330	2 + ?	Pininfarina			
6125 GT		6125 GT	330 GT	330	2 + 2	Pininfarina			
6127 GT		6127 GT	330 GT	330	2 + 2	Pininfarina			
6129 GT*		6129 GT	330 GT	330	2 + 2	Pininfarina	Maranello Conc.	U.K.	U.K.
6131 GT*		6131 GT	330 GT	330	2 + 2	Pininfarina	Maranello Conc.	U.K.	U.K.
6133 GT		6133 GT	330 GT	330	2 + 2	Pininfarina			
6135 GT		6135 GT	330 GT	330	2 + 2	Pininfarina			
6137 GT		6137 GT	330 GT	330	2 + 2	Pininfarina			
6139 GT		6139 GT	330 GT	330	2 + 2	Pininfarina			
6141 GT		6141 GT	330 GT	330	2 + 2	Pininfarina			
6143 GT		6143 GT	330 GT	330	2 + 2	Pininfarina			
6145 GT		6145 GT	330 GT	330	2 + 2	Pininfarina			
6147 GT		6147 GT	330 GT	330	2 + 2	Pininfarina			
6149 GT		6149 GT	330 GT	330	2 + 2	Pininfarina			
6151 GT		6151 GT	330 GT	330	2 + 2	Pininfarina			
6153 GT		6153 GT	330 GT	330	2 + 2	Pininfarina			
6155 GT*		6155 GT	330 GT	330	2 + 2	Pininfarina	Maranello Conc.	U.K.	U.K.
6157 GT		6157 GT	330 GT	330	2 + 2	Pininfarina			U.S.A.
6159 GT		6159 GT	330	330	2 + 2	Pininfarina			
6161 GT		6161 GT	330 GT	330	2 + 2	Pininfarina			
6163 GT		6163 GT	330 GT	330	2 + 2	Pininfarina			
6165 GT		6165 GT	330 GT	330	2 + 2	Pininfarina			
6167 GT*		6167 GT	250 LM	LM	Berlinetta	Scaglietti	Maranello Conc.	U.K.	U.S.A.?
		Completed in 1966?Raced in 1967,& 1968. All aluminium body.							
6169 GT		6169 GT	330 GT	330	2 + 2	Pininfarina			
6171 GT		6171 GT	330 GT	330	2 + 2	Pininfarina			U.S.A.
6173 GT*		6173 GT	250 LM	LM	Berlinetta	Scaglietti	SC Ambrosia	Italy	U.S.A.
		Completed on 1/4/65.Raced in 1965.Crashed and rebuilt in U.S.A.. All aluminium body.							
6175 GT		6175 GT	330 GT	330	2 + 2	Pininfarina			
6177 GT*		6177 GT	330 GT	330	2 + 2	Pininfarina	Maranello Conc.	U.K.	U.K.
6179 GT*		6179 GT	330 GT	330	2 + 2 RHD	Pininfarina	Maranello Conc.	U.K.	
6181 GT		6181 GT	330 GT	330	2 + 2	Pininfarina			
6183 GT		6183 GT	330 GT	330	2 + 2	Pininfarina			
6185 GT		6185 GT	330 GT	330	2 + 2	Pininfarina			
6187 GT		6187 GT	330 GT	330	2 + 2	Pininfarina			
6189 GT		6189 GT	330 GT	330	2 + 2	Pininfarina			
6191 GT		6191 GT	330 GT	330	2 + 2	Pininfarina			
6193 GT		6193 GT	330 GT	330	2 + 2	Pininfarina			
6195 GT		6195 GT	330 GT	330	2 + 2	Pininfarina			
6197 GT*		6197 GT	330 GT	330	2 + 2	Pininfarina	Maranello Conc.	U.K.	
6199 GT*		6199 GT	330 GT	330	2 + 2	Pininfarina	Maranello Conc.	U.K.	U.K.
6201 GT*		6201 GT	330 GT	330	2 + 2	Pininfarina	Maranello Conc.	U.K.	U.K.
6203 GT		6203 GT	330 GT	330	2 + 2	Pininfarina			
6205 GT		6205 GT	330 GT	330	2 + 2	Pininfarina			
6207 GT		6207 GT	330 GT	330	2 + 2	Pininfarina			
6209 GT		6209 GT	330 GT	330	2 + 2	Pininfarina			
6211 GT		6211 GT	330 GT	330	2 + 2	Pininfarina			
6213 GT		6213 GT	330 GT	330	2 + 2	Pininfarina			
6215 GT		6215 GT	330 GT	330	2 + 2	Pininfarina			
6217 GT		6217 GT	250 LM	LM	Berlinetta	Scaglietti	McDonald	Canada	Switzerland
		Completed on 14/1/65. Drogo Nose fitted ex-factory.All aluminium body.							
6219 GT		6219 GT	330 GT	330	2 + 2	Pininfarina			
6221 GT		6221 GT	330 GT	330	2 + 2	Pininfarina			
6223 GT		6223 GT	330 GT	330	2 + 2	Pininfarina			
6225 GT		6225 GT	330 GT	330	2 + 2	Pininfarina			
6227 GT		6227 GT	330 GT	330	2 + 2	Pininfarina			
6229 GT		6229 GT	330 GT	330	2 + 2	Pininfarina			
6231 GT		6231 GT	330 GT	330	2 + 2	Pininfarina			

Chassis No.	Picture Ref	Engine No.	Type	Model	Body Style	Coach-builder	First Owner	Original Location	Present Location
6233 GT		6233 GT	250LM	LM	Berlinetta	Scaglietti	Cord	U.S.A.	Italy
		Completed in June 1965. Fibreglass body.							
6235 GT		6235 GT	330 GT	330	2 + 2	Pininfarina			
6237 GT		6237 GT	330 GT	330	2 + 2	Pininfarina			
6239 GT		6239 GT	330 GT	330	2 + 2	Pininfarina			
6241 GT		6241 GT	330 GT	330	2 + 2	Pininfarina			
6243 GT		6243 GT	330 GT	330	2 + 2	Pininfarina			
6245 GT		6245 GT	330 GT	330	2 + 2	Pininfarina			
6247 GT		6247 GT	330 GT	330	2 + 2	Pininfarina			
6249 GT		6249 GT	330 GT	330	2 + 2	Pininfarina			
6251 GT		6251 GT	330 GT	330	2 + 2	Pininfarina			
6253 GT		6253 GT	330 GT	330	2 + 2	Pininfarina			
6255 GT		6255 GT	330 GT	330	2 + 2	Pininfarina			U.S.A.
6257 GT		6257 GT	330 GT	330	2 + 2	Pininfarina			
6259 GT		6259 GT	330 GT	330	2 + 2	Pininfarina			
6261 GT		6261 GT	330 GT	330	2 + 2	Pininfarina			
6263 GT		6263 GT	330 GT	330	2 + 2	Pininfarina			
6265 GT		6265 GT	330 GT	330	2 + 2	Pininfarina			
6267 SF		6267 SF	500	Superfast	Coupé	Pinifarina	Prince Bernhard	Holland	U.S.A.
		Delivered on 6/8/65.							
6269 GT		6269 GT	330 GT	330	2 + 2	Pininfarina			
6271 GT		6271 GT	330 GT	330	2 + 2	Pininfarina			
		Believed to be Paris Salon show car.							
6273 GT		6273 GT	330 GT	330	2 + 2	Pininfarina			
		Believed to be Paris Salon show car.							
6275 GT		6275 GT	330 GT	330	2 + 2	Pininfarina			
6277 GT		6277 GT	330 GT	330	2 + 2	Pininfarina			
6279 GT		6279 GT	330 GT	330	2 + 2	Pininfarina			
6281 GT		6281 GT	330 GT	330	2 + 2	Pininfarina			France
6283 GT		6283 GT	330 GT	330	2 + 2	Pininfarina			
6285 GT		6285 GT	330 GT	330	2 + 2	Pininfarina			
6287 GT		6287 GT	330 GT	330	2 + 2	Pininfarina			
6289 GT		6289 GT	330 GT	330	2 + 2	Pininfarina			
6291 GT		6291 GT	330 GT	330	2 + 2	Pininfarina			
6293 GT		6293 GT	330 GT	330	2 + 2	Pininfarina			
6295 GT		6295 GT	330 GT	330	2 + 2	Pininfarina			
6297 GT*?		6297 GT	330 GT	330	2 + 2	Pininfarina			Australia
6299 GT		6299 GT	330 GT	330	2 + 2	Pininfarina			Denmark
6301 GT*		6301 GT	330	GT	2 + 2	Pininfarina	Maranello Conc.	U.K.	U.K.?
6303 SF		6303 SF	500 Series I	Superfast	Coupé	Pininfarina	Livanos	Greece	U.S.A.
		Sold on 23/4/65.							
6305 SF		6305 SF	500 Series I	Superfast	Coupé	Pininfarina	Mouzino		U.S.A.
		Sold on 14/5/65.							
6307 SF		6307 SF	500 Series I	Superfast	Coupé	Pininfarina			U.S.A.
		Sold on 29/5/65.							
6309 SF		6309 SF	500 Series I	Superfast	Coupé	Pininfarina	Sachs		
		Sold on 15/7/65.							
6311 GT		6311 GT	330	GT	2 + 2	Pininfarina			
6313 GT*		6313 GT	250 LM	LM	Berlinetta	Scaglietti	Ecurie Francor-champs	Belgium	Australia
		Sold on 22/4/65. Raced in 1964 and 1965. All aluminium body.							
6315 GT		6315 GT	275	GTS	Spyder	Pininfarina			
		Believed shown at the 1964 Paris Salon.							
6317 GT		6317 GT	330	GT	2 + 2	Pininfarina			
6319 GT		6319 GT	330	GT	2 + 2	Pininfarina			
6321 GT*		6321 GT	250 LM	LM	Berlinetta	Scaglietti	David McKay	Australia	U.S.A.
		Completed October 1964. Raced in 1965 through 1967. All Aluminium body.							
6323 GT		6323 GT	330	GT	2 + 2	Pininfarina			
6325 GT		6325 GT	330	GT	2 + 2	Pininfarina			
6327 GT		6327 GT	330	GT	2 + 2	Pininfarina			
6329 GT		6329 GT	330	GT	2 + 2	Pininfarina			
6331 GT		6331 GT	330	GT	2 + 2	Pininfarina			
6333 GT		6333 GT	330	GT	2 + 2	Pininfarina			
6335 GT		6335 GT	330	GT	2 + 2	Pininfarina			
6337 GT		6337 GT	330	GT	2 + 2	Pininfarina			
6339 GT		6339 GT	330	GT	2 + 2	Pininfarina			
6341 GT		6341 GT	330	GT	2 +2	Pininfarina			
6343 GT		6343 GT	330	GT	2 + 2	Pininfarina			
6345 SF*		6345 SF	500 Series I	Superfast	Coupé	Pininfarina	R.Wilkins	U.K.	Destroyed
		Shown at the 1965 London Motor Show.							
6347 GT		6347 GT	330	GT	2 + 2	Pininfarina			
6349 GT		6349 GT	330	GT	2 + 2	Pininfarina			
6351 SF*		6351 SF	500 Series I	Superfast	Coupé	Pininfarina	Hood	U.K.	U.K.?
6353 GT		6353 GT	330	GT	2 + 2	Pininfarina			
6355 GT		6355 GT	330	GT	2 + 2	Pininfarina			U.K.

Chassis No.	Picture Ref	Engine No.	Type	Model	Body Style	Coach-builder	First Owner	Original Location	Present Location
6357 GT		6357 GT	275	GTB	Berlinetta	Scaglietti			
6359 GT		6359 GT	330	GT	2 + 2	Pininfarina			
6361 GT		6361 GT	330	GT	2 + 2	Pininfarina			
6363 GT		6363 GT	330	GT	2 + 2	Pininfarina			
6365 GT		6365 GT	330	GT	2 + 2	Pininfarina			
6367 GT		6367 GT	330	GT	2 + 2	Pininfarina			
6369 GT		6369 GT	330	GT	2 + 2	Pininfarina			
6371 GT		6371 GT	330	GT	2 + 2	Pininfarina			
6373 GT		6373 GT	330	GT	2 + 2	Pininfarina			U.S.A.
6375 GT		6375 GT	330	GT	2 + 2	Pininfarina			
6377 GT		6377 GT	330	GT	2 + 2	Pininfarina			
6379 GT		6379 GT	330	GT	2 + 2	Pininfarina			
6381 GT		6381 GT	330	GT	2 + 2	Pininfarina			
6383 GT		6383 GT	330	GT	2 + 2	Pininfarina			
6385 GT		6385 GT	330	GT	2 + 2	Pininfarina			
6387 GT		6387 GT	330	GT	2 + 2	Pininfarina			
6389 GT		6389 GT	330	GT	2 + 2	Pininfarina			Canada
6391 GT		6391 GT	330	GT	2 + 2	Pininfarina			Holland
6393 GT		6393 GT	330	GT	2 + 2	Pininfarina			
6395 GT		6395 GT	330	GT	2 + 2	Pininfarina			
6397 GT		6397 GT	330	GT	2 + 2	Pininfarina			
6399 GT		6399 GT	330	GT	2 + 2	Pininfarina			
6401 GT		6401 GT	330	GT	2 + 2	Pininfarina			
6403 GT		6403 GT	330	GT	2 + 2	Pininfarina			
6405 GT		6405 GT	330	GT	2 + 2	Pininfarina			
6407 GT		6407 GT	330	GT	2 + 2	Pininfarina			
6409 GT		6409 GT	330	GT	2 + 2	Pininfarina			
6411 GT		6411 GT	330	GT	2 + 2	Pininfarina			
6413 GT		6413 GT	330	GT	2 + 2	Pininfarina			
6415 GT		6415 GT	330	GT	2 + 2	Pininfarina			
6417 GT*		6417 GT	275	GTS	Spyder	Pininfarina			U.K.
	Shown at the 1964 London Motor Show.								
6419 GT		6419 GT	330	GT	2 + 2	Pininfarina			
6421 GT		6421 GT	330	GT	2 + 2	Pininfarina			
6423 GT		6423 GT	330	GT	2 + 2	Pininfarina			
6425 GT		6425 GT	330	GT	2 + 2	Pininfarina			
6427 GT		6427 GT	330	GT	2 + 2	Pininfarina			
6429 GT		6429 GT	330	GT	2 + 2	Pininfarina			
6431 GT		6431 GT	330	GTC	Coupé	Pininfarina			
	Believed to be the first prototype for the 330GTC.								
6433 GT		6433 GT	330	GT	2 + 2	Pininfarina			
6435 GT		6435 GT	330	GT	2 + 2	Pininfarina			
6437 GT		6437 GT	275	GTB	Berlinetta	Scaglietti			U.S.A.
	3 carb. Short nose.								
6439 GT		6439 GT	330	GT	2 + 2	Pininfarina			
6441 GT		6441 GT	330	GT	2 + 2	Pininfarina			
6443 GT		6443 GT	330	GT	2 + 2	Pininfarina			
6445 GT		6445 GT	330	GT	2 + 2	Pininfarina			
6447 GT		6447 GT	330	GT	2 + 2	Pininfarina			
6449 GT		6449 GT	275	GTB	Berlinetta	Scaglietti			
6451 GT		6451 GT	330	GT	2 + 2	Pininfarina			
6453 GT		6453 GT	330	GT	2 + 2	Pininfarina			
	Salon Torimo 64 E. Ferrari								
6455 GT		6455 GT	330	GT	2 + 2	Pininfarina			
6457 GT		6457 GT	275	GTB	Berlinetta	Scaglietti			
6459 GT		6459 GT	330	GT	2 + 2	Pininfarina			U.S.A.
6461 GT		6461 GT	275	GTS	Spyder	Pininfarina			
6463 GT		6463 GT	330	GT	2 + 2	Pininfarina			
6465 GT		6465 GT	330	GT	2 + 2	Pininfarina			
6467 GT		6467 GT	330	GT	2 + 2	Pininfarina			
6469 GT		6469 GT	330	GT	2 + 2	Pininfarina			
6471 GT		6471 GT	275	GTB	Berlinetta	Scaglietti			
6473 GT		6473 GT	330	GT	2 + 2	Pininfarina			
6475 GT		6475 GT	330	GT	2 + 2	Pininfarina			
6477 GT*		6477 GT	330	GT	2 + 2	Pininfarina	Maranello Conc.	U.K.	U.K.
6479 GT		6479 GT	330	GT	2 + 2	Pininfarina			
6481 GT		6481 GT	330	GT	2 + 2	Pininfarina			
6483 GT		6483 GT	330	GT	2 + 2	Pininfarina			
6485 GT		6485 GT	330	GT	2 + 2	Pininfarina			
6487 GT		6487 GT	330	GT	2 + 2	Pininfarina			
6489 GT		6489 GT	275	GTB	Berlinetta	Scaglietti			
	Outside filler cap.								
6491 GT		6491 GT	330	GT	2 + 2	Pininfarina			
6493 GT		6493 GT	330	GT	2 + 2	Pininfarina			

Chassis No.	Picture Ref	Engine No.	Type	Model	Body Style	Coach-builder	First Owner	Original Location	Present Location
6495 GT		6495 GT	330	GT	2 + 2	Pininfarina			
6497 GT		6497 GT	330	GT	2 + 2	Pininfarina			
6499 GT		6499 GT	330	GT	2 + 2	Pininfarina			
6501 GT*		6501 GT	330	GT	2 + 2	Pininfarina			U.K.
	Shown at the 1964 London Motor Show.								
6503 GT*		6503 GT	330	GT	2 + 2	Pininfarina			U.K.
6505 GT		6505 GT	275	GTB	Berlinetta	Scaglietti			
6507 GT		6507 GT	275	GTB	Berlinetta	Scaglietti			
6509 GT		6509 GT	330	GT	2 + 2	Pininfarina			
6511 GT		6511 GT	330	GT	2 + 2	Pininfarina			U.S.A.
6513 GT		6513 GT	330	GT	2 + 2	Pininfarina			
6515 GT		6515 GT	330	GT	2 + 2	Pininfarina			
6517 GT		6517 GT	275	GTB	Berlinetta	Scaglietti			Switzerland
	3 carb. Short nose.								
6519 GT*		6519 GT	330	GT	2 + 2	Pininfarina			
6521 GT*		6521 GT	275	GTB	Berlinetta	Scaglietti			U.K..
	Shown at the 1964 London Motor Show. 6 Carbs. Short nose.								
6523 GT		6523 GT	330	GT	2 + 2	Pininfarina			
6525 GT		6525 GT	330	GT	2 + 2	Pininfarina			
6527 GT*		6527 GT	275	GTB	Berlinetta	Scaglietti			U.K.
	Shown at the 1964 London Motor Show. .6 carb. Short nose.								
6529 GT		6529 GT	275	GTB	Berlinetta	Scaglietti			
6531 GT		6531 GT	330	GT	2 + 2	Pininfarina			
6533 GT		6533 GT	330	GT	2 + 2	Pininfarina			
6535 GT		6535 GT	330	GT	2 + 2	Pininfarina			
6537 GT		6537 GT	330	GT	2 + 2	Pininfarina			
6539 GT		6539 GT	330	GT	2 + 2	Pininfarina			
6541 GT		6541 GT	330	GT	2 + 2	Pininfarina			
6543 GT		6543 GT	275	GTB	Berlinetta	Scaglietti			
6545 GT		6545 GT	330	GT	2 + 2	Pininfarina			
6547 GT		6547 GT	330	GT	2 + 2	Pininfarina			
6549 GT		6549 GT	330	GT	2 + 2	Pininfarina			
6551 GT		6551 GT	330	GT	2 + 2	Pininfarina			U.S.A.
6553 GT		6553 GT	330	GT	2 + 2	Pininfarina			
6555 GT		6555 GT	330	GT	2 + 2	Pininfarina			
6557 GT		6557 GT	275	GTB	Berlinetta	Scaglietti			
	6 carb.								
6559 GT		6559 GT	330	GT	2 + 2	Pininfarina			
6561 GT		6561 GT	330	GT	2 + 2	Pininfarina			
6563 GT		6563 GT	275	GTB	Berlinetta	Scaglietti			
6565 GT		6565 GT	330	GT	2 + 2	Pininfarina			
6567 GT		6567 GT	330	GT	2 + 2	Pininfarina			
6569 GT		6569 GT	275	GTB	Berlinetta	Scaglietti			Austria
	3 carb. Short nose.								
6571 GT		6571 GT	330	GT	2 + 2	Pininfarina			
6573 GT		6573 GT	330	GT	2 + 2	Pininfarina			
6575 GT		6575 GT	275	GTB	Berlinetta	Scaglietti			
6577 GT		6577 GT	275	GTB	Berlinetta	Scaglietti			
6579 GT		6579 GT	330	GT	2 + 2	Pininfarina			
6581 GT		6581 GT	330	GT	2 + 2	Pininfarina			
6583 GT		6583 GT	330	GT	2 + 2	Pininfarina			
6585 GT		6585 GT	275	GTB	Berlinetta	Scaglietti			
6587 GT		6587 GT	275	GTB	Berlinetta	Scaglietti			
6589 GT		6589 GT	275	GTB	Berlinetta	Scaglietti			
6591 GT		6591 GT	330	GT	2 + 2	Pininfarina			
6593 GT		6593 GT	330	GT	2 + 2	Pininfarina			
6595 GT*		6595 GT	330	GT	2 + 2	Pininfarina			U.K.
6597 GT		6597 GT	330	GT	2 + 2	Pininfarina			
6599 GT		6599 GT	275	GTB	Berlinetta	Scaglietti			
6601 GT		6601 GT	275	GTB	Berlinetta	Scaglietti			
6603 GT		6603 GT	275	GTB	Berlinetta	Scaglietti			
	6 carb								
6605 SF		6605 SF	500 Series I	Superfast	Coupé	Pininfarina	Shah of Iran	Iran	
	Sold on 8/6/65.								
6607 GT*		6607 GT	330	GT	2 + 2	Pininfarina			U.K.
6609 GT		6609 GT	275	GTB	Berlinetta	Scaglietti			
6611 GT		6611 GT	275	GTB	Berlinetta	Scaglietti			
6613 GT		6613 GT	330	GT	2 + 2	Pininfarina			
	Chicago Auto Show 1965								
6615 SF		6615 SF	500 Series I	Superfast	Coupé	Pininfarina		Germany	U.S.A.
	Sold on 21/9/65.								
6617 GT		6617 GT	275	GTB	Berlinetta	Scaglietti			
6619 GT		6619 GT	275	GTB	Berlinetta	Scaglietti			
6621 GT		6621 GT	275	GTB	Berlinetta	Scaglietti			

Chassis No.	Picture Ref	Engine No.	Type	Model	Body Style	Coach-builder	First Owner	Original Location	Present Location
6623 GT		6623 GT	330	GT	2 + 2	Pininfarina			
6625 GT		6625 GT	330	GT	2 + 2	Pininfarina			
	Brussels Motor Show 1965								
6627 GT		6627 GT	330	GT	2 + 2	Pininfarina			
6629 GT		6629 GT	275	GTB	Berlinetta	Scaglietti			
6631 GT		6631 GT	275	GTB	Berlinetta	Scaglietti			
6633 GT		6633 GT	330	GT	2 + 2	Pininfarina			
6635 GT		6635 GT	330	GT	2 + 2	Pininfarina			
6637GT		6637GT	330	GT	2 + 2	Pininfarina			
6639 GT		6639 GT	275	GTB	Berlinetta	Scaglietti			
	6 carb.								
6641 GT		6641 GT	330	GT	2 + 2	Pininfarina			
6643 GT		6643 GT	275	GTB	Berlinetta	Scaglietti			
6645 GT		6645 GT	275	GTB	Berlinetta	Scaglietti			
6647 GT		6647 GT	330	GT	2 + 2	Pininfarina			
6649 GT		6649 GT	330	GT	2 + 2	Pininfarina			
6651 GT		6651 GT	275	GTB	Berlinetta	Scaglietti			
6653 GT		6653 GT	275	GTB	Berlinetta	Scaglietti			
6655 GT		6655 GT	275	GTB	Berlinetta	Scaglietti			
6657 GT		6657 GT	330	GT	2 + 2	Pininfarina			U.K.
6659 SF*		6659 SF	500 Series I	Superfast	Coupé	Pininfarina	E.Miller	U.K.	U.K.
	Sold on 4/9/65.								
6661 SF*		6661 SF	500 Series I	Superfast	Coupé	Pininfarina	J.Durlacher	U.K.	U.K.
	Sold on 9/6/65.								
6663 GT		6663 GT	275	GTB	Berlinetta	Scaglietti			
	6 carb.								
6665 GT		6665 GT	275	GTB	Berlinetta	Scaglietti			
	6 carb.								
6667 GT		6667 GT	330	GT	2 + 2	Pininfarina			
6669 GT		6669 GT	275	GTB	Berlinetta	Scaglietti			
6671 GT		6671 GT	275	GTB	Berlinetta	Scaglietti			
6673 SF*		6673 SF	500 Series I	Superfast	Coupé	Pininfarina	Hyams	U.K.	U.K.
	Sold on 22/7/65.								
6675 GT*		6675 GT	330	GT	2 + 2	Pininfarina			U.K.
6677 GT*		6677 GT	275	GTB	Berlinetta	Scaglietti			U.K.
6677 GT*	All aluminium body.6 carbs.								
6679 SF*		6679 SF	500 Series I	Superfast	Coupé	Pininfarina	Peter Sellers	U.K.	U.K.
	Sold on 30/9/65.								
6681 GT		6681 GT	275	GTB	Berlinetta	Scaglietti			U.S.A.
	3 carb.Short nose.								
6683 GT*		6683 GT	275	GTB	Berlinetta	Scaglietti			U.K.
6685 GT		6685 GT	330	GT	2 + 2	Pininfarina			
6687 GT		6687 GT	330	GT	2 + 2	Pininfarina			U.S.A.
6689 GT		6689 GT	330	GT	2 + 2	Pininfarina			
6691 GT		6691 GT	275	GTB	Berlinetta	Scaglietti			
6693 GT		6693 GT	275	GTB	Berlinetta	Scaglietti			
6695 GT		6695 GT	275	GTB	Berlinetta	Scaglietti			
6697 GT*		6697 GT	330	GT	2 + 2	Pininfarina			U.K.
6699 GT		6699 GT	330	GT	2 + 2	Pininfarina			
6701 GT		6701 GT	275 GTB	Competition	Berlinetta	Scaglietti			United Arab Emerites
	Built in 1965 as special competition version with special chassis and body with a dry sump 6 carb engine.								
6703 GT		6703 GT	275	GTB	Berlinetta	Scaglietti			
6705 GT		6705 GT	275	GTB	Berlinetta	Scaglietti			
6707 GT		6707 GT	275	GTB	Berlinetta	Scaglietti			
6709 GT		6709 GT	275	GTB	Berlinetta	Scaglietti			U.K.
	3 carb.Short nose.								
6711 GT		6711 GT	275	GTB	Berlinetta	Scaglietti			
6713 GT		6713 GT	330	GT	2 + 2	Pininfarina			
6715 GT		6715 GT	275	GTB	Berlinetta	Scaglietti			
	All aluminium body.								
6717 GT		6717 GT	275	GTB	Berlinetta	Scaglietti			
6719 GT*		6719 GT	275	GTB	Berlinetta	Scaglietti			U.K.
6721 GT		6721 GT	275	GTB	Berlinetta	Scaglietti			U.S.A.
	3 carb.Short nose.								
6723 GT*		6723 GT	275	GTB	Berlinetta	Scaglietti			U.K.
6725 GT		6725 GT	275	GTB	Berlinetta	Scaglietti			U.K.
6727 GT*		6727 GT	330	GT	2 + 2	Pininfarina			
6729 GT		6729 GT	330	GT	2 + 2	Pininfarina			
6731 GT		6731 GT	275	GTB	Berlinetta	Scaglietti			
	6 carb.								
6733 GT		6733 GT	275	GTB	Berlinetta	Scaglietti			
6735 GT		6735 GT	330	GT	2 + 2	Pininfarina			
6737 GT		6737 GT	330	GT	2 + 2	Pininfarina			
6739 GT*		6739 GT	330	GT	2 + 2	Pininfarina			U.K.

Chassis No.	Picture Ref	Engine No.	Type	Model	Body Style	Coach-builder	First Owner	Original Location	Present Location
6741 GT		6741 GT	275	GTB	Berlinetta	Scaglietti			Switzerland
6743 GT		6743 GT	330	GT	2 + 2	Pininfarina			
6745 GT		6745 GT	330	GT	2 + 2	Pininfarina			
6747 GT*		6747 GT	330	GT	2 + 2	Pininfarina			U.K.
6749 GT		6749 GT	275	GTB	Berlinetta	Scaglietti			
6751 GT		6751 GT	275	GTB	Berlinetta	Scaglietti			
6753 GT		6753 GT	330	GT	2 + 2	Pininfarina			
6755 GT		6755 GT	330	GT	2 + 2	Pininfarina			
6757 GT		6757 GT	330	GT	2 + 2	Pininfarina			
6759 GT		6759 GT	330	GT	2 + 2	Pininfarina			France
6761 GT		6761 GT	275	GTB	Berlinetta	Scaglietti			
6763 GT		6763 GT	330	GT	2 + 2	Pininfarina			
6765 GT		6765 GT	275	GTB	Berlinetta	Scaglietti			U.S.A.
6767 GT	3 carb.Short nose.	6767 GT	330	GT	2 + 2	Pininfarina			
6769 GT*	Geneva Auto Show 1965	6769 GT	330	GT	2 + 2	Pininfarina			U.K.
6771 GT		6771 GT	330	GT	2 + 2	Pininfarina			
6773 GT		6773 GT	275	GTB	Berlinetta	Scaglietti			
6775 GT		6775 GT	330	GT	2 + 2	Pininfarina			
6777 GT*		6777 GT	330	GT	2 + 2	Pininfarina			U.K.
6779 GT	6 carb.	6779 GT	275	GTB	Berlinetta	Scaglietti			
6781 GT*		6781 GT	330	GT	2 + 2	Pininfarina			U.K.
6783 GT*		6783 GT	330	GT	2 + 2	Pininfarina			U.K.
6785 GT		6785 GT	275	GTB	Berlinetta	Scaglietti			
6787 GT		6787 GT	275	GTB	Berlinetta	Scaglietti			
6789 GT	3 carb.Short Nose.	6789 GT	275	GTB	Berlinetta	Scaglietti			U.S.A.
6791 GT		6791 GT	275	GTB	Berlinetta	Scaglietti			
6793 GT		6793 GT	330	GT	2 + 2	Pininfarina			
6795 GT		6795 GT	330	GT	2 + 2	Pininfarina			
6797 GT		6797 GT	330	GT	2 + 2	Pininfarina			
6799 GT		6799 GT	330	GT	2 + 2	Pininfarina			
6801 GT		6801 GT	330	GT	2 + 2	Pininfarina			
6803 GT		6803 GT	330	GT	2 + 2	Pininfarina			
6805 GT	Brussels Motor Show	6805 GT	275	GTS	Spyder	Pininfarina			
6807 GT		6807 GT	275	GTS	Spyder	Pininfarina			
6809 GT		6809 GT	275	GTS	Spyder	Pininfarina			
6811 GT		6811 GT	330	GT	2 + 2	Pininfarina			
6813 GT		6813 GT	330	GT	2 + 2	Pininfarina			
6815 GT		6815 GT	330	GT	2 + 2	Pininfarina			
6817 GT		6817 GT	275	GTS	Spyder	Pininfarina			
6819 GT		6819 GT	275	GTS	Spyder	Pininfarina			
6821 GT		6821 GT	330	GT	2 + 2	Pininfarina			
6823 GT		6823 GT	330	GT	2 + 2	Pininfarina			
6825 GT		6825 GT	330	GT	2 + 2	Pininfarina			
6827 GT		6827 GT	275	GTB	Berlinetta	Scaglietti			
6829 GT		6829 GT	330	GT	2 + 2	Pininfarina			
6831 GT		6831 GT	275	GTB	Berlinetta	Scaglietti			
6833 GT		6833 GT	330	GT	2 + 2	Pininfarina			
6835 GT		6835 GT	330	GT	2 + 2	Pininfarina			
6837 GT		6837 GT	330	GT	2 + 2	Pininfarina			
6839 GT	6 carb.All aluminium body.	6839 GT	275	GTB	Berlinetta	Scaglietti			
6841 GT		6841 GT	275	GTB	Berlinetta	Scaglietti			
6843 GT		6843 GT	330	GT	2 + 2	Pininfarina			
6845 GT		6845 GT	330	GT	2 + 2	Pininfarina			
6847 GT		6847 GT	330	GT	2 + 2	Pininfarina			
6849 GT		6849 GT	330	GT	2 + 2	Pininfarina			
6851 GT		6851 GT	330	GT	2 + 2	Pininfarina			
6853 GT		6853 GT	275	GTS	Spyder	Pininfarina			
6855 GT		6855 GT	275	GTS	Spyder	Pininfarina			
6857 GT		6857 GT	330	GT	2 + 2	Pininfarina			
6859 GT		6859 GT	330	GT	2 + 2	Pininfarina			
6861 GT		6861 GT	330	GT	2 + 2	Pininfarina			
6863 GT		6863 GT	330	GT	2 + 2	Pininfarina			
6865 GT		6865 GT	275	GTS	Spyder	Pininfarina			
6867 GT		6867 GT	275	GTS	Spyder	Pininfarina			
6869 GT		6869 GT	330	GT	2 + 2	Pininfarina			
6871 GT		6871 GT	330	GT	2 + 2	Pininfarina			
6873 GT	Geneva Auto Show 1965	6873 GT	330	GT	2 + 2	Pininfarina			

Chassis No.	Picture Ref	Engine No.	Type	Model	Body Style	Coach-builder	First Owner	Original Location	Present Location
6875 GT*		6875 GT	330	GT	2 + 2	Pininfarina			U.K.
6877 GT		6877 GT	275	GTS	Spyder	Pininfarina			
6879 GT*		6879 GT	330	GT	2 + 2	Pininfarina			U.K.
6881 GT	3 carb. Short nose.	6881 GT	275	GTB	Berlinetta	Scaglietti			Spain
6883 GT*		6883 GT	330	GT	2 + 2	Pininfarina			U.K.
6885 GT	Built in 1965 as special competition car with special chassis and body with dry sump 6 carb engine. Raced in 1965. All aluminium body.	6885 GT	275 GTB	Competition	Berlinetta	Scaglietti			U.S.A.
6887 GT		6887 GT	275	GTB	Berlinetta	Scaglietti			
6889 GT		6889 GT	275	GTS	Spyder	Pininfarina			
6891 GT		6891 GT	275	GTB	Berlinetta	Scaglietti			
6893 GT		6893 GT	275	GTB	Berlinetta	Scaglietti			
6895 GT		6895 GT	275	GTB	Berlinetta	Scaglietti			
6897 GT		6897 GT	275	GTB	Berlinetta	Scaglietti			Ireland
6899 GT	3 carb. Short nose.	6899 GT	275	GTB	Berlinetta	Scaglietti			
6901 GT*		6901 GT	275	GTB	Berlinetta	Scaglietti			U.K.
6903 GT		6903 GT	275	GTB	Berlinetta	Scaglietti			
6905 GT		6905 GT	275	GTB	Berlinetta	Scaglietti			
6907 GT	All aluminium body.	6907 GT	275	GTB	Berlinetta	Scaglietti			
6909 GT		6909 GT	275	GTS	Spyder	Pininfarina			
6911 GT		6911 GT	330	GT	2 + 2	Pininfarina			
6913 GT		6913 GT	275	GTB	Berlinetta	Scaglietti			U.K.
6915 GT	3 carb. Short nose.	6915 GT	275	GTB	Berlinetta	Scaglietti			
6917 GT	Display chassis.	6917 GT	275	GTB	Berlinetta	Scaglietti			
6919 GT		6919 GT	275	GTS	Spyder	Pininfarina			
6921 GT		6921 GT	330	GT	2 + 2	Pininfarina			
6923 GT		6923 GT	275	GTS	Spyder	Pininfarina			
6925 GT		6925 GT	275	GTB	Berlinetta	Scaglietti			
6927 GT	All aluminium body.	6927 GT	330	GT	2 + 2	Pininfarina			
6929 GT		6929 GT	330	GT	2 + 2	Pininfarina			
6931 GT*		6931 GT	275	GTB	Berlinetta	Scaglietti			U.K.
6933 GT		6933 GT	275	GTB	Berlinetta	Scaglietti			U.S.A.
6935 GT	3 carb. Short nose.	6935 GT	275	GTB	Berlinetta	Scaglietti			U.S.A.
6937 GT	3 carb. Short nose.	6937 GT	330	GT	2 + 2	Pininfarina			
6939 GT		6939 GT	330	GT	2 + 2	Pininfarina			
6941 GT*	First with 5 speeds.	6941 GT	275	GTB	Berlinetta	Scaglietti			U.K.
6943 GT	6 carb. Short nose.	6943 GT	275	GTB	Berlinetta	Scaglietti			
6945 GT		6945 GT	330	GT	2 + 2	Pininfarina			
6947 GT		6947 GT	330	GT	2 + 2	Pininfarina			
6949 GT		6949 GT	275	GTB	Berlinetta	Scaglietti			
6951 GT		6951 GT	275	GTB	Berlinetta	Scaglietti			
6953 GT		6953 GT	330	GT	2 + 2	Pininfarina			
6955 GT		6955 GT	330	GT	2 + 2	Pininfarina			
6957 GT		6957 GT	330	GT	2 + 2	Pininfarina			
6959 GT	Geneva Auto Show 1965	6959 GT	275	GTS	Spyder	Pininfarina			
6961 GT		6961 GT	330	GT	2 + 2	Pininfarina			
6963 GT		6963 GT	275	GTS	Spyder	Pininfarina			
6965 GT		6965 GT	330	GT	2 + 2	Pininfarina			
6967 GT		6967 GT	275	GTB	Berlinetta	Scaglietti			
6969 GT		6969 GT	330	GT	2 + 2	Pininfarina			
6971 GT		6971 GT	330	GT	2 + 2	Pininfarina			
6973 GT		6973 GT	275	GTB	Berlinetta	Scaglietti			
6975 GT		6975 GT	330	GT	2 + 2	Pininfarina			
6977 GT		6977 GT	275	GTS	Spyder	Pininfarina			
6979 GT		6979 GT	330	GT	2 + 2	Pininfarina			
6981 GT		6981 GT	330	GT	2 + 2	Pininfarina			
6983 GT		6983 GT	275	GTB	Berlinetta	Scaglietti			
6985 GT		6985 GT	330	GT	2 + 2	Pininfarina			
6987 GT		6987 GT	275	GTS	Spyder	Pininfarina			
6989 GT*		6989 GT	275	GTS	Spyder	Pininfarina			U.K.
6991 GT		6991 GT	330	GT	2 + 2	Pininfarina			
6993 GT		6993 GT	330	GT	2 + 2	Pininfarina			
6995 GT	6 carb.	6995 GT	275	GTB	Berlinetta	Scaglietti			

Chassis No.	Picture Ref	Engine No.	Type	Model	Body Style	Coach-builder	First Owner	Original Location	Present Location
6997 GT		6997 GT	330	GT	2 + 2	Pininfarina			
6999 GT		6999 GT	275	GTS	Spyder	Pininfarina			
7001 GT		7001 GT	275	GTB	Berlinetta	Scaglietti			
7003 GT		7003 GT	275	GTB	Berlinetta	Scaglietti			Sweden
	3 carb. Short nose.								
7005 GT		7005 GT	330	GT	2 + 2	Pininfarina			
7007 GT		7007 GT	275	GTS	Spyder	Pininfarina			
7009 GT		7009 GT	275	GTB	Berlinetta	Scaglietti			
7011 GT		7011 GT	330	GT	2 + 2	Pininfarina			
7013 GT		7013 GT	275	GTS	Spyder	Pininfarina			
7015 GT		7015 GT	330	GT	2 + 2	Pininfarina			
7017 GT		7017 GT	330	GT	2 + 2	Pininfarina			
7019 GT		7019 GT	275	GTS	Spyder	Pininfarina			
7021 GT		7021 GT	275	GTS	Spyder	Pininfarina			
7023 GT		7023 GT	330	GT	2 + 2	Pininfarina			
7025 GT		7025 GT	330	GT	2 + 2	Pininfarina			
7027 GT		7027 GT	275	GTS	Spyder	Pininfarina			
7029 GT		7029 GT	330	GT	2 + 2	Pininfarina			
7031 GT		7031 GT	275	GTS	Spyder	Pininfarina			
7033 GT		7033 GT	330	GT	2 + 2	Pininfarina			
7035 GT		7035 GT	275	GTS	Spyder	Pininfarina			
7037 GT		7037 GT	275	GTB	Berlinetta	Scaglietti			
7039 GT		7039 GT	275	GTS	Spyder	Pininfarina			
7041 GT		7041 GT	330	GT	2 + 2	Pininfarina			
7043 GT		7043 GT	330	GT	2 + 2	Pininfarina			
7045 GT		7045 GT	275	GTB	Berlinetta	Scaglietti			
	6 carb.								
7047 GT		7047 GT	330	GT	2 + 2	Pininfarina			
7049 GT		7049 GT	275	GTS	Spyder	Pininfarina			
7051 GT		7051 GT	330	GT	2 + 2	Pininfarina			
7053 GT		7053 GT	275	GTB	Berlinetta	Scaglietti			
7055 GT		7055 GT	330	GT	2 + 2	Pininfarina			
7057 GT		7057 GT	275	GTS	Spyder	Pininfarina			
7059 GT		7059 GT	330	GT	2 + 2	Pininfarina			
7061 GT		7061 GT	275	GTB	Berlinetta	Scaglietti			
7063 GT		7063 GT	330	GT	2 + 2	Pininfarina			
7065 GT		7065 GT	275	GTS	Spyder	Pininfarina			
7067 GT		7067 GT	275	GTB	Berlinetta	Scaglietti			
7069 GT		7069 GT	330	GT	2 + 2	Pininfarina			
7071 GT		7071 GT	275	GTS	Spyder	Pininfarina			
7073 GT		7073 GT	275	GTB	Berlinetta	Scaglietti			
7075 GT		7075 GT	275	GTB	Berlinetta	Scaglietti			U.S.A.
	3 carb. Short nose.								
7077 GT		7077 GT	330	GT	2 + 2	Pininfarina			
7079 GT		7079 GT	275	GTS	Spyder	Pininfarina			
7081 GT		7081 GT	330	GT	2 + 2	Pininfarina			
7083 GT		7083 GT	330	GT	2 + 2	Pininfarina			
7085 GT		7085 GT	275	GTB	Berlinetta	Scaglietti			U.S.A.
	3 carb. Short nose.								
7087 GT		7087 GT	330	GT	2 + 2	Pininfarina			
7089 GT		7089 GT	275	GTS	Spyder	Pininfarina			
7091 GT		7091 GT	330	GT	2 + 2	Pininfarina			
7093 GT		7093 GT	275	GTB	Berlinetta	Scaglietti			
7095 GT		7095 GT	330	GT	2 + 2	Pininfarina			
7097 GT		7097 GT	275	GTB	Berlinetta	Scaglietti			
7099 GT		7099 GT	330	GT	2 + 2	Pininfarina			
7101 GT		7101 GT	275	GTB	Berlinetta	Scaglietti			
7103 GT		7103 GT	330	GT	2 + 2	Pininfarina			
7105 GT*		7105 GT	275	GTS	Spyder	Pininfarina			U.K.
7107 GT		7107 GT	275	GTB	Berlinetta	Scaglietti			
7109 GT		7109 GT	275	GTB	Berlinetta	Scaglietti			France.
	3 carb. Short nose.								
7111 GT		7111 GT	275	GTB	Berlinetta	Scaglietti			
7113 GT		7113 GT	330	GT	2 + 2	Pininfarina			
7115 GT		7115 GT	330	GT	2 + 2	Pininfarina			
7117 GT		7117 GT	275	GTB	Berlinetta	Scaglietti			
7119 GT		7119 GT	330	GT	2 + 2	Pininfarina			
7121 GT		7121 GT	275	GTS	Spyder	Pininfarina			
7123 GT		7123 GT	330	GT	2 + 2	Pininfarina			
7125 GT		7125 GT	330	GT	2 + 2	Pininfarina			
	Rebodied in 1987 with fibreglass replica California body.								
7127 GT*		7127 GT	275	GTB	Berlinetta	Scaglietti			U.K.
	6 carbs. Short nose.								
7129 GT		7129 GT	330	GT	2 + 2	Pininfarina			

Chassis No.	Picture Ref	Engine No.	Type	Model	Body Style	Coach-builder	First Owner	Original Location	Present Location
7131 GT*		7131 GT	330	GT	2 + 2	Pininfarina			U.K.
7133 GT		7133 GT	275	GTS	Spyder	Pininfarina			
7135 GT		7135 GT	275	GTB	Berlinetta	Scaglietti			U.S.A.
	3 carb. Short nose.								
7137 GT		7137 GT	330	GT	2 + 2	Pininfarina			
7139 GT		7139 GT	330	GT	2 + 2	Pininfarina			
7141 GT		7141 GT	330	GT	2 + 2	Pininfarina			
7143 GT		7143 GT	275	GTS	Spyder	Pininfarina			
7145 GT*		7145 GT	275	GTB	Berlinetta	Scaglietti			U.K.
	3 carb. Short nose.								
7147 GT		7147 GT	275	GTB	Berlinetta	Scaglietti			U.K.
	3 carb. Short nose.								
7149 GT		7149 GT	330	GT	2 + 2	Pininfarina			
7151 GT		7151 GT	330	GT	2 + 2	Pininfarina			
7153 GT*		7153 GT	275	GTS	Spyder	Pininfarina			U.K.
7155 GT*		7155 GT	275	GTB	Berlinetta	Scaglietti			U.K.
	3 carb. Short nose.								
7157 GT		7157 GT	330	GT	2 + 2	Pininfarina			
7159 GT		7159 GT	275	GTB	Berlinetta	Scaglietti			
7161 GT		7161 GT	330	GT	2 + 2	Pininfarina			
7163 GT		7163 GT	275	GTS	Spyder	Pininfarina			
7165 GT		7165 GT	275	GTB	Berlinetta	Scaglietti			
7167 GT		7167 GT	330	GT	2 + 2	Pininfarina			
7169 GT*		7169 GT	275	GTB	Berlinetta	Scaglietti			U.K.
	3 carb. Short nose.								
7171 GT*		7171 GT	275	GTS	Spyder	Pininfarina			U.K.
7173 GT*		7173 GT	275	GTB	Berlinetta	Scaglietti			U.K.
	6 carb. Short nose.								
7175 GT		7175 GT	330	GT	2 + 2	Pininfarina			
7177 GT		7177 GT	275	GTB	Berlinetta	Scaglietti			
7179 GT*		7179 GT	330	GT	2 + 2	Pininfarina			U.K.
7181 GT		7181 GT	275	GTB	Berlinetta	Scaglietti			
7183 GT		7183 GT	330	GT	2 + 2	Pininfarina			
7185 GT		7185 GT	275 GTB	Competition	Berlinetta	Scaglietti			U.S.A.
	Built in 1965 as special competition car with special chassis and body with dry sump 6 carb engine. All aluminium body.								
7187 GT		7187 GT	330	GT	2 + 2	Pininfarina			
7189 GT		7189 GT	275	GTS	Spyder	Pininfarina			
7191 GT*		7191 GT	330	GT	2 + 2	Pininfarina			U.K.
7193 GT		7193 GT	275	GTB	Berlinetta	Scaglietti			
7195 GT		7195 GT	330	GT	2 + 2	Pininfarina			
7197 GT		7197 GT	275	GTB	Berlinetta	Scaglietti			
7199 GT		7199 GT	275	GTB	Berlinetta	Scaglietti			
7201 GT		7201 GT	330	GT	2 + 2	Pininfarina			
7203 GT		7203 GT	275	GTS	Spyder	Pininfarina			
7205 GT		7205 GT	275	GTS	Spyder	Pininfarina			
7207 GT		7207 GT	275	GTB	Berlinetta	Scaglietti			
7209 GT		7209 GT	275	GTS	Spyder	Pininfarina			
7211 GT		7211 GT	275	GTB	Berlinetta	Scaglietti			
7213 GT		7213 GT	330	GT	2 + 2	Pininfarina			
7215 GT		7215 GT	275	GTS	Spyder	Pininfarina			
7217 GT		7217 GT	275	GTB	Berlinetta	Scaglietti			
	6 carb. Reported as 'Speciale':.								
7219 GT		7219 GT	330	GT	2 + 2	Pininfarina			
7221 GT		7221 GT	275	GTB	Berlinetta	Scaglietti			U.S.A.
	3 carb. Short nose.								
7223 GT		7223 GT	275	GTB	Berlinetta	Scaglietti			
7225 GT*		7225 GT	330	GT	2 + 2	Pininfarina			U.K.
7227 GT		7227 GT	275	GTS	Spyder	Pininfarina			
7229 GT		7229 GT	330	GT	2 + 2	Pininfarina			
7231 GT		7231 GT	330	GT	2 + 2	Pininfarina			
7233 GT		7233 GT	275	GTB	Berlinetta	Scaglietti			
7235 GT		7235 GT	275	GTS	Spyder	Pininfarina			
7237 GT		7237 GT	275	GTB	Berlinetta	Scaglietti			
7239 GT		7239 GT	275	GTB	Berlinetta	Scaglietti			
7241 GT		7241 GT	275	GTB	Berlinetta	Scaglietti			
	6 carb.								
7243 GT		7243 GT	275	GTB	Berlinetta	Scaglietti			Australia.
	3 carb. Short nose.								
7245 GT		7245 GT	330	GT	2 + 2	Pininfarina			
7247 GT		7247 GT	275	GTB	Berlinetta	Scaglietti			
	6 carb.								
7249 GT		7249 GT	275	GTB	Berlinetta	Scaglietti			
7251 GT		7251 GT	330	GT	2 + 2	Pininfarina			
7253 GT		7253 GT	330	GT	2 + 2	Pininfarina			

Chassis No.	Picture Ref	Engine No.	Type	Model	Body Style	Coach-builder	First Owner	Original Location	Present Location
7255 GT*		7255 GT	330	GT	2 + 2	Pininfarina			U.K.
7257 GT		7257 GT	275	GTS	Spyder	Pininfarina			
7259 GT		7259 GT	330	GT	2 + 2	Pininfarina			
7261 GT		7261 GT	275	GTB	Berlinetta	Scaglietti			
7263 GT		7263 GT	275	GTB	Berlinetta	Scaglietti			
7265 GT*		7265 GT	330	GT	2 + 2	Pininfarina			U.K.
7267 GT		7267 GT	330	GT	2 + 2	Pininfarina			
7269 GT		7269 GT	275	GTB	Berlinetta	Scaglietti			
7271 GT		7271 GT	275	Competition	Berlinetta	Scaglietti			Holland
	*The first of a batch of 11? cars built in late 1965 for competition. 6 carb. All aluminium body.*								
7273 GT		7273 GT	330	GT	2 + 2	Pininfarina			
7275 GT		7275 GT	275	GTS	Spyder	Pininfarina			
7277 GT		7277 GT	275	GTS	Spyder	Pininfarina			
7279 GT		7279 GT	330	GT	2 + 2	Pininfarina			
7281 GT		7281 GT	330	GT	2 + 2	Pininfarina			
7283 GT*		7283 GT	275	GTS	Spyder	Pininfarina			U.K.
7285 GT		7285 GT	275	GTS	Spyder	Pininfarina			
7287 GT		7287 GT	275	GTS	Spyder	Pininfarina			
7289 GT		7289 GT	275	GTS	Spyder	Pininfarina			
7291 GT*		7291 GT	330	GT	2 + 2	Pininfarina			U.K.
7293 GT*		7293 GT	275	GTS	Spyder	Pininfarina			U.K.
7295 GT		7295 GT	275	GTB	Berlinetta	Scaglietti			
7297 GT		7297 GT	275	GTS	Spyder	Pininfarina			
7299 GT		7299 GT	275	GTB	Berlinetta	Scaglietti			
7301 GT		7301 GT	275	GTS	Spyder	Pininfarina			
7303 GT		7303 GT	330	GT	2 + 2	Pininfarina			
7305 GT		7305 GT	275	GTS	Spyder	Pininfarina			
7307 GT*		7307 GT	275GTB	Competition	Berlinetta	Scaglietti			
	*All aluminium body.*								
7309 GT		7309 GT	275	GTS	Spyder	Pininfarina			
7311 GT		7311 GT	275	GTB	Berlinetta	Scaglietti			
7313 GT*		7313 GT	330	GT	2 + 2	Pininfarina			U.K.
7315 GT		7315 GT	275	GTB	Berlinetta	Scaglietti			U.S.A.
	*Prototype fibreglass floor pans.*								
7317 GT		7317 GT	275	GTS	Spyder	Pininfarina			
7319 GT		7319 GT	275	GTB	Berlinetta	Scaglietti			
7321 GT		7321 GT	330	GT	2 + 2	Pininfarina			
7323 GT*		7323 GT	330	GT	2 + 2	Pininfarina			U.K.
7325 GT		7325 GT	275	GTS	Spyder	Pininfarina			
7327 GT		7327 GT	275	GTB	Berlinetta	Scaglietti			
7329 GT		7329 GT	330	GT	2 + 2	Pininfarina			
7331 GT		7331 GT	275	GTS	Spyder	Pininfarina			
7333 GT		7333 GT	275	GTB	Berlinetta	Scaglietti			
7335 GT		7335 GT	330	GT	2 + 2	Pininfarina			
7337 GT		7337 GT	275	GTS	Spyder	Pininfarina			
7339 GT		7339 GT	330	GT	2 + 2	Pininfarina			
7341 GT		7341 GT	275	GTB	Berlinetta	Scaglietti			
7343 GT		7343 GT	330	GT	2 + 2	Pininfarina			
7345 GT		7345 GT	275	GTS	Spyder	Pininfarina			
7347 GT		7347 GT	275	GTB	Berlinetta	Scaglietti			
7349 GT		7349 GT	330	GT	2 + 2	Pininfarina			
7351 GT		7351 GT	275	GTB	Berlinetta	Scaglietti			
7353 GT*		7353 GT	330	GT	2 + 2	Pininfarina			U.K.
7355 GT		7355 GT	330	GT	2 + 2	Pininfarina			
7357 GT		7357 GT	275	GTB	Berlinetta	Scaglietti			
7359 GT		7359 GT	275	GTS	Spyder	Pininfarina			
7361 GT		7361 GT	275	GTS	Spyder	Pininfarina			
7363 GT		7363 GT	330	GT	2 + 2	Pininfarina			
7365 GT		7365 GT	275	GTB	Berlinetta	Scaglietti			
7367 GT		7367 GT	275	GTS	Spyder	Pininfarina			
7369 GT		7369 GT	330	GT	2 + 2	Pininfarina			
7371 GT		7371 GT	275	GTB	Berlinetta	Scaglietti			U.S.A.
	*3 carb. Short nose.*								
7373 GT		7373 GT	275	GTB	Berlinetta	Scaglietti			
7375 GT		7375 GT	330	GT	2 + 2	Pininfarina			
7377 GT		7377 GT	330	GT	2 + 2	Pininfarina			
7379 GT		7379 GT	275	GTS	Spyder	Pininfarina			
7381 GT		7381 GT	275	GTB	Berlinetta	Scaglietti			
7383 GT		7383 GT	275	GTS	Spyder	Pininfarina			
7385 GT		7385 GT	275	GTB	Berlinetta	Scaglietti			
7387 GT		7387 GT	330	GT	2 + 2	Pininfarina			
7389 GT		7389 GT	275	GTS	Spyder	Pininfarina			
7391 GT		7391 GT	275	GTB	Berlinetta	Scaglietti			
7393 GT		7393 GT	330	GT	2 + 2	Pininfarina			

Chassis No.	Picture Ref	Engine No.	Type	Model	Body Style	Coach-builder	First Owner	Original Location	Present Location
7395 GT*		7395 GT	275	GTS	Spyder	Pininfarina			U.K.
7397 GT*		7397 GT	275	GTB	Berlinetta	Scaglietti			U.K.
	6 carb. Short nose.								
7399 GT		7399 GT	330	GT	2 + 2	Pininfarina			
7401 GT		7401 GT	275	GTB	Berlinetta	Scaglietti			
	6 carb.								
7403 GT		7403 GT	275	GTS	Spyder	Pininfarina			
7405 GT		7405 GT	330	GT	2 + 2	Pininfarina			
7407 GT*		7407 GT	275 GTB	Competition	Berlinetta	Scaglietti			U.K.
	Built in 1965 as a specially prepared competition car. 6 carb. All aluminium body.								
7409 GT		7409 GT	275	GTS	Spyder	Pininfarina			
7411 GT		7411 GT	330	GT	2 + 2	Pininfarina			
7413 GT*		7413 GT	275	GTB	Berlinetta	Scaglietti			U.K.
	6 carb. Short nose.								
7415 GT		7415 GT	330	GT	2 + 2	Pininfarina			
7417 GT		7417 GT	330	GT	2 + 2	Pininfarina			
7419 GT*		7419 GT	275	GTS	Spyder	Pininfarina			U.K.
7421 GT		7421 GT	275 GTB	Competition	Berlinetta	Scaglietti			U.S.A.
	Built in 1965 as special competition car. 6 carb. All aluminium body.								
7423 GT		7423 GT	275	GTS	Spyder	Pininfarina			U.S.A.
7425 GT		7425 GT	275	GTB	Berlinetta	Scaglietti			
7427 GT		7427 GT	275	GTS	Spyder	Pininfarina			U.S.A.
7429 GT		7429 GT	330	GT	2 + 2	Pininfarina			
7431 GT		7431 GT	275	GTB	Berlinetta	Scaglietti			
7433 GT		7433 GT	330	GT	2 + 2	Pininfarina			
7435 GT		7435 GT	275	GTS	Spyder	Pininfarina			
7437 GT		7437 GT	275 GTB	Competition	Berlinetta	Scaglietti			U.S.A.
	Built in 1965 as special competition car. 6 carb. All aluminium body.								
7439 GT		7439 GT	330	GT	2 + 2	Pininfarina			
7441 GT		7441 GT	275	GTS	Spyder	Pininfarina			
7443 GT		7443 GT	275	GTB	Berlinetta	Scaglietti			
7445 GT		7445 GT	330	GT	2 + 2	Pininfarina			
7447 GT		7447 GT	275	GTB	Berlinetta	Scaglietti			
7449 GT		7449 GT	275	GTS	Spyder	Pininfarina			
7451 GT		7451 GT	275	GTB	Berlinetta	Scaglietti			
7453 GT		7453 GT	275	GTS	Spyder	Pininfarina			
7455 GT		7455 GT	330	GT	2 + 2	Pininfarina			
7457 GT		7457 GT	275	GTS	Spyder	Pininfarina			
7459 GT		7459 GT	275	GTB	Berlinetta	Scaglietti			
7461 GT		7461 GT	330	GT	2 + 2	Pininfarina			
7463 GT		7463 GT	275	GTB	Berlinetta	Scaglietti			U.S.A.
	3 carb. Short nose.								
7465 GT		7465 GT	275	GTS	Spyder	Pininfarina			
7467 GT		7467 GT	330	GT	2 + 2	Pininfarina			
7469 GT		7469 GT	275	GTS	Spyder	Pininfarina			
7471 GT		7471 GT	330	GT	2 + 2	Pininfarina			
7473 GT		7473 GT	275	GTB	Berlinetta	Scaglietti			
7475 GT		7475 GT	275	GTS	Spyder	Pininfarina			
7477 GT		7477 GT	275 GTB	Competition	Berlinetta	Scaglietti			U.S.A.
	Built in 1965 as special competition car. 6 carb. All aluminium body.								
7479 GT		7479 GT	275	GTS	Spyder	Pininfarina			
7481 GT		7481 GT	330	GT	2 + 2	Pininfarina			
7483 GT		7483 GT	330	GT	2 + 2	Pininfarina			
7485 GT		7485 GT	275	GTB	Berlinetta	Scaglietti			
7487 GT		7487 GT	275	GTS	Spyder	Pininfarina			
7489 GT		7489 GT	330	GT	2 + 2	Pininfarina			
7491 GT		7491 GT	275	GTB	Berlinetta	Scaglietti			
7493 GT		7493 GT	275	GTS	Spyder	Pininfarina			
7495 GT		7495 GT	275	GTB	Berlinetta	Scaglietti			
	All aluminium body.								
7497 GT		7497 GT	330	GT	2 + 2	Pininfarina			
7499 GT		7499 GT	365	GT	2 + 2	Pininfarina			
7501 GT		7501 GT	275	GTS	Spyder	Pininfarina			
7503 GT		7503 GT	275	GTB	Berlinetta	Scaglietti			
7505 GT		7505 GT	275	GTS	Spyder	Pininfarina			
7507 GT		7507 GT	330	GT	2 + 2	Pininfarina			
7509 GT		7509 GT	275	GTB	Berlinetta	Scaglietti			U.S.A.
	3 carb. Short nose.								
7511 GT		7511 GT	275	GTB	Berlinetta	Scaglietti			
7513 GT		7513 GT	275	GTS	Spyder	Pininfarina			
7515 GT		7515 GT	330	GT	2 + 2	Pininfarina			
7517 GT*		7517 GT	275 GTB	Competition	Berlinetta	Scaglietti			U.K.
	Built in 1965 as special competition car. 6 carb. All aluminium body.								
7519 GT		7519 GT	330	GT	2 + 2	Pininfarina			

Chassis No.	Picture Ref	Engine No.	Type	Model	Body Style	Coach-builder	First Owner	Original Location	Present Location
7521 GT		7521 GT	275	GTS	Spyder	Pininfarina			U.S.A.
7523 GT		7523 GT	275	GTB	Berlinetta	Scaglietti			
7525 GT		7525 GT	275	GTS	Spyder	Pininfarina			
7527 GT		7527 GT	330	GT	2 + 2	Pininfarina			
7529 GT		7529 GT	275	GTB	Berlinetta	Scaglietti			
7531 GT		7531 GT	275	GTS	Spyder	Pininfarina			
7533 GT		7533 GT	330	GT	2 + 2	Pininfarina			
7535 GT		7535 GT	275	GTB	Berlinetta	Scaglietti			
7537 GT		7537 GT	330	GT	2 + 2	Pininfarina			
7539 GT		7539 GT	275	GTB	Berlinetta	Scaglietti			
7541 GT		7541 GT	275	GTS	Spyder	Pininfarina			
7543 GT		7543 GT	275	GTS	Spyder	Pininfarina			
7545 GT*		7545 GT	275 GTB	Competition	Berlinetta	Scaglietti			Australia
	Built in 1965 as a special competition car. 6 carb. All aluminium body.								
7547 GT		7547 GT	330	GT	2 + 2	Pininfarina			
7549 GT		7549 GT	275	GTS	Spyder	Pininfarina			
7551 GT		7551 GT	275	GTB	Berlinetta	Scaglietti			
	Prototype fibreglass floor panels.								
7553 GT		7553 GT	330	GT	2 + 2	Pininfarina			
7555 GT		7555 GT	275	GTB	Berlinetta	Scaglietti			France
	3 carb. Short nose.								
7557 GT		7557 GT	330	GT	2 + 2	Pininfarina			
7559 GT		7559 GT	275	GTS	Spyder	Pininfarina			
7561 GT		7561 GT	275	GTB	Berlinetta	Scaglietti			
7563 GT		7563 GT	275	GTS	Spyder	Pininfarina			
7565 GT		7565 GT	275	GTB	Berlinetta	Scaglietti			
7567 GT		7567 GT	330	GT	2 + 2	Pininfarina			U.S.A.
7569 GT*		7569 GT	275	GTS	Spyder	Pininfarina			U.K.
7571 GT		7571 GT	275	GTS	Spyder	Pininfarina			
7573 GT		7573 GT	275	GTS	Spyder	Pininfarina			
	Believed to be Paris Salon show car.								
7575 GT		7575 GT	330	GT	2 + 2	Pininfarina			
7577 GT		7577 GT	275 GTB	Competition	Berlinetta	Scaglietti			U.S.A.
	Built in 1965 as special competition car. Also reported as possibly having a steel body. 6 carb. All aluminium body.								
7579 GT		7579 GT	275	GTB	Berlinetta	Scaglietti			
7581 GT		7581 GT	330	GT	2 + 2	Pininfarina			
1966									
7583 GT		7583 GT	275	GTS	Spyder	Pininfarina			
7585 GT*		7585 GT	275	GTS	Spyder	Pininfarina			U.K.
7587 GT		7587 GT	275	GTB	Berlinetta	Scaglietti			Germany
	3 carb. Short nose.								
7589 GT		7589 GT	330	GT	2 + 2	Pininfarina			
7591 GT		7591 GT	275	GTB	Berlinetta	Scaglietti			
	Might be 330GT.								
7593 GT		7593 GT	275	GTB	Berlinetta	Scaglietti			
7595 GT		7595 GT	330	GT	2 + 2	Pininfarina			
7597GT*		7597GT	275	GTB	Berlinetta	Scaglietti			U.K.
7599 GT		7599 GT	275	GTS	Spyder	Pininfarina			
7601 GT		7601 GT	330	GT	2 + 2	Pininfarina			
7603 GT		7603 GT	275	GTB	Berlinetta	Scaglietti			
7605 GT		7605 GT	275	GTS	Spyder	Pininfarina			
7607 GT		7607 GT	330	GT	2 + 2	Pininfarina			
7609 GT		7609 GT	275	GTB	Berlinetta	Scaglietti			
7611 GT		7611 GT	275	GTS	Spyder	Pininfarina			
7613 GT		7613 GT	330	GT	2 + 2	Pininfarina			
7615 GT		7615 GT	275	GTS	Spyder	Pininfarina			
7617 GT		7617 GT	275	GTB	Berlinetta	Scaglietti			
7619 GT		7619 GT	275	GTS	Spyder	Pininfarina			U.S.A.
7621 GT		7621 GT	330	GT	2 + 2	Pininfarina			
7623 GT		7623 GT	275 GTB	Competition	Berlinetta	Scaglietti			U.S.A.
	Built in 1965 as special competition car. 6 carb. All aluminium body.								
7625 GT		7625 GT	330	GT	2 + 2	Pininfarina			
7627 GT		7627 GT	275	GTS	Spyder	Pininfarina			
7629 GT		7629 GT	275	GTB	Berlinetta	Scaglietti			Japan
	3 carb. Short nose.								
7631 GT		7631 GT	275	GTS	Spyder	Pininfarina			
7633 GT		7633 GT	275	GTB	Berlinetta	Scaglietti			
7635 GT		7635 GT	275	GTS	Spyder	Pininfarina	Luigi Chinetti	U.S.A.	U.S.A.
	Appeared on cover of Road & Track, September, 1966.								
7637 GT		7637 GT	275	GTB	Berlinetta	Scaglietti			
7639 GT		7639 GT	275	GTS	Spyder	Pininfarina			
7641 GT		7641 GT	275 GTB	Competition	Berlinetta	Scaglietti			U.S.A.
	Built in 1965 as special competition car. 6 carb. All aluminium body.								
7643 GT		7643 GT	275	GTS	Spyder	Pininfarina			

Chassis No.	Picture Ref	Engine No.	Type	Model	Body Style	Coach-builder	First Owner	Original Location	Present Location
7645 GT		7645 GT	275	GTB	Berlinetta	Scaglietti			
7647 GT*		7647 GT	330	GT	2 + 2	Pininfarina	Maranello Conc.	U.K.	U.K.
7649 GT		7649 GT	275	GTS	Spyder	Pininfarina			
7651 GT		7651 GT	275	GTB	Berlinetta	Scaglietti			U.S.A.
7653 GT		7653 GT	275	GTS	Spyder	Pininfarina			
7655 GT		7655 GT	275	GTS	Spyder	Pininfarina			U.S.A.
7657 GT		7657 GT	275	GTB	Berlinetta	Scaglietti			
7659 GT		7659 GT	275	GTS	Spyder	Pininfarina			U.S.A.
7661 GT		7661 GT	275	GTB	Berlinetta	Scaglietti			
7663 GT*		7663 GT	330	GT	2 + 2	Pininfarina	Maranello Conc.	U.K.	U.K.
7665 GT		7665 GT	275	GTB	Berlinetta	Scaglietti			
7667 GT		7667 GT	275	GTS	Spyder	Pininfarina			
7669 GT		7669 GT	330	GT	2 + 2	Pininfarina			
7671 GT		7671 GT	275	GTS	Spyder	Pininfarina			
7673 GT		7673 GT	330	GT	2 + 2	Pininfarina			
7675 GT		7675 GT	275	GTB	Berlinetta	Scaglietti			
7677 GT		7677 GT	275	GTB	Berlinetta	Scaglietti			
7679 GT		7679 GT	330	GT	2 + 2	Pininfarina			
7681 GT*		7681 GT	275	GTS	Spyder	Pininfarina	Maranello Conc.	U.K.	U.K.
7683 GT		7683 GT	275	GTB	Berlinetta	Scaglietti			U.S.A.
7685 GT*		7685 GT	330	GT	2 + 2	Pininfarina	Maranello Conc.	U.K.	U.K.
7687 GT		7687 GT	330	GT	2 + 2	Pininfarina			
7689 GT		7689 GT	275	GTB	Berlinetta	Scaglietti			U.S.A.
7691 GT		7691 GT	275	GTS	Spyder	Pininfarina			
7693 GT		7693 GT	330	GT	2 + 2	Pininfarina			
7695 GT*		7695 GT	330	GT	2 + 2	Pininfarina	Maranello Conc.	U.K.	U.K..
7697 GT		7697 GT	330	GT	2 + 2	Pininfarina			
7699 GT*		7699 GT	275	GTB	Berlinetta	Scaglietti			U.K.
7701 GT		7701 GT	275	GTS	Spyder	Pininfarina			
7703 GT		7703 GT	330	GT	2 + 2	Pininfarina			
7705 GT		7705 GT	275	GTS	Spyder	Pininfarina			
7707 GT		7707 GT	275	GTB	Berlinetta	Scaglietti			
	Long nose prototype.								
7709 GT		7709 GT	330	GT	2 + 2	Pininfarina			
7711 GT		7711 GT	275	GTB	Berlinetta	Scaglietti			U.S.A.
7713 GT		7713 GT	330	GT	2 + 2	Pininfarina			U.S.A.
7715 GT*		7715 GT	275	GTB	Berlinetta	Scaglietti	Maranello Conc.	U.K.	Germany
7717 GT		7717 GT	330	GT	2 + 2	Pininfarina			
7719 GT		7719 GT	275	GTS	Spyder	Pininfarina			
7721 GT		7721 GT	330	GT	2 + 2	Pininfarina			
7723 GT		7723 GT	275	GTB	Berlinetta	Scaglietti			U.S.A.
7725 GT		7725 GT	330	GT	2 + 2	Pininfarina			U.S.A.
7727 GT		7727 GT	275	GTS	Spyder	Pininfarina			U.S.A.
7729 GT		7729 GT	330	GT	2 + 2	Pininfarina			
7731 GT		7731 GT	275	GTS	Spyder	Pininfarina			
7733 GT		7733 GT	275	GTB	Berlinetta	Scaglietti			Switzerland
7735 GT		7735 GT	275	GTB	Berlinetta	Scaglietti			
7737 GT		7737 GT	275	GTS	Spyder	Pininfarina			
7739 GT		7739 GT	275	GTB	Berlinetta	Scaglietti			
7741 GT		7741 GT	275	GTS	Spyder	Pininfarina			
7743 GT		7743 GT	275	GTB	Berlinetta	Scaglietti			
7745 GT		7745 GT	275	GTS	Spyder	Pininfarina			
7747 GT		7747 GT	275	GTB	Berlinetta	Scaglietti			
7749 GT		7749 GT	275	GTS	Spyder	Pininfarina			
7751 GT		7751 GT	275	GTB	Berlinetta	Scaglietti			
7753 GT		7753 GT	275	GTS	Spyder	Pininfarina			
	Shown at the 1964 Turin Motor Show.								
7755 GT		7755 GT	330	GT	2 + 2	Pininfarina			
7757 GT		7757 GT	330	GT	2 + 2	Pininfarina			
7759 GT		7759 GT	330	GT	2 + 2	Pininfarina			
7761 GT		7761 GT	330	GT	2 + 2	Pininfarina			
7763 GT		7763 GT	330	GT	2 + 2	Pininfarina			
7765 GT		7765 GT	275	GTB	Berlinetta	Scaglietti			
7767 GT		7767 GT	275	GTS	Spyder	Pininfarina			
7769 GT		7769 GT	275	GTB	Berlinetta	Scaglietti			
7771 GT*		7771 GT	275	GTS	Spyder	Pininfarina	Maranello Conc.	U.K.	U.K.
7773 GT		7773 GT	275	GTB	Berlinetta	Scaglietti			
7775 GT		7775 GT	330	GT	2 + 2	Pininfarina			
7777 GT		7777 GT	330	GT	2 + 2	Pininfarina			
7779 GT		7779 GT	275	GTS	Spyder	Pininfarina			
7781 GT		7781 GT	275	GTB	Berlinetta	Scaglietti			
7783 GT		7783 GT	275	GTS	Spyder	Pininfarina			
7785 GT		7785 GT	275	GTB	Berlinetta	Scaglietti			U.S.A.
7787 GT		7787 GT	275	GTS	Spyder	Pininfarina			

Chassis No.	Picture Ref	Engine No.	Type	Model	Body Style	Coach-builder	First Owner	Original Location	Present Location
7789 GT*		7789 GT	275	GTB	Berlinetta	Scaglietti	Maranello Conc.	U.K.	U.K.
7791 GT*		7791 GT	275	GTS	Spyder	Pininfarina	Maranello Conc.	U.K.	U.K..
	Shown at the 1965 London Motor Show.								
7793 GT		7793 GT	275	GTB	Berlinetta	Scaglietti			
7795 GT*		7795 GT	275	GTS	Spyder	Pininfarina			U.S.A.
	6 carb.Sold to U.S.A..								
7797 GT*		7797 GT	275	GTB	Berlinetta	Scaglietti	Maranello Conc.	U.K.	U.K.
7799 GT		7799 GT	275	GTS	Spyder	Pininfarina			
7801 GT		7801 GT	330	GT	2 + 2	Pininfarina			
7803 GT		7803 GT	275	GTB	Berlinetta	Scaglietti			
7805 GT		7805 GT	275	GTS	Spyder	Pininfarina			
7807 GT		7807 GT	275	GTB	Berlinetta	Scaglietti			
7809 GT		7809 GT	275	GTB	Berlinetta	Scaglietti			U.S.A.
	6 carb.Long nose.All aluminium body.								
7811 GT		7811 GT	275	GTS	Spyder	Pininfarina			
7813 GT		7813 GT	275	GTS	Spyder	Pininfarina			
7815 GT		7815 GT	330	GT	2 + 2	Pininfarina			U.S.A.
7817 SF		7817 SF	500 Series II	Superfast	Coupé	Pininfarina	?	U.S.A.	
	Sold on 11/11/65.								
7819 GT		7819 GT	275	GTB	Berlinetta	Scaglietti			Holland
7821 GT		7821 GT	275	GTB	Berlinetta	Scaglietti			
7823 GT		7823 GT	330	GT	2 + 2	Pininfarina			
7825 GT		7825 GT	275	GTS	Spyder	Pininfarina			
7827 GT		7827 GT	275	GTB	Berlinetta	Scaglietti			U.S.A.
	The last short nose built.								
7829 GT*		7829 GT	330	GT	2 + 2	Pininfarina	Maranello Conc.	U.K.	U.K.
7831 GT*		7831 GT	330	GT	2 + 2	Pininfarina	Maranello Conc.	U.K.	U.K.
7833 GT		7833 GT	275	GTS	Spyder	Pininfarina			
7835 GT		7835 GT	275	GTS	Spyder	Pininfarina			
7837 GT		7837 GT	330	GT	2 + 2	Pininfarina			
7839 GT		7839 GT	275	GTS	Spyder	Pininfarina			
7841 GT		7841 GT	275	GTS	Spyder	Pininfarina			
7843 GT*		7843 GT	330	GT	2 + 2	Pininfarina	Maranello Conc.	U.K.	U.K.
7845 GT*		7845 GT	275	GTS	Spyder	Pininfarina			U.S.A.
	6 carb.Sold to U.S.A..								
7847 GT		7847 GT	275	GTS	Spyder	Pininfarina			
7849 GT*		7849 GT	330	GT	2 + 2	Pininfarina			U.K.
7851 GT		7851 GT	330	GT	2 + 2	Pininfarina			
7853 GT		7853 GT	275	GTS	Spyder	Pininfarina			
7855 GT		7855 GT	275	GTB	Berlinetta	Scaglietti			
7857 GT		7857 GT	330	GT	2 + 2	Pininfarina			
7859 GT		7859 GT	330	GT	2 + 2	Pininfarina			
7861 GT		7861 GT	275	GTS	Spyder	Pininfarina			
7863 GT		7863 GT	330	GT	2 + 2	Pininfarina			
7865 GT		7865 GT	275	GTS	Spyder	Pininfarina			
7867 GT		7867 GT	275	GTS	Spyder	Pininfarina			
7869 GT		7869 GT	275	GTB	Berlinetta	Scaglietti			
7871 GT		7871 GT	275	GTB	Berlinetta	Scaglietti			
7873 GT		7873 GT	275	GTB	Berlinetta	Scaglietti			U.S.A.
7875 GT		7875 GT	330	GT	2 + 2	Pininfarina			
7877 GT		7877 GT	330	GT	2 + 2	Pininfarina			
7879 GT		7879 GT	330	GT	2 + 2	Pininfarina			
7881 GT		7881 GT	275	GTB	Berlinetta	Scaglietti			
7883 GT		7883 GT	330	GT	2 + 2	Pininfarina			
7885 GT		7885 GT	275	GTS	Spyder	Pininfarina			
7887 GT		7887 GT	275	GTB	Berlinetta	Scaglietti			
7889 GT		7889 GT	330	GT	2 + 2	Pininfarina			
7891 GT		7891 GT	275	GTS	Spyder	Pininfarina			
7893 GT		7893 GT	275	GTB	Berlinetta	Scaglietti			
7895 GT		7895 GT	330	GT	2 + 2	Pininfarina			
7897 GT		7897 GT	275	GTS	Spyder	Pininfarina			
7899 GT		7899 GT	275	GTB	Berlinetta	Scaglietti			
7901 GT		7901 GT	330	GT	2 + 2	Pininfarina			
7903 GT		7903 GT	275	GTS	Spyder	Pininfarina			
7905 GT		7905 GT	275	GTB	Berlinetta	Scaglietti			France
7907 GT		7907 GT	275	GTS	Spyder	Pininfarina			
7909 GT		7909 GT	330	GT	2 + 2	Pininfarina			
7911 GT		7911 GT	275	GTB	Berlinetta	Scaglietti			
7913 GT*		7913 GT	275	GTS	Spyder	Pininfarina			U.S.A.
	6 carb.Sold to U.S.A..								
7915 GT		7915 GT	275	GTS	Spyder	Pininfarina			
7917 GT		7917 GT	330	GT	2 + 2	Pininfarina			
7919 GT		7919 GT	330	GT	2 + 2	Pininfarina			
7921 GT		7921 GT	275	GTS	Spyder	Pininfarina			

Chassis No.	Picture Ref	Engine No.	Type	Model	Body Style	Coach-builder	First Owner	Original Location	Present Location
7923 GT		7923 GT	275	GTB	Berlinetta	Scaglietti			U.S.A.
7925 GT		7925 GT	330	GT	2 + 2	Pininfarina			
7927 GT		7927 GT	275	GTB	Berlinetta	Scaglietti			
	All aluminium body.								
7929 GT		7929 GT	275	GTS	Spyder	Pininfarina			U.S.A.
7931 GT		7931 GT	275	GTB	Berlinetta	Scaglietti			
7933 GT		7933 GT	275	GTB	Berlinetta	Scaglietti			
7935 GT		7935 GT	275	GTS	Spyder	Pininfarina			
7937 GT		7937 GT	275	GTS	Spyder	Pininfarina			
7939 GT		7939 GT	275	GTS	Spyder	Pininfarina			
7941 GT		7941 GT	330	GT	2 + 2	Pininfarina			
7943 GT		7943 GT	330	GT	2 + 2	Pininfarina			
7945 GT		7945 GT	275	GTS	Spyder	Pininfarina			
7947 GT		7947 GT	330	GT	2 + 2	Pininfarina			
7949 GT		7949 GT	275	GTS	Spyder	Pininfarina			
7951 GT		7951 GT	330	GT	2 + 2	Pininfarina			U.S.A.
7953 GT		7953 GT	275	GTB	Berlinetta	Scaglietti			U.S.A.
	6 carb.All aluminium body.								
7955 GT		7955 GT	275	GTB	Berlinetta	Scaglietti			
	6 carb.								
7957 GT		7957 GT	275	GTS	Spyder	Pininfarina			
7959 GT		7959 GT	275	GTB	Berlinetta	Scaglietti			Switzerland
7961 GT		7961 GT	275	GTB	Berlinetta	Scaglietti			U.S.A.
	6 carb. All aluminium body.								
7963 GT	P1/271	7963 GT	330	2 + 2	Station Wagon	Vignale			U.S.A.
	Shown at the 1968 Turin Motor Show.A one off prototype built on a 330GT 2+2 chassis. Built to the order of Luigi Chinetti based on a design by American Bob Peak.								
7965 GT		7965 GT	275	GTS	Spyder	Pininfarina			
7967 GT		7967 GT	275	GTS	Spyder	Pininfarina			
7969 GT		7969 GT	275	GTB	Berlinetta	Scaglietti			
7971 GT		7971 GT	275	GTB	Berlinetta	Scaglietti			
7973 GT		7973 GT	330	GT	2 + 2	Pininfarina			
7975 SA		7975 SA	500 Series II	Superfast	Coupé	Pininfarina	Shah of Iran	Iran	U.K.
	Sold on 27/11/65.								
7977 GT		7977 GT	275	GTS	Spyder	Pininfarina			
7979 GT		7979 GT	330	GT	2 + 2	Pininfarina			
7981 GT		7981 GT	275	GTB	Berlinetta	Scaglietti			
7983 GT		7983 GT	275	GTB	Berlinetta	Scaglietti			U.S.A.
	All aluminium body.								
7985 GT		7985 GT	275	GTS	Spyder	Pininfarina			
7987 GT		7987 GT	275	GTS	Spyder	Pininfarina			U.S.A.
7989 GT		7989 GT	275	GTS	Spyder	Pininfarina			U.S.A.
7991 GT		7991 GT	275	GTB	Berlinetta	Scaglietti			Germany
	All aluminium body.								
7993 GT		7993 GT	275	GTB	Berlinetta	Scaglietti			Switzerland
	6 carb.All aluminium body.								
7995 GT		7995 GT	275	GTB	Berlinetta	Scaglietti	Shah of Iran	Iran	U.S.A.
	6 carb.All aluminium body.								
7997 GT*		7997 GT	275	GTS	Spyder	Pininfarina			U.S.A.
	6 carb.Sold to U.S.A..								
7999 GT		7999 GT	275	GTS	Spyder	Pininfarina			
8001 GT		8001 GT	275	GTS	Spyder	Pininfarina			
8003 GT		8003 GT	275	GTS	Spyder	Pininfarina			
8005 GT		8005 GT	275	GTS	Spyder	Pininfarina			
8007 GT*		8007 GT	275	GTS	Spyder	Pininfarina			U.S.A.
	6 carb.Sold to U.S.A..								
8009 GT		8009 GT	275	GTS	Spyder	Pininfarina			
8011 GT		8011 GT	275	GTB	Berlinetta	Scaglietti			
8013 GT		8013 GT	275	GTB	Berlinetta	Scaglietti			
8015 GT		8015 GT	275	GTS	Spyder	Pininfarina			U.S.A.
8017 GT		8017 GT	275	GTB	Berlinetta	Scaglietti			
8019 SF		8019 SF	500 Series II	Superfast	Coupé	Pininfarina			U.S.A.
	Shown at the 1966 Brussels Motor Show.								
8021 GT		8021 GT	275	GTB	Berlinetta	Scaglietti			
8023 GT		8023 GT	275	GTB	Berlinetta	Scaglietti			
	Maybe 330GT 2+2.								
8025 GT		8025 GT	330	GT	2 + 2	Pininfarina			U.S.A.
8027 GT		8027 GT	275	GTB	Berlinetta	Scaglietti			
	6 carb.								
8029 GT		8029 GT	275	GTB	Berlinetta	Scaglietti			
	6 carb.All aluminium body.								
8031 GT		8031 GT	275	GTB	Berlinetta	Scaglietti			
8033 GT		8033 GT	275	GTB	Berlinetta	Scaglietti			
8035 GT		8035 GT	275	GTB	Berlinetta	Scaglietti			

Chassis No.	Picture Ref	Engine No.	Type	Model	Body Style	Coach-builder	First Owner	Original Location	Present Location
8037 GT		8037 GT	275	GTB	Berlinetta	Scaglietti			
8039 GT		8039 GT	275	GTB	Berlinetta	Scaglietti			
8041 GT		8041 GT	275	GTB	Berlinetta	Scaglietti			France
8043 GT		8043 GT	275	GTB	Berlinetta	Scaglietti			
8045 GT		8045 GT	275	GTB	Berlinetta	Scaglietti			
	All aluminium body.								
8047 GT*		8047 GT	275	GTB	Berlinetta	Scaglietti	Maranello Conc.	U.K.	U.K.
	Shown at the 1965 London Motor Show. 6 carb. All aluminium body.								
8049 GT		8049 GT	275	GTB	Berlinetta	Scaglietti			
	All aluminium body.								
8051 GT		8051 GT	275	GTB	Berlinetta	Scaglietti			U.S.A.
	6 carb. All aluminium body.								
8053 GT		8053 GT	275	GTB	Berlinetta	Scaglietti			U.S.A.
	6 carb. All aluminium body.								
8055 GT*		8055 GT	275	GTB	Berlinetta	Scaglietti	Maranello Conc.	U.K.	Australia
	6 carb. All aluminium body.								
8057 GT		8057 GT	275	GTB	Berlinetta	Scaglietti			
	All aluminium body.								
8059 GT		8059 GT	275	GTB	Berlinetta	Scaglietti			
	All aluminium body.								
8061 GT		8061 GT	275	GTB	Berlinetta	Scaglietti			
	All aluminium body.								
8063 GT		8063 GT	275	GTB	Berlinetta	Scaglietti			
8065 GT		8065 GT	275	GTB	Berlinetta	Scaglietti			France
	All aluminium body.								
8067 GT		8067 GT	275	GTB	Berlinetta	Scaglietti			U.S.A.
	6 carb. All aluminium body.								
8069 GT		8069 GT	275	GTB	Berlinetta	Scaglietti			
	All aluminium body.								
8071 GT*		8071 GT	275	GTB	Berlinetta	Scaglietti	Maranello Conc.	U.K.	U.K.
	6 carb.								
8073 GT		8073 GT	330	GT	2 + 2	Pininfarina			
8075 GT		8075 GT	330	GT	2 + 2	Pininfarina			
8077 GT*		8077 GT	275	GTB	Berlinetta	Scaglietti	Maranello Conc.	U.K.	U.K.
	6 carb. All aluminium body.								
8079 GT		8079 GT	275	GTB	Berlinetta	Scaglietti			U.S.A.
	6 carb. All aluminium body.								
8081 GT		8081 GT	275	GTB	Berlinetta	Scaglietti			U.S.A.
	All aluminium body.								
8083 SF		8083 SF	500 Series II	Superfast	Coupé	Pininfarina	Bailard		U.S.A.
	Sold on 10/12/65.								
8085 GT		8085 GT	275	GTB	Berlinetta	Scaglietti			
8087 GT		8087 GT	275	GTB	Berlinetta	Scaglietti			
	All aluminium body.								
8089 GT		8089 GT	275	GTB	Berlinetta	Scaglietti			
8091 GT		8091 GT	275	GTB	Berlinetta	Scaglietti			
8093 GT		8093 GT	330	GT	2 + 2	Pininfarina			
8095 GT		8095 GT	330	GT	2 + 2	Pininfarina			
8097 GT*		8097 GT	330	GT	2 + 2	Pininfarina	Maranello Conc.	U.K.	U.K.
8099 GT		8099 GT	330	GT	2 + 2	Pininfarina			U.S.A.
8101 GT		8101 GT	330	GT	2 + 2	Pininfarina			
8103 GT		8103 GT	330	GT	2 + 2	Pininfarina			
8105 GT*		8105 GT	330	GT	2 + 2	Pininfarina			U.K.
8107 GT		8107 GT	330	GT	2 + 2	Pininfarina			
8109 GT		8109 GT	330	GT	2 + 2	Pininfarina			
8111 GT		8111 GT	275	GTB	Berlinetta	Scaglietti			
	All aluminium body.								
8113 GT		8113 GT	275	GTB	Berlinetta	Scaglietti			
	All aluminium body.								
8115 GT*		8115 GT	330	GT	2 + 2	Pininfarina			U.K.
8117 GT		8117 GT	275	GTB	Berlinetta	Scaglietti			U.S.A.
	All aluminium body.								
8119 GT		8119 GT	275	GTB	Berlinetta	Scaglietti			
8121 GT		8121 GT	275	GTB	Berlinetta	Scaglietti			
	6 carb. All aluminium body.								
8123 GT		8123 GT	275	GTB	Berlinetta	Scaglietti			Switzerland
	All aluminium body.								
8125 GT		8125 GT	275	GTB	Berlinetta	Scaglietti			U.S.A.
	All aluminium body.								
8127 GT		8127 GT	330	GT	2 + 2	Pininfarina			
8129 GT		8129 GT	330	GT	2 + 2	Pininfarina			
8131 GT		8131 GT	330	GT	2 + 2	Pininfarina			
8133 GT*		8133 GT	330	GT	2 + 2	Pininfarina	Maranello Conc.	U.K.	U.K.

Chassis No.	Picture Ref	Engine No.	Type	Model	Body Style	Coach-builder	First Owner	Original Location	Present Location
8135 GT		8135 GT	275	GTB	Berlinetta	Scaglietti			U.S.A.
	All aluminium body.								
8137 GT		8137 GT	275	GTB	Berlinetta	Scaglietti			U.S.A.
	6 carb. All aluminium body.								
8139 GT*		8139 GT	330	GT	2 + 2	Pininfarina	Maranello Conc.	U.K.	U.K.
8141 GT		8141 GT	330	GT	2 + 2	Pininfarina			
8143 GT		8143 GT	275	GTB	Berlinetta	Scaglietti			U.S.A.
	All aluminium body.								
8145 GT		8145 GT	275	GTB	Berlinetta	Scaglietti			
8147 GT		8147 GT	330	GT	2 + 2	Pininfarina			
8149 GT		8149 GT	330	GT	2 + 2	Pininfarina			
8151 GT		8151 GT	275	GTB	Berlinetta	Scaglietti			Holland
8153 GT		8153 GT	330	GT	2 + 2	Pininfarina			
8155 GT		8155 GT	275	GTB	Berlinetta	Scaglietti			
8157 GT		8157 GT	275	GTB	Berlinetta	Scaglietti			U.S.A.
	6 carb. All aluminium body.								
8159 GT		8159 GT	275	GTB	Berlinetta	Scaglietti			U.S.A.
	All aluminium body.								
8161 GT		8161 GT	330	GT	2 + 2	Pininfarina			
8163 GT		8163 GT	275	GTB	Berlinetta	Scaglietti			
8165 GT		8165 GT	250	LM	Berlinetta	Scaglietti	Filipinetti	CH	U.K.
	Last LM								
8167 GT		8167 GT	330	GT	2 + 2	Pininfarina			U.S.A.
8169 GT		8169 GT	330	GT	2 + 2	Pininfarina			U.S.A.
8171 GT		8171 GT	330	GT	2 + 2	Pininfarina			
8173 GT		8173 GT	330	GT	2 + 2	Pininfarina			
8175 GT		8175 GT	330	GT	2 + 2	Pininfarina			
8177 GT		8177 GT	330	GT	2 + 2	Pininfarina			
8179 GT*		8179 GT	275	GTB	Berlinetta	Scaglietti			South Africa
8181 GT*		8181 GT	275	GTB	Berlinetta	Scaglietti	Maranello Conc.	U.K.	U.K.
	6 carb.								
8183 GT		8183 GT	330	GT	2 + 2	Pininfarina			U.S.A.
8185 GT		8185 GT	330	GT	2 + 2	Pininfarina			
8187 GT		8187 GT	275	GTB	Berlinetta	Scaglietti			
8189 GT		8189 GT	330	GT	2 + 2	Pininfarina			U.S.A.
8191 GT		8191 GT	275	GTB	Berlinetta	Scaglietti			U.K.
	All aluminium body.								
8193 GT		8193 GT	275	GTB	Berlinetta	Scaglietti			Switzerland
8195 GT		8195 GT	330	GT	2 + 2	Pininfarina			
8197 GT		8197 GT	330	GT	2 + 2	Pininfarina			
8199 GT		8199 GT	275	GTB	Berlinetta	Scaglietti			
8201 GT		8201 GT	330	GT	2 + 2	Pininfarina			U.S.A.
8203 GT		8203 GT	330	GT	2 + 2	Pininfarina			
8205 GT		8205 GT	330	GT	2 + 2	Pininfarina			U.S.A.
8207 GT		8207 GT	330	GT	2 + 2	Pininfarina			U.S.A.
8209 GT		8209 GT	275	GTB	Berlinetta	Scaglietti			
8211 GT		8211 GT	330	GT	2 + 2	Pininfarina			
8213 GT		8213 GT	275	GTB	Berlinetta	Scaglietti			U.S.A.
	All aluminium body.								
8215 GT		8215 GT	330	GT	2 + 2	Pininfarina			U.S.A.
8217 GT		8217 GT	330	GT	2 + 2	Pininfarina			
8219 GT*		8219 GT	275	GTB	Berlinetta	Scaglietti	Maranello Conc.	U.K.	U.K.
	All aluminium body.								
8221 GT*		8221 GT	275	GTB	Berlinetta	Scaglietti			U.K.
	6 carb.								
8223 GT		8223 GT	330	GT	2 + 2	Pininfarina			
8225 GT		8225 GT	275	GTB	Berlinetta	Scaglietti			U.S.A.
	6 carb. All aluminium body.								
8227 GT		8227 GT	330	GT	2 + 2	Pininfarina			
8229 GT		8229 GT	275	GTB	Berlinetta	Scaglietti			
	6 carb.								
8231 GT		8231 GT	330	GT	2 + 2	Pininfarina			U.S.A.
8233 GT		8233 GT	275	GTB	Berlinetta	Scaglietti			U.S.A.
	6 carb.								
8235 GT		8235 GT	330	GT	2 + 2	Pininfarina			
8237 GT		8237 GT	330	GT	2 + 2	Pininfarina			
8239 GT		8239 GT	330	GT	2 + 2	Pininfarina			
8241 GT*		8241 GT	275	GTB	Berlinetta	Scaglietti			U.K.
8243 GT		8243 GT	330	GT	2 + 2	Pininfarina			
8245 GT		8245 GT	330	GT	2 + 2	Pininfarina			U.S.A.
8247 GT		8247 GT	275	GTB	Berlinetta	Scaglietti			
	All aluminium body.								
8249 GT		8249 GT	275	GTB	Berlinetta	Scaglietti			U.S.A.
	6 carb. All aluminium body.								

Chassis No.	Picture Ref	Engine No.	Type	Model	Body Style	Coach-builder	First Owner	Original Location	Present Location
8251 GT		8251 GT	330	GT	2 + 2	Pininfarina			
8253 SF		8253 SF	500 Series II	Superfast	Coupé	Pininfarina	Friden	U.S.A.	U.S.A.
	Sold on 20/1/66.								
8255 GT		8255 GT	275	GTB	Berlinetta	Scaglietti			
8257 GT		8257 GT	330	GT	2 + 2	Pininfarina			
8259 GT		8259 GT	275	GTB	Berlinetta	Scaglietti			Switzerland
	6 carb.All aluminium body.								
8261 GT		8261 GT	330	GT	2 + 2	Pininfarina			
8263 GT		8263 GT	275	GTB	Berlinetta	Scaglietti			U.S.A.
	6 carb.All aluminium body.								
8265 GT		8265 GT	330	GT	2 + 2	Pininfarina			
8267 GT		8267 GT	330	GT	2 + 2	Pininfarina			
8269 GT		8269 GT	330	GT	2 + 2	Pininfarina			
8271 GT		8271 GT	330	GT	2 + 2	Pininfarina			
8273 SF		8273 SF	500 Series II	Superfast	Coupé	Pininfarina	Knowles		U.S.A.
	Sold on 31/1/66.								
8275 GT		8275 GT	330	GT	2 + 2	Pininfarina			
8277 GT*		8277 GT	275	GTB	Berlinetta	Scaglietti	Maranello Conc.	U.K.	U.K.
8279 GT		8279 GT	330	GT	2 + 2	Pininfarina			U.S.A.
8281 GT		8281 GT	330	GT	2 + 2	Pininfarina			
8283 GT		8283 GT	330	GT	2 + 2	Pininfarina			
8285 GT		8285 GT	330	GT	2 + 2	Pininfarina			U.S.A.
8287 GT		8287 GT	275	GTS	Spyder	Pininfarina			
8289 GT		8289 GT	330	GT	2 + 2	Pininfarina			
8291 GT		8291 GT	330	GT	2 + 2	Pininfarina			
8293 GT		8293 GT	330	GT	2 + 2	Pininfarina			
8295 GT		8295 GT	330	GT	2 + 2	Pininfarina			
8297 GT		8297 GT	275	GTB	Berlinetta	Scaglietti			Holland
	6 carb.								
8299 SF		8299 SF	500 Series II	Superfast	Coupé	Pininfarina			
	Sold on 8/2/66.Shown at the 1966 New York Auto Show.								
8301 GT		8301 GT	330	GT	2 + 2	Pininfarina			
8303 GT		8303 GT	275	GTS	Spyder	Pininfarina			
8305 GT		8305 GT	275	GTB	Berlinetta	Scaglietti			
8307 GT		8307 GT	330	GT	2 + 2	Pininfarina			
8309 GT		8309 GT	330	GT	2 + 2	Pininfarina			
8311 GT		8311 GT	275	GTB	Berlinetta	Scaglietti			U.S.A.
	6 carb.All aluminium body.Torque tube.								
8313 GT		8313 GT	275	GTS	Spyder	Pininfarina			
8315 GT		8315 GT	330	GT	2 + 2	Pininfarina			
8317 GT		8317 GT	275	GTB	Berlinetta	Scaglietti			
8319 GT		8319 GT	330	GT	2 + 2	Pininfarina			
8321 GT		8321 GT	330	GT	2 + 2	Pininfarina			
8323 GT		8323 GT	275	GTB	Berlinetta	Scaglietti			
8325 GT		8325 GT	330	GT	2 + 2	Pininfarina			U.S.A.
8327 GT		8327 GT	275	GTB	Berlinetta	Scaglietti			
8329 GT		8329 GT	330	GTC	Coupé	Pininfarina			
	Geneva Show								
8331 GT		8331 GT	330	GT	2 + 2	Pininfarina			
8333 GT		8333 GT	330	GT	2 + 2	Pininfarina			
8335 GT		8335 GT	275	GTS	Spyder	Pininfarina			
8337 GT		8337 GT	275	GTB	Berlinetta	Scaglietti			Holland
	6 carb.								
8339 GT		8339 GT	330	GT	2 + 2	Pininfarina			U.S.A.
8341 GT		8341 GT	275	GTB	Berlinetta	Scaglietti			U.S.A.
	6 carb.								
8343 GT		8343 GT	275	GTB	Berlinetta	Scaglietti			U.S.A.
	6 carb.All aluminium body.								
8345 GT		8345 GT	330	GT	2 + 2	Pininfarina			U.S.A.
8347		8347	365	California	Spyder	Pininfarina	D.Fabbri	Italy	
	Sold on 26/7/66.								
8349 GT		8349 GT	275	GTB	Berlinetta	Scaglietti			U.S.A.
8351 GT		8351 GT	330	GT	2 + 2	Pininfarina			
8353 GT		8353 GT	275	GTS	Spyder	Pininfarina			
8355 GT		8355 GT	275	GTB	Berlinetta	Scaglietti			U.S.A.
8357 GT		8357 GT	330	GT	2 + 2	Pininfarina			
8359 GT		8359 GT	275	GTB	Berlinetta	Scaglietti			U.S.A.
8361 GT		8361 GT	330	GT	2 + 2	Pininfarina			U.S.A.
8363 GT		8363 GT	330	GT	2 + 2	Pininfarina			
8365 GT		8365 GT	275	GTB	Berlinetta	Scaglietti			
8367 GT		8367 GT	330	GT	2 + 2	Pininfarina			
8369 GT		8369 GT	275	GTS	Spyder	Pininfarina			
8371 GT		8371 GT	275	GTB	Berlinetta	Scaglietti			U.K.
8373 GT		8373 GT	330	GT	2 + 2	Pininfarina			

Chassis No.	Picture Ref	Engine No.	Type	Model	Body Style	Coach-builder	First Owner	Original Location	Present Location
8375 GT		8375 GT	275	GTS	Spyder	Pininfarina			
8377 GT*		8377 GT	275	GTB	Berlinetta	Scaglietti	Maranello Conc.	U.K.	U.K.
8379 GT		8379 GT	330	GT	2 + 2	Pininfarina			
8381 GT		8381 GT	275	GTB	Berlinetta	Scaglietti			
8383 GT		8383 GT	330	GT	2 + 2	Pininfarina			
8385 GT		8385 GT	275	GTB	Berlinetta	Scaglietti			U.S.A.
8387 GT		8387 GT	330	GT	2 + 2	Pininfarina			U.S.A.
8389 GT		8389 GT	275	GTB	Berlinetta	Scaglietti			
8391 GT*		8391 GT	275	GTB	Berlinetta	Scaglietti	Maranello Conc.	U.K.	U.K.
8393 GT		8393 GT	330	GT	2 + 2	Pininfarina			
8395 GT		·8395 GT	275	GTB	Berlinetta	Scaglietti			
8397 GT		8397 GT	275	GTS	Spyder	Pininfarina			
8399 GT		8399 GT	330	GT	2 + 2	Pininfarina			
8401 GT		8401 GT	330	GT	2 + 2	Pininfarina			
8403 GT		8403 GT	275	GTB	Berlinetta	Scaglietti			U.S.A.
8405 GT	6 carb.	8405 GT	330	GT	2 + 2	Pininfarina			
8407 GT		8407 GT	275	GTB	Berlinetta	Scaglietti			
8409 GT		8409 GT	330	GT	2 + 2	Pininfarina			
8411 GT		8411 GT	330	GT	2 + 2	Pininfarina			U.S.A.
8413 GT		8413 GT	275	GTB	Berlinetta	Scaglietti			
8415 GT		8415 GT	330	GT	2 + 2	Pininfarina			
8417 GT*		8417 GT	330	GT	2 + 2	Pininfarina	Maranello Conc.	U.K.	U.K.
8419 GT		8419 GT	275	GTB	Berlinetta	Scaglietti			
8421 GT		8421 GT	330	GT	2 + 2	Pininfarina			
8423 GT	6 carb.	8423 GT	275	GTB	Berlinetta	Scaglietti			
8425 GT		8425 GT	330	GT	2 + 2	Pininfarina			
8427 GT		8427 GT	330	GT	2 + 2	Pininfarina			
8429 GT		8429 GT	330	GT	2 + 2	Pininfarina			
8431 GT	6 carb.	8431 GT	275	GTB	Berlinetta	Scaglietti			U.S.A.
8433 GT		8433 GT	330	GT	2 + 2	Pininfarina			
8435 GT		8435 GT	330	GT	2 + 2	Pininfarina			
8437 GT*		8437 GT	330	GT	2 + 2	Pininfarina	Maranello Conc.	U.K.	U.K.
8439 GT		8439 GT	275	GTB	Berlinetta	Scaglietti			
8441 GT		8441 GT	330	GT	2 + 2	Pininfarina			
8443 GT		8443 GT	330	GT	2 + 2	Pininfarina			
8445 GT		8445 GT	275	GTB	Berlinetta	Scaglietti			
8447 GT		8447 GT	330	GT	2 + 2	Pininfarina			U.S.A.
8449 GT		8449 GT	330	GTC	Coupé	Pininfarina			
8451 GT		8451 GT	275	GTB	Berlinetta	Scaglietti			
8453 GT		8453 GT	330	GT	2 + 2	Pininfarina			
8455 GT		8455 GT	275	GTB	Berlinetta	Scaglietti			
8457 GT		8457 GT	275	GTB	Berlinetta	Scaglietti			
8459 SF*	Sold on 1/3/66.	8459 SF	500 Series II	Superfast	Coupé	Pininfarina	J.Durlacher	U.K.	
8461 GT*		8461 GT	330	GT	2 + 2	Pininfarina	Maranello Conc.	U.K.	U.K.
8463 GT		8463 GT	330	GT	2 + 2	Pininfarina			
8465 GT		8465 GT	275	GTB	Berlinetta	Scaglietti			
8467 GT		8467 GT	330	GT	2 + 2	Pininfarina			
8469 GT		8469 GT	330	GT	2 + 2	Pininfarina			
8471 GT		8471 GT	275	GTB	Berlinetta	Scaglietti			
8473 GT		8473 GT	330	GT	2 + 2	Pininfarina			
8475 GT		8475 GT	330	GT	2 + 2	Pininfarina			
8477 GT		8477 GT	275	GTB	Berlinetta	Scaglietti			U.S.A.
8479 GT	6 carb.	8479 GT	330	GT	2 + 2	Pininfarina			U.S.A.
8481 GT		8481 GT	330	GT	2 + 2	Pininfarina			
8483 GT		8483 GT	275	GTB	Berlinetta	Scaglietti			
8485 GT		8485 GT	330	GT	2 + 2	Pininfarina			
8487 GT		8487 GT	330	GT	2 + 2	Pininfarina			
8489 GT		8489 GT	275	GTB	Berlinetta	Scaglietti			
8491 GT		8491 GT	330	GT	2 + 2	Pininfarina			
8493 GT		8493 GT	275	GTB	Berlinetta	Scaglietti			
8495 GT	6 carb.	8495 GT	330	GT	2 + 2	Pininfarina			Switzerland
8497 GT		8497 GT	275	GTB	Berlinetta	Scaglietti			
8499 GT		8499 GT	330	GT	2 + 2	Pininfarina			
8501 GT		8501 GT	275	GTB	Berlinetta	Scaglietti			
8503 GT*	6 carb.	8503 GT	275	GTB	Berlinetta	Scaglietti	Maranello Conc.	U.K.	U.K.
8505 GT		8505 GT	330	GT	2 + 2	Pininfarina			
8507 GT		8507 GT	275	GTB	Berlinetta	Scaglietti			

Chassis No.	Picture Ref	Engine No.	Type	Model	Body Style	Coach-builder	First Owner	Original Location	Present Location
8509 GT		8509 GT	330	GT	2 + 2	Pininfarina			
8511 GT		8511 GT	275	GTB	Berlinetta	Scaglietti			
8513 GT		8513 GT	275	GTB	Berlinetta	Scaglietti			
8515 GT		8515 GT	330	GT	2 + 2	Pininfarina			
8517 GT		8517 GT	275	GTB	Berlinetta	Scaglietti			
8519 GT		8519 GT	330	GT	2 + 2	Pininfarina			
8521 GT		8521 GT	275	GTB	Berlinetta	Scaglietti			U.S.A.
8523 GT		8523 GT	330	GT	2 + 2	Pininfarina			U.S.A.
8525 GT	6 carb.	8525 GT	275	GTB	Berlinetta	Scaglietti			U.S.A.
8527 GT		8527 GT	330	GT	2 + 2	Pininfarina			
8529 GT		8529 GT	330	GTC	Coupé	Pininfarina			Holland
8531 GT	May be 275GTB.	8531 GT	330	GT	2 + 2	Pininfarina			
8533 GT		8533 GT	330	GT	2 + 2	Pininfarina			U.S.A.
8535 GT		8535 GT	330	GT	2 + 2	Pininfarina			
8537 GT		8537 GT	330	GT	2 + 2	Pininfarina			
8539 GT		8539 GT	275	GTB	Berlinetta	Scaglietti			U.S.A.
8541 GT		8541 GT	275	GTB	Berlinetta	Scaglietti			Sweden
8543 GT		8543 GT	330	GT	2 + 2	Pininfarina			U.S.A.
8545 GT		8545 GT	275	GTB	Berlinetta	Scaglietti			U.S.A.
8547 GT		8547 GT	330	GT	2 + 2	Pininfarina			
8549 GT		8549 GT	275	GTB	Berlinetta	Scaglietti			U.S.A.
8551 GT		8551 GT	330	GT	2 + 2	Pininfarina			
8553 GT		8553 GT	330	GT	2 + 2	Pininfarina			
8555 GT		8555 GT	330	GT	2 + 2	Pininfarina			U.S.A.
8557 GT		8557 GT	275	GTB	Berlinetta	Scaglietti			
8559 GT		8559 GT	330	GT	2 + 2	Pininfarina			
8561 GT		8561 GT	330	GT	2 + 2	Pininfarina			
8563 GT*		8563 GT	330	GT	2 + 2	Pininfarina	Maranello Conc.	U.K.	U.K.
8565 SF	Sold on 2/4/66.	8565 SF	500 Series II	Superfast	Coupé	Pininfarina	John von Neumann	U.S.A.	
8567 GT	6 carb.	8567 GT	275	GTB	Berlinetta	Scaglietti			
8569 GT		8569 GT	330	GT	2 + 2	Pininfarina			U.S.A.
8571 GT		8571 GT	330	GT	2 + 2	Pininfarina			
8573 GT		8573 GT	275	GTB	Berlinetta	Scaglietti			
8575 GT		8575 GT	330	GT	2 + 2	Pininfarina			
8577 GT	6 carb. All aluminium body.	8577 GT	275	GTB	Berlinetta	Scaglietti			U.S.A.
8579 GT*	6 carb.	8579 GT	275	GTB	Berlinetta	Scaglietti			U.K.
8581 GT		8581 GT	330	GT	2 + 2	Pininfarina			
8583 GT		8583 GT	275	GTB	Berlinetta	Scaglietti			France
8585 GT		8585 GT	330	GT	2 + 2	Pininfarina			
8587 GT		8587 GT	330	GT	2 + 2	Pininfarina			
8589 GT		8589 GT	330	GT	2 + 2	Pininfarina			
8591 GT		8591 GT	330	GT	2 + 2	Pininfarina			
8593 GT		8593 GT	275	GTB	Berlinetta	Scaglietti			
8595 GT		8595 GT	330	GTC	Coupé	Pininfarina			U.S.A.
8597 GT		8597 GT	275	GTB	Berlinetta	Scaglietti			
8599 GT		8599 GT	330	GT	2 + 2	Pininfarina			
8601 GT		8601 GT	330	GT	2 + 2	Pininfarina			
8603 GT		8603 GT	275	GTB	Berlinetta	Scaglietti			U.S.A.
8605 GT		8605 GT	330	GT	2 + 2	Pininfarina			U.S.A.
8607 GT		8607 GT	330	GT	2 + 2	Pininfarina			
8609 GT		8609 GT	330	GT	2 + 2	Pininfarina			
8611 GT	6 carb.	8611 GT	275	GTB	Berlinetta	Scaglietti			U.S.A.
8613 GT		8613 GT	330	GT	2 + 2	Pininfarina			
8615 GT		8615 GT	275	GTB	Berlinetta	Scaglietti			
8617 GT		8617 GT	330	GT	2 + 2	Pininfarina			
8619 GT		8619 GT	275	GTB	Berlinetta	Scaglietti			
8621 GT		8621 GT	275	GTS	Spyder	Pininfarina			
8623 GT		8623 GT	330	GT	2 + 2	Pininfarina			
8625 GT		8625 GT	275	GTB	Berlinetta	Scaglietti			U.S.A.
8627 GT		8627 GT	330	GT	2 + 2	Pininfarina			U.S.A.
8629 GT		8629 GT	330	GT	2 + 2	Pininfarina			
8631 GT		8631 GT	275	GTS	Spyder	Pininfarina			
8633 GT		8633 GT	275	GTB	Berlinetta	Scaglietti			U.S.A.
8635 GT		8635 GT	330	GT	2 + 2	Pininfarina			
8637 GT		8637 GT	330	GT	2 + 2	Pininfarina			
8639 GT		8639 GT	275	GTS	Spyder	Scaglietti			
8641 GT		8641 GT	275	GTB	Berlinetta	Scaglietti			

Chassis No.	Picture Ref	Engine No.	Type	Model	Body Style	Coach-builder	First Owner	Original Location	Present Location
8643 GT		8643 GT	330	GT	2 + 2	Pininfarina			
8645 GT		8645 GT	330	GT	2 + 2	Pininfarina			
8647 GT*		8647 GT	275	GTB	Berlinetta	Scaglietti			U.K.
	6 carb.								
8649 GT		8649 GT	330	GT	2 + 2	Pininfarina			
8651 GT		8651 GT	330	GT	2 + 2	Pininfarina			
8653 GT		8653 GT	275	GTS	Spyder	Pininfarina			U.S.A.
	The last 275GTS produced.								
8655 GT		8655 GT	330	GT	2 + 2	Pininfarina			
8657 GT		8657 GT	330	GT	2 + 2	Pininfarina			U.S.A.
8659 GT		8659 GT	275	GTB	Berlinetta	Scaglietti			U.K.
8661 GT*		8661 GT	330	GT	2 + 2	Pininfarina	Maranello Conc.	U.K.	U.K.
8663 GT*		8663 GT	330	GT	2 + 2	Pininfarina			
8665 GT		8665 GT	330	GT	2 + 2	Pininfarina			U.S.A.
8667 GT		8667 GT	330	GT	2 + 2	Pininfarina			
8669 GT		8669 GT	275	GTB	Berlinetta	Scaglietti			
	6 carb.								
8671 GT		8671 GT	330	GT	2 + 2	Pininfarina			
8673 GT*		8673 GT	330	GT	2 + 2	Pininfarina			
8675 GT		8675 GT	275	GTB	Berlinetta	Scaglietti			U.S.A.
8677 GT		8677 GT	275	GTB	Berlinetta	Scaglietti			
8679 GT		8679 GT	330	GT	2 + 2	Pininfarina			
8681 GT*		8681 GT	275	GTB	Berlinetta	Scaglietti	Maranello Conc.	U.K.	U.K.
8683 GT		8683 GT	330	GTC	Coupé	Pininfarina			
8685 GT		8685 GT	330	GT	2 + 2	Pininfarina			
8687 GT		8687 GT	330	GT	2 + 2	Pininfarina			
8689 GT		8689 GT	330	GT	2 + 2	Pininfarina			U.S.A.
8691 GT		8691 GT	275	GTB	Berlinetta	Scaglietti			U.S.A.
	6 carb. All aluminium body.								
8693 GT*		8693 GT	330	GT	2 + 2	Pininfarina			
8695 GT		8695 GT	330	GT	2 + 2	Pininfarina			
8697 GT		8697 GT	275	GTB	Berlinetta	Scaglietti			
8699 GT*		8699 GT	275	GTB	Berlinetta	Scaglietti	Maranello Conc.	U.K.	U.K.
8701 GT		8701 GT	330	GT	2 + 2	Pininfarina			
8703 GT		8703 GT	330	GT	2 + 2	Pininfarina			
8705 GT		8705 GT	330	GT	2 + 2	Pininfarina			
8707 GT		8707 GT	275	GTB	Berlinetta	Scaglietti			U.S.A.
8709 GT		8709 GT	330	GT	2 + 2	Pininfarina			
8711 GT		8711 GT	330	GT	2 + 2	Pininfarina			
8713 GT		8713 GT	330	GT	2 + 2	Pininfarina			
8715 GT		8715 GT	330	GT	2 + 2	Pininfarina			
8717 GT		8717 GT	275	GTB	Berlinetta	Scaglietti			U.S.A.
8719 GT		8719 GT	330	GT	2 + 2	Pininfarina			
8721 GT		8721 GT	330	GT	2 + 2	Pininfarina			
8723 GT		8723 GT	330	GTC	Coupé	Pininfarina			
8725 GT		8725 GT	330	GT	2 + 2	Pininfarina			
8727 GT		8727 GT	330	GTC	Coupé	Pininfarina			
8729 GT		8729 GT	275	GTB	Berlinetta	Scaglietti			U.S.A.
8731 GT		8731 GT	330	GT	2 + 2	Pininfarina			
8733 GT		8733 GT	330	GT	2 + 2	Pininfarina			
8735 GT		8735 GT	330	GT	2 + 2	Pininfarina			
8737 GT		8737 GT	275	GTB	Berlinetta	Scaglietti			
8739 SF		8739 SF	500 Series II	Superfast	Coupé	Pininfarina	Battendar	U.S.A.	U.S.A.
	Sold on 30/4/66.								
8741 GT		8741 GT	330	GT	2 + 2	Pininfarina			U.S.A.
8743 GT		8743 GT	275	GTB	Berlinetta	Scaglietti			U.S.A.
	6 carb.								
8745 GT		8745 GT	330	GT	2 + 2	Pininfarina			U.S.A.
8747 GT		8747 GT	275	GTB	Berlinetta	Scaglietti			
8749 GT		8749 GT	275	GTB	Berlinetta	Scaglietti			Germany
8751 GT		8751 GT	330	GT	2 + 2	Pininfarina			
8753 GT		8753 GT	330	GTC	Coupé	Pininfarina			
8755 GT		8755 GT	330	GT	2 + 2	Pininfarina			U.S.A.
8757 GT		8757 GT	275	GTB	Berlinetta	Scaglietti			
8759 GT		8759 GT	330	GT	2 + 2	Pininfarina			
8761 GT		8761 GT	330	GTC	Coupé	Pininfarina			
8763 GT		8763 GT	275	GTB	Berlinetta	Scaglietti			
8765 GT		8765 GT	330	GT	2 + 2	Pininfarina			
8767 GT		8767 GT	330	GT	2 + 2	Pininfarina			
8769 GT		8769 GT	275	GTB4	Berlinetta	Scaglietti			
	Believed to be prototype GTB 4-cam.								
8771 GT		8771 GT	330	GT	2 + 2	Pininfarina			
8773 GT		8773 GT	330	GTC	Coupé	Pininfarina			
8775 GT		8775 GT	275	GTB	Berlinetta	Scaglietti			

Chassis No.	Picture Ref	Engine No.	Type	Model	Body Style	Coach-builder	First Owner	Original Location	Present Location
8777 GT		8777 GT	275	GTB	Berlinetta	Scaglietti			U.S.A.
8779 GT		8779 GT	330	GT	2 + 2	Pininfarina			
8781 GT		8781 GT	330	GT	2 + 2	Pininfarina			
8783 GT		8783 GT	330	GT	2 + 2	Pininfarina			
8785 GT		8785 GT	330	GTC	Coupé	Pininfarina			
8787 GT		8787 GT	330	GT	2 + 2	Pininfarina			
8789 GT		8789 GT	275	GTB	Berlinetta	Scaglietti			U.S.A.
8791 GT		8791 GT	330	GTC	Coupé	Pininfarina			
8793 GT		8793 GT	330	GT	2 + 2	Pininfarina			U.S.A.
8795 GT		8795 GT	275	GTB	Berlinetta	Scaglietti			
8797 GT		8797 GT	330	GTC	Coupé	Pininfarina			
8799 GT		8799 GT	330	GT	2 + 2	Pininfarina			
8801 GT		8801 GT	275	GTB	Berlinetta	Scaglietti			U.S.A.
	6 carb.								
8803 GT		8803 GT	330	GTC	Coupé	Pininfarina			
8805 GT		8805 GT	330	GT	2 + 2	Pininfarina			
8807 GT		8807 GT	330	GTC	Coupé	Pininfarina			
8809 GT		8809 GT	330	GT	2 + 2	Pininfarina			
8811 GT		8811 GT	330	GTC	Coupé	Pininfarina			
8813 GT		8813 GT	275	GTB	Berlinetta	Scaglietti			
8815 GT		8815 GT	365	P	3 Seat Coupé	Pininfarina	Giovanni Agnelli	Italy	France
	Built for the head of FIAT. Central seating position!								
8817 SF		8817 SF	500 Series II	Superfast	Coupé	Pininfarina			U.S.A.
	Sold on 30/6/66.								
8819 GT		8819 GT	330	GT	2 + 2	Pininfarina			
8821 GT		8821 GT	330	GTC	Coupé	Pininfarina			
8823 GT		8823 GT	330	GTC	Coupé	Pininfarina			
8825 GT		8825 GT	330	GT	2 + 2	Pininfarina			
8827 GT		8827 GT	330	GTC	Coupé	Pininfarina			
8829 GT		8829 GT	330	GT	2 + 2	Pininfarina			
8831 GT		8831 GT	330	GT	2 + 2	Pininfarina			
8833 GT		8833 GT	330	GTC	Coupé	Pininfarina			
8835 GT		8835 GT	275	GTB	Berlinetta	Scaglietti			
8837 GT		8837 GT	330	GT	2 + 2	Pininfarina			
8839 GT		8839 GT	330	GTC	Coupé	Pininfarina			
8841 GT		8841 GT	275	GTB	Berlinetta	Scaglietti			
	All aluminium body.								
8843 GT		8843 GT	330	GTC	Coupé	Pininfarina			
8845 GT		8845 GT	330	GT	2 + 2	Pininfarina			
8847 GT		8847 GT	275	GTB	Berlinetta	Scaglietti			
	6 carb.								
8849 GT		8849 GT	330	GTC	Coupé	Pininfarina			
8851 GT		8851 GT	330	GT	2 + 2	Pininfarina			
8853 GT		8853 GT	275	GTB	Berlinetta	Scaglietti			
8855 GT		8855 GT	330	GT	2 + 2	Pininfarina			U.S.A.
8857 GT		8857 GT	330	GTC	Coupé	Pininfarina			
8859 GT		8859 GT	275	GTB	Berlinetta	Scaglietti			U.S.A.
	6 carb.All aluminium body.								
8861 GT		8861 GT	330	GT	2 + 2	Pininfarina			
8863 GT		8863 GT	275	GTB	Berlinetta	Scaglietti			
8865 GT		8865 GT	330	GT	2 + 2	Pininfarina			
8867 GT		8867 GT	330	GTC	Coupé	Pininfarina			U.S.A.
8869 GT		8869 GT	275	GTB	Berlinetta	Scaglietti			
8871 GT		8871 GT	330	GT	2 + 2	Pininfarina			U.S.A.
8873 GT		8873 GT	330	GTC	Coupé	Pininfarina			
8875 GT		8875 GT	330	GT	2 + 2	Pininfarina			
8877 GT		8877 GT	275	GTB	Berlinetta	Scaglietti			South Africa?
8879 GT		8879 GT	330	GTC	Coupé	Pininfarina			
8881 GT		8881 GT	330	GT	2 + 2	Pininfarina			U.S.A.
8883 GT		8883 GT	330	GTC	Coupé	Pininfarina			
8885 GT		8885 GT	330	GT	2 + 2	Pininfarina			
8887 GT		8887 GT	330	GTC	Coupé	Pininfarina			
8889 GT		8889 GT	330	GT	2 + 2	Pininfarina			
8891 GT		8891 GT	275	GTB	Berlinetta	Scaglietti			U.S.A.
	6 carb.All aluminium body.								
8893 GT		8893 GT	330	GT	2 + 2	Pininfarina			U.S.A.
8895 GT		8895 GT	275	GTB	Berlinetta	Scaglietti			
8897 SF*		8897 SF	500 Series II	Superfast	Coupé	Pininfarina	Ronnie Hoare	U.K.	U.K.
	Sold on 1/8/66.								
8899 GT		8899 GT	330	GTS	Spyder	Pininfarina			
	Prototype 330GTS.Shown at the 1966 Paris Salon.								
8901 GT		8901 GT	275	GTB	Berlinetta	Scaglietti			
	6 carb.All aluminium body.Outside filler cap.								
8903 GT		8903 GT	330	GT	2 + 2	Pininfarina			

Chassis No.	Picture Ref	Engine No.	Type	Model	Body Style	Coach-builder	First Owner	Original Location	Present Location
8905 GT		8905 GT	330	GTC	Coupé	Pininfarina			
8907 GT		8907 GT	275	GTB	Berlinetta	Scaglietti			
8909 GT		8909 GT	330	GT	2 + 2	Pininfarina			
8911 GT		8911 GT	330	GTC	Coupé	Pininfarina			
8913 GT		8913 GT	330	GT	2 + 2	Pininfarina			
8915 GT		8915 GT	330	GTC	Coupé	Pininfarina			
8917 GT		8917 GT	330	GT	2 + 2	Pininfarina			U.S.A.
8919 GT		8919 GT	330	GT	2 + 2	Pininfarina			
8921 GT		8921 GT	275	GTB	Berlinetta	Scaglietti			U.S.A.
	6 carb.								
8923 GT		8923 GT	330	GTC	Coupé	Pininfarina			
8925 GT		8925 GT	330	GT	2 + 2	Pininfarina			
8927 GT		8927 GT	330	GTC	Coupé	Pininfarina			
8929 GT		8929 GT	330	GT	2 + 2	Pininfarina			
8931 GT		8931 GT	275	GTB	Berlinetta	Scaglietti			
8933 GT		8933 GT	275	GTB	Berlinetta	Scaglietti			U.S.A.
8935 GT		8935 GT	330	GTC	Coupé	Pininfarina			
8937 GT		8937 GT	330	GT	2 + 2	Pininfarina			U.S.A.
8939 GT		8939 GT	330	GTC	Coupé	Pininfarina			
8941 GT		8941 GT	330	GT	2 + 2	Pininfarina			
8943 GT		8943 GT	330	GT	2 + 2	Pininfarina			U.S.A.
8945 GT		8945 GT	330	GTC	Coupé	Pininfarina			
8947 GT		8947 GT	330	GT	2 + 2	Pininfarina			
8949 GT		8949 GT	330	GTC	Coupé	Pininfarina			
8951 GT		8951 GT	275	GTB	Berlinetta	Scaglietti			U.S.A.
8953 GT		8953 GT	330	GT	2 + 2	Pininfarina			U.S.A.
8955 GT		8955 GT	275	GTB	Berlinetta	Scaglietti			U.S.A.
8957 GT		8957 GT	330	GTC	Coupé	Pininfarina			
8959 GT		8959 GT	330	GT	2 + 2	Pininfarina			
8961 GT		8961 GT	275	GTB	Berlinetta	Scaglietti			
8963 GT		8963 GT	330	GTC	Coupé	Pininfarina			
8965 GT		8965 GT	330	GT	2 + 2	Pininfarina			
8967 GT		8967 GT	330	GT	2 + 2	Pininfarina			
8969 GT		8969 GT	330	GTC	Coupé	Pininfarina			
8971 GT		8971 GT	365	P	3 Seat Coupé	Pininfarina	Luigi Chinetti?	U.S.A.?	U.S.A.
	Central seating position.								
8973 GT		8973 GT	275	GTB	Berlinetta	Scaglietti			
8975 GT		8975 GT	330	GT	2 + 2	Pininfarina			
8977 GT		8977 GT	330	GTC	Coupé	Pininfarina			
8979 GT		8979 GT	275	GTB	Berlinetta	Scaglietti			U.S.A.
	The last 275GTB produced.								
8981 GT		8981 GT	330	GT	2 + 2	Pininfarina			
8983 GT		8983 GT	330	GTC	Coupé	Pininfarina			
8985 GT		8985 GT	330	GT	2 + 2	Pininfarina			
8987 GT		8987 GT	330	GTC	Coupé	Pininfarina			
8989 GT*		8989 GT	330	GT	2 + 2	Pininfarina	Maranello Conc.	U.K.	U.K.
8991 GT		8991 GT	330	GTC	Coupé	Pininfarina			
8993 GT		8993 GT	330	GT	2 + 2	Pininfarina			
8995 GT		8995 GT	330	GTC	Coupé	Pininfarina			
8997 GT		8997 GT	330	GT	2 + 2	Pininfarina			
8999 GT		8999 GT	330	GTC	Coupé	Pininfarina			
9001 GT		9001 GT	330	GT	2 + 2	Pininfarina			
9003 GT		9003 GT	330	GTC	Coupé	Pininfarina			
9005 GT		9005 GT	330	GT	2 + 2	Pininfarina			
9007 GT		9007 GT	275GTB/C	Competition	Berlinetta	Scaglietti			
	Special competition car. The first of twelve. Lightweight all aluminium body. Dry sump engine.								
9009 GT		9009 GT	330	GTC	Coupé	Pininfarina			
9011 GT		9011 GT	330	GT	2 + 2	Pininfarina			
9013 GT		9013 GT	330	GTC	Coupé	Pininfarina			
	First shown at the 1966? Paris Salon.								
9015 GT		9015 GT	275GTB/C	Competition	Berlinetta	Scaglietti			
	Special competition car. Lightweight all aluminium body. Dry sump engine.								
9017 GT		9017 GT	330	GT	2 + 2	Pininfarina			
9019 GT		9019 GT	330	GTC	Coupé	Pininfarina			
9021 GT		9021 GT	275 GTB	GTB	Berlinetta	Scaglietti			
9023 GT		9023 GT	330	GT	2 + 2	Pininfarina			
9025 GT		9025 GT	330	GTC	Coupé	Pininfarina			
9027 GT*		9027 GT	275GTB/C	Competition	Berlinetta	Scaglietti			
	Special competition car. Lightweight all aluminium body. Dry sump engine.								
9029 GT		9029 GT	330	GT	2 + 2	Pininfarina			
9031 GT		9031 GT	330	GTC	Coupé	Pininfarina			
9033 GT		9033 GT	330	GT	2 + 2	Pininfarina			
9035 GT*	P1/309	9035 GT	275GTB/C	Competition	Berlinetta	Scaglietti			
	Special competition car. Lightweight all aluminium body. Dry sump engine.								

Chassis No.	Picture Ref	Engine No.	Type	Model	Body Style	Coach-builder	First Owner	Original Location	Present Location
9037 GT		9037 GT	330	GTC	Coupé	Pininfarina			
9039 GT		9039 GT	330	GTC	Coupé	Pininfarina			
9O41 GT*		9O41 GT	275GTB/C	Competition	Berlinetta	Scaglietti			
	Special competition car. Lightweight all aluminium body.Dry sump engine.								
9043 GT		9043 GT	330	GT	2 + 2	Pininfarina			
9045 GT		9045 GT	330	GTC	Coupé	Pininfarina			
9047 GT		9047 GT	330	GT	2 + 2	Pininfarina			
9049 GT		9049 GT	330	GTC	Coupé	Pininfarina			
9051 GT		9051 GT	275GTB/C	Competition	Berlinetta	Scaglietti			
	Special competition car. Lightweight all aluminium body.Dry sump engine.								
9053 GT		9053 GT	330	GT	2 + 2	Pininfarina			
9055 GT		9055 GT	330	GTC	Coupé	Pininfarina			
9057 GT		9057 GT	275GTB/C	Competition	Berlinetta	Scaglietti			
	Special competition car. Lightweight all aluminium body.Dry sump engine.								
9059 GT		9059 GT	330	GT	2 + 2	Pininfarina			
9061 GT		9061 GT	330	GTC	Coupé	Pininfarina			
9063 GT		9063 GT	275GTB/C	Competition	Berlinetta	Scaglietti			
	Special competition car. Lightweight all aluminium body.Dry sump engine.								
9065 GT		9065 GT	275	GTB	Berlinetta	Scaglietti			
9067 GT		9067 GT	275GTB/C	Competition	Berlinetta	Scaglietti			
	Special competition car. Lightweight all aluminium body.Dry sump engine.								
9069 GT		9069 GT	330	GTC	Coupé	Pininfarina			
9071 GT*		9071 GT	330	GT	2 + 2	Pininfarina	Maranello Conc.	U.K.	U.K.
	Shown at the 1966? London Motor Show.								
9073 GT		9073 GT	275GTB/C	Competition	Berlinetta	Scaglietti			
	Special competition car. Lightweight all aluminium body.								
9075 GT		9075 GT	330	GTC	Coupé	Pininfarina			
9077 GT		9077 GT	330	GTC	Coupé	Pininfarina			
9079 GT*		9079 GT	275GTB/C	Competition	Berlinetta	Scaglietti			
	Special competition car. Lightweight all aluminium body.Dry sump engine.								
9081 GT		9081 GT	330	GTC	Coupé	Pininfarina			
9083 GT		9083 GT	330	GT	2 + 2	Pininfarina			
9085 GT		9085 GT	275GTB/C	Competition	Berlinetta	Scaglietti			
	Special competition car. Lightweight all aluminium body.Dry sump engine.								
9087 GT		9087 GT	330	GT	2 + 2	Pininfarina			
9089 GT*		9089 GT	330	GT	2 + 2	Pininfarina			
9091 GT		9091 GT	330	GTC	Coupé	Pininfarina			
9093 GT*		9093 GT	330	GTC	Coupé	Pininfarina	Maranello Conc.	U.K.	U.K.
	Shown at the 1966? London Motor Show.								
9095 GT		9095 GT	330	GT	2 + 2	Pininfarina			
9097 GT		9097 GT	330	GT	2 + 2	Pininfarina			
9099 GT		9099 GT	330	GTC	Coupé	Pininfarina			
9101 GT		9101 GT	330	GT	2 + 2	Pininfarina			
9103 GT		9103 GT	330	GTC	Coupé	Pininfarina			
9105 GT		9105 GT	330	GT	2 + 2	Pininfarina			
9107 GT		9107 GT	330	GTC	Coupé	Pininfarina			
9109 GT		9109 GT	330	GT	2 + 2	Pininfarina			
9111 GT		9111 GT	330	GTC	Coupé	Pininfarina			
9113 GT		9113 GT	330	GT	2 + 2	Pininfarina			
9115 GT		9115 GT	330	GTC	Coupé	Pininfarina			
9117 GT*		9117 GT	275	GTB4	Berlinetta	Scaglietti	Maranello Conc.	U.K.	U.K.
	Shown at the 1966 London Motor Show.								
9119 GT		9119 GT	330	GT	2 + 2	Pininfarina			
9121 GT		9121 GT	330	GTC	Coupé	Pininfarina			
9123 GT		9123 GT	330	GT	2 + 2	Pininfarina			
9125 GT		9125 GT	330	GTC	Coupé	Pininfarina			
9127		9127	365	California	Spyder	Pininfarina	Ms de Cuevas	U.S.A.	
	Sold on 10/10/66.								
9129 GT		9129 GT	330	GT	2 + 2	Pininfarina		U.S.A.	
9131 GT		9131 GT	330	GTC	Coupé	Pininfarina			
9133 GT		9133 GT	330	GT	2 + 2	Pininfarina			
9135 GT		9135 GT	330	GTC	Coupé	Pininfarina			
9137 GT		9137 GT	330	GT	2 + 2	Pininfarina			
9139 GT		9139 GT	330	GTC	Coupé	Pininfarina			
9141 GT		9141 GT	330	GT	2 + 2	Pininfarina			
9143 GT		9143 GT	330	GT	2 + 2	Pininfarina			
9145 GT		9145 GT	330	GT	2 + 2	Pininfarina			
9147 GT		9147 GT	330	GT	2 + 2	Pininfarina			
9149 GT		9149 GT	330	GT	2 + 2	Pininfarina			
9151 GT		9151 GT	330	GT	2 + 2	Pininfarina			
9153 GT		9153 GT	330	GT	2 + 2	Pininfarina			
	Shown at the 1966 Turin Motor Show.								
9155 GT*		9155 GT	330	GTS	Spyder	Pininfarina	Maranello Conc.	U.K.	U.K.
	Shown at the 1966 London Motor Show.								

Chassis No.	Picture Ref	Engine No.	Type	Model	Body Style	Coach-builder	First Owner	Original Location	Present Location
9157 GT		9157 GT	275	GTB	Berlinetta	Scaglietti			
9159 GT		9159 GT	330	GTC	Coupé	Pininfarina			
9161 GT		9161 GT	330	GT	2 + 2	Pininfarina			
9163 GT		9163 GT	330	GTC	Coupé	Pininfarina			
9165 GT		9165 GT	330	GT	2 + 2	Pininfarina			
9167 GT		9167 GT	330	GTC	Coupé	Pininfarina			
9169 GT		9169 GT	330	GTC	Coupé	Pininfarina			
9171 GT		9171 GT	330	GTC	Coupé	Pininfarina			
9173 GT		9173 GT	330	GTC	Coupé	Pininfarina			U.S.A.
9175 GT		9175 GT	330	GTC	Coupé	Pininfarina			
9177 GT		9177 GT	330	GT	2 + 2	Pininfarina			
9179 GT		9179 GT	330	GT	2 + 2	Pininfarina			
9181 GT		9181 GT	330	GTC	Coupé	Pininfarina			
9183 GT		9183 GT	330	GT	2 + 2	Pininfarina			
9185 GT		9185 GT	330	GTC	Coupé	Pininfarina			
9187 GT		9187 GT	330	GT	2 + 2	Pininfarina			
9189 GT		9189 GT	330	GTC	Coupé	Pininfarina			
9191 GT		9191 GT	330	GTC	Coupé	Pininfarina			
9193 GT		9193 GT	330	GT	2 + 2	Pininfarina			
9195 GT		9195 GT	330	GTC	Coupé	Pininfarina			
9197 GT		9197 GT	330	GTC	Coupé	Pininfarina			
9199 GT		9199 GT	330	GTS	Spyder	Pininfarina			
	Shown at the 1966 Turin Motor Show.								
9201 GT		9201 GT	330	GTC	Coupé	Pininfarina			
9203 GT		9203 GT	33O	GT	2 + 2	Pininfarina			
9205 GT		9205 GT	330	GT	2 + 2	Pininfarina			
9207 GT		9207 GT	330	GTC	Coupé	Pininfarina			
9209 GT		9209 GT	330	GT	2 + 2	Pininfarina			
9211 GT		9211 GT	330	GT	2 + 2	Pininfarina			
9213 GT		9213 GT	330	GT	2 + 2	Pininfarina			
9215 GT		9215 GT	330	GTC	Coupé	Pininfarina			
9217 GT		9217 GT	330	GTC	Coupé	Pininfarina			
9219 GT		9219 GT	330	GT	2 + 2	Pininfarina			
9221 GT		9221 GT	330	GT	2 + 2	Pininfarina			
9223 GT		9223 GT	330	GTC	Coupé	Pininfarina			
9225 GT		9225 GT	275	GTB4	Berlinetta	Scaglietti			
9227 GT		9227 GT	330	GT	2 + 2	Pininfarina			
9229 GT		9229 GT	330	GT	2 + 2	Pininfarina			
9231 GT		9231 GT	330	GTC	Coupé	Pininfarina			
9233 GT		9233 GT	275	GTB4	Berlinetta	Scaglietti			
9235 GT		9235 GT	330	GT	2 + 2	Pininfarina			
9237 GT		9237 GT	330	GTC	Coupé	Pininfarina			
9239 GT		9239 GT	330	GTC	Coupé	Pininfarina			
9241 GT		9241 GT	330	GTC	Coupé	Pininfarina			
9243 GT		9243 GT	330	GTC	Coupé	Pininfarina			U.S.A.
9245 GT		9245 GT	330	GTC	Coupé	Pininfarina			
9247 GT		9247 GT	275	GTB	Berlinetta	Scaglietti			
9249 GT		9249 GT	330	GTC	Coupé	Pininfarina			
				1967					
9251 GT*		9251 GT	330	GTC	Coupé	Pininfarina	Maranello Conc.	U.K.	U.K.
9253 GT		9253 GT	275	GTB4	Berlinetta	Scaglietti			
9255 GT		9255 GT	275	GTB4	Berlinetta	Scaglietti			
9257 GT		9257 GT	330	GTC	Coupé	Pininfarina			
9259 GT		9259 GT	330	GTC	Coupé	Pininfarina			
9261 GT*		9261 GT	275	GTB4	Berlinetta	Scaglietti	Maranello Conc.	U.K.	U.K.
9263 GT		9263 GT	330	GT	2 + 2	Pininfarina			
9265 GT		9265 GT	330	GTC	Coupé	Pininfarina			
9267 GT		9267 GT	330	GT	2 + 2	Pininfarina			
9269 GT		9269 GT	330	GT	2 + 2	Pininfarina			
9271 GT		9271 GT	330	GT	2 + 2	Pininfarina			
9273 GT		9273 GT	330	GTC	Coupé	Pininfarina			
9275 GT		9275 GT	330	GT	2 + 2	Pininfarina			
9277 GT		9277 GT	330	GTC	Coupé	Pininfarina			
9279 GT		9279 GT	330	GT	2 + 2	Pininfarina			
9281 GT		9281 GT	330	GTC	Coupé	Pininfarina			
9283 GT		9283 GT	330	GTC	Coupé	Pininfarina			
9285 GT		9285 GT	275	GTB4	Berlinetta	Scaglietti			
9287 GT		9287 GT	330	GTC	Coupé	Pininfarina			
9289 GT*		9289 GT	330	GTC	Coupé	Pininfarina	Maranello Conc.	U.K.	U.K.
9291 GT		9291 GT	330	GT	2 + 2	Pininfarina			
9293 GT		9293 GT	330	GTC	Coupé	Pininfarina			
9295 GT		9295 GT	330	GTC	Coupé	Pininfarina			
9297 GT		9297 GT	330	GTS	Spyder	Pininfarina			U.S.A.
9299 GTS		9299 GTS	330	GT	Spyder	Pininfarina			

Chassis No.	Picture Ref	Engine No.	Type	Model	Body Style	Coach-builder	First Owner	Original Location	Present Location
9301 GT		9301 GT	330	GTC	Coupé	Pininfarina			
9303 GT		9303 GT	330	GTC	Spyder	Pininfarina			
9305 GT		9305 GT	330	GT	2 + 2	Pininfarina			
9307 GT		9307 GT	330	GTC	Coupé	Pininfarina			
9309 GT		9309 GT	330	GT	2 + 2	Pininfarina			
9311 GT		9311 GT	330	GTC	Coupé	Pininfarina			
9313 GT		9313 GT	330	GTC	Coupé	Pininfarina			
9315 GT		9315 GT	330	GT	2 + 2	Pininfarina			
9317 GT*		9317 GT	330	GTC	Coupé	Pininfarina	Maranello Conc.	U.K.	U.K.
9319 GT		9319 GT	330	GT	2 + 2	Pininfarina			U.S.A.
9321 GT		9321 GT	330	GTC	Coupé	Pininfarina			
9323 GT*		9323 GT	330	GTC	Coupé	Pininfarina	Maranello Conc.	U.K.	U.K.
9325 GT		9325 GT	330	GT	2 + 2	Pininfarina			
9327 GT		9327 GT	330	GTC	Coupé	Pininfarina			
9329 GT		9329 GT	330	GTC	Coupé	Pininfarina			
9331 GT		9331 GT	330	GT	2 + 2	Pininfarina			
9333 GT		9333 GT	330	GTC	Coupé	Pininfarina			
9335 GT		9335 GT	330	GTC	Coupé	Pininfarina			
9337 GT		9337 GT	275	GTB4	Berlinetta	Scaglietti			
9339 GT		9339 GT	330	GTC	Coupé	Pininfarina			
9341 GT		9341 GT	330	GTC	Coupé	Pininfarina			
9343 GT		9343 GT	330	GTS	Spyder	Pininfarina			
9345 GT		9345 GT	275	GTB	Berlinetta	Scaglietti			
9347 GT		9347 GT	330	GT	2 + 2	Pininfarina			
9349 GT		9349 GT	330	GT	2 + 2	Pininfarina			
9351 GT		9351 GT	330	GTC	Coupé	Pininfarina			
9353 GT		9353 GT	330	GTC	Coupé	Pininfarina			
9355 GT		9355 GT	275	GTB	Berlinetta	Scaglietti			
9357 GT		9357 GT	330	GT	2 + 2	Pininfarina			
9359 GT		9359 GT	330	GTC	Coupé	Pininfarina			
9361 GT		9361 GT	330	GTC	Coupé	Pininfarina			
9363 GT		9363 GT	275	GTB	Berlinetta	Scaglietti			
9365 GT		9365 GT	330	GTC	Coupé	Pininfarina			
9367 GT		9367 GT	330	GTC	Coupé	Pininfarina			
9369 GT		9369 GT	330	GTS	Spyder	Pininfarina			U.S.A.
9371 GT		9371 GT	275	GTB4	Berlinetta	Scaglietti			
9373 GT		9373 GT	330	GT	2 + 2	Pininfarina			
9375 GT		9375 GT	330	GTC	Coupé	Pininfarina			
9377 GT		9377 GT	275	GTB4	Berlinetta	Scaglietti			
9379 GT		9379 GT	330	GT	2 + 2	Pininfarina			
9381 GT		9381 GT	330	GTS	Spyder	Pininfarina			
	Shown at the 1966 Brussels Motor Show.								
9383 GT		9383 GT	275	GTB4	Berlinetta	Scaglietti			
9385 GT		9385 GT	330	GT	2 + 2	Pininfarina			
9387 GT		9387 GT	330	GTC	Coupé	Pininfarina			
9389 GT		9389 GT	275	GTB4	Berlinetta	Scaglietti			
9391 GT		9391 GT	330	GT	2 + 2	Pininfarina			
9393 GT		9393 GT	330	GTC	Coupé	Pininfarina			
9395 GT		9395 GT	275	GTB	Berlinetta	Scaglietti			
9397 GT		9397 GT	330	GT	2 + 2	Pininfarina			
9399 GT		9399 GT	330	GTC	Coupé	Pininfarina			
9401 GT		9401 GT	275	GTB4	Berlinetta	Scaglietti			
9403 GT		9403 GT	330	GT	2 + 2	Pininfarina			
9405 GT		9405 GT	330	GT	2 + 2	Pininfarina			
9407 GT		9407 GT	275	GTB4	Berlinetta	Scaglietti			
9409 GT		9409 GT	330	GT	2 + 2	Pininfarina			
9411 GT		9411 GT	330	GTC	Coupé	Pininfarina			
9413 GT		9413 GT	275	GTB4	Berlinetta	Scaglietti			
9415 GT		9415 GT	330	GTC	Coupé	Pininfarina			
9417 GT		9417 GT	275	GTB4	Berlinetta	Scaglietti			
9419 GT		9419 GT	330	GT	2 + 2	Pininfarina			
9421 GT		9421 GT	275	GTB4	Berlinetta	Scaglietti			
9423 GT		9423 GT	330	GT	2 + 2	Pininfarina			
9425 GT		9425 GT	275	GTB4	Berlinetta	Scaglietti			
9427 GT		9427 GT	330	GTS	Spyder	Pininfarina			
9429 GT		9429 GT	330	GT	2 + 2	Pininfarina			
9431 GT		9431 GT	275	GTB4	Berlinetta	Scaglietti			
9433 GT		9433 GT	330	GTC	Coupé	Pininfarina			
9435 GT		9435 GT	330	GT	2 + 2	Pininfarina			
9437 GT		9437 GT	275GTB4/S	NART	Spyder	Scaglietti	Luigi Chinetti	U.S.A.	U.S.A.
	The first NART Spyder. Raced in 1967. Featured in the movie 'The Thomas Crown Affair'. All aluminium body.								
9439 GT	P1/343?	9439 GT	330	GTC	Coupé Speciale	Pininfarina			U.S.A.
	Believed to be one of several 330GTC Speciale built by Pininfarina.								
9441 GT		9441 GT	330	GTC	Coupé	Pininfarina			

Chassis No.	Picture Ref	Engine No.	Type	Model	Body Style	Coach-builder	First Owner	Original Location	Present Location
9443 GT		9443 GT	330	GT	2 + 2	Pininfarina			
9445 GT		9445 GT	275	GTB4	Berlinetta	Scaglietti			
9447		9447	365	California	Spyder	Pininfarina			U.S.A.
	Sold on 19/12/66. Shown at the 1966 Turin Motor Show.								
9449 GT		9449 GT	330	GTC	Coupé	Pininfarina			U.S.A.
9451 GT		9451 GT	275	GTB4	Berlinetta	Scaglietti			
9453 GT		9453 GT	330	GT	2 + 2	Pininfarina			
9455 GT		9455 GT	330	GTC	Coupé	Pininfarina			
9457 GT		9457 GT	275	GTB4	Berlinetta	Scaglietti			
9459 GT		9459 GT	330	GTC	Coupé	Pininfarina			
9461 GT		9461 GT	330	GT	2 + 2	Pininfarina			
9463 GT		9463 GT	275	GTB4	Berlinetta	Scaglietti			
9465 GT		9465 GT	330	GTC	Coupé	Pininfarina			
9467 GT		9467 GT	275	GTB4	Berlinetta	Scaglietti			
9469 GT		9469 GT	330	GTS	Spyder	Pininfarina			
9471 GT*		9471 GT	330	GT	2 + 2	Pininfarina	Maranello Conc.	U.K.	U.K.
9473 GT		9473 GT	330	GTC	Coupé	Pininfarina			
9475 GT		9475 GT	274	GTB4	Berlinetta	Scaglietti			
9477 GT		9477 GT	330	GT	2 + 2	Pininfarina			
9479 GT		9479 GT	275	GTB4	Berlinetta	Scaglietti			
9481 GT		9481 GT	330	GTS	Spyder	Pininfarina			U.S.A.
9483 GT		9483 GT	330	GT	2 + 2	Pininfarina			
9485 GT		9485 GT	275	GTB4	Berlinetta	Scaglietti			
9487 GT		9487 GT	330	GTC	Coupé	Pininfarina			
9489 GT		9489 GT	275	GTB4	Berlinetta	Scaglietti			
9491 GT		9491 GT	330	GT	2 + 2	Pininfarina			
9493 GT		9493 GT	330	GTC	Coupé	Pininfarina			
9495 GT		9495 GT	275	GTB4	Berlinetta	Scaglietti			
9497 GT		9497 GT	330	GTC	Coupé	Pininfarina			
9499 GT		9499 GT	330	GT	2 + 2	Pininfarina			
9501 GT		9501 GT	275	GTB4	Berlinetta	Scaglietti			
9503 GT		9503 GT	330	GTC	Coupé	Pininfarina			
9505 GT		9505 GT	275	GTB4	Berlinetta	Scaglietti			
9507 GT		9507 GT	330	GTC	Coupé	Pininfarina			
9509 GT		9509 GT	330	GTC	Coupé	Pininfarina			
9511 GT		9511 GT	275	GTB4	Berlinetta	Scaglietti			
9513 GT		9513 GT	330	GTS	Spyder	Pininfarina			
9515 GT		9515 GT	330	GTC	Coupé	Pininfarina			
9517 GT		9517 GT	275	GTB4	Berlinetta	Scaglietti			
9519 GT		9519 GT	330	GTC	Coupé	Pininfarina			
9521 GT		9521 GT	330	GT	2 + 2	Pininfarina			
9523 GT		9523 GT	275	GTB4	Berlinetta	Scaglietti			
9525 GT		9525 GT	330	GTC	Coupé	Pininfarina			
9527 GT		9527 GT	330	GTC	Coupé	Pininfarina			
9529 GT		9529 GT	330	GTC	Coupé	Pininfarina			
9531 GT		9531 GT	275	GTB4	Berlinetta	Scaglietti			
9533 GT		9533 GT	330	GT	2 + 2	Pininfarina			U.S.A.
	Single headlight.								
9535 GT		9535 GT	330	GTC	Coupé	Pininfarina			U.S.A.
9537 GT		9537 GT	330	GTC	Coupé	Pininfarina			U.S.A.
9539 GT		9539 GT	275	GTB4	Berlinetta	Scaglietti			
9541 GT		9541 GT	330	GT	2 + 2	Pininfarina			
9543 GT		9543 GT	330	GTC	Coupé	Pininfarina			
9545 GT		9545 GT	275	GTB4	Berlinetta	Scaglietti			
9547 GT		9547 GT	330	GT	Coupé	Pininfarina			
9549 GT		9549 GT	330	GT	2 + 2	Pininfarina			
9551 GT		9551 GT	275	GTB4	Berlinetta	Scaglietti			
9553 GT		9553 GT	330	GTC	Coupé	Pininfarina			
9555 GT		9555 GT	330	GTC	Coupé	Pininfarina			
9557 GT*		9557 GT	330	GT	2 + 2	Pininfarina	Maranello Conc.	U.K.	U.K.
9559 GT		9559 GT	275	GTB4	Berlinetta	Scaglietti			
9561 GT		9561 GT	330	GTC	Coupé	Pininfarina			
9563 GT		9563 GT	330	GTC	Coupé	Pininfarina			U.S.A.
9565 GT		9565 GT	275	GTB4	Berlinetta	Scaglietti			
9567 GT		9567 GT	330	GTC	Coupé	Pininfarina			
9569 GT		9569 GT	330	GTC	Coupé	Pininfarina			
9571 GT	P1/343?	9571 GT	330	GTC	Coupé Speciale	Pininfarina			
	Special Coupé built by Pininfarina on 330GTC chassis.								
9573 GT		9573 GT	275	GTB4	Berlinetta	Scaglietti			
9575 GT		9575 GT	330	GTC	Coupé	Pininfarina			
9577 GT		9577 GT	330	GTC	Coupé	Pininfarina			
9579 GT		9579 GT	275	GTB4	Berlinetta	Scaglietti			
9581 GT		9581 GT	330	GTC	Coupé	Pininfarina			
9583 GT		9583 GT	330	GTC	Coupé	Pininfarina			

Chassis No.	Picture Ref	Engine No.	Type	Model	Body Style	Coach-builder	First Owner	Original Location	Present Location
9585 GT		9585 GT	275	GTB4	Berlinetta	Scaglietti			
9587 GT		9587 GT	330	GTC	Coupé	Pininfarina			U.S.A.
	Factory A/C.								
9589 GT		9589 GT	330	GTC	Coupé	Pininfarina			
9591 GT		9591 GT	275	GTB4	Berlinetta	Scaglietti			
9593 GT		9593 GT	330	GTC	Coupé	Pininfarina			
9595 GT		9595 GT	330	GTC	Coupé	Pininfarina			
9597 GT		9597 GT	275	GTB4	Berlinetta	Scaglietti			
9599 GT		9599 GT	330	GTC	Coupé	Pininfarina			
9601 GT		9601 GT	330	GTC	Coupé	Pininfarina			U.S.A.
9603 GT		9603 GT	275	GTB4	Berlinetta	Scaglietti			
9605 GT		9605 GT	330	GTC	Coupé	Pininfarina			
9607 GT		9607 GT	330	GTC	Coupé	Pininfarina			
9609 GT		9609 GT	275	GTB4	Berlinetta	Scaglietti			
9611 GT		9611 GT	330	GTC	Coupé	Pininfarina			
9613 GT		9613 GT	330	GTC	Coupé	Pininfarina			
9615		9615	365	California	Spyder	Pininfarina		Spain	
	Sold on 30/1/67.								
9617 GT		9617 GT	275	GTB4	Berlinetta	Scaglietti			
9619 GT		9619 GT	330	GTC	Coupé	Pininfarina			
9621 GT		9621 GT	330	GTC	Coupé	Pininfarina			
9623 GT		9623 GT	275	GTB4	Berlinetta	Scaglietti			
9625 GT		9625 GT	330	GTS	Spyder	Pininfarina			
9627 GT		9627 GT	330	GTS	Spyder	Pininfarina			
	Shown at the 1967 Geneva Motor Show.								
9629 GT		9629 GT	330	GT	2 + 2	Pininfarina			
9631		9631	365	California	Spyder	Pininfarina			U.S.A..
	Shown at the 1967 Geneva Motor Show.								
9633 GT		9633 GT	330	GTC	Coupé	Pininfarina			
9635 GT		9635 GT	275	GTB4	Berlinetta	Scaglietti			
9637 GT		9637 GT	330	GT	2 + 2	Pininfarina			
9639 GT		9639 GT	330	GTS	Spyder	Pininfarina			
9641 GT		9641 GT	330	GT	Coupé	Pininfarina			
9643 GT		9643 GT	275	GTB4	Berlinetta	Scaglietti			
9645 GT		9645 GT	330	GT	2 + 2	Pininfarina			
9647 GT		9647 GT	330	GTC	Coupé	Pininfarina			
9649 GT		9649 GT	275	GTB4	Berlinetta	Scaglietti			
9651 GT		9651 GT	330	GTC	Coupé	Pininfarina			
9653 GT		9653 GT	330	GTC Speciale	Coupé	Pininfarina			U.S.A.
	Specially built for Princess Lillian de Rethy of Belgium.								
9655 GT		9655 GT	330	GTS	Spyder	Pininfarina			
9657 GT		9657 GT	275	GTB4	Berlinetta	Scaglietti			Canada
	Specially revised by Ferrari and Pininfarina.								
9659 GT		9659 GT	330	GTC	Coupé	Pininfarina			
9661 GT		9661 GT	330	GTC	Coupé	Pininfarina			
9663 GT		9663 GT	275	GTB4	Berlinetta	Scaglietti			Switzerland
9665 GT		9665 GT	330	GT	2 + 2	Pininfarina			
9667 GT		9667 GT	330	GT	2 + 2	Pininfarina			
9669 GT		9669 GT	275	GTB4	Berlinetta	Scaglietti			
9671 GT		9671 GT	330	GTC	Coupé	Pininfarina			
9673 GT		9673 GT	330	GT	2 + 2	Pininfarina			
9675 GT		9675 GT	330	GT	2 + 2	Pininfarina			
9677 GT		9677 GT	275	GTB4	Berlinetta	Scaglietti			
9679 GT		9679 GT	330	GTC	Coupé	Pininfarina			
9681 GT		9681 GT	330	GTS	Spyder	Pininfarina			
9683 GT		9683 GT	275	GTB4	Berlinetta	Scaglietti			
9685 GT		9685 GT	330	GTC	Coupé	Pininfarina			
9687 GT		9687 GT	330	GTS	Spyder	Pininfarina			
9689 GT		9689 GT	275	GTB4	Berlinetta	Scaglietti			
9691 GT		9691 GT	330	GTS	Spyder	Pininfarina			
9693 GT		9693 GT	330	GT	2 + 2	Pininfarina			U.S.A.
9695 GT		9695 GT	275	GTB4	Berlinetta	Scaglietti			
9697 GT		9697 GT	330	GTC	Coupé	Pininfarina			
9699 GT		9699 GT	330	GTS	Spyder	Pininfarina			U.S.A.
	European model.								
9701 GT		9701 GT	275	GTB4	Berlinetta	Scaglietti			
9703 GT		9703 GT	275	GTB4	Berlinetta	Scaglietti			
9705 GT		9705 GT	330	GTC	Coupé	Pininfarina			
9707 GT		9707 GT	330	GT	2 + 2	Pininfarina			
9709 GT		9709 GT	275	GTB4	Berlinetta	Scaglietti			
9711 GT		9711 GT	330	GTC	Coupé	Pininfarina			
9713 GT		9713 GT	275	GTB4	Berlinetta	Scaglietti			
9715 GT		9715 GT	330	GTS	Spyder	Pininfarina			
9717 GT		9717 GT	330	GT	2 + 2	Pininfarina			

Chassis No.	Picture Ref	Engine No.	Type	Model	Body Style	Coach-builder	First Owner	Original Location	Present Location
9719 GT		9719 GT	330	GT	2 + 2	Pininfarina			
9721 GT		9721 GT	275	GTB4	Berlinetta	Scaglietti			
9723 GT		9723 GT	330	GT	2 + 2	Pininfarina			
9725 GT		9725 GT	275	GTB4	Berlinetta	Scaglietti			
9727 GT		9727 GT	330	GT	2 + 2	Pininfarina			
9729 GT		9729 GT	275	GTB4	Berlinetta	Scaglietti			U.S.A.
9731 GT		9731 GT	330	GT	2 + 2	Pininfarina			
9733 GT		9733 GT	330	GTS	Spyder	Pininfarina			
9735 GT		9735 GT	275	GTB4	Berlinetta	Scaglietti			
9737 GT		9737 GT	275	GTB4	Berlinetta	Scaglietti			
9739 GT		9739 GT	330	GT	2 + 2	Pininfarina			
9741 GT		9741 GT	330	GTC	Coupé	Pininfarina			
9743 GT		9743 GT	275	GTB4	Berlinetta	Scaglietti			
9745 GT		9745 GT	330	GT	2 + 2	Pininfarina			
9747 GT		9747 GT	275	GTB4	Berlinetta	Scaglietti			
9749 GT		9749 GT	330	GTS	Spyder	Pininfarina			
9751 GT		9751 GT	275GTB4/S	NART	Spyder	Scaglietti	Luigi Chinetti	U.S.A.	U.S.A.
9753 GT		9753 GT	330	GT	2 + 2	Pininfarina			
9755 GT		9755 GT	275	GTB4	Berlinetta	Scaglietti			
9757 GT*		9757 GT	330	GT	2 + 2	Pininfarina	Maranello Conc.	U.K.	U.K.
9759 GT		9759 GT	365	GT	2 + 2	Pininfarina			
9761 GT		9761 GT	275	GTB4	Berlinetta	Scaglietti			U.S.A.
9763 GT		9763 GT	330	GT	2 + 2	Pininfarina			
9765 GT		9765 GT	330	GTS	Spyder	Pininfarina			U.S.A.
9767 GT		9767 GT	275	GTB4	Berlinetta	Scaglietti			
9769 GT		9769 GT	330	GTC	Coupé	Pininfarina			
9771 GT		9771 GT	330	GTS	Spyder	Pininfarina			
9773 GT		9773 GT	330	GT	2 + 2	Pininfarina			
9775 GT		9775 GT	275	GTB4	Berlinetta	Scaglietti			
9777 GT		9777 GT	330	GTS	Spyder	Pininfarina			
9779 GT		9779 GT	275	GTB4	Berlinetta	Scaglietti			
9781 GT		9781 GT	330	GTS	Spyder	Pininfarina			
9783 GT		9783 GT	275	GTB4	Berlinetta	Scaglietti			
9785 GT		9785 GT	330	GTC	Coupé	Pininfarina			
9787 GT		9787 GT	330	GTS	Spyder	Pininfarina			
9789 GT		9789 GT	275	GTB4	Berlinetta	Scaglietti			
9791 GT		9791 GT	330	GTS	Spyder	Pininfarina			
9793 GT		9793 GT	330	GT	2 + 2	Pininfarina			
9795 GT		9795 GT	275	GTB4	Berlinetta	Scaglietti			
9797 GT		9797 GT	330	GTS	Spyder	Pininfarina			
9799 GT		9799 GT	330	GTC	Coupé	Pininfarina			
9801		9801	365	California	Spyder	Pininfarina	Luigi Chinetti	U.S.A.	U.S.A.
		Sold on 22/3/67. Shown at the 1967 New York Auto Show.							
9803 GT		9803 GT	275	GTB4	Berlinetta	Scaglietti			
9805 GT		9805 GT	330	GTS	Spyder	Pininfarina			
9807 GT		9807 GT	330	GTC	Coupé	Pininfarina			
9809 GT		9809 GT	330	GT	2 + 2	Pininfarina			
9811 GT		9811 GT	330	GT	2 + 2	Pininfarina			
9813 GT		9813 GT	275	GTB4	Berlinetta	Scaglietti			
9815 GT		9815 GT	330	GTC	Coupé	Pininfarina			
9817 GT		9817 GT	275	GTB4	Berlinetta	Scaglietti			
9819 GT		9819 GT	330	GTC	Coupé	Pininfarina			
9821 GT		9821 GT	330	GTC	Coupé	Pininfarina			
9823 GT		9823 GT	330	GT	2 + 2	Pininfarina			
9825 GT		9825 GT	275	GTB4	Berlinetta	Scaglietti			
9827 GT		9827 GT	330	GTC	Coupé	Pininfarina			
9829 GT		9829 GT	330	GTC	Coupé	Pininfarina			
9831 GT		9831 GT	275	GTB4	Berlinetta	Scaglietti			
9833 GT		9833 GT	330	GTC	Coupé	Pininfarina			
9835 GT		9835 GT	330	GT	2 + 2	Pininfarina			
9837 GT		9837 GT	330	GTC	Coupé	Pininfarina			
9839 GT		9839 GT	330	GTC	Coupé	Pininfarina			
9841 GT		9841 GT	330	GT	2 + 2	Pininfarina			
9843 GT		9843 GT	330	GTC	Coupé	Pininfarina			
9845 GT		9845 GT	330	GTC	Coupé	Pininfarina			
9847 GT		9847 GT	330	GTC	Coupé	Pininfarina			U.S.A.
9849		9849	365	California	Spyder	Pininfarina	Bud Bickel	U.S.A.	U.S.A.
9851 GT		9851 GT	275	GTB4	Berlinetta	Scaglietti			
9853 GT		9853 GT	330	GTC	Coupé	Pininfarina			
9855 GT		9855 GT	275	GTB4	Berlinetta	Scaglietti			
9857 GT		9857 GT	330	GTC	Coupé	Pininfarina			
9859 GT		9859 GT	275	GTB4	Berlinetta	Scaglietti			
9861 GT		9861 GT	330	GTC	Coupé	Pininfarina			
9863 GT		9863 GT	330	GTC	Coupé	Pininfarina			

Chassis No.	Picture Ref	Engine No.	Type	Model	Body Style	Coach-builder	First Owner	Original Location	Present Location
9865 GT		9865 GT	275	GTB4	Berlinetta	Scaglietti			
9867 GT		9867 GT	330	GTC	Coupé	Pininfarina			
9869 GT		9869 GT	330	GTC	Coupé	Pininfarina			
9871 GT		9871 GT	275	GTB4	Berlinetta	Scaglietti			
9873 GT		9873 GT	330	GTC	Coupé	Pininfarina			
9875 GT		9875 GT	330	GTC	Coupé	Pininfarina			
9877 GT		9877 GT	275	GTB4	Berlinetta	Scaglietti			
9879 GT		9879 GT	330	GTC	Coupé	Pininfarina			
9881 GT		9881 GT	330	GTC	Coupé	Pininfarina			
9883 GT		9883 GT	275	GTB4	Berlinetta	Scaglietti			
9885 GT		9885 GT	330	GT	Coupé	Pininfarina			
9887 GT		9887 GT	275	GTB4	Berlinetta	Scaglietti			
9889		9889	365	California	Spyder	Pininfarina	M.Joffolini		
9891 GT		9891 GT	275	GTB4	Berlinetta	Scaglietti			
9893 GT		9893 GT	330	GTC	Coupé	Pininfarina			
9895 GT		9895 GT	330	GTC	Coupé	Pininfarina			
9897 GT		9897 GT	275	GTB4	Berlinetta	Scaglietti			
9899 GT		9899 GT	330	GTC	Coupé	Pininfarina			
9901 GT		9901 GT	330	GTC	Coupé	Pininfarina			
9903 GT		9903 GT	275	GTB4	Berlinetta	Scaglietti			
9905 GT		9905 GT	330	GTC	Coupé	Pininfarina			
9907 GT		9907 GT	330	GTC	Coupé	Pininfarina			
9909 GT		9909 GT	275	GTB4	Berlinetta	Scaglietti			
9911 GT		9911 GT	330	GT	Coupé	Pininfarina			
9913 GT		9913 GT	330	GT	Coupé	Pininfarina			
9915 GT		9915 GT	330	GT	2+2	Pininfarina			
9917 GT		9917 GT	275	GTB4	Berlinetta	Scaglietti			
9919 GT		9919 GT	330	GT	Coupé	Pininfarina			
9921 GT		9921 GT	275	GTB4	Berlinetta	Scaglietti			
9923 GT		9923 GT	330	GTC	Coupé	Pininfarina			
9925 GT		9925 GT	275	GTB4	Berlinetta	Scaglietti			
9927 GT		9927 GT	330	GTC	Coupé	Pininfarina			
9929 GT		9929 GT	330	GT	2 + 2	Pininfarina			
9930 GT		9930 GT	275	GTB4	Berlinetta	Scaglietti			
9933 GT		9933 GT	330	GT	2 + 2	Pininfarina			
9935		9935	365	California	Spyder	Pininfarina	M.Jenksbury	U.S.A.	
9937 GT		9937 GT	275	GTB4	Berlinetta	Scaglietti			
9939 GT		9939 GT	330	GTC	Coupé	Pininfarina			
9941 GT		9941 GT	275	GTB4	Berlinetta	Scaglietti			
9943 GT		9943 GT	330	GTC	Coupé	Pininfarina			
9945 GT		9945 GT	330	GTC	Coupé	Pininfarina			
9947 GT		9947 GT	275	GTB4	Berlinetta	Scaglietti			
9949 GT		9949 GT	330	GTC	Coupé	Pininfarina			
9951 GT		9951 GT	275	GTB4	Berlinetta	Scaglietti			
9953 GT		9953 GT	330	GTC	Coupé	Pininfarina			
9955 GT		9955 GT	330	GTC	Coupé	Pininfarina			
9957 GT		9957 GT	275	GTB4	Berlinetta	Scaglietti			
9959 GT		9959 GT	330	GTC	Coupé	Pininfarina			
9961 GT		9961 GT	275	GTB4	Berlinetta	Scaglietti			
9963 GT		9963 GT	330	GTC	Coupé	Pininfarina			U.S.A.
9965 GT		9965 GT	330	GT	2 + 2	Pininfarina			
9967 GT		9967 GT	275	GTB4	Berlinetta	Scaglietti			
9969 GT		9969 GT	330	GT	2 + 2	Pininfarina			
9971 GT		9971 GT	275	GTB4	Berlinetta	Scaglietti			
9973 GT		9973 GT	330	GTC	Coupé	Pininfarina			
9975 GT		9975 GT	275	GTB4	Berlinetta	Scaglietti			
9977 GT		9977 GT	330	GT	2 + 2	Pininfarina			
9979 GT		9979 GT	330	GTC	Coupé	Pininfarina			
9981 GT		9981 GT	275	GTB4	Berlinetta	Scaglietti			
9983 GT		9983 GT	330	GTC	Coupé	Pininfarina			
9985*		9985	365	California	Spyder	Pininfarina			U.K.
9987 GT		9987 GT	275	GTB4	Berlinetta	Scaglietti			
9989 GT		9989 GT	275	GTB4	Berlinetta	Scaglietti			
9991 GT		9991 GT	330	GT	2 + 2	Pininfarina			
9993 GT		9993 GT	275	GTB4	Berlinetta	Scaglietti			
9995 GT		9995 GT	330	GTS	Spyder	Pininfarina			
9997 GT		9997 GT	330	GTC	Coupé	Pininfarina			
9999 GT		9999 GT	275	GTB4	Berlinetta	Scaglietti			
10001 GT		10001 GT	330	GTC	Coupé	Pininfarina			
10003 GT		10003 GT	330	GTS	Spyder	Pininfarina			
10005 GT		10005 GT	275	GTB4	Berlinetta	Scaglietti			
10007 GT		10007 GT	330	GTC	Coupé	Pininfarina			
10009 GT		10009 GT	330	GTC	Coupé	Pininfarina			
10011 GT		10011 GT	275	GTB4	Berlinetta	Scaglietti			

Chassis No.	Picture Ref	Engine No.	Type	Model	Body Style	Coach-builder	First Owner	Original Location	Present Location
10013 GT		10013 GT	330	GTC	Coupé	Pininfarina			
10015 GT		10015 GT	330	GT	2+2	Pininfarina			
10017 GT		10017 GT	275	GTB4	Berlinetta	Scaglietti			U.S.A.
10019 GT		10019 GT	330	GT	2+2	Pininfarina			
10021 GT		10021 GT	275	GTB4	Berlinetta	Scaglietti			
10023 GT		10023 GT	330	GTC	Coupé	Pininfarina			
10025 GT		10025 GT	275	GTB4	Berlinetta	Scaglietti			
10027 GT		10027 GT	330	GT	2+2	Pininfarina			
10029 GT		10029 GT	330	GT	2+2	Pininfarina			
10031 GT		10031 GT	275	GTB4	Berlinetta	Scaglietti			
10033 GT		10033 GT	330	GTC	Coupé	Pininfarina			
10035 GT		10035 GT	275	GTB4	Berlinetta	Scaglietti			
10037 GT		10037 GT	330	GTS	Spyder	Pininfarina			U.S.A.
10039 GT		10039 GT	275	GTB4	Berlinetta	Scaglietti			
10041 GT		10041 GT	330	GT	2+2	Pininfarina			
10043 GT		10043 GT	330	GT	2+2	Pininfarina			
10045 GT		10045 GT	275	GTB4	Berlinetta	Scaglietti			
10047 GT		10047 GT	275	GTB4	Berlinetta	Scaglietti			
10049 GT		10049 GT	330	GTC	Coupé	Pininfarina			
10051 GT		10051 GT	275	GTB4	Berlinetta	Scaglietti			
10053 GT		10053 GT	330	GTS	Spyder	Pininfarina			
10055 GT		10055 GT	275	GTB4	Berlinetta	Scaglietti			
10057 GT		10057 GT	330	GT	2+2	Pininfarina			
10059 GT		10059 GT	275	GTB4	Berlinetta	Scaglietti			
10061 GT		10061 GT	330	GTC	Coupé	Pininfarina			
10063 GT		10063 GT	275	GTB4	Berlinetta	Scaglietti			
10065 GT		10065 GT	330	GTC	Coupé	Pininfarina			
10067 GT		10067 GT	275	GTB4	Berlinetta	Scaglietti			U.S.A.
10069 GT		10069 GT	330	GT	2+2	Pininfarina			
10071 GT		10071 GT	275	GTB4	Berlinetta	Scaglietti			U.S.A.
10073 GT		10073 GT	330	GTS	Spyder	Pininfarina			
10075 GT		10075 GT	275	GTB4	Berlinetta	Scaglietti			
10077		10077	365	California	Spyder	Pininfarina		U.S.A.	
10079 GT		10079 GT	330	GTC	Coupé	Pininfarina			U.S.A.
10081 GT		10081 GT	275	GTB4	Berlinetta	Scaglietti			
10083 GT		10083 GT	330	GT	2+2	Pininfarina			
10085 GT		10085 GT	330	GT	2+2	Pininfarina			
10087 GT		10087 GT	275	GTB4	Berlinetta	Scaglietti			
10089 GT		10089 GT	330	GT	2+2	Pininfarina			
10091 GT		10091 GT	330	GT	2+2	Pininfarina			
10093 GT		10093 GT	275	GTB4	Berlinetta	Scaglietti			
10095 GT		10095 GT	330	GTC	Coupe	Pininfarina			
10097 GT		10097 GT	330	GTC	Coupe	Pininfarina			
10099 GT		10099 GT	275	GTB4	Berlinetta	Scaglietti			
10101 GT		10101 GT	330	GTC	Coupe	Pininfarina			
10103 GT		10103 GT	275	GTB4	Berlinetta	Scaglietti			
10105 GT		10105 GT	330	GTC	Coupe	Pininfarina			
10107 GT	P1/343?	10107 GT	330	GTC	Coupe Speciale	Pininfarina			
	Special body built on 330GTC chassis.								
10109 GT		10109 GT	275	GTB4	Berlinetta	Scaglietti			
10111 GT		10111 GT	330	GTS	Spyder	Pininfarina			
10113 GT		10113 GT	330	GTS	Spyder	Pininfarina			
10115 GT		10115 GT	275	GTB4	Berlinetta	Scaglietti			
10117 GT		10117 GT	330	GT	2+2	Pininfarina			
10119 GT		10119 GT	275	GTB4	Berlinetta	Scaglietti			
10121 GT		10121 GT	330	GT	2+2	Pininfarina			U.S.A.
10123 GT		10123 GT	275	GTB4	Berlinetta	Scaglietti			
10125 GT		10125 GT	330	GT	2+2	Pininfarina			U.S.A.
	Single headlight Series II.								
10127 GT		10127 GT	330	GTS	Spyder	Pininfarina			
10129 GT		10129 GT	275	GTB4	Berlinetta	Scaglietti			
10131 GT		10131 GT	330	GT	2+2	Pininfarina			
10133 GT		10133 GT	275	GTB4	Berlinetta	Scaglietti			
10135 GT		10135 GT	330	GTS	Spyder	Pininfarina			
10137 GT		10137 GT	330	GT	2+2	Pininfarina			
10139 GT		10139 GT	275 GTB4/S	NART	Spyder	Scaglietti	Luigi Chinetti	U.S.A.	U.S.A.
10141 GT		10141 GT	330	GTS	Spyder	Pininfarina			
10143 GT		10143 GT	330	GTC	Coupe	Pininfarina			
10145 GT		10145 GT	330	GT	2+2	Pininfarina			
10147 GT		10147 GT	275	GTB4	Berlinetta	Scaglietti			
10149 GT		10149 GT	330	GT	2+2	Pininfarina			
10151 GT		10151 GT	275	GTB4	Berlinetta	Scaglietti			
10153 GT		10153 GT	330	GT	2+2	Pininfarina			

Chassis No.	Picture Ref	Engine No.	Type	Model	Body Style	Coach-builder	First Owner	Original Location	Present Location
10155		10155	365	California	Spyder	Pininfarina		Germany	U.S.A.
	Sold on 23/6/67.								
10157 GT		10157 GT	330	GTC	Coupe	Pininfarina			
10159 GT		10159 GT	275	GTB4	Berlinetta	Scaglietti			
10161 GT		10161 GT	330	GT	2+2	Pininfarina			
10163 GT		10163 GT	275	GTB4	Berlinetta	Scaglietti			
10165 GT		10165 GT	330	GT	2+2	Pininfarina			
10167 GT		10167 GT	330	GTS	Spyder	Pininfarina			
10169 GT		10169 GT	275	GTB4	Berlinetta	Scaglietti			
10171 GT		10171 GT	330	GTC	Coupe	Pininfarina			
10173 GT		10173 GT	330	GTS	Spyder	Pininfarina			
10175 GT		10175 GT	330	GT	2+2	Pininfarina			
10177 GT		10177 GT	275	GTB4	Berlinetta	Scaglietti			
10179 GT		10179 GT	330	GTC	Coupe	Pininfarina			
10181 GT		10181 GT	330	GT	2+2	Pininfarina			
10183 GT		10183 GT	330	GTC	Coupe	Pininfarina			
10185 GT		10185 GT	275	GTB4	Berlinetta	Scaglietti			
10187 GT		10187 GT	330	GTC	Coupe	Pininfarina			
10189 GT		10189 GT	330	GTS	Spyder	Pininfarina			
10191 GT		10191 GT	275	GTB4	Berlinetta	Scaglietti			
10193 GT		10193 GT	330	GT	2+2	Pininfarina			
	The last 330GT 2+2 produced.								
10195 GT		10195 GT	275	GTB4	Berlinetta	Scaglietti			
10197 GT		10197 GT	330	GTC	Coupe	Pininfarina			
10199 GT		10199 GT	330	GTC	Coupe	Pininfarina			
10201 GT		10201 GT	275	GTB4	Berlinetta	Scaglietti			
10203 GT		10203 GT	330	GTS	Spyder	Pininfarina			
10205 GT		10205 GT	275	GTB4	Berlinetta	Scaglietti			
10207 GT		10207 GT	275	GTB4	Berlinetta	Scaglietti			
10209 GT		10209 GT	330	GTC	Coupe	Pininfarina			
10211 GT		10211 GT	330	GTC	Coupe	Pininfarina			
10213 GT		10213 GT	275	GTB4	Berlinetta	Scaglietti			
10215 GT		10215 GT	330	GTC	Coupe	Pininfarina			U.S.A.
10217 GT		10217 GT	275	GTB4	Berlinetta	Scaglietti			
10219 GT		10219 GT	275 GTB4/S	NART	Spyder	Scaglietti	Luigi Chinetti	U.S.A.	U.S.A.
10221 GT		10221 GT	330	GTC	Coupe	Pininfarina			
10223 GT		10223 GT	275	GTB4	Berlinetta	Scaglietti			
10225 GT		10225 GT	330	GTS	Spyder	Pininfarina			
10227 GT		10227 GT	275	GTB4	Berlinetta	Scaglietti			
10229 GT		10229 GT	330	GTC	Coupe	Pininfarina			
10231 GT		10231 GT	275	GTB4	Berlinetta	Scaglietti			
10233 GT		10233 GT	275	GTB4	Berlinetta	Scaglietti			
10235 GT		10235 GT	330	GTC	Coupe	Pininfarina			
10237 GT		10237 GT	275	GTB4	Berlinetta	Scaglietti			
10239 GT		10239 GT	330	GTC	Coupe	Pininfarina			
10241 GT	P1/343	10241 GT	330	GTC	Coupe Speciale	Pininfarina			
	Special coupé body built on a 330GTC chassis.								
10243 GT		10243 GT	275	GTB4	Berlinetta	Scaglietti			
10245 GT		10245 GT	275	GTB4	Berlinetta	Scaglietti			
10247 GT		10247 GT	330	GTC	Coupe	Pininfarina			
10249 GT		10249 GT	275 GTB4/S	NART	Spyder	Scaglietti	Luigi Chinettti	U.S.A.	U.S.A.
10251 GT		10251 GT	330	GTC	Coupe	Pininfarina			
10253 GT		10253 GT	275	GTB4	Berlinetta	Scaglietti			
10255 GT		10255 GT	330	GTC	Coupe	Pininfarina			
10257 GT		10257 GT	275	GTB4	Berlinetta	Scaglietti			U.S.A.
10259 GT		10259 GT	275	GTB4	Berlinetta	Scaglietti			
10261 GT		10261 GT	330	GTC	Coupe	Pininfarina			
10263 GT		10263 GT	275	GTB4	Berlinetta	Scaglietti			
10265 GT		10265 GT	330	GTC	Coupe	Pininfarina			
10267 GT		10267 GT	330	GTC	Coupe	Pininfarina			
10269 GT		10269 GT	275	GTB4	Berlinetta	Scaglietti			
10271 GT		10271 GT	275	GTB4	Berlinetta	Scaglietti			
10273 GT		10273 GT	330	GTC	Coupe	Pininfarina			
10275 GT		10275 GT	275	GTB4	Berlinetta	Scaglietti			
10279 GT		10279 GT	330	GTC	Coupe	Pininfarina			
10281 GT		10281 GT	275	GTB4	Berlinetta	Scaglietti			
10283 GT		10283 GT	330	GTC	Coupe	Pininfarina			
10285 GT		10285 GT	275	GTB4	Berlinetta	Scaglietti			
10287 GT		10287 GT	365 GTB4	Daytona	Berlinetta	Pininfarina			
	Believed to be the first 365GTB4 prototype.								
10289 GT		10289 GT	330	GTC	Coupe	Pininfarina			
10291 GT		10291 GT	275	GTB4	Berlinetta	Scaglietti			
10293 GT		10293 GT	330	GTC	Coupe	Pininfarina			
10295 GT		10295 GT	275	GTB4	Berlinetta	Scaglietti			

Chassis No.	Picture Ref	Engine No.	Type	Model	Body Style	Coach-builder	First Owner	Original Location	Present Location
10297 GT		10297 GT	330	GTC	Coupe	Pininfarina			
10299 GT		10299 GT	275	GTB4	Berlinetta	Scaglietti			
10301 GT		10301 GT	330	GTC	Coupe	Pininfarina			
10303 GT		10303 GT	275	GTB4	Berlinetta	Scaglietti			
10305 GT		10305 GT	330	GTC	Coupe	Pininfarina			
10307 GT		10307 GT	275	GTB4	Berlinetta	Scaglietti			
10309 GT		10309 GT	330	GTC	Coupe	Pininfarina			
10311 GT		10311 GT	275	GTB4	Berlinetta	Scaglietti			
10313 GT		10313 GT	330	GTC	Coupe	Pininfarina			
10315 GT		10315 GT	275	GTB4	Berlinetta	Scaglietti			
10317 GT		10317 GT	330	GTC	Coupe	Pininfarina			
10319 GT		10319 GT	275	GTB4	Berlinetta	Scaglietti			
10321 GT		10321 GT	275	GTB4	Berlinetta	Scaglietti			
10323 GT		10323 GT	330	GTS	Spyder	Pininfarina			U.S.A.
	Shown at the 1967 Frankfurt Motor Show.								
10325 GT		10325 GT	275	GTB4	Berlinetta	Scaglietti			
10327		10327	365	California	Spyder	Pininfarina			U.S.A.
10329 GT		10329 GT	275	GTB4	Berlinetta	Scaglietti			
10331 GT		10331 GT	330	GTC	Coupe	Pininfarina			
10333 GT		10333 GT	275	GTB4	Berlinetta	Scaglietti			
10335 GT		10335 GT	330	GTS	Spyder	Pininfarina			U.S.A.
10337 GT		10337 GT	275	GTB4	Berlinetta	Scaglietti			
10339 GT		10339 GT	275	GTB4	Berlinetta	Scaglietti			
10341 GT		10341 GT	330	GTS	Spyder	Pininfarina			
10343 GT		10343 GT	275	GTB4	Berlinetta	Scaglietti			
10345 GT		10345 GT	275	GTB4	Berlinetta	Scaglietti			
10347 GT		10347 GT	330	GT	Coupe	Pininfarina			
10349 GT		10349 GT	275	GTB4	Berlinetta	Scaglietti			
10351 GT		10351 GT	275	GTB4	Berlinetta	Scaglietti			
10353 GT		10353 GT	330	GTC	Coupe	Pininfarina			
10355 GT		10355 GT	275	GTB4	Berlinetta	Scaglietti			
10357 GT		10357 GT	275	GTB4	Berlinetta	Scaglietti			
10359 GT		10359 GT	330	GTS	Spyder	Pininfarina			
10361 GT		10361 GT	275	GTB4	Berlinetta	Scaglietti			
10363 GT		10363 GT	330	GTC	Coupe	Pininfarina			
10365 GT		10365 GT	275	GTB4	Berlinetta	Scaglietti			
10367 GT		10367 GT	330	GTC	Coupe	Pininfarina			
10369*		10369	365	California	Spyder	Pininfarina			
	Destroyed.								
10371 GT		10371 GT	275	GTB4	Berlinetta	Scaglietti			
10373 GT		10373 GT	330	GTC	Coupe	Pininfarina			
10375 GT		10375 GT	330	GTS	Spyder	Pininfarina			
10377 GT		10377 GT	330	GTC	Coupe	Pininfarina			
10379 GT		10379 GT	275	GTB4	Berlinetta	Scaglietti			
10381 GT		10381 GT	275	GTB4	Berlinetta	Scaglietti			
10383 GT		10383 GT	330	GTC	Coupe	Pininfarina			
10385 GT		10385 GT	275	GTB4	Berlinetta	Scaglietti			
10387 GT		10387 GT	275	GTB4	Berlinetta	Scaglietti			
10389 GT		10389 GT	330	GTC	Coupe	Pininfarina			
10391 GT		10391 GT	275	GTB4	Berlinetta	Scaglietti			
10393 GT		10393 GT	330	GTC	Coupe	Pininfarina			
10395 GT		10395 GT	275	GTB4	Berlinetta	Scaglietti			
10397 GT		10397 GT	330	GTC	Coupe	Pininfarina			
10399 GT		10399 GT	275	GTB4	Berlinetta	Scaglietti			
10401 GT		10401 GT	330	GTC	Coupe	Pininfarina			
10403 GT		10403 GT	275	GTB4	Berlinetta	Scaglietti			
10405 GT		10405 GT	275	GTB4	Berlinetta	Scaglietti			
10407 GT		10407 GT	330	GTS	Spyder	Pininfarina			U.S.A.
	Shown at the 1967 Paris Salon.								
10409 GT		10409 GT	275	GTB4	Berlinetta	Scaglietti			
10411 GT		10411 GT	330	GTC	Coupe	Pininfarina			
10413 GT		10413 GT	275	GTB4	Berlinetta	Scaglietti			
10415 GT		10415 GT	330	GTC	Coupe	Pininfarina			
10417 GT		10417 GT	275	GTB4	Berlinetta	Scaglietti			
10419 GT		10419 GT	330	GTS	Spyder	Pininfarina			
10421 GT		10421 GT	330	GTC	Coupe	Pininfarina			
10423 GT		10423 GT	275	GTB4	Berlinetta	Scaglietti			
10425 GT		10425 GT	330	GTC	Coupe	Pininfarina			
10427 GT		10427 GT	275	GTB4	Berlinetta	Scaglietti			
10429 GT		10429 GT	330	GTC	Coupe	Pininfarina			
10431 GT		10431 GT	365	GT	2+2	Pininfarina			
10433 GT		10433 GT	330	GTC	Coupe	Pininfarina			
10435 GT		10435 GT	275	GTB4	Berlinetta	Scaglietti			U.S.A.
10437 GT		10437 GT	330	GTC	Coupe	Pininfarina			

Chassis No.	Picture Ref	Engine No.	Type	Model	Body Style	Coach-builder	First Owner	Original Location	Present Location
10439 GT		10439 GT	275	GTB4	Berlinetta	Scaglietti			
10441 GT		10441 GT	330	GTC	Coupe	Pininfarina			
10443 GT		10443 GT	275	GTB4	Berlinetta	Scaglietti			
10445 GT		10445 GT	330	GTC	Coupe	Pininfarina			
10447 GT		10447 GT	275	GTB4	Berlinetta	Scaglietti			
10449 GT		10449 GT	330	GTC	Coupe	Pininfarina			
10451 GT		10451 GT	275	GTB4	Berlinetta	Scaglietti			
10453 GT		10453 GT	275 GTB4/S	NART	Spyder	Scaglietti	Luigi Chinetti	U.S.A.	U.S.A.
	Originally owned by Steve McQueen.								
10455 GT		10455 GT	330	GTC	Coupe	Pininfarina			
10457 GT		10457 GT	330	GTC	Coupe	Pininfarina			
10459 GT		10459 GT	275	GTB4	Berlinetta	Scaglietti			
10461 GT		10461 GT	275	GTB4	Berlinetta	Scaglietti			
10463 GT		10463 GT	330	GTC	Coupe	Pininfarina			
10465 GT		10465 GT	275	GTB4	Berlinetta	Scaglietti			U.S.A.
10467 GT		10467 GT	330	GTC	Coupe	Pininfarina			
10469 GT		10469 GT	275	GTB4	Berlinetta	Scaglietti			
10471 GT		10471 GT	330	GTC	Coupe	Pininfarina			
10473 GT		10473 GT	275	GTB4	Berlinetta	Scaglietti			
10475 GT		10475 GT	330	GTC	Coupe	Pininfarina			
10477 GT		10477 GT	330	GTC	Coupe	Pininfarina			

1968

Chassis No.	Picture Ref	Engine No.	Type	Model	Body Style	Coach-builder	First Owner	Original Location	Present Location
10479 GT		10479 GT	365	GT	2+2	Pininfarina			
	Reported as the prototype 365GT 2+2 and believed shown at the 1967 London Motor Show.								
10481 GT		10481 GT	275	GTB4	Berlinetta	Scaglietti			
10483 GT		10483 GT	330	GTC	Coupe	Pininfarina			
10485 GT		10485 GT	275	GTB4	Berlinetta	Scaglietti			
10487 GT		10487 GT	330	GTC	Coupe	Pininfarina			
10489 GT		10489 GT	330	GTC	Coupe	Pininfarina			
10491 GT		10491 GT	275	GTB4	Berlinetta	Scaglietti			
10493 GT		10493 GT	330	GTC	Coupe	Pininfarina			
10495 GT		10495 GT	330	GTC	Coupe	Pininfarina			
10497 GT		10497 GT	275	GTB4	Berlinetta	Scaglietti			
10499 GT		10499 GT	330	GTS	Spyder	Pininfarina			U.S.A.
10501 GT		10501 GT	330	GTC	Coupe	Pininfarina			
10503 GT		10503 GT	330	GTC	Coupe	Pininfarina			
10505 GT		10505 GT	330	GTS	Spyder	Pininfarina			U.S.A.
10507 GT		10507 GT	275	GTB4	Berlinetta	Scaglietti			
10509 GT		10509 GT	330	GTC	Coupe	Pininfarina			
10511 GT		10511 GT	275	GTB4	Berlinetta	Scaglietti			
10513 GT		10513 GT	330	GTC	Coupe	Pininfarina			
10515 GT		10515 GT	275	GTB4	Berlinetta	Scaglietti			
10517 GT		10517 GT	330	GTC	Coupe	Pininfarina			
10519 GT		10519 GT	275	GTB4	Berlinetta	Scaglietti			
10521 GT		10521 GT	330	GTC	Coupe	Pininfarina			
10523 GT		10523 GT	275	GTB4	Berlinetta	Scaglietti			
10525 GT		10525 GT	275	GTB4	Berlinetta	Scaglietti			
10527 GT		10527 GT	275	GTB4	Berlinetta	Scaglietti			
10529 GT		10529 GT	330	GTC	Coupe	Pininfarina			
10531 GT		10531 GT	275	GTB4	Berlinetta	Scaglietti			
10533 GT		10533 GT	275	GTB4	Berlinetta	Scaglietti			
10535 GT		10535 GT	330	GTC	Coupe	Pininfarina			
10537 GT		10537 GT	275	GTB4	Berlinetta	Scaglietti			
10539 GT		10539 GT	330	GTC	Coupe	Pininfarina			
10541 GT		10541 GT	330	GTC	Coupe	Pininfarina			
10543 GT		10543 GT	275	GTB4	Berlinetta	Scaglietti			
10545 GT		10545 GT	275	GTB4	Berlinetta	Scaglietti			
10547 GT		10547 GT	330	GTC	Coupe	Pininfarina			
10549 GT		10549 GT	275	GTB4	Berlinetta	Scaglietti			
10551 GT		10551 GT	330	GTS	Spyder	Pininfarina			
10553 GT		10553 GT	330	GTS	Spyder	Pininfarina			
10555 GT		10555 GT	330	GTC	Coupe	Pininfarina			
10557 GT		10557 GT	275	GTB4	Berlinetta	Scaglietti			
10559 GT		10559 GT	275	GTB4	Berlinetta	Scaglietti			
10561 GT		10561 GT	330	GTS	Spyder	Pininfarina			
10563 GT		10563 GT	275	GTB4	Berlinetta	Scaglietti			
10565 GT		10565 GT	275	GTB4	Berlinetta	Scaglietti			
10567 GT		10567 GT	330	GTS	Spyder	Pininfarina			
10569 GT		10569 GT	275	GTB4	Berlinetta	Scaglietti			
10571 GT		10571 GT	330	GTC	Coupe	Pininfarina			
10573 GT		10573 GT	330	GTC	Coupe	Pininfarina			
10575 GT		10575 GT	330	GTC	Coupe	Pininfarina			
10577 GT		10577 GT	275	GTB4	Berlinetta	Scaglietti			
10579 GT		10579 GT	330	GTC	Coupe	Pininfarina			

Chassis No.	Picture Ref	Engine No.	Type	Model	Body Style	Coach-builder	First Owner	Original Location	Present Location
10581 GT		10581 GT	330	GTC	Coupe	Pininfarina			
10583 GT		10583 GT	275	GTB4	Berlinetta	Scaglietti			
10585 GT		10585 GT	330	GTC	Coupe	Pininfarina			
10587 GT		10587 GT	330	GTC	Coupe	Pininfarina			
10589 GT		10589 GT	275	GTB4	Berlinetta	Scaglietti			
10591 GT		10591 GT	330	GTC	Coupe	Pininfarina			
10593 GT		10593 GT	330	GTC	Coupe	Pininfarina			
10595 GT		10595 GT	275	GTB4	Berlinetta	Scaglietti			U.S.A.
10597 GT		10597 GT	275	GTB4	Berlinetta	Scaglietti			
10599 GT		10599 GT	330	GTS	Spyder	Pininfarina			
10601 GT		10601 GT	275	GTB4	Berlinetta	Scaglietti			
10603 GT		10603 GT	275	GTB4	Berlinetta	Scaglietti			
10605 GT		10605 GT	330	GTS	Spyder	Pininfarina			
10607 GT		10607 GT	275	GTB4	Berlinetta	Scaglietti			
10609 GT		10609 GT	275	GTB4	Berlinetta	Scaglietti			
10611 GT		10611 GT	330	GTC	Coupe	Pininfarina			
10613 GT		10613 GT	275	GTB4	Berlinetta	Scaglietti			
10615 GT		10615 GT	275	GTB4	Berlinetta	Scaglietti			
10617 GT		10617 GT	330	GTC	Coupe	Pininfarina			
10619 GT		10619 GT	275	GTB4	Berlinetta	Scaglietti			U.S.A.
10621 GT		10621 GT	275	GTB4	Berlinetta	Scaglietti			
10623 GT		10623 GT	330	GTC	Coupe	Pininfarina			
10625 GT		10625 GT	275	GTB4	Berlinetta	Scaglietti			
10627 GT		10627 GT	275	GTB4	Berlinetta	Scaglietti			
10629 GT		10629 GT	330	GTC	Coupe	Pininfarina			
10631 GT		10631 GT	330	GTC	Coupe	Pininfarina			
10633 GT		10633 GT	330	GTS	Spyder	Pininfarina			
10635 GT		10635 GT	275	GTB4	Berlinetta	Scaglietti			
10637 GT		10637 GT	330	GTC	Coupe	Pininfarina			
10639 GT		10639 GT	330	GTC	Coupe	Pininfarina			
10641 GT		10641 GT	330	GTC	Coupe	Pininfarina			U.S.A.
10643 GT		10643 GT	275	GTB4	Berlinetta	Scaglietti			U.S.A.
10645 GT		10645 GT	330	GTC	Coupe	Pininfarina			
10647 GT		10647 GT	330	GTC	Coupe	Pininfarina			
10649 GT		10649 GT	275	GTB4	Berlinetta	Scaglietti			U.S.A.
10651 GT		10651 GT	330	GTC	Coupe	Pininfarina			
10653 GT		10653 GT	330	GTC	Coupe	Pininfarina			
10655 GT		10655 GT	275	GTB4	Berlinetta	Scaglietti			
10657 GT		10657 GT	330	GTC	Coupe	Pininfarina			
10659 GT	P1/339?	10659 GT	330	GTC	Coupe	Pininfarina			
		Believed to have been rebodied by Zagato to the order of Luigi Chinetti.							
10661 GT		10661 GT	330	GTC	Coupe	Pinin Farina			
10663 GT		10663 GT	275	GTB4	Berlinetta	Scaglietti			U.S.A.
10665 GT		10665 GT	330	GTC	Coupe	Pininfarina			
10667 GT		10667 GT	330	GTC	Coupe	Pininfarina			
10669 GT		10669 GT	275	GTB4	Berlinetta	Scaglietti			
10671 GT		10671 GT	330	GTC	Coupe	Pininfarina			
10673 GT		10673 GT	330	GTC	Coupe	Pininfarina			
10675 GT		10675 GT	275	GTB4	Berlinetta	Scaglietti			
10677 GT		10677 GT	330	GTC	Coupe	Pininfarina			
10679 GT		10679 GT	330	GTC	Coupe	Pininfarina			
10681 GT		10681 GT	275	GTB4	Berlinetta	Scaglietti			
10683 GT		10683 GT	330	GTC	Coupe	Pininfarina			
10685 GT		10685 GT	330	GTC	Coupe	Pininfarina			
10687 GT		10687 GT	275	GTB4	Berlinetta	Scaglietti			
10689 GT		10689 GT	330	GTS	Spyder	Pininfarina			
10691 GT		10691 GT	275 GTB4/S	NART	Spyder	Scaglietti	Luigi Chinetti	U.S.A.	U.S.A.
10693 GT		10693 GT	330	GTC	Coupe	Pininfarina			
10695 GT		10695 GT	330	GTC	Coupe	Pininfarina			
10697 GT		10697 GT	275	GTB4	Berlinetta	Scaglietti			
10699 GT		10699 GT	330	GTC	Coupe	Pininfarina			
10701 GT		10701 GT	275	GTB4	Berlinetta	Scaglietti			
10703 GT		10703 GT	330	GTS	Spyder	Pininfarina			
10705 GT		10705 GT	275 GTB4 OR 330GTC		Berlinetta	Scaglietti			
10707 GT		10707 GT	275	GTB4	Berlinetta	Scaglietti			
10709 GT		10709 GT	275 GTB4/S	NART	Spyder	Scaglietti	Luigi Chinetti	U.S.A.	U.S.A.
10711 GT		10711 GT	275	GTB4	Berlinetta	Scaglietti			
10713 GT		10713 GT	330	GTC	Coupe	Pininfarina			U.S.A.
10715 GT		10715 GT	275	GTB4	Berlinetta	Scaglietti			
10717 GT		10717 GT	275	GTB4	Berlinetta	Scaglietti			
10719 GT		10719 GT	330	GTS	Spyder	Pininfarina			
10721 GT		10721 GT	275	GTB4	Berlinetta	Scaglietti			
10723 GT		10723 GT	275	GTB4	Berlinetta	Scaglietti			
10725 GT		10725 GT	330	GTC	Coupe	Pininfarina			

Chassis No.	Picture Ref	Engine No.	Type	Model	Body Style	Coach-builder	First Owner	Original Location	Present Location
10727 GT		10727 GT	275	GTB4	Berlinetta	Scaglietti			
10729 GT		10729 GT	330	GTC	Coupe	Pininfarina			
10731 GT		10731 GT	330	GTS	Spyder	Pininfarina			
10733 GT		10733 GT	330	GTC	Coupe	Pininfarina			
10735 GT		10735 GT	330	GTC	Coupe	Pininfarina			
10737 GT		10737 GT	330	GTS	Spyder	Pininfarina			
10739 GT		10739 GT	330	GTC	Coupe	Pininfarina			
10741 GT		10741 GT	330	GTC	Coupe	Pininfarina			
10743 GT		10743 GT	275	GTB4	Berlinetta	Scaglietti			
10745 GT		10745 GT	330	GTC	Coupe	Pininfarina			
10747 GT		10747 GT	330	GTC	Coupe	Pininfarina			
10749 GT		10749 GT	275 GTB4/S	NART	Spyder	Scaglietti	Luigi Chinetti	U.S.A.	U.S.A.
10751 GT		10751 GT	330	GTC	Coupe	Pininfarina			
10753 GT		10753 GT	330	GTS	Spyder	Pininfarina			
10755 GT		10755 GT	330	GTC	Coupe	Pininfarina			
10757 GT		10757 GT	275	GTB4	Berlinetta	Scaglietti			
10759 GT		10759 GT	330	GTS	Spyder	Pininfarina			
10761 GT		10761 GT	330	GTC	Coupe	Pininfarina			
10763 GT		10763 GT	330	GTS	Spyder	Pininfarina			
10765 GT		10765 GT	275	GTB4	Berlinetta	Scaglietti			
10767 GT		10767 GT	330	GTC	Coupe	Pininfarina			
10769 GT		10769 GT	330	GTC	Coupe	Pininfarina			
10771 GT		10771 GT	275	GTB4	Berlinetta	Scaglietti			
10773 GT		10773 GT	330	GTS	Spyder	Pininfarina			
	Stolen in 1981 in Paris, France.								
10775 GT		10775 GT	330	GTC	Coupe	Pininfarina			
10777 GT		10777 GT	275	GTB4	Berlinetta	Scaglietti			
10779 GT		10779 GT	330	GTC	Coupe	Pininfarina			
10781 GT		10781 GT	330	GTS	Spyder	Pininfarina			
10783 GT		10783 GT	275	GTB4	Berlinetta	Scaglietti			
10785 GT		10785 GT	275	GTB4	Berlinetta	Scaglietti			
10787 GT		10787 GT	330	GTC	Coupe	Pininfarina			
10789 GT		10789 GT	330	GTS	Spyder	Pininfarina			
10791 GT		10791 GT	365	GT	2+2	Pininfarina			U.S.A.
	Shown at the 1967 Brussels Motor Show.								
10793 GT		10793 GT	330	GTC	Coupe	Pininfarina			
10795 GT		10795 GT	330	GTC	Coupe	Pininfarina			
10797 GT		10797 GT	330	GTS	Spyder	Pininfarina			
10799 GT		10799 GT	330	GTC	Coupe	Pininfarina			
10801 GT		10801 GT	330	GTC	Coupe	Pininfarina			U.S.A.
10803 GT		10803 GT	275	GTB4	Berlinetta	Scaglietti			
10805 GT		10805 GT	330	GTC	Coupe	Pininfarina			
10807 GT		10807 GT	330	GTC	Coupe	Pininfarina			
10809 GT		10809 GT	330	GTC	Coupe	Pininfarina			
10811 GT		10811 GT	330	GTC	Coupe	Pininfarina			
10813 GT		10813 GT	275	GTB4	Berlinetta	Scaglietti			
10815 GT		10815 GT	275	GTB4	Berlinetta	Scaglietti			
10817 GT		10817 GT	330	GTS	Spyder	Pininfarina			
10819 GT		10819 GT	275	GTB4	Berlinetta	Scaglietti			
10821 GT		10821 GT	275	GTB4	Berlinetta	Scaglietti			
10823 GT		10823 GT	330	GTC	Coupe	Pininfarina			
10825 GT		10825 GT	330	GTC	Coupe	Pininfarina			
10827 GT		10827 GT	275	GTB4	Berlinetta	Scaglietti			
10829 GT		10829 GT	??	??	??	??			
10831 GT		10831 GT	330	GTC	Coupe	Pininfarina			
10833 GT		10833 GT	330	GTC	Coupe	Pininfarina			
10835 GT		10835 GT	275	GTB4	Berlinetta	Scaglietti			
10837 GT		10837 GT	365	GT	2+2	Pininfarina			
10839 GT		10839 GT	330	GTC	Coupe	Pininfarina			
10841 GT		10841 GT	330	GTC	Coupe	Pininfarina			
10843 GT		10843 GT	275	GTB4	Berlinetta	Scaglietti			
10845 GT		10845 GT	330	GTS	Spyder	Pininfarina			
10847 GT		10847 GT	275	GTB4	Berlinetta	Scaglietti			
10849 GT		10849 GT	330	GTC	Coupe	Pininfarina			
10851 GT		10851 GT	275	GTB4	Berlinetta	Scaglietti			
10853 GT		10853 GT	330	GTC	Coupe	Pininfarina			
10855 GT		10855 GT	275	GTB4	Berlinetta	Scaglietti			
10857 GT		10857 GT	330	GTC	Coupe	Pininfarina			
10859 GT		10859 GT	330	GTC	Coupe	Pininfarina			
10861 GT		10861 GT	275	GTB4	Berlinetta	Scaglietti			
10863 GT		10863 GT	330	GTC	Coupe	Pininfarina			
10865 GT		10865 GT	330	GTC	Coupe	Pininfarina			
10867 GT		10867 GT	275	GTB4	Berlinetta	Scaglietti			
10869 GT		10869 GT	275	GTB4	Berlinetta	Scaglietti			

Chassis No.	Picture Ref	Engine No.	Type	Model	Body Style	Coach-builder	First Owner	Original Location	Present Location
10871 GT		10871 GT	330	GTC	Coupe	Pininfarina			
10873 GT		10873 GT	330	GTC	Coupe	Pininfarina			
10875 GT		10875 GT	275	GTB4	Berlinetta	Scaglietti			
10877 GT		10877 GT	330	GTS	Spyder	Pininfarina			
10879 GT		10879 GT	330	GTC	Coupe	Pininfarina			
10881 GT		10881 GT	275	GTB4	Berlinetta	Scaglietti			
10883 GT		10883 GT	330	GTS	Spyder	Pininfarina			
10885 GT		10885 GT	330	GTC	Coupe	Pininfarina			
10887 GT		10887 GT	275	GTB4	Berlinetta	Scaglietti			
10889 GT		10889 GT	330	GTC	Coupe	Pininfarina			
10891 GT		10891 GT	330	GTC	Coupe	Pininfarina			
10893 GT		10893 GT	330	GTC	Coupe	Pininfarina			
10895 GT		10895 GT	275	GTB4	Berlinetta	Scaglietti			
10897 GT		10897 GT	330	GTC	Coupe	Pininfarina			
10899 GT		10899 GT	275	GTB4	Berlinetta	Scaglietti			
10901 GT		10901 GT	330	GTS	Spyder	Pininfarina			
10903 GT		10903 GT	330	GTC	Coupe	Pininfarina			
10905 GT		10905 GT	275	GTB4	Berlinetta	Scaglietti			
10907 GT		10907 GT	330	GTC	Coupe	Pininfarina			
10909 GT		10909 GT	330	GTC	Coupe	Pininfarina			
10911 GT		10911 GT	275	GTB4	Berlinetta	Scaglietti			
10913 GT		10913 GT	330	GTS	Spyder	Pininfarina			
10915 GT		10915 GT	330	GTC	Coupe	Pininfarina			
10917 GT		10917 GT	275	GTB4	Berlinetta	Scaglietti			
10919 GT		10919 GT	330	GTC	Coupe	Pininfarina			
10921 GT		10921 GT	330	GTC	Coupe	Pininfarina			
10923 GT		10923 GT	330	GTC	Coupe	Pininfarina			
10925 GT		10925 GT	275	GTB4	Berlinetta	Scaglietti			
10927 GT		10927 GT	330	GTC	Coupe	Pininfarina			
10929 GT		10929 GT	330	GTC	Coupe	Pininfarina			U.S.A.
10931 GT		10931 GT	275	GTB4	Berlinetta	Scaglietti			
10933 GT		10933 GT	365	GT	2+2	Pininfarina			
10935 GT		10935 GT	330	GTC	Coupe	Pininfarina			
10937 GT		10937 GT	330	GTC	Coupe	Pininfarina			U.S.A.
10939 GT		10939 GT	275	GTB4	Berlinetta	Scaglietti			
10941 GT		10941 GT	330	GTC	Coupe	Pininfarina			
10943 GT		10943 GT	275	GTB4	Berlinetta	Scaglietti			
10945 GT		10945 GT	330	GTC	Coupe	Pininfarina			
10947 GT		10947 GT	330	GTC	Coupe	Pininfarina			
10949 GT		10949 GT	275	GTB4	Berlinetta	Scaglietti			
10951 GT		10951 GT	330	GTC	Coupe	Pininfarina			
10953 GT		10953 GT	275	GTB4	Berlinetta	Scaglietti			
10955 GT		10955 GT	365	GT	2+2	Pininfarina			
10957 GT		10957 GT	330	GTC	Coupe	Pininfarina			
10959 GT		10959 GT	330	GTC	Coupe	Pininfarina			
10961 GT		10961 GT	330	GTS	Spyder	Pininfarina			
10963 GT		10963 GT	330	GTC	Coupe	Pininfarina			
10965 GT		10965 GT	275	GTB4	Berlinetta	Scaglietti			
10967 GT		10967 GT	330	GTC	Coupe	Pininfarina			
10969 GT		10969 GT	275	GTB4	Berlinetta	Scaglietti			Unmknown
10971 GT		10971 GT	330	GTC	Coupe	Pininfarina			
10973 GT		10973 GT	275	GTB4	Berlinetta	Scaglietti			
10975 GT		10975 GT	330	GTC	Coupe	Pininfarina			
10977 GT		10977 GT	330	GTC	Coupe	Pininfarina			
10979 GT		10979 GT	330	GTC	Coupe	Pininfarina			U.S.A.
10981 GT	*European version.*	10981 GT	275	GTB4	Berlinetta	Scaglietti			
10983 GT		10983 GT	330	GTC	Coupe	Pininfarina			
10985 GT		10985 GT	330	GTC	Coupe	Pininfarina			
10987 GT		10987 GT	275	GTB4	Berlinetta	Scaglietti			
10989 GT		10989 GT	330	GTC	Coupe	Pininfarina			
10991 GT		10991 GT	275	GTB4	Berlinetta	Scaglietti			
10993 GT		10993 GT	365	GT	2+2	Pininfarina			
10995 GT		10995 GT	275	GTB4	Berlinetta	Scaglietti			
10997 GT		10997 GT	330	GTC	Coupe	Pininfarina			
10999 GT		10999 GT	330	GTS	Spyder	Pininfarina			
11001 GT		11001 GT	365GTB4	Daytona	Berlinetta	Scaglietti			
11003 GT	*The second 365GTB4 prototype.*	11003 GT	275	GTB4	Berlinetta	Scaglietti			
11005 GT		11005 GT	330	GTC	Coupe	Pininfarina			
11007 GT		11007 GT	330	GTC	Coupe	Pininfarina			
11009 GT		11009 GT	330	GTC	Coupe	Pininfarina			
11011 GT		11011 GT	330	GTS	Spyder	Pininfarina			U.S.A.
11013 GT		11013 GT	275	GTB4	Berlinetta	Scaglietti			

Chassis No.	Picture Ref	Engine No.	Type	Model	Body Style	Coach-builder	First Owner	Original Location	Present Location
11015 GT		11015 GT	330	GTS	Spyder	Pininfarina			
11015 GT		11015 GT	330	GTC	Coupe	Pininfarina			
11017 GT		11017 GT	330	GTC	Coupe	Pininfarina			
11019 GT		11019 GT	275	GTB4	Berlinetta	Scaglietti			
11021 GT		11021 GT	330	GTS	Spyder	Pininfarina			
11023 GT		11023 GT	330	GTS	Spyder	Pininfarina			U.S.A.
11025 GT		11025 GT	330	GTC	Coupe	Pininfarina			
11027 GT		11027 GT	330	GTS	Spyder	Pininfarina			
11029 GT		11029 GT	330	GTC	Coupe	Pininfarina			
11031 GT		11031 GT	330	GTC	Coupe	Pininfarina			
11033 GT		11033 GT	330	GTS	Spyder	Pininfarina			U.S.A.
11035 GT		11035 GT	330	GTC	Coupe	Pininfarina			
11037 GT		11037 GT	365	GT	2+2	Pininfarina			
11039 GT		11039 GT	330	GTC	Coupe	Pininfarina			
11041 GT		11041 GT	330	GTC	Coupe	Pininfarina			
11043 GT		11043 GT	330	GTC	Coupe	Pininfarina			
11045 GT		11045 GT	330	GTS	Spyder	Pininfarina			
11047 GT		11047 GT	330	GTC	Coupe	Pininfarina			
11049 GT		11049 GT	330	GTC	Coupe	Pininfarina			
11051 GT		11051 GT	365	GT	2+2	Pininfarina			
	Shown at the 1968 Geneva Motor Show.								
11053 GT		11053 GT	330	GTC	Coupe	Pininfarina			U.S.A.
11055 GT		11055 GT	330	GTS	Spyder	Pininfarina			
11057 GT		11057 GT	275 GTB4/S	NART	Spyder	Scaglietti			U.S.A.
	Sold new in Europe. The last NART Spyder made.								
11059 GT		11059 GT	330	GTC	Coupe	Pininfarina			
11061 GT		11061 GT	365	GT	2+2	Pininfarina			
11063 GT		11063 GT	275	GTB4	Berlinetta	Scaglietti			
11065 GT		11065 GT	330	GTC	Coupe	Pininfarina			
11067 GT		11067 GT	365	GT	2+2	Pininfarina			
11069 GT		11069 GT	275	GTB4	Berlinetta	Scaglietti			
11071 GT		11071 GT	330	GTS	Spyder	Pininfarina			
11073 GT		11073 GT	330	GTC	Coupe	Pininfarina			
11075 GT		11075 GT	330	GTC	Coupe	Pininfarina			
11077 GT		11077 GT	330	GTC	Coupe	Pininfarina			
11079 GT		11079 GT	330	GTC	Coupe	Pininfarina			
11081 GT		11081 GT	330	GTS	Spyder	Pininfarina			
11083 GT		11083 GT	330	GTC	Coupe	Pininfarina			
11085 GT		11085 GT	330	GTS	Spyder	Pininfarina			
11087 GT		11087 GT	330	GTC	Coupe	Pininfarina			
11089 GT		11089 GT	330	GTC	Coupe	Pininfarina			
11091 GT		11091 GT	330	GTS	Spyder	Pininfarina			
11093 GT		11093 GT	330	GTC	Coupe	Pininfarina			
11095 GT		11095 GT	365	GT	2+2	Pininfarina			
11097 GT		11097 GT	330	GTC	Coupe	Pininfarina			
11099 GT		11099 GT	330	GTC	Coupe	Pininfarina			
11101 GT		11101 GT	365	GT	2+2	Pininfarina			U.S.A.
11103 GT		11103 GT	330	GTC	Coupe	Pininfarina			
11105 GT		11105 GT	330	GTC	Coupe	Pininfarina			
11107 GT		11107 GT	330	GTC	Coupe	Pininfarina			
11109 GT		11109 GT	365	GT	2+2	Pininfarina			
11111 GT		11111 GT	330	GTC	Coupe	Pininfarina			
11113 GT		11113 GT	330	GTC	Coupe	Pininfarina			
11115 GT		11115 GT	365	GT	2+2	Pininfarina			
11117 GT		11117 GT	330	GTC	Coupe	Pininfarina			
11119 GT		11119 GT	330	GTC	Coupe	Pininfarina			
11121 GT		11121 GT	365	GT	2+2	Pininfarina			
11123 GT		11123 GT	330	GTC	Coupe	Pininfarina			
11125 GT		11125 GT	330	GTC	Coupe	Pininfarina			
11127 GT		11127 GT	365	GT	2+2	Pininfarina			
11129 GT		11129 GT	330	GTC	Coupe	Pininfarina			
11131 GT		11131 GT	330	GTC	Coupe	Pininfarina			
11133 GT		11133 GT	365	GT	2+2	Pininfarina			
11135 GT		11135 GT	330	GTC	Coupe	Pininfarina			
11137 GT		11137 GT	330	GTC	Coupe	Pininfarina			
11139 GT		11139 GT	365	GT	2+2	Pininfarina			
11141 GT		11141 GT	330	GTC	Coupe	Pininfarina			
11143 GT		11143 GT	330	GTC	Coupe	Pininfarina			
11145 GT		11145 GT	365	GT	2+2	Pininfarina			
11147 GT		11147 GT	330	GTC	Coupe	Pininfarina			
11149 GT		11149 GT	330	GTC	Coupe	Pininfarina			
11151 GT		11151 GT	365	GT	2+2	Pininfarina			
11153 GT		11153 GT	330	GTC	Coupe	Pininfarina			
11155 GT		11155 GT	365	GT	2+2	Pininfarina			

Chassis No.	Picture Ref	Engine No.	Type	Model	Body Style	Coach-builder	First Owner	Original Location	Present Location
11157 GT		11157 GT	330	GTC	Coupe	Pininfarina			
11159 GT		11159 GT	330	GTC	Coupe	Pininfarina			
11161 GT		11161 GT	365	GT	2+2	Pininfarina			
11163 GT		11163 GT	330	GTC	Coupe	Pininfarina			
11165 GT		11165 GT	330	GTC	Coupe	Pininfarina			
11167 GT		11167 GT	330	GTC	Coupe	Pininfarina			
11169 GT		11169 GT	330	GTC	Coupe	Pininfarina			
11171 GT		11171 GT	330	GTC	Coupe	Pininfarina			
11173 GT		11173 GT	330	GTS	Spyder	Pininfarina			
11175 GT		11175 GT	330	GTC	Coupe	Pininfarina			
11177 GT		11177 GT	330	GTC	Coupe	Pininfarina			
11179 GT		11179 GT	330	GTS	Spyder	Pininfarina			
11181 GT		11181 GT	330	GTC	Coupe	Pininfarina			
11183 GT		11183 GT	330	GTC	Coupe	Pininfarina			

ADDITIONAL INFORMATION

The following six 365GT 2 + 2 cars were built by the factory with automatic transmission:

12755	13169
13165	13171
13167	13173

All six were shipped to the U.S.A.

365GTB/4 Spyder

As these 'Daytona' Spyders are much in demand and highly valued, we present the following list which is believed to be acccurate except as noted.

12851 Prototype	14779 US	15919 W/Hardtop	16859 US
14365	14813 US	15963 RHD	16891 US
14371 RHD	14823 US	15969 RHD	16895 US
14373 RHD	14829 US	16451 US	16901 US
14375	14857 US	16455 US	16903 US
14383	14863 US	16463 US	16911 US
14387	14901 US	16465 US	16913 US
14389	14913 US	16467 US	16915 US
14391	14993 US	16473 US	16949 US
14395	15007 US	16475 US	16987 US
14403 US	15171 US	16481 US	16995 US
14415	15179 US	16483 US	17001 US
14463 US	15239	16489 US	17013 US
14469 US	15277 US	16497 US	17025
14471 US	15283 US	16499 US	17039 US
14473 US	15297 US	16545 US	17041 US
14537	15369	16549 US	17045 US
14539 US	15383 ??	16567 US	17047 US
14543 US	15417 US	16573 US	17051 US
14547 Targa top	15429 US	16597 ??	17053 US
14549	15433 US	16689 US	17055 US
14553 US	15525	16697 US	17057 US
14557 US	15535	16705 US	17059 US
14563 US	15579 US	16783 US	17061 US
14565 US	15593 US	16793 US	17063 US
14605	15687	16799 US	17065 US
14671 US	15811 RHD	16801 US	17067 US
14699 US	15845	16835 US	17069 US
14737 US	15909 RHD	16839 US	17071 US
14739 US	15911	16847 US	17073 US
14761 US	15917 RHD	16857 US